Works like a Charm

SUNY series, Insinuations: Philosophy, Psychoanalysis, Literature

Charles Shepherdson, editor

Works like a Charm

Incentive Rhetoric and the Economization of Everyday Life

ROBERT O. McDONALD

Cover art: Anonymous. *Contest between Apollo and Marsyas.* ca. 1543. The Metropolitan Museum of Art.

Published by State University of New York Press, Albany

For information, contact State University of New York Press, Albany, NY
www.sunypress.edu

Library of Congress Cataloging-in-Publication Data

Name: McDonald, Robert O., author.
Title: Works like a charm : incentive rhetoric and the economization of everyday life / Robert O. McDonald.
Description: Albany : State University of New York Press, [2023] | SUNY series, Insinuations: Philosophy, Psychoanalysis, Literature | Includes bibliographical references and index.
Identifiers: ISBN 9781438494098 (hardcover : alk. paper) | ISBN 9781438494104 (ebook) | ISBN 9781438494081 (pbk. : alk. paper)
Further information is available at the Library of Congress.

10 9 8 7 6 5 4 3 2 1

To absent friends

Contents

Acknowledgments

I am indebted to my mentors and teachers: Joshua Gunn, Barry Brummett, Sharon Jarvis, Diane Davis, Larry Grossberg, Bill Balthrop, Fredric Jameson, Carole Blair, Michael Palm, Todd Ochoa, Benjamin Waterhouse, Mark Longaker, Crystal Colombini, James Arnt Aune and Rob Asen. In particular, I extend my deepest gratitude to my advisors, the immensely different but immensely formative, Dana Cloud and Christian Lundberg. This project, however indirectly, would have been impossible without the friendship of my peers, including Matt Morris, Kurt Zemlicka, Alex McVey, Adam Rottinghaus, Calum Matheson, Chris Dahlie, Armond Towns, Grant Bollmer, Heather Woods, Lucy Burgchardt, Andrew Davis, Carolyn Hardin, Allison Schlobohm, Dana DeSoto, Amy Fallah, Josh Scacco, Atilla Halsby, Marnie Ritchie, Kevin Musgrave, Dustin Greenwalt, Leslie Rossman, and Anna Kornbluh. Two friends deserve special mention, without whom I would have never considered graduate study in the first place: Bryan McCann and Kevin Johnson. Thank you, from the bottom of my heart.

This project has received institutional assistance, for which I am truly grateful. The University of Kansas' New Faculty General Research Fund played a pivotal role in funding my archival work at the University of Chicago's Hanna Holborn Gray Special Collections Research Center, to which I am also thankful. The University of Kansas' Hall Center for the Humanities has also been generous, and I am humbled by receiving its Friends of the Hall Center Book Publication Award. The work performed by Lindsey Kraus, my research assistant, in gathering materials, organizing citations, and other innumerable tasks, is staggering, above and beyond any expectations I had. Thank you. I am also grateful for the collegial support from my department, the Department of Communication Studies, in particular, Jay Childers, Dave Tell, and Beth Innocenti. I also thank

Ben Chappell for accepting me into the Hall Center for the Humanities Faculty Colloquium on the cultural lives of neoliberalism, where part of this project was born.

Finally, I am grateful for the help, the solidarity, and the love from my partner, Ashley Muddiman, who witnessed this project grow from its inception to now. I can never ever repay you for this support.

An earlier version of chapter 1 was published in the *Quarterly Journal of Speech* 104, no. 4, 400–21 (2018) and an earlier version of chapter 2 appeared in *Advances in the History of Rhetoric* 21, no. 2, 115–30 (2018).

Introduction

The Metastatic Logic of the Incentive

> Economists, the prophets of incentives, quite logically respond to their own incentives to service their various constituencies, and as they never cease to insist, life is nothing but a sequence of trade-offs. Whenever they make reference to the 'public good' or 'general welfare' in the course of their endeavors, they frequently mean nothing more than the brute fact of *caveat emptor*.
>
> —Philip Mirowski, *Never Let a Serious Crisis Go to Waste*[1]

This book is a story about a magic word. To say it at a business roundtable, a Congressional hearing, during oral arguments at the Supreme Court, inside a workplace, or during a faculty meeting, indicates a special knowledge—a shortcut to understanding what motivates people. It is a word that cuts across the social field. It is universally applicable, promiscuous even, and promises a simplified way to render a chaotic world sensible. It is a word that summarizes an entire approach to human behavior. It is a word invoked by the powerful, the well connected, the true believers. Its enthusiastic proponents have won Bank of Sweden prizes in economic sciences, have been appointed to presidential administrations, have written for top news outlets, have become influential federal judges, and have testified in front of—and elected to—the United States Congress. This is also a book about an extremely ordinary word. Chances are, you have said it aloud to children, coworkers, students, and friends. It springs to mind whenever you need to induce a behavior you desire. When signing up for a health insurance plan, or weighing options for a car purchase, the word has flickered across your computer screen, enticing you to act. The word is incentive. It acts as a charm, an incantation, a word that "sets the tune" of its listener's behavior. As *Freakonomics* authors Steven D. Levitt and Stephen J. Dubner emphatically put it, "*Incentives are the cornerstone of modern life*."[2] To be "incentive-driven" is the human condition: we satisfy our desires within a universal system of rewards and penalties, in accordance with our unique individual preferences. While the term originated from economic theory, it now describes all manner of social interaction, from love to healthy eating. Incentives purport to explain how businesses motivate workers, when people turn off the light at night to sleep, and even how courts come to their rulings. Former Federal Circuit Court Judge Richard Posner, the most widely cited US legal authority, relied upon incentives as part of his judicial philosophy, informed by the precepts of neoclassical economics. For Posner, "The 'economist's basic analytical tool for studying markets' can be used to study other behavior."[3]

Despite its neutral appearance, there is nothing innocent about the appearance of "incentives" in matters of social importance. The incentive framework smuggles in a quintessentially economic view of society to noneconomic domains. When a mother incentivizes her daughter to run errands by promising a visit to a taco truck, when a criminal justice reform activist looks to "change the incentives" for prosecutors, or when a sports journalist casually remarks that "like all human beings, major league players respond to incentives," they are not simply selecting from an available set of equivalent terms to describe the world around them.[4] Rather, utterances like these represent the colonization of common sense by the discipline of economics by applying an individualized, conscious, cost/benefit analysis to the complexities of social life. The seepage of economic thought into these formations is neither natural nor inevitable; its deployment is no impartial description of social reality. Incentive rhetoric embodies the leading edge of the economization of everyday life—the reduction of social complexity to a knowable set of assumptions about what motivates people and what causes their actions. To be sure, not all incentives are created equal: the legal system incentivizes individuals to refrain from murder by harshly punishing the act, while a public radio station incentivizes individuals to make charitable donations by offering canvas tote bags and window decals. My aim is less to provide a framework for adjudicating one's own comfort with its various appearances in society but to index what is symbolically exchanged in its adoption. This work addresses the consequences when a diverse vocabulary for motives is traded for a single signifier that is, without exception, yoked to the discipline of economics and foregrounds a quintessentially "economic" vision of the social bond. The specific content of any one incentive is less socially important to me than the form that has metastasized into entirely new domains. In other words, I am concerned with why a food bank and the World Bank use the same exact term to explain people's actions.

What makes incentive rhetoric so powerful, so pervasive, and so present in our lives? The answer concerns economics' own account of its causal claims and what specific type of insights it generates in its way of seeing. Economics, Hoover contends, originated as a "science of causes," whose conceptions of causality from Hume and others "remain implicit in economics today."[5] Incentives work as an account of causality—by incentivizing behavior, one can elicit any manner of result, be it rational economic activity or positive public health outcomes. The power of the incentive framework is also its universality; its insights operate identically in the other direction. Some economic policies, social policies, and workplace policies produce "perverse incentives" that contravene not the precepts of economic thinking but the supposedly rational and efficient outcomes promised by the ideologists of capital. In the tradition of rhetoric, metastasis is the trope that denotes an expansion, and a transfer of cause from one domain to another, and understanding incentives as a metastatic vocabulary helps explain why they appear unavoidable. Metastasis is the tropic engine for incentive discourse in these ways: by curving alternative explanations for outcomes toward those intrinsic to economic analysis, the field of what economics can explain expands.

This version of economic causality, however, is not simple or straightforward. Thus, to understand the contemporary ideological power of incentive discourse is to recognize the strange temporality of its claims. Incentive-based causality, this book argues, is a *retroactive* phenomenon, in that the "meaning" of any action is only established by retroactively positing any outcome as *having been caused* by the ironclad laws of economics. Incentive discourse retroactively distills all human motivation into the narrow axioms of consumer behavior, borrowed from neoclassical economic thought, and its epistemological presumptions. The word "incentive" names (and covers) the gap of causality—and, like any gap, it has a form: any outcome becomes understandable once we discover the "hidden forces" of markets that pervade our existence. Incentives offer an account not of what specifically motivates individuals but a formal axiom that claims they are motivated and a promise for how to discover their motives; the analysis retroactively distills what must have caused an action from extant resources. However, this figural occlusion elides questions surrounding structural economic inequalities, and what results is an extreme individualization of responsibility for complex, conjunctural matters. (For instance, economists have argued that if a woman leaves her job to care for children, she is incentivized by a "weakness for children," rather than meaningful employment—therefore no ameliorative legislation or social action ought to be enacted.[6]) As a set of public persuasive acts, incentive rhetoric prescribes a vision of the social bond contoured fundamentally by economic precepts: we must behave like economically rational agents *because we already do*. This approach, which replaces alternative explanations for outcomes with the "one social science" of economics, narrows explanatory faculties and black-boxes genuine questions about complex, noneconomic determinants of social change. When incentives become a univocal explanatory matrix, individuals are held responsible for their (constrained) choices, all structural inequalities can be safely tucked away as results of prior incentive structures, and institutions are at license to prescribe behaviors for their populations. "Incentives" give rhetorical cover to enormously uneven distributions of outcomes in today's society by retroactively ascribing an operative incentive structure that motivated individuals to accept their lot in life; it should come as no surprise that such logics thrive in moments of extreme wealth inequality.

What Is an Incentive?

In chapter 2, I trace a concrete history of the term from antiquity, but for now, a provisional definition of "incentive" will demonstrate how the term extends beyond its original resting place. The *Oxford Dictionary of Economics* defines the term primarily as causal inducement within the workplace: "Rewards or penalties designed to induce one set of economic agents to act in such a way as to produce results that another economic agent wants. As rewards for good results, incentives can include higher pay, better working conditions, better job security, better promotion prospects, or prestige. . . . Incentives cannot be based on inputs or outputs unobservable by management: to motivate these it is necessary to rely on self-respect or team spirit."[7] Workplace incentives solve a motivational problem for employers and managers—they "provide a tool to increase motivation, shape the way people work, and make businesses more productive."[8] Nonmonetary incentives can be "material" like a corner office, or "immaterial," like a title, but unsurprisingly, money remains the best incentive within the workplace, according to a meta-analysis performed by Boswell, Colvin, and Darnold.[9] Similarly, researchers from the *Harvard Business Review* found that while performance pay incentives are the most effective in inducing work and stimulating job satisfaction, they do increase the perception that the extra pay only comes "through an intensification of the work process."[10] Incentives also frequently refer to "tax incentives" offered by governments to induce action in constituents, either individually or for corporations. For instance, when Amazon took bids for a new headquarters in 2018, 238 separate cities offered up bids, largely offering lavish tax incentives and abatements totaling in the billions of dollars to attract the corporation to set up shop.[11] The city of Chicago offered to pay part of the income tax bills of its employees, Columbus offered a 2.8-billion-dollar property tax exemption, and Atlanta offered a car exclusively for Amazon personnel on Atlanta's mass transit system and fifty free parking spots and a lounge for Amazon executives at the Hartsfield-Jackson International Airport."[12]

Today, the logic of the incentive describes monetary and nonmonetary interactions on a single plane; this textbook term has entered new realms but has not shed its neoclassical foundations. As Gregory Mankiw puts it in his *Principles of Macroeconomics*, "People respond to incentives" is the discipline's foundational axiom.[13] Economist Gary Becker advocates a parsimonious rubric for all social questions organized around the centrality of the incentive: human beings (1) have stable preferences (they do not change their beliefs or desires under any circumstances whatsoever), (2) they are utility-maximizing (they act to satisfy those desires), and (3) they operate as if they are working within market structures (in that individuals weigh the "prices" of their behaviors and desires before acting). He writes: "The heart of my argument is that human behavior is not compartmentalized, sometimes based on maximizing, sometimes not, sometimes motivated by stable preferences, sometimes by volatile ones, sometimes resulting in an optimal allocation of information, sometimes not. Rather, all human behavior can be viewed as involving participants who maximize their utility from a stable set of preferences and accumulate an optimal amount of information and other inputs in a variety of markets."[14] Becker's formulation anticipates Arnsperger and Varoufakis's critical definition of neoclassical economics, in which three axioms encapsulate the discipline: methodological equilibration, methodological individualism, and methodological instrumentalism.[15] This approach presupposes that market mechanisms coordinate all behavior, that individuals are the basic (and only) unit of analysis, and that individuals maximize their utility, or happiness, as they see fit. This conceptually slim edifice articulates any present outcome as the result of prior incentives and massages a complex reality into evidence for an efficient market process. Whether monetary or nonmonetary, inter- or intrapersonal, observable or unobservable, incentives discursively mediate vastly disparate orders of being into becoming fungible with one another and provide economic theory with a coherent rationale for all human behavior, which neatly lines up with neoclassical economic axioms of consumer behavior. The logic of the incentive, thanks in large part to influential economists, has spread into domains far beyond that of simple commodity relations.

The cultural metastasis of incentives does not mean that people are motivated by money more than ever but rather that all cultural practices are presumed to obey the tenets of economic theory. In their 2014 self-help book, *Think Like a Freak*, *Freakonomics* authors Levitt and Dubner follow Becker in that they both centralize incentives into an analysis of human behavior and metastasize it to incorporate virtually every motive imaginable: "If there is one mantra a Freak lives by, it is this: people respond to incentives . . . Different types of incentives—financial, social, moral, legal, and others—push people's buttons in different directions, in different magnitudes . . . But if you want to think like a Freak, you must learn to be a master of incentives—the good, the bad, and the ugly."[16] To speak of incentives is tricky because its prevalence stems in part from its conceptual promiscuity. The promiscuity of the concept stems from its status as a load-bearing term for the discipline of economics: if it is the proper object of study for economics and economics is, in the words of one of its theoreticians, "anything an economist studies," then "incentive" is nothing less than the description of quite literally any action in modern life. According to Benjamin Powell, a fellow of the Mercatus Center, a right-wing think tank associated with George Mason University, it is private property itself, combined with a price system, which provides incentives for individuals to both conserve and protect their resources as well as engage in productive economic activity.[17] In this sense, "incentive" functions synecdochically for the capitalist mode of production itself, human beings are at root incentive-driven animals, and capitalism is the best system for coordinating them.

To summarize, the incentive binds neoclassical economics' axioms of behavior, for it lurks below, and motivates, all action (whether it be choosing a brand of peas, a romantic partner, an optimal amount of environmental pollution, or whether to murder someone). Any articulation of reward or motive is redescribed as an economic input, so "personal habits and addictions, peer pressure, parental influences on the tastes of children, advertising, love and sympathy, and other neglected behavior" become material for analysis using a neoclassical economic approach.[18] Thus it is better to think of an incentive less as a "thing" on its own but a name with a twofold status: a signifier attached to economics' object of desire. It is not the commodity that one purchases, it is a measure of its desirability. It is not a monetary reward for one's hard work but rather the measure of one's desire to obtain the wage. Its peculiar status—as signifier, that which represents the subject for another signifier—and as an object of desire, is what makes incentive such a tricky, and useful vehicle for the discipline of economics and its spread into new arenas.

The Imperial Ambitions of Economics

The prevalence of economics, economists and economic theory in contemporary culture is unquestionable—in everything from popular entertainment, journalism, the nonprofit sector, and politics, economics functions as a governing metaphor for imagining the social bond, interpersonal relations, and even the underlying structure of the natural world.[19] Mainstream economics has formidable reach due in part to its imperial ambitions. Jack Hirshleifer, in an essay celebrating the American Economics Association's centenary, writes approvingly of economics' ambitions: "It is ultimately impossible to carve off a distinct territory for economics, bordering upon but separated from other social disciplines. Economics interpenetrates them all, and is reciprocally penetrated by them. *There is only one social science.*"[20] Hirshleifer calls economics "the universal grammar of social science" and praises its "imperialist invasive power" because "our analytical categories—scarcity, cost, preferences, opportunities, etc.—are truly universal in applicability."[21] Economist Maurice Allais, in his 1990 Bank of Sweden prize lecture, stated: "I have been gradually led to a twofold conviction: human psychology remains fundamentally the same at all times and in all places; and the present is determined by the past according to invariant laws. It seems to me that, to a very large extent, the social sciences must, like the physical sciences, be based on the search for relationships and quantities *invariant in time and in space.*"[22]

Economist Ernest Fehr argues against the insistence on attentiveness to context: "That view lacks any grounding. In this regard, I really like the strong theoretical emphasis of economics and our desire for unifying explanations. It distinguishes us from biologists and psychologists, and provides us with a normative anchor."[23] Imperialism is an apt metaphor for what economics does to other disciplines and to the lifeworld. Empires do not merely materially dominate their colonies, nor do they simply extract and make the people of their colonies poorer. They alter the conditions of production under a new law of value and irrevocably change the horizons of the colonized, while simultaneously incorporating new signs of value under their aegis, thus turning these signs into shibboleths.

Fine and Milonakis call the preeminence that economists are afforded in public policy discourse, and the seepage of economics into such fields, "economics imperialism," or the seepage of economic assumptions and methods into other disciplines.[24] Earle, Moran, and Ward-Perkins term our contemporary conjuncture an "Econocracy"—a government run by and for economists and economic approaches to solving problems.[25] Of all of the social sciences, only economics is associated with a "Nobel," although it is not a Nobel Prize in a strict sense but rather a prize handed out by the central bank of Sweden. Of all the social sciences, only economics has a White House advisory board. In the legal field, as of 2020, twenty-nine faculty members of the country's top-ranked law school, Yale University, have at least one degree in economics. The aforementioned Judge Posner— the single-most cited legal scholar nationwide—explicitly advocates the "law and economics" market-based approach to all matters, legal, moral and ethical. The application of a market framework onto the juridical subject, with an emphasis on protecting property rights and presuming selfish behavior by claimants has been extraordinarily successful, thanks to funding efforts by billionaire libertarian Charles Koch and the intellec- tual efforts of influential faculty in law schools nationwide. According to Nancy MacLean, "By 1990 . . . a stunning 40 percent of the U.S. federal judiciary had been treated to a Koch-backed curriculum."[26] The University of Chicago, whose economics department birthed the eponymous (and infamous) "Chicago School" of economics, is a leader in this subdiscipline: the law school endows several chairships in law and economics, and organizes a yearly institute on the topic.[27] A 2017 participant, Mateusz Grochowski, was quoted in the school's newsletter as saying the institute "was inspiring and incentivizing."[28]

Other fields, including political science, have witnessed economics enter through the front door. In 2020, at least twenty-nine members of

Harvard's Kennedy School of Government had a degree in the field, most of them graduate degrees. Within academic publishing, rational choice theory, or the adoption of economic tools for political science, has fairly recently arrived within the field as a way to interpret the behaviors of political actors (institutions, voters, politicians) as well as to entreat them to behave according to these economic precepts. To wit: the subject heading "rational choice theory" in the Political Science Complete database yields 550 results from 1965 to 2017; of this number, 455 have appeared since the year 1997, and 515 have appeared since 1987. In other words, 93 percent of all articles engaging with rational choice theory have been published in the last three decades. The tenets of rational choice in economics, law, and now politics have consequences for how public policy is shaped (and defended in court): The Obama administration's signature legislative achievement, the Affordable Care Act, mentions "incentives" 105 times in its text, referring to monetary payments for individual enrollees as well as for health providers that meet certain patient outcomes.[29]

But as Grossberg puts it, coding social activity as "economic" demands critical attention, particularly upon a discipline that has presided over some serious empirical shortcomings.[30] Infamously, following the 2008 financial crisis, Queen Elizabeth II of England asked a group of economists at the London School of Economics why they failed to see the crash coming. The bemused economists returned a three-page letter to Buckingham Palace, attributing the crisis to "a failure of the collective imagination of many bright people" and that the financial sector was "guilty of wishful thinking combined with hubris."[31] Grossberg writes,

> What other discipline claims the right to directly shape real policies, while building analytic tools that enable it to operate by abstracting models that are only weakly if at all connected to reality? What other discipline could claim to be the only true science in the human sciences, while still clinging to its founding texts . . . as if they were sacred? . . . What other discipline can claim to be authoritative, even a 'science,' and yet have such a bad record?[32]

The social power of economics and economists within the academy and within the think-tank, NGO, and political realms has much to do with its status as an affirmative science: economics (and economics alone) is capable of narrating a compelling, coherent, and uncomplicated story about the shape of the present. The very parsimony of economic analysis, whose roots stem back to Adam Smith, William Stanley Jevons, and Alfred Marshall, authorizes its spread across the social field, to solve purportedly "non-economic" problems through recourse to economic axioms. Its ingratiation with the powerful is no historical accident.[33]

Why Psychoanalysis?

It is precisely because incentives are not a natural component of human existence—incentives are frequently imposed upon individuals through forced choices—that they are part of a hegemonic struggle over what is "common sense." And because they are foundational to an "imperial" discipline, it matters less whether they provide an adequate representation of the world as a whole, what matters is that they are an operant, internally coherent signifying structure. The failed predictions, unrealistic assumptions, or moral ambiguities of mainstream economics are not its weaknesses but instead are evidence of economics' status as primarily a signifying system: a system of tropic connections and disconnections largely indifferent to "real-world" referents. As Jacques Lacan puts it in his "Presentation on Psychical Causality," "if a man who thinks he is a king is mad, a king who thinks he is a king is no less so."[34] That is, the hyperboles, errors, and imperialistic claims have never prevented an "untrue" discourse to take root. Seen from this angle, Adam Kotsko's judgment of neoliberalism a "political theology," is apropos, for neoliberalism provides "an account of the sources of legitimacy for our social institutions and of the moral order of the world."[35] Theology similarly functions as a signifying system with no external verifiable referent, no "transcendental signifier" that grounds it, and yet discursively stitches up an unstable, chaotic world.[36] The psychoanalytic perspective requires seeing how speech is an instantiation—an insistence—on what is empirically not present. Speech fills in a causal gap precisely because of the lack of a "transcendental signifier" that provides the final word. Thus to demystify the discourse of incentives, and neoclassical economics more broadly, requires taking its signifying practices to the letter.

The language of economic inquiry, its aspirations as a universal social science, the very grammar of our interactional being, and its pretensions at quantifying nonempirical objects, demands a vocabulary capable of sizing it up—hence my introduction of psychoanalysis as an interpretive framework. Incentives function as indexes of desire, act synecdochically for the capitalist mode of production, and all the while, the justifications for their usage are laundered through the symbolic order. Psychoanalytic inquiry attends to these three aspects—it is a style of inquiry that foregrounds desire, its objects, and its intersections with speech. Hence an attention to the rhetorical life of the incentive, this peculiar object, will begin to help explain why economics is so uniquely powerful in everyday life. Following Deirdre McCloskey's (and others') inauguration of the "rhetoric of economics" field of inquiry, scholars have drawn attention to precisely how economic discourse exerts social effects via rhetorical mechanisms. Goodnight and Green retell the story of the dot-com bubble as a fundamentally mimetic process; Hanan, Ghosh, and Brooks deploy the memory studies term "mnesis" to explore how neoclassical economic theory's ontological rhetoric collapses different orders of time to theoretically justify economic equilibrium.[37] Colombini uses the kinesthetic metaphor of "walking away" from homes with underwater mortgages to explore potential resistant practices following the 2009 foreclosure crisis in America.[38] And Abbott traces the public circulation of "confidence" following the 2008 financial crisis, and sees it as the guiding metaphor of the Bush administration's strategic response thereto.[39]

Recent critical scholarship has recently taken up Lacanian psychoanalysis as a method for interpreting texts on a variety of publicly significant matters, and my adoption of Lacan's work follows his careful attention to an economy of tropes in public discourse. The privileged site for Lacan, a practitioner his entire professional life, was speech: "These patients speak to us in the same language as ourselves. Without this component, we would be in total ignorance. It's therefore the economy of discourse, the relationship between meaning and meaning, the relationship between their discourse and the common organization of discourse, that allows us to ascertain that a certain delusion is involved."[40] Lacan's rhetorical artifact is not the discrete utterance of an all-knowing subject, nor is it the epiphenomenal effect of a dominant ideology, but a practice that is mutually interpenetrated by each. Rickert writes: "If it is through signifiers that function not so much as *representations* of the world and people but as their *representatives*, then the relations between language and audience are mystified each time we isolate the two as separate entities."[41] In the absence of a symbolic guarantee, or "click" between signifier and signified, speech mediates this gap, or lack-in-being; it is both a technology of desire and of fulfillment. Speech renders an inconsistent world as "whole," but in so doing, its leakages, breakages, and especially repetitions testify to the presence of the unconscious.

The unconscious, Lacan reminds us, resides in speech, immanent to each utterance. Lacan's twin aphorisms, that the unconscious is structured like a language, and the unconscious is the discourse of the Other, stake out positions that allow psychoanalysis to interpret verbal ejaculations of public import. The irresolvable conflict between "structure" and "agency" is a false problem when supplemented with the unconscious: albeit not predictable from the outset or determined in advance, structure (language) interacts with agency (speech), and obeys certain formal and contextual rules. The grammar of the unconscious, Lacan writes in "The Instance of the Letter in the Unconscious," relies upon the figures of metaphor and metonymy, or condensation and displacement.[42] Metaphor and metonymy, or condensation and displacement, are minimal formal principles of connection, circulation, and difference for any language to operate. And simultaneously, just as Marx argued that humankind can only solve the problems it can set out for itself, the unconscious is made up only of the social, cultural, and historical material that circulates around any speaking subject, the "raw material" (as in Freud's dream-work) of everyday life that constitutes it. A rhetorical unconscious helps explain why, in so many different arenas of life, "incentive" seems to spring to mind for speakers of all kinds. It is doubtlessly encouraged by the powerful (and much of this work attends to the speech of powerful political figures who advocate on its behalf), yet it also appears as a natural, neutral term that summarizes, better than any other, the conflagration of desire, reward, and effort.

A psychoanalytic contribution entails a careful parsing of the mechanisms by which rhetorical mechanisms activate, compel, habituate, and rationalize discursive practices. Much like the way analysands slip psychologically significant admissions into their sessions, the repetition of phrases by speakers in public signals a discursive investment; depending on the translation into English, Lacan refers to this process as the "agency" or the "insistence" of the letter. Lacanian authors have employed various technical terms to explain the engines of circulation, repetition, and purchase on subjects, such as the *objet a*, *jouissance* (enjoyment), the "fundamental fantasy" ($\$ \Diamond a$), and *cathexis*.[43] *Objet a* is Lacan's term for the "object-cause" of desire, the quotient of desire that remains in the gap in speech, between the signifier and the signified, or colloquially, that which is "in you, but more than you." To attend to the *objet a* is to recognize that any desired object contains a surplus. Desire is not reducible to a job promotion, new item of clothing, or monetary reward; desire is that which lurks beneath each, an engine that spurs every subsequent desire. The same mechanism operates within speech. As Lacan reminds us, when one speaks, one either says too much or too little—the word is insufficient. At an unconscious level, the speaking subject is aware of two possibilities existing in tandem: both the inadequacy of the signifier to match the signified and an anxiety that the signified is not what one intended in the first place.

The *objet a* is a nonempirical object but one that exerts effects nonetheless and can be located in the disturbances it elicits in speech. Foregrounding the interaction between speech and *objet a* offers a methodological and analytical advantage: economists employ "incentive" as a nonempirical, measurable object that nevertheless exerts effects on subjects. "Incentive" joins together the enigmas of cause and effect and provides, through its habituated repetition, a stable, knowable, and rational world, in which all activity can be attributable to the ironclad laws of economics: prices, preferences, and utility. Thus, in the speech of economists, theorists, ideologists, cheerleaders, and policymakers, "incentive" functions as the *objet a* for the discipline itself, making a "whole" discourse where before there resided a hole of causality. By insisting on the attributive value of "incentive" rather than its causal value, one can identify how it is economics' own object of desire, the thing it seeks in every social interaction, to retroactively render any outcome as quintessentially economic. The supposed neutrality of the term, its function as a form rather than a content, masks its libidinal value for the discourse of economics, for it offers pretentions at causality and a way to retroactively assign casual power to narrow economic precepts.

Plan for the Work

Overall, this work aims to address the question, "Why are incentives everywhere now?" by accentuating the key words in the question: *incentives*, *everywhere*, and *now*. Chapter 1 introduces a set of terms from a politically engaged psychoanalysis, with particular attentiveness to the method's rhetorical dimensions. Psychoanalysis and the language of trope offer a materialist account of economics' contemporary pervasiveness and the symbolic dimensions of its power. An enormously consequential discourse, with pretentions to explain everything in modern life, demands a critical framework that can match its precision on the topic of desires and their objects. In this chapter, I explore the psychoanalytic concept of "retroactive causality" and the trope of "metastasis" to explain why incentives appear to be *everywhere*: incentive rhetoric stakes robust claims about causality, which accounts for how easily its explanatory matrix can spread into new and disparate sites. As described by Quintilian, Cicero, and others, the trope of metastasis designates a rhetorical shift from one cause to another: "Incentive" emblematizes the trope by shifting the cause of any action into that of "the economic." Retroactive causality takes this one step further and elucidates how the causal claims that economists advocate are merely a logical distillation that generates a stable economic cause for any outcome in the present, which renders any outcome (particularly any social inequality) justifiable.

Chapter 2 tells a story about the term "incentive," from its roots in antiquity to the twentieth century, which explains why *incentive*, instead of any other term, has such cultural preponderance. The term's contemporary slipperiness and promiscuity is built into its origins. "Incentive" arrives from the Latin *incentivum*, meaning "that which sets the tune" and in its earliest translations offers the sense of a "spell" or "charm" that allures its listeners. The connection between the magic of an incentive and the magical speech associated with classical rhetoric is clear: Marsyas, the satyr, skillfully played the "incentive pipe" to sway his listeners, the same way Socrates would beguile listeners in the *Symposium*. Here I foreground the Lacanian concept of the *objet a*, a nonempirical quantity that acts as the motivating force behind all economic action; the *objet a* is both internal and external (or "extimate") and becomes the proper object of the discipline of economics. Alfred Marshall and Paul Samuelson, two towering figures in neoclassical economic thought, both adopt the term to describe a signal to induce economically motivated action. The discipline of economics adopts "incentive" to incorporate all goal-directed behavior and then yokes this behavior to the pursuit of the money commodity. "Incentive" is externalized into an objective feature of the price system that generates automatic, economically rational responses. Much like how after Marsyas loses his life after challenging Apollo to a contest of musical skill and his trickling blood forms a river, incentives have trickled into everyday culture as a way to attribute cause to an inherently unstable world.

Chapter 3 marks a pivotal moment for the contemporary prevalence of incentives. One economist is largely responsible for the metastasis of incentives across all social fields: Gary Becker. This chapter gives the reason why incentives are everywhere *now*: Becker gained worldwide fame, and a Bank of Sweden Prize in Economic Sciences in 1992, for the theory of an "economic approach to human behavior," in which literally any action can be interpreted according to narrow economic axioms—without reference to context or history. This chapter lays out the rhetorical structure of the incentive that incorporates each of his components: stable preferences, price mechanisms, and utility maximization. Becker's metastatic "economic approach" produces a justification for virtually any inequality imaginable, through the retroactive detection of an incentive: Becker's opposition to environmental laws, public schooling, unions, antidiscrimination laws, and so on, is the result of a methodological deduction from this incentive-based approach. Becker's approach allows for the detection of an economy of enjoyment that underwrites, and operates beneath, commodity-based inter-actions, such that the rationality of the market is continuously affirmed, and no inequality can ever be deemed unjust. I conclude the chapter by exploring how Becker's unflinching approach is, in some ways, a challenge to the fields of economics and rhetoric.

Chapter 4 takes up debates over equal pay legislation in Congress as emblematic of the Lacanian concept of the "Real": opponents of equal pay simultaneously contend that while the gender pay gap does not exist, if it did, there would be perfectly good reasons for it. The pay gap presents no "neutral ground" upon which to view it and acts as a stain or hitch that blocks the presentation of an "objective" reality. I examine the legislative fates of two bills here: the Lilly Ledbetter Fair Pay Restoration Act, and the Paycheck Fairness Act, and how incentive rhetoric was deployed in order to sink the latter. Whereas the Lilly Ledbetter Act was named for a woman, it was desexed, and made applicable to the liberal juridical subject writ large. By contrast, the fairly minor labor market reforms promised by the Paycheck Fairness Act were characterized as jeopardizing the free market system entirely. Central to opposition was the invocation of "women's incentives," or the natural desires that women have to care for children and the elderly, that would be either unfairly rewarded or threatened were this bill to pass. Simply put, the "non-monetary incentives" that result from the nature of gendered social reproduction are retroactively laundered into justifications for the continued underpayment and mistreatment of women. Lacan's concepts of "masculine" and "feminine" *jouissance* explain how these justifications functioned rhetorically, with commentators, members of Congress, and testifiers against the bill attempted to answer the question, "What does Woman want?"

Chapters 5 and 6 evaluate the global phenomenon of "nudges" as the political culmination of the logic of the incentive. Behavioral "nudges" emerge from the idea that people occasionally make poor choices, not just for themselves, but for society as a whole; state actors are then authorized to step in and correct these mistakes with a "nudge" in the proper direction. Nudges have been deployed on issues ranging from environmental regulation to healthy eating, education, organ donations, and healthcare, in which "choice architects" nudge individuals into generating economically rational outcomes. This also entails "incentivizing" socially beneficial behaviors, or inducing ethical or responsible behavior by corporations, institutions, and so on. Nudges function as the sublimation of the "economic approach to human behavior": rather than rejecting outright the idea that all human beings behave economically rationally, nudges instead presume that the economic approach on the whole is valid, but that policymakers can systematically adjust the behaviors of individuals by altering the "prices" of their actions. Despite the fact that they tend to promote social and ethical goals, nudges fully embody the tenets of neoclassical economics.

Chapter 5 characterizes nudges as that which instantiates "political neurosis." Nudges force individuals to make choices within marketlike spaces designed to reveal their true incentive but at the cost of denying collectivities universal public goods. Neurosis, understood by Lacan as organized around a repression that guards against an excess of enjoyment, characterize the subjective disposition of a nudge. When offered the appearance of a choice, one is not offered certainty but a question about the Other's desire, phrased as "What does the Other want of me?" Nudges are figures, not only of symbolic exhaustion but also of symbolic impotence: states cannot even appear to offer universal political goods; they can only incentivize individuals to make "good choices" to pursue them. Chapter 6 presents the consequences and limits of the widespread use of nudges in statecraft. Here, I examine two cases wherein nudges and incentives failed to cope with the social crises surrounding the COVID-19 pandemic. With reference to Lacan's distinction between the "aim" and "goal" of a subject, as well as the "decline of symbolic efficiency" hypothesis, I evaluate how political figures argued that supplemental unemployment benefits provided "disincentives to work" and that labor must be disciplined through privation. Despite the pretenses of incentives as suasive devices, I expose the coercion upon which incentives rest. Next, I examine the efficacy of vaccination incentives offered by states and cities and why they failed to have an effect on the unvaccinated population. The inefficacious vaccination incentives were victims of the success of incentives writ large, which privileges individual decision-making and weighing of costs and benefits; by addressing people exclusively as individual rational choosers, and not members of communities, incentives failed to hit their mark. The expansion of the logic of private property to not only one's own possessions, but the signifiers that emanate from these possessions, entails that the economic way of looking at behavior is insulated against any attempt to nudge people in a socially beneficial manner through market mechanisms.

The concluding chapter takes up the massive challenge that economics as a discipline continues to pose, not simply to our concepts of representation but also to the social bond as a whole. The rhetoric of incentives provides a coherent rationale for all human activity as caused by an unseen but measurable market force; its public justifications retroactively account for virtually every inequality. Just as nudges do, incentives demonstrate a critique of political representation (in the colloquial sense) and at a conceptual level—only market mechanisms could ever hope to properly represent the desires of individuals. In this chapter, I advance five dialectical postulates of incentives that summarize their commitments and provide actionable rejoinders to each, involving both "mass politics" colloquially understood, and a politically engaged psychoanalytic reading practice. The "hidden forces" of desire that a study of incentives unearths these desires, so only economists are capable of correctly interpreting social reality. The imperialistic discipline of economics succeeds by representing the cause of any behavior as fundamentally economic. In its stead, Lacan's concepts of desire and of the signifier (and the complex interrelation of the two) demonstrate two things: First, all desire is structurally metonymic. This may appear to be a concession to mainstream economics: that any attempt to "guarantee" an outcome ultimately ends up in its diversion. Second, despite this, mediation matters. That is, as mentioned, incentivization does not solve but only displaces the problem of social reality onto that of the economic. Incentives are a framework that rhetorically justifies the commodification of social reality, and are thus an index of the social power of commodity relations.

Contra its depiction by a deconstructive framework, a signifier in the Lacanian sense is fundamentally one of nonidentity—no signifier is adequate to itself (or self-identical), and no signifier equates to the thing it purports to represent. To rephrase Lacan's definition of the signifier, incentives represent a cause for another signifier. If incentive rhetoric names a gap and offers a fixity in the guise of a form, the psychoanalytic task is to resist that fixity, unbind its artifice, and hold the gap open for new ways of being apart from market forces. As Fredric Jameson develops the idea in "An American Utopia," psychoanalysis' base unit of interpretation is never the individual but rather the social existence of an individual in a network of signifiers.[44] The kinds of psychological maladies Freud identified in his milieu—perversion, neurosis, psychosis—are not simply the patient's own but symptomatic of an ill society. Incentive rhetoric arises as the answer to a set of serious social questions; it should be no surprise that extreme income inequality, fiscal austerity, and the retreat of the welfare state, particularly in the United States, are concomitant with the foregrounding of orthodox economic principles that claim human nature is quintessentially economic. The only way out of the logic of the incentive, and of the economization of everyday life, is to refuse methodological individualism and embrace social relations beyond that of the limiting form of the commodity.

Chapter 1

Incentives, Retroactive Causality, and the Rhetorical Unconscious

The cultural preponderance of incentives in cultural formations is no neutral development—it smuggles in the tenets of neoclassical economic theory to virtually all choices and promotes a quintessentially economic vision of the social bond. Incentive rhetoric appears to have a mind of its own: incentives "spread" across various domains, and they spring to mind in all manner of circumstances not apparently governed by the field of economics. Doubtlessly, economists and political operatives insert the discourse of incentives from their pulpits into various areas—the deliberate deployment of incentives formalizes social relations as identical to commodity interactions. Yet my gamble for its colloquial uptake is not simply that this term is transmitted by the powerful into the heads of ordinary people but rather functions at an unconscious level because of its pretensions toward a robust explanation of causality. Metastasis is the formal name for this operation. Thus, here I introduce key terms from Lacanian psychoanalysis to offer a critical exploration of how incentives function as causal mechanisms. The psychoanalytic unconscious offers a way to view metastasis as a nonsubjective rhetorical agency—not simply a tool used by speakers to transfer cause from one position to another, as Quintilian and others posit, but how this shift occurs nearly spontaneously in their speech. The habituated repetition of a term in significant cultural sites signals an affective investment, a surplus meaning attached to a signifier. For Lacan, when we speak, we always say "too much": "[The unconscious] presumes as well an entire mechanism that makes the case that—whatever you say in thinking about it, or in not thinking about it,

19

whatever you formulate—once you have mounted the treadmill of idle chatter, your discourse always says more than what you are saying."[1] Metastasis does not appear in the figures of rhetoric Lacan names in his *oeuvre* for interpreting speech, but it has tremendous analytic utility.[2]

Quintilian's translation of metastasis as "transference" is an analytically propitious coincidence, for transference is a key psychoanalytic term in several respects. Sigmund Freud, in *The Interpretation of Dreams*, describes it as the process by which some accidental feature of a subject's daily life is taken up by the unconscious and acquires psychological value—the affect of an unconscious signifier is transferred onto the more recent phenomenon.[3] For example, an analysand's unexpressed anxiety about their career may become transferred to the image of a car they saw speeding through a stop sign the previous day. Later, Lacan centralizes the concept of transference in analytic training—what we call "the transference" involves the analysand on the proverbial couch, free-associating, with the analyst out of sight. The purpose of this setup is to fight against the lure of intersubjectivity that communication invites: the two egos of analysand and analyst must not meet, for the possibility lurks that one or both parties will begin to seek in the Other what they lack elsewhere. The analyst may wish to appear as if they actually do hold the secret of the analysand's misery, or the analysand may wish to appear either worse or better depending on what they believe the analyst wants of them. Speech is both the terrain and the tool that breaks the imaginary intersubjective bond of two individuals. As Derek Hook writes, "It is only via highlighting the functions of the signifier, stressing what is unintentionally said within the enunciative properties of speech itself, highlighting thus how the unconscious is the discourse of the Other, that we may reach beyond the deadlock of dyadic intersubjectivity."[4] When rhetoricians mistakenly refer to the materiality of discourse with the accompanying fantasy that speech magically exerts "material" effects, they evade what is radical in Lacan's formulation.[5] The "materiality" of discourse is the medium of language, and its capacity to exert intrasubjective effects on its speaker. When a signifier becomes ineluctable for a speaker, that is a result of the enjoyment lodged in its invocation and repetition.

Within the transference proper is the process of transfer of affect from one "thing"—say, a psychical trauma—to another, the proper word that will unlock and retroactively undo it. But crucially, transference is intended as a radical process, which allows an analysand to discover their own cure through speech; it is only the analyst's job to "provoke desire" in them.[6]

Thus transference, and psychoanalysis overall, is a critical vocabulary for the transfer of cause from the "self" somewhere else, to paraphrase Freud, to transform neurotic misery into ordinary human unhappiness. Hence, this is why attention to the signifying practices of mainstream economics is so valuable at this conjunctural moment: "Incentive" is the enigmatic signifier in economic discourse that actually does promise a "solution" to the world's problems. It "sticks out" in discourse and carries with it greater weight than any equivalent metonym. Psychoanalytic transference works as a counter-movement to the metastasis of neoclassical economics onto cultural formations by shifting the stasis away from economics onto the proper domains of the political, the cultural, the historical, and the terrain of class struggle. If economics binds the plurivocal signifiers of the world to its own narrow precepts, psychoanalysis unbinds them and points to the fragility of the chains that link them together.

The language of trope overall offers a rich vocabulary for this kind of inquiry: "For Lacan, 'trope' marks the idea that no connection in the life of the subject or its discourses is given in advance. Rather, such connections are the result of habituated accidental connections between signs, representations and the world."[7] Lundberg calls rhetoric the enterprise of "*signifying in a condition of failed unicity* and a way of *feigning unicity in the context of failed unicity*"; speech is a compensatory mechanism that stitches up gaps in an inconsistent reality.[8] Tropes are the mechanisms by which subjects feign unicity, they signal the nodal point where a signifier momentarily intersects with an affect to produce enjoyment. Thus psychoanalytic praxis looks for how certain tropes acquire a privileged status and how certain terms become symptomatic of libidinal investment; Lundberg draws attention to how "ritually repeated connections" elicit libidinal investment, acting as a motor force for repetition.[9] And as Rickert puts it, "The signifiers, images, and objects that circulate in socio-symbolic space, however, are never neutral in regard to our comportment toward them. Above and beyond the mechanism of identification, they are continuously penetrated or suffused with *jouissance*."[10] I invoke *jouissance* advisedly. While it can name an unbearable affect, or pulsion beyond pleasure, for my purposes, *jouissance* is the excess within signification that admits a beyond to signification. While the embodied, extra-discursive meanings of the term certainly have utility, for rhetoricians, the concept rears its head within the symbolic order when it symptomatically "sticks out" in a signifying regime.

Lacan's "insistence" of the letter in the unconscious means just that: Once introduced into a subject's psychic reality, a privileged signifier becomes ineluctable, inescapable. When the desire to manage infinite complexity merges with a promise of causal explanation, "incentive" lodges itself into a signifying regime. Braunstein refuses to "say which came first, whether *jouissance* or the word . . . There is only *jouissance* for the being who speaks and because he speaks."[11] Rosman expands upon this idea, suggesting that "*jouissance* and language are co-terminus," and we must insist on evaluating the full weight of co-terminus.[12] Language and *jouissance* are entangled, with the gap between signifier and signified as the space of enjoyment; their structural incommensurability evokes the desire for repetition. Their coincision, their coemergence is also their mutual terminus, their limit. Lacan's work also affords a means of thinking through causality in ways especially pertinent to the issue of incentives. Lacan posits that the conditions for meaning are never pregiven, or even reducible to empiricist, doxastic, or even pragmatist principles. Rather, meaning is established retroactively through tropic mechanisms—the signifier arcs backward in time to render the "blooming, buzzing confusion" of a subject's reality coherent. Lundberg, for instance, takes issue with the conventionalist view of "meaning" in rhetoric, and forwards the economy-of-trope perspective to emphasize how meaning results from momentary nodal points that elicit enjoyment.[13] But the more essential point should not be missed: it is only through the rhetorical labor of the trope that the accidental, habitual activity of the subject solidifies, and becomes a desire to repeat. "Meaning" may indeed name a momentary node of investment but becomes durable through the presence of the trope. Once something like "incentive" becomes a stable explanatory matrix, as Rickert writes, "conceptual stability is achieved retroactively, and insofar as this occurs through hegemonic foundations, we should see that these stabilities can achieve striking sedimentation."[14] The Lacanian concept of retroactive causality explains how incentive rhetoric functions to produce a coherent, quintessentially economic explanation of any and all events.

Retroaction, Cause, and
Metastasis in Psychoanalytic Thought

Psychoanalysis' concept of retroaction comes from Freud's "Wolf Man" case, in which his patient developed severe obsessional neurosis, including hallucinations and animal phobia (hence his pseudonym). Through dream analysis, Freud traced his patient's present-day troubles back to his childhood self witnessing his parents *coitus a tergo* on a hot summer afternoon; the traumatic "primal scene" purportedly caused his present psychological troubles. Yet Freud's innovation is that for the unconscious, time runs backward: The Wolf Man *retroactively willed his cause into being*—witnessing his parents in the act of sex only became traumatic long after the fact. Freud both notes how "*banal*" the act was, and later, rebuking his earlier "seduction theory" of analysis, hypothesizes that "perhaps what the child observed was not a coitus between his parents, but an animal coitus, which he then displaced."[15] His original traumatic experience, whether real or not, functioned not as a cause but as a signifier; witnessing "the real thing" (of copulation) was not traumatic in-itself but became so at the moment "sex" acquired a taboo significance—a meaning—in his present symbolic network. This is not to suggest that causality is always fictitious or that trauma is somehow unreal—far from it. Naming an experience *as* trauma and giving it the dignity it deserves also confers retroactive solidity upon a traumatizing interaction. Hence psychoanalysis' insistence on the painstaking—occasionally interminable—process of "the talking cure" involves unearthing those prior repressed affects and articulating them in a way that is true for the subject—as Lacan claimed, what is at stake in analysis is not "reality," but "truth."[16]

In the field of human affairs, "cause" acts as a discursive surplus: the name conferred upon the gap in our understanding that renders past, present, and future as fundamentally explicable. Lacan ruminates on Aristotle's "four causes" discourses from the *Physics* and *Metaphysics* to pinpoint how causality appears retroactively through the symbolic order. Aristotle argues that any effect results from the intermingling of four causes: the formal, material, efficient, and final, summarized here: "*The substance* or the essence is a cause (for the *why* leads us back to the ultimate formula, and the first *why* is a cause and a principle); in another, it is the matter or the underlying subject; in a third, the source which begins motion; and in a fourth, the cause opposite to the previous, namely, the final cause or the good (for this is the end of every generation and every motion)."[17] I engage here with only the efficient and final causes, which for Lacan align with magic and religion.[18] What binds these regimes is not metaphysics but the primacy of the symbolic order: neither exists without speech. For Aristotle, the final cause is the purpose of any action: "The end, and this is the final cause [that for the sake of which—trans.]; for example, walking is for the sake of health. Why does he walk? We answer, 'In order to be healthy;' and having spoken thus, we think that we have given the cause."[19]

By walking, we set out the final cause ahead of us; we accomplish having caused the action by achieving its end.

For Lacan, Aristotle's vision of causality produces a world of determinism: Aristotle's vision of causality is teleological—every thing exists, or happens, for a purpose that is intertwined with its material, form, and agent. Paul Humphrey posits that Aristotle's "Prime Mover," or the primary cause of all motion in the universe, teleologically functions as the "final cause" of all action precisely because it is the "good toward which all things strive. That is, it acts as an object of desire."[20] Such an approach leaves no space for human action; we are the results of forces effectuating forms through raw material. Empiricist philosophers like David Hume drew attention to the problem of cause—one can never truly be sure what caused the billiard ball to strike the other and fall into the hole—and rightly deduced that any explanation is always a *post hoc* one, retroactively assigned from the position of the observer. For Lacan, these skeptics of causality may be misguided, but they nevertheless pinpoint a kernel of truth. What psychoanalysis adds to our notion of causality is attending to the inclusion of the unconscious, for whom cause is a concern. Causality is a human construct, especially the idea that the "final" cause of any outcome can be definitively pinned down; underlying any causal claim is the unspoken desire for certainty, to determine what *really* caused any outcome. Causality must always be constructed in a signifying chain, a fragile one, in which the inclusion of the speaking subject makes the question more (not less) transparent: did the billiard ball fall into the hole because of the cue's chemical composition, the combined laws of motion and geometry, because of practice, or because of my desire? Lacan explains that for the empiricists "the more cause was criticized, the more the requirements of what might be called determinism were imposed on thought. The less the cause is graspable the more everything seems *caused*—right up to the final term, the one called *the meaning of history*."[21] Lacan's position is neither that causality is fictitious nor that inviolable laws determine the universe in advance. Instead, he navigates a middle ground by locating in both positions the same anxiety: that causality as such designates a gap in our understanding. But to point out that causality is retroactive, and therefore unreal, does not solve the conundrum for the speaking subject; it merely passes it along to the discourse of science: "The gap between cause and effect to the extent that it gets filled in—and this is precisely what is called from a certain perspective, the progress of science—makes the function of cause fade away, I mean, wherever the gap gets filled in."[22] The "final cause," even if unreal, still exerts effects—as mentioned, psychoanalysis is concerned with the psychological "truth" of a subject, not their fragile "reality."

Lacan's critical reading of Aristotle allows us to posit situations in which causality is reversed. Because in human affairs, the "final cause" is always missing from the chain of events—in the absence of what Lacan calls the "big Other," a guarantor and registrar of our actions, the subject compensates for this absence and rhetorically deduces a chain of causality. Something lurks behind the cause, which Lacan designates as a "hidden object," an "object in syncope."[23] What results is a rhetorical form of retroactive causality, in which, through the view of the present, we attribute a "final cause." For example, if we ever unconsciously veer away from a stranger when crossing paths on an empty sidewalk, we fill in this gap of causality through a retroactive rhetorical reconstruction—we tell ourselves the concrete in our path was uneven, that we would have bumped into them had we not moved, or finally, the stranger did not notice anyway. The logic of the unconscious is not simply one of plurality but of opposition—it is not simply any potential replacement signifier but its opposite that takes its place in the chain.[24] This retroactive narration of the act covers over our guilt: not because we could not control our actions but likelier that we were in control but sought symbolic compensation for our unspoken desire to avoid a stranger.[25]

Psychoanalysis rescues causality from determinism by accentuating the symbolic order as surplus to any phenomenon. Says Lacan, "All the effects are subjected to the pressure of a transfactual, causal order which demands to join in their dance, but, if they held their hands tightly, as in the song, they would prevent the cause intruding in their round."[26] Subjects defer to cause precisely at the moment that natural "laws" fail—it is there that the signifier intervenes.

Psychoanalysis' "final cause" is not the expressive causality of the Prime Mover but its inverse—humans rescue idiosyncratic, idiotic, habituated, action from itself by retroactively attributing meaning to our actions. Philippe van Haute writes: "Consider, for example, a mother who holds her crying child up before the mirror and says, 'Look, that's Johnny! Isn't he a big boy!;' . . . The expression 'Look, that's Johnny! Isn't he a big boy!' establishes a meaning that was not there before; it introduces an order into reality that previously did not exist. It compellingly assigns our crying baby boy a place he could not previously have occupied ('big boy!')."[27] As Lacan claims, "This is a retroversion effect by which the subject becomes at each stage what he was before and announces himself—he will have been—only in the future perfect tense."[28] The "raw material" of "Johnny" preexists its symbolic designation, but the symbolic order confers what will have been there all along.[29] There is a recursion effect here: the proper name acts as "cause" for Johnny's behavior—"big boys don't cry," after all. Contra Aristotle, for whom a thing's purpose is lodged even in its material and form, Lacan highlights how this desire to locate purpose is itself compensatory, and indeed, rhetorical. The subject's desire to name a cause both retroactively domesticates the infinite complexity of the world and authorizes its habituated repetition—the signifier arcs forward in time and across conceptual space.

"Incentive" performs tremendous rhetorical labor for it stands in as an explanation of cause, so the question of outcomes can be reduced from an infinite contextual complexity to a single question: "By what were you incentivized?" Because incentive offers a stand-in for cause, I turn now to the trope of metastasis, for it best explains the capacity for incentive rhetoric to spread across the social field. Metastasis' etymology offers a clue to its function: "Metastasis" indicates a displacement, for something is placed (*stasis*) outside (*meta-*) its original context. Incentives are functionally metastatic in that they move beyond their original stasis of financial motivation onto domains not previously governed by its logic. Metastasis names the tropological movement that renders all outcomes as quintessentially economic. Colloquially, "metastasis" denotes the unfortunate effects of cancer, like when the disease metastasizes into another area of the body. I do not shy from this sense—the creep of economic language into everyday discourse and cultural texts is poisonous for alternative visions of the social bond. But this spread is, in the strongest sense of the term, artificial—the result of artifice. Rhetorical thinkers across the centuries—Cicero, Quintilian, Peacham, and Puttenham—offer an interlocking definition of metastasis, and while it goes through several transformations, a conceptual unity subsists.

For these thinkers, metastasis is a trope of purposeful displacement, deployed to shift the responsibility of an outcome. After introducing the trope's traditional definition, I innovate, with reference to psychoanalysis, by viewing metastasis as a nonsubjective tropological movement within a signifying system. In his *Institutio Oratoria*, Quintilian predicates his discussion of metastasis on an orator who must defend against accusations through objection, opposition, pleading ignorance, begging for mercy, and so on. Quintilian builds from Cicero's *de Oratore* and *Brutus/Orator* wherein Cicero defines the trope of metastasis as the "transference of responsibility onto someone else."[30] While Remer notes that Quintilian's focus was on judicial, rather than political oratory,[31] Quintilian's theorization approximates Cicero's own:

> If a defence can neither be sustained on the motive of the act itself, nor by extrinsic aid, our next course is to *transfer the charge,* if we find it possible, on another party . . . Sometimes, then, the blame is thrown on a person . . . Sometimes it is cast on some circumstance, as if *a person who had been directed to do something in the will of another ad had not done it, should say that it was rendered impossible by the laws,* This the Greeks call μεταστασις, "transference."[32]

For Quintilian, metastasis means transferring responsibility from one order of causality to another—from person to person, or person to circumstance.

For Peacham, metastasis works both as refutation and counter-accusation. He defines the term aggressively, as "a forme of speech by which we turne backe those thinges that are objected against us, to them which laid them to us . . . The use of this figure serveth both to repell objections, and also to reply by accusations, and all at one time."[33] Finally, Puttenham (like Cicero) registers metastasis' utility for persuasive ends: "Now as art and good policy in persuasion bids us to abide and not to stir from the point of our most advantage . . . so doth discretion will us sometimes to flit from one matter to another, as a thing meet to be forsaken, and another entered upon; I call him therefore the Flitting Figure, or Figure of Remove."[34] Puttenham's metastasis appears more defensive than the others, but there is an essential unity among these theorists. Metastasis involves a strategic transfer of a charge from one cause to another through aggressive counter-accusation or purposeful evasion; Puttenham merely advocates its utility to dodge-and-weave if in a position of rhetorical weakness.

If "incentives" strictly functioned metonymically for "reward" or "desire," these terms could easily be interchanged. The rhetorical "stickiness" of the term as a transcontextual explanatory device—that corporate governance, political corruption, and classroom behavior can be addressed by "fixing the incentives"—indicates the immense affective investment in the term as such. Incentive rhetorics function supraindividually, they simply "come to mind," even in an offhand manner. When video games slyly "incentivize" certain behaviors through subtle rewards,[35] or when advocates for dramatically liberalized handgun laws argue that "they can limit the harm and take away the incentive that these killers obtain from their warped desire to get media attention," we are a witnesses to a colonization of available discursive resources by the discourse of economics.[36] That the same term can function nearly identically in the workplace, in advertisements, and social interactions demonstrates its metastasis across cultural venues. Certainly, highly paid authors and presidential appointees who attempt to replace school nutrition standards with behavioral incentives for children to eat healthily are deliberately introducing incentives into the social bond, as Bank of Sweden prizewinner Richard Thaler and coauthor Cass Sunstein have argued.[37] For prominent economists, metastasizing incentives onto nonmarket domains is not accidental, or even innocent. Economist Gary Becker used his platform as a columnist for *Business Week* to prescribe incentive-based systems upon nearly every cultural and political issue imaginable. Yet we should take these two sides as symptomatic of the same rhetorical coin. For economists, there is no symbolic distance or artifice in ascribing importance to incentives—the tropic work has already been done. For noneconomists, uttering "incentives" indicates that the connection between one stasis and another are already linked within the symbolic order itself through the trope of metastasis. This is not even necessarily an intentional displacement, in the classical sense of the trope but rather occurs through the habituated rhetorical practices that code everyday life as essentially economic.

In the rhetorical tradition, speakers employ metastasis to intentionally shift blame from one cause to another. The methodological innovation of psychoanalysis is to discover how the speaker's unconscious similarly employs tropic mechanisms as an organizational and libidinal apparatus. Metastasis functions symptomatically in that it stands out; in this case, it refers to the offhand or automatic expression of "incentive" in any social setting. Several years ago, a colleague of mine in political science described to me the difficulties of online teaching at our doctoral institution. Because instructors do not own the intellectual property of the course, he wrote, "there's no incentive for grad students" to improve their courses, even if they have obvious errors or shortcomings. *New York Times* opinion writer Ezra Klein, writing about the United States Senate's filibuster rule, wrote in 2021, "I want to be clear: I don't think getting rid of the filibuster will usher in some new era of bipartisanship. But it would make governance easier, and lead to better incentives at the margin."[38] And many employers offer incentive systems as a component of their health insurance plans—if an employee drinks water, attends biometric screenings, or quits smoking, they earn "incentive points" to be exchanged for lower monthly premiums.[39] Each of these partake in some aspect of what an incentive is—a reward, the desire for an induced outcome, and so on. Yet the axis of selection of any equivalent metonym is circumscribed by the sheer prevalence of "incentives" in our contemporary culture.

This rhetorical stickiness, I argue, stems from the domain of economics using "incentive" as an explanation for cause, rendering a chaotic and contradictory world whole by inserting a hidden mechanism that promotes a rational explanation for all outcomes. For the psychoanalytic tradition, Freud's "Wolf Man" case study models how past and present are entangled in the subject's unconscious and how the attribution of cause solves problems for patients undergoing analysis. For the Wolf Man, his fascination, or fixation, with witnessing his parents' lovemaking became "stuck" in his unconscious—it was simultaneously enticing and horrifying and became his own vulgar explanation of his present psychological difficulties. Attributing causality to this primal experience domesticated his current symptoms and provided a stable through-line to his present psychological difficulties. The enigma of sexuality, of alterity-as-such, and the questions that it opened in him, was kept alive—kept enigmatic. That is, the Wolf Man "enjoyed" his symptom: It explained (away) his current problems by posing an answer that could not be dislodged: since his traumatic experience happened in the past, there is no way for it to be "undone." His explanation in the past arced backward to solidify an uncertain past but also arced forward to rationalize his current misery. The exact same mechanisms are at work in contemporary incentive rhetoric: Incentive rhetorics promise a robust and universal explanation of causality in everyday life, and this accounts for its durability, circulation, and habituation in sites far afield from that of commodity exchange.

The quandary of causality—the anxiety that it elicits—is not simply endemic to the signifying order. Contemporary culture intensifies anxieties around causality: deciphering what the markets want, how to make a comfortable living, why other people act the way they do, these are all perfectly reasonable questions, so the prevalence of "economic culture" should not surprise anyone, as self-help, survival, or as an object of fascination. Who would refuse a universal code to unlocking all human behavior, to manipulate infinite complexity, or to (ideologically) justify anyone's lot in life? Only three simplifying presumptions—individuals are self-interested, have stable preferences, and the "prices" of behaviors are known to individuals prior to any action—are necessary to render this complexity legible. Once incentives become rhetorically indispensable through their pretensions to causality, they can metastasize without limit onto the social field. The general term "incentive" names the specific motivating factor for any given individual and in so doing, stands in for—represents—the specific cause of that behavior. This rhetorical transference is what makes "incentive" structurally metastatic—the word substitutes for the cause, and can become mobile, as all tropes do.

Retroactive Causality as Political Attribution

Incentive rhetorics have social consequences. Here, I draw attention to the extreme individualization of social outcomes when laundered through the logic of the incentive—responsibility is transferred downward from structures to subjects. As mentioned, an incentive can be considered a reward (or penalty) for any behavior, as long as it is measurable and appears to exert causal effect on a subject. Incentives negotiate a strange space, not merely temporally but along the activity/passivity binary: on the one hand, as economics reminds us, it is a science of decision-making, and that the existence of choice is a foundational condition of all market (or marketlike) interactions. On the other, to presume that someone is "incentive-driven" means that they are compelled by an outside force, obedient to things like price signals or the promises of rewards. Incentive rhetorics become an ideological buffer zone for inequality, since every outcome can be retroactively accounted for as a previous set of forces—a different set of preferences, a higher psychic cost, an individual maximizing their utility differently than received theory suggests. The discourse of incentives renders all people retroactively responsible for the (contingent, constrained) choices they make because they are presumed to have voluntarily chosen the action from an available menu of market choices.

For example, upon Apple's introduction of $159 wireless headphones for iPhones, software engineer Sajid Mehmood proclaimed on Twitter, "The $159 AirPod price tag is really for your own sake. Incentivizes you not to lose them."[40] Because commands and coercion purport to be on the opposite end of the spectrum from "incentive-based" approaches, incentives presume that actions are always freely chosen from an available menu of options. Basu writes, "In traditional economics, it is presumed that if a person chooses an alternative x over y, then the person must receive at least as much utility from x as from y. Let me call this the 'choice equals utility' or 'choice equals preference' axiom. This is called 'selfish behavior,' by definition, in microeconomic theory and game theory."[41] This largely restates the concept of freedom within the capitalist mode of production—because no monarch coerces our activities, we freely choose them from within our circumstances. Basu's axiom indicates economics' normative justification for the status quo, since one can assume that any person was incentivized to take the actions they did.

The presumption of individual responsibility also restricts what can be considered coercion, since any choice can be reinterpreted as a voluntary cost/benefit problem. Basu uses his experience with a mugger to illustrate: "When the man pointed the knife at me and asked for my watch, he was giving me a choice: I could give him my watch or my life. I *chose* to keep my life . . . So having a choice cannot be equated with noncoercion. It is depriving me of my right—namely, the right to *both* my watch *and* life—that made it a case of coercion."[42] Basu's preference for remaining alive outweighed his preference for timekeeping, so his decision was rational—QED. In this view, people are paradoxically held responsible for choices from circumstances beyond their control, because they rationally respond to the "price signals" of external circumstances and attune their behavior thereto. James Buchanan and Gordon Tullock use the logic of incentivization to justify inequalities in capitalism as a social good in and of itself: "Inequality, and the incentives that go with it, are crucial in sending the right signals to economic actors."[43] For these thinkers, inequalities are not simply an outcome of the capitalist mode of production, they are a crucial part of its justificatory inner loop. And in a parallel case, in a 1992 *Business Week* column opposing welfare benefits, Becker argued that those who do not enroll in welfare programs value the incentive of personal dignity higher than money.[44] For Becker, the "incentive" of dignity filled a gap between program eligibility and enrollment; if dignity and money are fungible, then defunding welfare programs will result, hydraulically, in increased total social dignity. Retroactively narrating existing social relations—ignoring the difficulty of applying for benefits, the social stigma attached thereto, and deliberate attempts by states to render residents ineligible—becomes a justification for ending the system altogether. Paradoxically (or fortunately, depending on one's beliefs), increasing the stigmatization of welfare benefits justifies ending the programs.

Nudge authors Thaler and Sunstein use the existence of individuals who make "socially unacceptable" choices as evidence of the rectitude of an incentive-based approach to social policy. When a state raises the cost of these behaviors, actors who choose "higher priced" behaviors are presumed to voluntarily pay the penalty, be it monetary or social: "If people want to smoke cigarettes, to eat a lot of candy, to choose an unsuitable health care plan, or fail to save for retirement, libertarian paternalists will not force them to do otherwise—or even make things hard for them."[45] Even if someone's behavior does not appear perfectly "rational," it is rational to the extent that each individual maximizes their utility function as they see it. Hence, critics of "neoliberalism" or of economics more broadly miss the mark when they presume the discipline requires a highly selfish, or super-humanly calculating individual. One only needs an incentive-driven subject that acts to satisfy their desires to derive most of economics' conclusions. Yet Godelier notes that equating rational and economic is a conceptual sleight of hand, for it merely restates a "formal theory of purposive action" in economic terms: "We are thus confronted with a formal definition of 'the economic' which is good for nothing, and a principle of rationality which, in order to elucidate something in the economy, has to assume that the latter has already been correctly defined."[46] Every action taken is "economical" because economics assumes actors have stable preferences and maximize their utility as they see it; because it is economical, it is assumed to be rational. Because each action is presumably voluntary, the status quo is rhetorically justifiable.

The circularity of this explanation is emblematic of economics' retroactive causal loop in explaining real-world inequalities at a grand scale. For instance, in an article published in the *American Economic Review*, one of the so-called Top Five journals in the field, Ashraf and Galor use economic modeling to explain why European, North American, and certain Asian societies happen to be more materially wealthy than Native American and African ones. The argument suggests that it is a "Goldilocks" amount of genetic diversity (not too much, not too little) that causes economic development; this genetic diversity directly correlates with efficient production methods and, therefore, higher productivity: "While the low degree of diversity among Native American populations and the high degree of diversity among African populations have been detrimental forces in the development of these regions, the intermediate levels of genetic diversity prevalent among European and Asian populations have been conducive for development."[47] The authors claim that this genetic determinism explains the fate of societies in ways that are "not captured by geographical, institutional, and cultural factors."[48] As with the Wolf Man, Ashraf and Galor retroactively will the cause into being: while the authors do not mention slavery specifically, they do note that "European colonization significantly altered the genetic diversity and, hence, the composition of human capital in colonized countries."[49] The authors place the opportunity for economic development beyond any living human's reach and stake the fate of a society on its degree of genetic diversity, turning the contingent story of human history and the struggles therein into a teleological narrative of the supremacy of colonizing nations.

Yet with all teleologies, it is possible to detect an element of truth in the hypothesis that if economic wealth is caused by an optimal level of genetic diversity on a country-level basis, then European colonizers did in fact achieve this level by importing and enslaving the "optimal" amount of productive "human capital" from Africa. Ergo, slavery was the direct cause of the wealth of nations like the United States: much like a dream, a monstrous truth is conveyed in distorted form. In the hands of neoclassical economics, the causal mechanism is exactly reversed. Genetic diversity is the cause of material well-being, rather than the effect of chattel slavery and capitalist property relations. The authors, by placing the cause of this well-being in genetics and an unchangeable history, justify contin-ued inequalities by placing any ability to rectify them upon the stasis of immutable genetic factors: for Ashraf and Galor, contemporary outcomes in the capitalist mode of production are attributable to prehistoric factors, "determined tens of thousands of years ago."[50] From the perspective of psychoanalysis, this presents an extreme case of a cause being willed into being: While contemporary inequalities are doubtlessly deeply rooted and difficult to dislodge, the assignation of cause as genetic, unchangeable, and prehistoric absolves any living person the responsibility for changing these states of affairs. The obvious truth, of slavery and colonialism's legacies, sits in plain sight, like the "purloined letter" discovered by C. Auguste Dupin.

To conclude this chapter, I present a case from the world of sports that the authors of *Freakonomics* and its offshoot podcast series use to proclaim the causal power of incentives. I trace the extension of one published economic paper, from the *American Economic Review*, into the anecdote that opens the third *Freakonomics* book *Think Like a Freak*. This case is emblematic of the metastasis of incentive rhetoric onto cultural domains and with each step displaces the problematic of causality onto the uncontestable laws of economics. In this case, "incentives" retroactively account for nonempirical, unobservable causes to fill in the yawning gap of causality. Sport as a cultural practice involves discrete and calculable outcomes—players make or miss shots, balls remain in play or roll out of bounds, teams win or lose. Thus, incentives ought to function as a test case for motivated behavior, and in many cases, professional contracts in many sports do contain specific monetary incentives for reaching certain statistical marks.[51] However, the universal applicability of the essential neoclassical economic axioms (prices, preferences, utility) founders precisely where it should be most useful.

I begin with the original research. Writing in the *American Economic Review*, authors Levitt, Chiappori, and Groseclose study penalty-shot conversion rates in European professional football during the 1990s. In a penalty shot in football, the ball is placed on a spot twelve yards from the goal, the attacking player may strike the ball once, and the goalkeeper must remain on the goal line until the ball is kicked. Penalty shots, because they appear to have only two "true outcomes," are ripe for interpretation; either a goal is scored, or it is not. Yet a great deal of unconscious, dialectical complexity is at work beneath this apparent binary opposition. The authors claim that in a penalty shootout, the most economically "rational" shot is dead center since data suggests a goalkeeper will dive in one direction to block shots aimed at a corner of the goal.[52] At first blush, this is a reasonable presumption: goalkeepers calculate that shooters will choose a spot they can hit with power and act accordingly. Yet in order to arrive at this mathematically derived conclusion, the authors assume that both players move simultaneously, not based on empirical observation of the data set but rather on a simplifying inference about the ball's theoretical maximum velocity.[53] Because a football can theoretically travel upward of one hundred miles per hour, the authors presume that goalkeepers must dive simultaneously with the shot, since it is impossible for a goalkeeper to react in time. This simplification is, of course, belied by observed behavior—players frequently judge the movement of their opponents *before* striking the ball. This tactic is economically rational (it leads to the highest success rate) but not a passive reaction to the "rational" market signal; it is instead a psychologically and situationally complex interpersonal dialectic. Indeed, the authors admit that they "cannot reject that players optimally choose strategies, conditional on the opponent's behavior."[54] The economists' argument, that the rational shooter should kick toward the center of the goal, is rather a retroactive assignation, a post-hoc rationalization, in the guise of articulating the "efficient" strategy.

The mathematical and inferential simplifications of economics—reducing a complex social setting to strict neoclassical behavioral precepts—

obfuscate rather than reveal insights that surround an event. This game within a game is revelatory of the unconscious mechanisms that structure social interactions: whether one can "outsmart" one's opponent by standing still, leaping left, or leaping right crucially depends on whether the Other knows that one's actions, and desires, are enigmatic even to ourselves. The penalty shootout asks the question: what does the Other want of me? Yet the model's simplification, presuming simultaneous movement, elides this very complexity and transposes one binary opposition (presence/absence) into a simplified binary outcome (goal/no goal). In the last analysis, the causal mechanism may actually be reversed: one simply kicks where the opponent *is not*. As with the issue of optimal genetic diversity, referenced above, interpreting a social interaction as fundamentally economic hides a truth in plain sight. Eden Hazard, of Chelsea Football Club, scored nine consecutive penalties in the 2014–2015 season simply by waiting for his opponent to move and then kicking into the open space.

Although the academic research elides the specific causal mechanism, its uptake in a popular press book leans into "incentives" as a discrete and individualizing explanation for human behavior. In *Think Like a Freak*, Levitt (one of the aforementioned article's coauthors) and Dubner metastasize the incentive-based approach by introducing "noneconomic" incentives that affect the shooter's behavior. In the following lengthy passage, note the displacement—the metastasis—from economic analysis to an individualized narrative, wherein the authors enjoin readers to imagine themselves as the player in question:

> At this most turbulent moment, what is your true incentive? The answer might seem obvious: you want to score the goal to win the game for your team. If that's the case, the statistics plainly show you should kick the ball dead center. But is winning the game your truest incentive? . . . If you follow this selfish incentive—protecting your own reputation by not doing something potentially foolish—you are more likely to kick toward a corner. If you follow the communal incentive—trying to win the game for your nation even though you risk looking personally foolish—you will kick toward the center.[55]

Star football players across the decades, such as David Beckham, Sergio Ramos, and Roberto Baggio have been derided by their supporters for making the error that Levitt and Dubner characterize as the "selfish" incentive, shooting the ball high and losing important matches and tournaments for their teams. This is the alleged social expectation—go for glory, smash a spectacular shot, avoid looking foolish if the keeper remains motionless. (Even if a goalkeeper saves an aimed shot, the player will not be blamed to the same extent.) The "communal" incentive is instead to follow market wisdom and guide the ball gently down the middle. Other factors are registered as competing incentives, and the outcome is retroactively narrated as the result of the individual volition of the kicker—the "true incentive" is discovered as an external effect of the outcome, not of the process.

For the *Freakonomics* authors, discovering the "true incentive" is an act of retroactive causality; the incentive (whether selfish or communal) undergoes a rhetorical substitution with its outcome, cause is substituted for effect. Those who aim toward a corner and miss are incentivized by selfish fear; those who rationally roll the ball dead center are incentivized more by victory. Chaput characterizes *Freakonomic* rhetoric as ahistorical, asocial, amaterial, apolitical, and naturalizing—a quintessentially neoliberal discursive formation that claims to explain everything.[56] Economists often distinguish between professed and revealed preferences—one may profess a preference for scoring a goal, but by acting against market wisdom, one reveals a preference for something else. The "something else" in this case is the "revealed preference" to avoid ridicule, the true causal mechanism. Most of the readers of the *Freakonomics* series will not take penalty shots in the World Cup, but they will encounter the appearance of a choice and be forced to ask themselves "what do I truly desire?" Thus, the rhetorical function of this anecdote is to give rhetorical cover for individualized explanations for complex events in culture more broadly and to affirm that whether we like them or not, markets will always rationalize—or discipline—individual behaviors. Failure—from the competitive power of an opponent, poor scouting, a slick patch of grass, or any other explanation, is instead retroactively narrated as an individual choice based on a selfish incentive. "Incentive" functions as a placeholder to mark the *absence* of a robust explanation of social behavior, a black box for complexity in social explanations, and a placeholder that switches the "cause" of behavior from a rational economic response to stimuli into a moral, character-based explanation. Such is the Freakonomic *modus operandi*, in which received wisdom is almost always wrong, and underlying market data proves to be correct: one can always fail, but the market can never be failed. When incentives metastasize over the social field, the retroversion effect that

Lacan identifies in the signifier means that the domain of the economic supplants that of any other explanation.

Crucially, the authors transpose the data from professional football onto the World Cup, in which players represent their countries rather than their employers, yet no reference to the relevant motivational differences is registered. National pride—or the fear of disappointing one's country—may provide a more robust "incentive" for certain actions over professional pride. In fact, an incentive scheme that combined monetary reward with national pride had a backfire effect in the 2014 World Cup. The minister of sport for Côte d'Ivoire promised players a $50,000 "incentive payment" if they qualified for the tournament's knockout rounds.[57] Unfortunately, an Ivorian player committed a foul in the last moments of a match against Greece, who converted the penalty kick and advanced at Côte d'Ivoire's expense. A gap in the order of causality opens between a promised incentive and an outcome: Did the lure of a reward cause the player to be overzealous? What competing incentives comprised the proximate cause for the outcome? Would a higher payment have prevented the clumsy tackle? By pointing these questions downward, as Levitt and Dubner did, asking "What is your true incentive?" the more complex answer is displaced from our analytic purview. If our starting point and terminus of analysis is the methodologically derived individual we are left with voluntaristic, individualized decisions rather than material inequalities and unequal distributions of power. Our provisional answers to the enigma of causality become a source of enjoyment, a vantage point from which to say, "You were incentivized by *this*," an unseen expression of inviolable economic laws.

Conclusion: Hiding the Ball in Plain Sight

Albeit in an inverted manner, the example of a missed penalty shot in football testifies to a basic psychoanalytic problem: Why do our desires and our actions fail to match up? As Lacan put it, "To be a psychoanalyst is to open your eyes to the evident fact that nothing malfunctions more than human reality."[58] Fear of failure, of disappointing someone, of ascribing a knowledge greater than one's own to the Other: all weigh just as heavily as the desire for love and approbation. The discursive regime whose sole axiom is "humans are incentive-driven" binds these outcomes to a strict expression of economic laws, reducing social complexity into inputs that presume individuals (and always individuals) are utility maximizing, preference-driven creatures who obey price signals. "Incentives" metastasize—shift the cause—onto the economic because they, and they alone, claim to render whole a seemingly contradictory world. The analytically propitious gaps where the unconscious might reside are locked out. Yet, simultaneously, so is any explanation that admits the existence of class inequalities, or supraindividual differences in power. Ironically, the economic approach to understanding social phenomena forecloses both possibilities. Hence, I have offered a psychoanalytically accented set of reading practices, attending to speech acts that habitually insert "incentive" as substitute for cause in public discourse. The unconscious, Lacan reminds us, is the discourse of the Other; so paradoxically, by granting credence to the unconscious, we can begin a social rather than hopelessly individual explanation for why malfunctions occur. Each apparent "moment of truth" that economics purports to explain reverses the causal mechanism to economize the outcome, displacing the social or conjunctural cause from its place.

In this chapter, I have argued for what makes "incentive" *everywhere* now, with reference to a method that attends to how causality is established retroactively in the speaking subject's unconscious. Causality is an enigma that must be stitched up through the order of the signifier—absent a guarantee, or an unmovable solidity, cause is established in the present by arcing backward to establish its origins in the past. Psychoanalysis' concept of retroactive causality links to the rhetorical tradition via the trope of metastasis, which involves a placing of a cause outside of its original context; thinkers from antiquity to the Renaissance have theorized metastasis' strategic value in shifting responsibility from one cause to another. The intentional use of this trope must be supplemented with the power of the unconscious: the economic way of looking at behavior metastasizes over the social field, cancerlike, through the habituated repetition of "incentives" as a causal mechanism. In the imperial purview of economics, there is nothing that cannot be redescribed as an incentive, obedient to the ironclad laws of supply and demand. Once all of social reality can be calculated as economic input, all outcomes can be retroactively attributed as the result of a prior incentive force; any inequality can be justified as that which was chosen by the methodologically derived individual. The strange temporal loop of incentive rhetoric negotiates both activity and passivity, with individuals figured as both choosers and obedient to their preexisting incentive structures, which renders them responsible for any outcome that befalls them. The attributive value of incentives is libidinally valuable. It becomes a source of enjoyment, a vantage point to explain away the complexities of social life under the singular law of economic value. But what makes "incentive," as opposed to any other term, the specifically chosen one for the discipline of economics? In the following chapter, I retrieve a history of the term "incentive" from its roots in antiquity to explain exactly what makes it such a mobile and persistent term in contemporary discursive formations.

Chapter 2

This Is Not a Pipe, or Incentives from Antiquity to Modernity

According to Greek myth, the satyr Marsyas, master of the dual-piped flute, lost his skin and his life after challenging the sun god Apollo to a test of musical prowess and coming out on the losing end. Marsyas, the intemperate and randy aulist, was no match for Apollo, who combined instrumental music (his lyre) with his singing voice to win the contest. Allegorically, according to Kim, the myth functions as a fable for the value of Apollonian temperance, harmony, and balance over the Phrygian ribaldry, represented by the pipe: "The *Aulos* and its makers and players promoting complicated music must be banished from the state, for it is an art which seeks aural pleasure alone. Only the lyre and cithara should be kept in the city, the shepherd's pipe in the country."[1] Marsyas's ignominious death symbolizes not simply the hubris of challenging a god (and by extension, a social order that venerates gods) but of the mesmeric and captivating essence of his chosen instrument, the pipe. What was the satyr's great sin? His music short-circuited its listeners' conscious minds and compelled them to follow the tune that he set out for them. The pipe enticed its listeners to become single-minded, obeisant, driven solely by its sound and insensitive to other considerations.

The previous chapter was organized by the animating question: why are incentives *everywhere* now? This chapter places the emphasis differently: why are *incentives* everywhere now? Incentive rhetoric has metastasized across the cultural field by providing a causal, external, and measurable rubric for evaluating and molding human behavior. But the vectors of power—political, institutional, and intellectual—that have carried neoclassical economics to the center of culture and policymaking are buttressed by the particularly resonant rhetorical work that the term "incentive" itself does for the discipline of economics. If the prior chapter demonstrates that "incentive" is a metastasis-friendly term to insert market principles into every conceivable field, this chapter explains why the term incentive functions as an organizing principle for the discipline of neoclassical economics itself. There is a clue from its history, which I unearth here. From the Latin *incentivum*, or "that which sets the tune," incentives compel their listeners to take action, and this historical notion remains embedded within its contemporary usage. Yet incentive does not remain yoked exclusively to the world of music. "Incentive" and the word "incantation" are etymologically linked, so it is possible to think of "incentive" as a charm or chant that accomplishes the same task of bypassing one's reasoning faculties and that elicits an automatic response. As McKenzie and Lee point out, "Care has to be exercised in using incentives *because they are so powerful*."[2] In short, incentives are magic charms. Marsyas was killed not because he failed to outplay a god but because the stakes were too high for him to remain alive. His charming pipe short-circuited rationality and reason, and rendered its listeners servants to the desires elicited in them by his tune.

The idea that an external force compels people to act is nothing new to the discipline of rhetoric, going back to Plato's warning that "oratory is the art of enchanting the soul."[3] Ogden and Richards remind us that "word-magic" was the default position of the Greeks in drama and philosophy, and that "the whole human race has been so impressed by the properties of words as instruments for the control of objects, that in every age it has attributed to them occult powers."[4] Gorgias boasts in his Encomium of Helen, "Inspired incantations through speeches are inducers of pleasure and reducers of sorrow; by intercourse with the mind's belief, the power of the incantation enchants and persuades and moves it by sorcery."[5] And in Plato's Gorgias, the Sophist declares that with rhetoric's power "you will have the doctor as your slave, and the trainer as your slave."[6] Freud himself acknowledged that philosophy today overvalues "the magic of words and the belief that real events in the world" are affected, spell-like, by them.[7] Gunn reads occult rhetoric along the same lines, for their texts "assume the ability of specialized language to 'presence' elements of ultimate reality better than ordinary language."[8] Peters analogizes nineteenth-century communication to a literally mesmeric process and compares the power of the modern media to a spell: "Indeed, the word-magic so prominent in early human cultures—the belief that the name gives power over the thing—has not declined but increased in the twentieth century, thanks to the ability of the 'symbolic apparatus' to disseminate clichés."[9] McCloskey, no stranger to the relationship between rhetoric and economics, defines persuasive discourse as "sweet talk" in contradistinction to coercive state action.[10] To think of "incentive" as a magic charm means to see a through-line from its ancient musical origins to its contemporary value for neoclassical economic thought: through the use of "incentives" by early neoclassical economic thinkers, up to its widespread popularization in the twentieth century, "incentive" gradually becomes an autonomous, objective feature of market-based societies that compels productive economic behavior. The incentive ceases to be necessarily voiced or played by an individual but becomes an endemic feature of the capitalist mode of production itself. The incentive pipe becomes an incentive charm; the incentive charm becomes a price signal.

As referenced previously, Gregory Mankiw, author of one of the most widely assigned introductory economics textbooks in the United States, contends that the axiom "People respond to incentives" is one of his discipline's foundational principles:

> Because rational people make decisions by comparing costs and benefits, they respond to incentives . . . One economist went so far as to suggest that the entire field could be summarized as simply "People respond to incentives. The rest is commentary. Incentives are crucial to analyzing how markets work. For example, when the price of an apple rises, people decide to eat fewer apples. At the same time, apple orchards decide to hire more workers and harvest more apples. In other words, a higher price in a market provides an incentive for buyers to consume less and an incentive for sellers to produce more.[11]

Neoclassical economic theory centralizes not innate human endeavor as the source of economic activity but instead foregrounds the external, objective features of a market society as the genesis and aim of all action. The price system within a market society is what offers objective signals that must be exploited by incentive-driven actors for the market to reach equilibrium.[12] As Hanan, Ghosh, and Brooks argue, neoclassical economic thought presupposes the conditions for equilibrium as always-already having been satisfied in a pure past; rhetorically, the messy business of markets "clearing" must necessarily be smoothed over with the presumption that they always have.[13]

There is a secondary but no less important result of the gradual objectification of "incentives" once neoclassical economics captures the term. The axiom "people respond to incentives" testifies to the supposed manipulability of the human subject by corporations and policymakers—as "incentive-driven" animals, we act in accordance with whatever satisfies our needs within a market framework, and if powerful entities know this, then they can tailor their offerings thereto. Rather than a doctrine that documents the power of innate human freedom, neoclassical economics is an alibi for human passivity, inertness, and capacity for management.[14] The other side of reward is, of course, punishment: once rewards become objective features of market society, punishment is the implied outcome for those who fail to take advantage of them. Incentives, despite the appearance of univocality and positivity, coerce without obvious coercion. The statements "People respond to incentives" or "Economics is the study of incentives" entails that those who act contrary to any market's incentive structures are instead motivated by a "something else," which Gary Becker calls a "psychic cost" and other economists call a "revealed preference." In the neoclassical economic canon, incentives reveal desires that are latent within the subject, such that no outcome can be ever described as unfair, unjust, or unequal, merely the expression of diverse preference structures.[15] The more expansive the definition of what a market is, or what is covered by market mechanisms, the more that can be explained as someone rationally deciding their own destiny.

The incentive functions discursively as this "something else," the unseen force that guides behavior and that only economics can properly discern. It is the cause of desire for the (rational) economic actor herself but more crucially functions as an object of desire for economists, who are trained to seek it out in any situation—market based, or otherwise. Hence, I frame "the incentive" as emblematic of the *objet a*, or object-cause of desire, to account for a variety of dualities endemic to the term. The disparate concepts of cause/effect, desire/reward, past/present, and subject/object are all accounted for as an enigmatic object for the discipline of economics. Incentives are causal, objective, and measurable mechanisms, and understanding the history of the term allows us to witness their contemporary power. "Incentive" is economics' own name for the objective features of a market society that induces action, as well as the "something else" that accounts for market disequilibrium. I advance *objet a* to emphasize that "incentive" acts as an object of desire within the discipline of economics and to defamiliarize our commonsense relationship therewith: it is not the "thing" that motivates individuals to act economically rationally but is rather the discursive attributive force that economists themselves place into any economic setting. Finally, *objet a* functions conceptually here as an indicator of mobility. Lacan located the *objet a* as a leftover in language, part of the "metonymy of desire" that analysts seek to pin down. "Incentives" in the early twentieth century become disarticulated from speech and also objective, autonomous features of market societies; in the late twentieth century incentives are disarticulated from monetary price altogether and instead name unseen (but measurable) desires of rational economic agents. I invoke psychoanalysis to more carefully discern what makes this a necessary—and profitable—move for the discipline of economics itself.

In sum, to answer the question, "Why are *incentives* everywhere now?" means to see an incentive as a problem-solving device for the discipline of neoclassical economics. Incentives provide a coherent explanation for how human beings are motivated to do the things they do with only a passing reference to the subject's interiority. By wedding both internal and external motivation, activity and passivity, and especially desire and reward, incentives are central to the three pillars of the neoclassical economic project—methodological equilibration, methodological individualism, and methodological instrumentalism. The externalization and objectification of "incentives" via twentieth-century neoclassical economics is key to its eventual cultural metastasis. Once laundered through its theoretical tenets, financial motivation ceases to be the explanation for all peoples' goals; rather, market analysis becomes the model for interpreting all behavior, commodity-based or not. Once "incentive" becomes synonymous with all goal-directed behavior, there is nothing that cannot be reduced to an "economic" question, narrowly understood.

This chapter leads up to this metastasis and proceeds in two major phases. First I recount the history of "incentive" from its Latin origins in *incentivum* and *incentiva*: "Incentive" travels from "that which sets the tune" in a musical sense to the domain of magical, or charming speech. I then work through Lacan's reading of Plato's *Symposium*, wherein Lacan suggests that the *objet a*, or object-cause of desire, structures the dialogue. What makes Plato so attractive to his interlocutors is his ability to stir listeners with magic speech; his *agalma* (that which is in him, but more than him) is what sparks the unconscious desire of Alcibiades. It is here that I theorize that "incentive" functions as an *objet a* for the discipline, as the fantasmic signifier that causes, and satisfies, desire. Next, I evaluate how "incentive" functions within twentieth-century neoclassical economic theory, in particular, its transformation from a signifier of desire to a sign of reward. Neoclassical economics eventually externalizes incentives into a descriptor of price signals, which offer clear, objective motivators for economically rational activity. Market economies, according to orthodox economic theory, efficiently distribute resources because monetary rewards are built into the system itself; the equilibrium analysis is predicated upon on the presumption any desire is matched instantaneously with its satisfaction. Within the capitalist mode of production, the incentive pipe plays itself. Secondarily, the poetic sense of the term is constricted around the narrow sense of financial motivation. This constriction is momentary but absolutely vital for its eventual cultural metastasis, which is the subject of chapter 3. The metaphor of price governs the domain of incentives, and financial reward becomes the "special thing" added to social interactions that makes the world tick. The figure of Marsyas sets the tune of this chapter. His pipe works as the through-line from *incentivum* and its musical connotations to the contemporary power of incentive rhetoric that compel listeners beyond their conscious control; it also paves the way for "incentives" to automatically exert effects within market frameworks.

From *Incentivum* to Incentive

The English term "incentive" originates from the Latin *incentivum*, a noun that designates "the playing of the tune," which indicates both the playing of a pipe as well as a chant or incantation. The adjectival form borrows from the noun *incentio*, meaning "the playing of music," and the verb *incanto*, to consecrate with spells or sing.[16] The English word "incantation" itself comes from the Latin *incantationem*, a "noun of action from [the] past participle stem incantare."[17] Yet the pipe is rarely ever simply a pipe: the incentive pipe (and later, incentive speech) is thought to be overpowering to its listener and bypasses their faculties of self-reflection. As such, appearances of the Latin forms of "incentive" connote a series of social conflicts over prudence, control, and social harmony; the pipe is a dangerous instrument in the hands of a skilled player because of its capacity to bypass reflection and thought. Consider again the myth of Marsyas and Apollo. The story counterpoises the harmonious and orderly Apollonian system of laws with a wild, tempestuous (and above all, hubristic) Phrygian society. This social conflict—the serene harmonics of the seven-stringed lyre contrasted with the single-minded pipe—are latent within the pipe's incentive capacities. *Incentivam*, according to Varro's *On Agriculture*, a first-century BCE Roman treatise, is deployed as part of an allegorical reading of dominance and submission, with *incentiva* describing the right pipe of a dual-piped flute: "Wherefore the art of agriculture 'accompanies' the pastoral because it is subordinate, as the left pipe is to the stops of the right."[18] The *incentiva* pipe provides the melodic charm, with which the *succentiva* harmonizes. Thus, the social cleavage between the Phrygian countryside and the Apollonian city shifts to within Varro's aulos to a debate between the agricultural and pastoral, with *incentiva* playing the socially necessary melody and *succentiva* the agricultural harmony.

Works by Plutarch, a Greek essayist writing around the same time as Varro, have been translated by various authors to include "incentive" references as both melodic incitement and mesmerizing speech. "Incentive" appears as melodic incitement in Philemon Holland's 1603 translation of Plutarch's discourse on music, in which he recounts the social cleavages between auletic and cithearean melodic enchantments. Plutarch alludes to the *Orthios Nomos*, a genre of lyric song as "a tune or song exceeding high and incentive; which when *Timotheus* sung before King *Alexander*, he was so moved and incited, that presently he leapt foorth and tooke armes."[19] Goodwin, in an 1878 translation of Plutarch's essay on praise and envy, refers to "incentive" as magic speech, or the spur of persuasive discourse: "We know the counsel that brings persuasive deeds as well as words, a lively exemplar, and an immediate familiar incentive, insouls a man with courage, moves, yea, vehemently spurs him up to such a resolution of mind as cannot doubt the possibility and success of the attempt."[20] Helmbold's 1939 translation of Plutarch's discourse on brotherly love also includes a mention of "incentive" as speech to encourage action: "And indeed it is an uncle's duty to rejoice and take pride in the fair deeds and honours and offices of a brother's sons and to help to give them an incentive to honourable achievement, and, when they succeed, to praise them without stint."[21] We may see then, in these translations of the same work, the shifting senses of what "incentive" indicates, first as an allegorical reference to the power of a melodic enchantment that provokes action and then as speech that encourages the same.

The mesmeric qualities of the incentive pipe are also evident in the well-known tale of the Pied Piper. According to the legend which emerged in fourteenth-century Germany, a piper was hired to rid the village of Hamelin of its rat problem by playing his pipe, charming them, and leading them to drown in the Weser River. However, the mayor reneged on payment, and as punishment, the piper used his powers to lure the village's children to the same watery fate. As Gœthe put it in his 1802 poem on the legend, "Good-humoured though he is the Piper, he charms the children like a viper/the wildest ones follow along, as he sings his golden fairy song."[22] The Pied Piper's instrument magically compelled the children: they followed that which set the tune, their incentive. The veracity of the legend is immaterial to its hortatory function. The legend may have dramatized an actual plague, a bout of starvation that took the lives of Hamelin's children, or their emigration from the hamlet to other areas of Europe; however, its persistence testifies to some unconscious desire on behalf of the parents to either fantasize about no longer having children or, more likely, to assuage their guilt at having lost them by externalizing the cause of their demise. In this legend, the Pied Piper is responsible for their deaths, and yet only acted after the town's mayor failed to live up to his end of the bargain. Thus the parents' guilt is laundered through two separate layers of responsibility. The lesson of the Pied Piper stares its readers in the face and has for seven hundred years: Latent within the very idea of an incentive is the possibility that it can be used for good or ill, and any technique that induces singlemindedness can distort the actions of its listeners to socially unbeneficial outcomes.[23]

The first appearance of the word "incentive" specifically in English comes from an anonymous fifteenth-century English translation of Ranulfi Higden's fourteenth-century world history book, the *Polychronicon*, originally written in Latin. Higden deploys *incentivum* in the preface to his work, self-aggrandizingly praising the writers of history for their moral fortitude, honesty, and virtue, or *incentivum probitatis*.[24] The translator renders this phrase as "incentiue of manhode," a somewhat straightforward Anglicization. The straightforwardness of the translation is, paradoxically, unsatisfying from a creative standpoint, yet it does indicate that "incentive" and "incentivum" relate and share a relationship with desire and reward. Michael Drayton's 1612 *Poly-Olbion*, a history of the British Isles and people in poetic verse, more fruitfully demonstrates incentive's spellbinding sense: Drayton writes that the instruments and chorus of the Irish, Welsh, and Scots "charme" their compatriots, and produce a "musicall incentiue to warre" against their foes.[25] John Selden, who provided commentary and notes on the *Poly-Olbion*, makes Drayton's allusions explicit: the prowess of the Britons is deeply connected to the power of song, especially the

Marsyan dual-piped flute. He writes: "But to conjoin this fiery office with that quenching power of the *Bards*, spoken of by the Author, I imagine that they had also for this partial purpose skill in that kind of music they call *Phrygian*, being (as *Aristotle* says) . . . madding the mind with sprightful motion."[26] Selden frames this social conflict between the Citharean lyre and Phrygian pipe as it was in antiquity, a battle between temperance and cognition versus, essentially, passion and mesmerism. Selden describes the aulos pipe "as . . . dividing itself into two at the end, the other spread in the middle, as two segments of a circle, but one at both ends, I guess them intended near the same," and explicitly references "the poetic story of *Marsyas*" as inspiration for Drayton's tale.[27] To alight a listener, "madding the mind with sprightful motion," is to capture their unconscious desire and incite them to obey orders without thinking.

Before moving on, there is one path of "incentive" that cannot be definitively substantiated etymologically, but phonemically it may contribute to its contemporary prevalence and power. It is possible to read "incentive" as linked to "incense," or "incendiary," something akin to a fire that calls for automatic action. In the *Polychronicon*, "incentive" conveys a fiery connotation in the hands of the scholar John Trevisa, who translates the "incentivum probitatis" of historical writers as "blaiseþ and schyneþ clerliche þe riȝt rule of þewes," (or "blazes and shines clearly the right rule of those").[28] I interpret this apparent inexactitude as a signal that the phonemic resemblances between the terms indicate a general sense of motivation. A lit fire indicates a compulsion similar to a spellbinding tune, much like Milton's *Paradise Lost*, wherein "incentive" modifies a fuse, or matchstick: "Whereof to found thir Engins and thir Balls/Of missive ruin; part incentive reed/Provide, pernicious with one touch to fire."[29] From the perspective of the unconscious, this metaphorical detour offers some clue as to the term's rhetorical tenacity. Incentive as a "fiery" term accomplishes comparable rhetorical labor to a magic charm—think of the idiom "lighting a fire" beneath someone to motivate activity. Much like the spell, a fire is univocal and demands automatic action, similar to how Aristotle describes smoke as an inartistic proof, or sign, of fire.

The *Objet a* in Plato's *Symposium*

As several of the aforementioned authors make clear, Marsyas's mythological pipe functions allegorically—the incentive pipe articulates a latent desire in the listening subject, and they unconsciously obey that which plays the tune. So too was Plato well aware that Marsyas's pipe is a metaphor for desire, so I return to antiquity to yoke the concept of incentive speech as the psychoanalytic *objet a*, that which elicits, signals and indicates the desire of the Other. The *Symposium* itself drills in on the relationship between love and speech, with each speaker (Agathon, Phaedrus, Pausanias, Alcibiades, Socrates) identifying some aspect of desire that approaches it most closely. As Lacan explains, Socrates' interlocutors identify the philosopher's mesmerizing oral skills as akin to Marsyas' incentive pipe, something that stirs their unconscious desire.[30] Contemporary rhetoricians, such as Gunn, have used Lacan's other works to theorize that all communication is a demand for love, or fundamentally a demand for what the other does not possess.[31] Lacan reads the *Symposium* as a demonstration of multiple overlapping lacks, thus emblematizing how speech functions in the human experience. In this section I discuss how the *Symposium* equates Marsyas's pipe to Socrates's speech, then I theorize the *objet a* as a libidinal remainder within the symbolic order, and finally, express what it means for the discipline of economics to centralize this object as their object of study.

Alcibiades, the heartsick and jilted would-be lover of Socrates, makes a drunken accusation about the philosopher's oral power and directly equates Marsyas's incentive pipe and incentive speech:

> You may not play the pipes, like Marsyas, but what you do is much more amazing. He had only to open his mouth to delight men, but he needed a musical instrument to do it . . . His is the only music which carries people away, & reveals those who have a desire for the gods and their rites. Such is its divine power, and it makes no difference whether it's played by an expert, or a mere flute girl. You have the same effect on people. The only difference is that you do it with words alone, without the aid of any instrument.[32]

What Alcibiades is trying to describe, and get from Socrates is his *objet a*—the fragment of being that makes Socrates more than simply a man, the fascinating thing that is in him and yet more than him. Socrates's voice, in particular, serves as the *objet a* around which the discourse is organized. Quinet places Alcibiades's accusation in psychoanalytic terms, and likens its mesmerizing power to Marsyas's pipe: "As a flutist, Marsyas not only charms men but also puts them into a trance-like state."[33] Several years after his seminar on transference, Lacan would identify "the voice" as one of the few recognized *objets a* by psychoanalysis, and undoubtedly this dialogue contributed to its inclusion.[34] Socrates's voice conveyed an enigmatic signifier that moved—figuratively and literally—his interlocutors, as if charmed or entranced. (Consider the circumstances that later led to his execution: according to his accusers, Socrates's magic speech corrupted the youth of Athens and diverted them from productive ends.) It is not that Socrates's words *express* desire, but rather his words *elicit* desire in his listeners, exactly equivalent to the way that the pipe is not the desired object: their unconscious desires are funneled through the music that the pipe plays.

The detour through speech is absolutely necessary for understanding the power of incentives: As all of Plato's characters testify, in different ways, speech is magical not strictly because it brainwashes a listener into a trance but because it draws out from the listener their own unacknowledged desires. Plato and his interlocutors metaphorize the dialectical pursuit of truth as seduction, love, and magic; Alcibiades even one-ups Socrates's "scroll in your pocket" joke from the *Sophist* by explicitly referencing Socrates's oral skills as an advance on Marsyas's overreliance on his—*ahem*—instrument. Persuasion-as-seduction works metaphorically because it presupposes a listener's consanguinity—their willingness to be moved. The same insight is true for what the Socratic method is meant to accomplish in the first place—through speech, one never ends where one begins; speech as the interior Other entails that the subject's desire always remains unarticulated and found along the way. One engages in dialogue and debate using words, phrases, positions, and beliefs that are not one's own, not simply to "unearth" the truth, but to recognize that it emerges from a noncomplementary intersubjective exchange, through the play of signifiers.

To that point, the way Socrates elicits in the other the signifier of what they desire—the Socratic Method—is precisely why Lacan uses the *Symposium* "as a sort of account of psychoanalytic sessions."[35] The dialogue provides coordinates for teaching analysts how to elicit this signifier in patients, but Lacan wishes to avoid what befalls the symposium's interlocutors, which is then locating this desire within the body of the analyst and misrecognizing the analyst's desire as their own. That is, in an analytic situation, the analysand is faced with a question: what does the Other (the analyst) want of me? Ostensibly, the answer should be that the analyst desires their patient to improve, but the question is not directly answerable. Rather, the analysand may begin to suspect that the analyst wants to hear the "right" things, so instead of focusing on oneself, the analysand diverts the river of their desire into pleasing the analyst. Second, the analysand may fall victim to another delusion, that the analyst "really has" the answer; so instead of finding it within themselves, the analysand may probe and provoke the analyst into telling the analysand "what is really going on inside me," as if they do know better. Simultaneously, the analyst may fabricate the idea that they alone can cure the analysand, a delusion that the analyst "really has" the answer. The analyst may desire their own genius, just as much as they begin to desire the analysand for the same reason—they have something within them that is locatable and not within their speech—external to them.

This is why Lacan interprets the *Symposium* as a meditation on transference, or the interpersonal relation of analyst and analysand. Fink writes:

> In comparing Socrates's speech to that of Marsyas, Alcibiades stresses the power of its mesmerizing charm . . . In this passage, we may interpret this other sort of agalma, Socrates's voice as object a. As a flutist, Marsyas not only charms men but also puts them into a trance-like state. Alcibiades says that Socrates performs likewise with words rather than an instrument . . . Such is the mesmerising [sic] power of this agalmatic transference. Alcibiades further declares that Socrates is a modern Marsyas and in describing the effect of the Socratic words, he says he is enslaved by Socrates's voice and profound utterances.[36]

Of course, the aim of psychoanalytic treatment is to locate the *objet a*, or object-cause of the subject's desire; this object can only be found in the analysand's speech. Lacan rephrases his understanding of his own concept throughout his *oeuvre* (at different moments partaking in all three of his registers of experience—the Imaginary, Symbolic and Real), but the essential therapeutic aim remains the same. Some scholars, following Žižek's provocative implementations of the *objet a* in ideology critique have tended to grant the object a quasi-mythical status; I instead return it to its place in the domain of speech. Quinet writes, "*Object a* is language's effect on jouissance. . . . Just because *object a* is the product of language does not mean it is inside language: *object a* is to language what the inside hole is to the doughnut."[37] That is, language topologically produces its exterior space, an "out there" that ever eludes the grasp of the subject; the pursuit of satisfaction is precisely what keeps the desire for the object alive. The *objet a* organizes a subject's desire and offers them consistency; crucially, it is not a "thing" in and of itself but a disposition within language that keeps the spark of desire alive. For someone like the literary figure of Don Juan, or Giacomo Casanova, their *objet a* is the pursuit of a partner, not the partner themselves—the enjoyment is in the chase. When a subject is presented with the chance to satisfy their desire, such as a promotion, a cherished commodity purchase, or to consummate a sexual relationship with a desired person, psychoanalytic theory predicts that the subject will be inevitably frustrated or realize that it is not what they "truly" desired. In this sense, the *objet a* is not "it": The proper description for the *objet a* is "that's not 'it.'"

From this perspective, desire continually, habitually refers to a "something else," which is why it is helpful to view the *objet a* as a relationship at the level of meaning, not at the level of being. This is also why Lacan's deployment of rhetorical terms (like metonymy and metaphor) are so vital to elucidate it. Quinet formulates the *objet a* thusly: $\frac{\text{Language}}{\text{Jouissance}} \rightarrow object\ a$, meaning that *objet a* functions as a remainder of a division operation, and can also be read as the linguistic $\frac{\text{signifier}}{\text{signified}}$, with *jouissance* as a purely affective, extra-linguistic reference.[38] The *objet a* is never "the thing itself" but rather a desirous relationship with what the "thing" refers to. That the *objet a* is produced by language, a product of the curve that language imparts upon our being, demystifies the concept, and stops it from appearing as some sublime, metaphysical "thing." It is the quotient of the signifier/signified operation, with no signifier or signified being ultimately "the thing" that desire ultimately refers to. It is not produced within language, or solely out in the "Real" but acts as an incision upon both. Remainder, subtraction, absent reference: Even in a vocabulary specifically attuned to the contours of the unconscious and the tricky language of desire, psychoanalysis must rely on metonymy and example to elucidate the concept.

By contrast, economics has but one term for it—incentive—which performs all of the necessary rhetorical labor to summarize desire, satisfaction, and enjoyment. "Incentive" functions as the *objet a* for the discourse of neoclassical economics precisely because it is a mobile object, that which can refer to potentially any desire in any setting, and sutures both cause and effect, desire and reward, as well as subjective and objective motivations. According to its prophets, an incentive can be literally anything that induces motivated action. Marsyas's incentive pipe, and

Socrates's incentive speech, elicit the unconscious desire of the Other; this is crucial for how "incentives" are mobilized by contemporary economic thought. It is a form for organizing desire, not a content—it does not prescribe in advance by *what* people are motivated rather simply *that* they are motivated. The incentive sparks a desire; it is an enigmatic signifier that draws those who hear the charming tune toward it. However, when twentieth-century economics takes up "incentives" from its colloquial and historic usage, "incentive" undergoes a terminological constriction. Because by and large economics presupposes that coercion is inimical to commerce, any action taken must be prima facie evidence of a subject's desire. There must be some reward, either tangible or intangible, that motivates a subject. Twentieth-century neoclassical economics grasps "incentives" and turns them into an objective, scientific measure of desire, then transposes that seemingly quintessential amount into the name for a tangible reward. The term loses aspects of its poetic connotations and is instead wedded to the price signal, an impersonal and objective measurement. Thus, the enigmatic signifier (of desire) is yoked to the concrete sign (of reward): money.[39]

The Incentive, from Signifier to Sign

External and causal: It is this dual sense of "incentive" that makes it such an attractive organizing formulation for the discipline of economics—it weds both subjective and objective motive, and it appears to describe both internal (unconscious) desires as well as objective signals that cannot be disobeyed. What neoclassical economic thought does to the ancient sense of "incentive" is an objective measurability—the transformation of "incentive" from a descriptor of motive to a scientific "object" in and of itself. In this section, I detail the uptake of "incentives" from within the neoclassical economic canon, exemplified by twentieth-century economists Alfred Marshall and Paul Samuelson. Marshall deploys "incentives" within his work at the founding of the discipline and reformulates Jeremy Bentham's utilitarian philosophy around the money commodity as a measurable marker of human effort; Samuelson's work as the great synthesizer and systematizer of the neoclassical tradition indexes how "incentive" becomes interchangeable as the name for the objective (pricing) features of market economies. Mankiw's earlier observation, that economics is the study of incentives (and the rest is just details), is apropos because of how ineluctable they are for justifying a moral order according to its founding precepts. Within neoclassical economic thought, "incentive" becomes metonymic for the capitalist mode of production writ large, objective features such as a commodity's price, aphoristic articles of faith like the law of supply and demand, and even its moral underpinnings, like the necessity of wealth inequality.

Robert L. Heilbroner, renowned economic historian, contends that Alfred Marshall introduced "a new figure . . . of the economy," akin to Hobbes's monarch that organized the philosopher's own moment.[40] Heilbroner writes: "The new figure is The Individual, whose calculations not only symbolize the workings of the market system, but are in fact the rock on which the economy itself ultimately rests."[41] The triple features of neoclassical economics, methodological individualism, methodological instrumentalism, and methodological equilibration, find clear expression in Marshall's work, and he yokes each of them together with the term "incentive" as a way to provide a measurable marker of effort and desire within the capitalist mode of production. His work is also pivotal for his adaptation of utilitarian philosopher Jeremy Bentham's thought into economics; Bentham's "Felicific Calculus" attempted to empirically map out the "pleasures and pains" that constituted the decision-making units for individuals and societies. Marshall acknowledges Bentham's impossible project and devises a simplifying assumption to make his utilitarian approach work both normatively and descriptively. Along with other early neoclassical pioneers, such as Stanley Jevons and Léon Walras, Marshall is credited with formalizing the field and implementing several of its most persistent postulates: a theory of marginal utility, graphing supply and demand functions, and the "law" of diminishing returns. As Heilbroner makes clear, Marshall's lasting contribution was to project a global picture of economics' world vision into the decision-making processes of individuals. No longer a science that studies the movements of commodities, economics became instead a science of goal-directed behavior.

Key to the story of "incentives" is Marshall's advances in the proper object of economics itself. His aims are self-professedly ordinary; he claims to describe behavior in their "ordinary" or "common usage." Contrary to his more mathematical and scientistic contemporaries, Marshall offers a kind of humble Kantianism. What an "incentive" is for Marshall is a signal of desire: to discover what someone values, determine how much one would pay for it, or how hard one would work to earn it. What Marshall does with his measurement of incentives is bundle a series of indirections into what can be measurable by economics within a utility function. The money commodity is certainly not the only (and perhaps not even the best) measure of human endeavor but is the closest approximation and thus adequate to the task. However, this admission of indirection is precisely what allows for economics to incorporate much more into the domain of economics, rather than circumscribe it to commodity interactions. "Incentive" in Marshall's work performs a double duty, for it denotes both a desire for a thing as well as its satisfaction. This suturing is necessary for equilibrium analysis to function properly, for it justifies market clearance in theory in advance of its accomplishment in practice.

In his landmark *Principles of Economics*, published in 1890, Marshall outlines why economics as an academic discipline is better suited to answer questions about human activity than others. He writes: "The advantage which economics has over other branches of social science appears to arise from the fact that it concerns itself chiefly with those desires, aspirations and other affectations of human nature, the outward manifestations of which appear as incentives to action in a form which is easily measurable, and which therefore are amenable to treatment by scientific machinery."[42] For Marshall, it is not just that human behavior can be observed scientifically, for any statistician could measure patterns of behavior. But rather, his gambit is that human beings behave according to the theories of neoclassical economics—with defined consumption preferences and initial outlays of resources, each of which obey the ironclad laws of supply and demand. The affectations of human nature—the very things that motivate human beings—are made visible by the capitalist mode of production and thus can be studied by the domain of economics. And even these claims are, if not dubious, contestable: as economic historian Philip Mirowski's *More Heat Than Light* painstakingly elucidates, the discipline of physics in the nineteenth century influenced the foundational assumptions of neoclassical economics—the seemingly random movement of stock prices, the law of diminishing returns, supply and demand curves, and especially the notion of market equilibrium, all have precisely adopted analogues from the domain of physics. Market behavior and the behavior of particles in a vacuum did not spontaneously appear identical, but the representation of the latter affected how the former was theorized.[43]

Specifically, Marshall is concerned with developing a positivistic interpretation of all human behavior—one that can avoid the trap of looking "inside" people's heads for their motivations or desires:

But the economist studies mental states rather through their manifestations than in themselves; and if he finds they afford evenly balanced incentives to action, he treats them *primâ facie* as for his purpose equal. He follows indeed in a more patient and thoughtful way, and with greater precautions, what everybody is always doing every day in ordinary life . . . He estimates the incentives to action by their effects just in the same way as people do in common life.[44]

"Incentive" is a representational placeholder for any affect that motivates someone to act and appears only when it tangibly materializes in effort. Marshall's agnosticism about motives—not asking why people do what they do but that if they endeavor in any way it becomes visible in economic activity—is both a reformulation of Jeremy Bentham's utilitarian philosophy, as well as an extraordinarily useful rhetorical tool for contemporary economists. Bentham's tabulations of pleasures and pains are similarly ordinary-seeming; he writes in his *Introduction to the Principles of Morals and Legislation*, "No subtilty, no metaphysics; we need not consult Plato nor Aristotle. *Pain* and *pleasure* are what every body feels them to be; the peasant as well as the prince, the uneducated man as well as the philosopher."[45] Because pain and pleasure are universal experiences, they can be mobilized as a rational accounting system for all human activity. And while Bentham does have a list of fourteen simple pleasures (including benevolence, amity, skill, and imagination), fourteen matching pains (either opposition to a pleasure, or its absence), and eleven primary motives for action, ultimately each of these are reducible to the pleasure/pain dialectic.[46] Yet even his dialectic masks a fundamental unity. For Bentham, each of the "pains" are mere absences or negations of their presences as pleasures, so the system is ultimately univocally organized around the concept of "pleasure." This univocality is especially important for Marshall's adaptation of his framework, for Marshall's advance is to adapt the language of "pleasure," and the pursuit thereof, into a scientific study of effort and desire by measuring the movements of money.

Marshall writes: "Thus though it is true that 'money' or 'general purchasing power' or 'command over material wealth,' is the centre around which economic science clusters; this is so, not because money or material wealth is regarded as the main aim of human effort, nor even as affording the main subject-matter of study for the economist, but because in this world of ours it is the one convenient means of measuring human motive on a large scale."[47] Convenience is not the only alibi for Marshall's terminological reduction of effort to money. The economist reinforces his "money-as-motive" thesis in two ways: first, he offers a widened version of "economic" activity as simply goal-directed action for gain, and second, he sums all potential contexts (both internal and external, both cultural and individual) into a single utility function. Marshall contends that "this indirect comparison can be applied to all classes of desire," which means he does not simply restrict economic analysis to what we restrictively consider "the economy."[48] Maurice Godelier contends that once the definition of "economic" is stretched to include all purposive behavior, "it is no longer possible to distinguish between economic activity and activity directed towards obtaining pleasure, power or salvation. At this rate, while all purposive action comes to be called economic in principle, no action actually remains economic in fact."[49] Godelier prefers to restrict "the economic" to "the production, distribution and consumption of goods and services," granting a certain autonomy to habits, practices, and activities that obey their own logics, even if they intersect with economic activity. By contrast, Marshall, at the very outset of the formalization of neoclassical economics as a discrete discipline, opens the floodgates to bring all activity under the auspices of individualized utility function. Indeed, Marshall claims that the way to draw comparisons between different actors' behaviors is to measure extra-economic motives, with money as the common measure.

Because the aim is to understand aggregated behavior, not psychologize individuals, one cannot assume an "animal instinct" was more or less powerful than a rational or "cultured" inkling. From Marshall, we get the economist's invocation of the phrase *ceteris paribus*—"all things being equal."[50] Marshall writes, "Thus measuring a mental state, as men do in ordinary life, by its motor force or the incentive which it affords to action, no new difficulty is introduced by the fact that some of the motives which we have to take account belong to man's higher nature, and others to his lower."[51] Either influence is functionally equivalent if it produces identical action. This motivational agnosticism is also why he endorses profit-seeking behavior as (a form of) deontological ethics: "Money is a means towards ends, and if the ends are noble, the desire for the means is not ignoble."[52] By analyzing human action from this angle, the economist can begin to take note of the incentives that motivate behavior, whether the incentive is a cultural influence or a monetary reward, once one accepts that the action is taken by a utility-maximizing agent. One need not begin with the human as the hyperrational computational machine if one instead believes that market mechanisms are themselves the necessary computational mechanism.

Taken together, Marshall gives us a fairly coherent picture of human motivation: assume that all human action can be indexed according to the money commodity, equate money to a measure of desire and effort, assume nothing about a subject's interiority or influences on motivations, observe behavior, and finally (begin and) end by assuming neoclassical postulates about behavior are true. What we end with is a concept of an "incentive" as a marker of desire and effort that is made visible in economic activity, narrowly conceived. But despite the fact that for Marshall, "money" and "incentive" are linked via desire and effort, his work points to the metonymic function of both—"money" is an indirect way of accessing desire and an analytically necessary simplification for accounting for the infinite multitude of influences on any one person's behavior and certainly on any aggregate population. In sum, Marshall's methodological advance was to yoke motivation, effort, and desire around a legible object: the money commodity. People may be driven by virtually any incentive, but for that incentive to register for the discipline of neoclassical economics, it must be rendered visible within "economic activity" narrowly understood. Marshall's constriction of desire's signifier to the tangible sign of reward is operationalized by later economists and economic thinkers.

The Incentive, from Object to Objective

In the mid-twentieth century, the discipline's uptake of incentives as an organizing metaphor mirrored that of economic policymakers and industrial leaders. The transformation from what Marshall called the "short, stout links" of logic, and the "ordinary business of life" happens via mathematization, the rhetorical mark of which is the externalization of "incentive" from an index of desire to an index of reward. In this section, I trace how "incentives" become rhetorically externalized, and central to the neoclassical economic project in the mid-twentieth century.

Mainstream economics achieves this by positing decision-making individuals as the primary object of study, strictly analogous to the postulates of utility maximization and methodological individualism. But a simultaneous countermovement occurs: individuals are the proper object of study if and only if the "rules" of the capitalist mode of production are a perfect method of representation for desires that motivate rational behavior. This double movement can be read as a shift in the discursive status of "incentive" in economics. Under the influence of eminent economists like Paul Samuelson, "incentives" become fully externalized as objective features of market economies writ large. That is, the price signal is all the incentive one needs to act rationally (and gainfully) act in accordance with one's desires. As a result, the full expression of this system means that any alteration to the market system becomes a distortion of its perfection. As the neoclassical adage goes, if one goes about changing the distribution of the economic "pie," one "may lessen its total."[53] In practice, this means that an "incentive economy" privileges tangible financial reward, despite paying lip service to the idea that money is not the only thing that motivates people. By simultaneously centralizing the money commodity as the only object capable of approximating human effort, as Marshall had, and claiming its status as a non-all object, Samuelson's intellectual tradition wins in both directions. The money commodity incentive follows the logic of the *objet a*: one cannot reduce all action to the pursuit of money, but if one subtracts it from an economy of desire, the entire system falls apart.

The reduction of human effort to the money commodity in neoclassical economic theory finds its concrete expression when the insight is operationalized within the workplace itself. Whatever desires cannot be captured in reduction to the money commodity must remain structurally uncountable, a "something else" that cannot find its expression within the boundaries of mainstream economic theory. With these two innovations in mind, "incentive" becomes disarticulated from a measure of effort or desire, and instead becomes sutured to the features of a market society writ large. This ostensibly refers to the compelling power that prices have in a market economy (that is, low prices stimulate consumer purchases, and high prices stimulate production) but it also entails a justification of the theoretical postulates of competitive markets and utility maximization. Once incentives become external stimuli and not the expression of individual, idiosyncratic desires, they can metaphorically take the place of any other motivation and become a universal explanatory mechanism for all human behavior. In the works of twentieth-century economists and policymakers, "incentive" functions as an *objet a*, for they summarize the definitional commitments of neoclassical economics, tightly constricted around the promise of financial reward.

Upon the presentation of his 1970 Bank of Sweden prize in "economic sciences," Paul Samuelson was credited by the award committee for "contribut[ing] to raising the general analytical and methodological level in economic science."[54] Samuelson, one of the most influential economists of the twentieth century, is credited with systematizing economic thinking and coined the term the "grand neoclassical synthesis," which at the time meant a détente between Keynesian macroeconomics and neoclassical microeconomics.[55] The term "incentive" appears in Samuelson as an external reward for behavior, and I employ his work as representative of the discipline at the time. Samuelson follows Marshall in "economizing" incentives and renders them as the expression of the priorities of a market system. An incentive, by the mid-twentieth century, is no longer an enigmatic signifier of desire but a sign (in the guise of price) that automatically causes economically rational behavior. The "incentive" in twentieth-century neoclassical economics becomes an external, autonomous effect of the hard-and-fast laws of supply and demand, and the theoretical postulates of competitive markets serve as the proof for why people behave the way they do. In other words, the market system itself induces rational action.

Samuelson, and by extension, twentieth-century economics, adopted Marshall's foregrounding of "The Individual" as the central figure of economics—the movements of commodities at a macro level are only legible against the backdrop of methodological individualism. As McCloskey puts it, Samuelson was one of the primary economists "who reduced economics to the reasoning of a constrained maximizer, Seeking Man."[56] Samuelson writes: "It is possible to derive operationally meaningful restrictive hypotheses on consumers' demand functions from the assumption that consumers behave so as to maximize an ordinal preference scale of quantities of consumptions goods and services."[57] Just as with Marshall, rationality is not reducible to being aware of, or predicting, all outcomes in advance; it simply means that one has clearly defined preferences and works to satisfy them given certain constraints. The constraints that most people face, which prevent most people from satisfying their infinite desires, are budgetary ones—meaning that one simply does not have enough money to satisfy all of their desires and/or that the prices of their preferred commodities are too high. The principle of rationality is externalized from individuals onto markets. Markets rationalize infinitely desirous behavior through the price mechanism.

Any critical view on economics that foregrounds the principle of individual rationality (as unrealistic, solipsistic, or context-free) fails to realize that this strong definition of rationality, at least in twentieth-century mainstream economics, is inessential. As long as an individual is forward-looking and desirous, their actions are considered "rational," and market mechanisms do the rest. A better critical approach is to undercut this minimal principle of rationality from two angles. The first is that while economic actors are not expected to be clairvoyant, they are expected to be held responsible for their choices. Economics' selfish behavior axiom presumes that any rational actor who makes a choice does so as a wager that they will have derived utility from that choice over the array of possible alternatives. If an economic actor chooses a cigarette instead of a municipal bond, their actions are taken as prima facie rational and can be held responsible for their actions. Or as Amadae writes, "If individuals were to dig their own graves, the mere fact of their action serves to indicate that it comports with their preferences."[58] As I discuss in chapter 4, the constrained choices that women make (choosing low-paying jobs, leaving the workforce to raise children, and so on) are then deployed as data to justify continual mistreatment of women, for they freely made these choices from an available menu of options.

The second critique to be leveled at economics' provisional definition of rationality is the fiction that one's desires are ever self-evident, or self-transparent. The idea of an unconscious desire, or a desire for unhappiness, is foreign to the discipline of economics, except in the most tautological way: in which any unconscious desire still manifests itself in rational action and therefore in some way satisfies one's utility function. The overarching claims that Samuelson makes about preferences are predicated on a circularity, one that he freely admits: "The consumer's market behavior is explained in terms of preferences, which are in turn defined only by behavior. The result can very easily be circular, and in many formulations undoubtedly is."[59] Even for an eminent neoclassical economist, is impossible to derive a foundational, self-authorizing inference about an empirical body of discrete individuals. There must be a nonempirical supplement that necessarily underwrites any claim that economics makes about its own field of inquiry—in Lacanian psychoanalysis, this object is the *objet a*.[60] For Samuelson, the circularity of preferences (one's preferences are evidenced by one's actions, something cannot be a preference unless it is made visible by an action) requires no ultimate grounding or explanation—the point is to derive the rules by which decision-making rational actors behave. Yet economics relies on a bridging term—the incentive—to make this circular system function. In Lacanese, economics offers no "phallic signifier" of desire, no "final word" on what causes people to behave the way they do, and so "incentive" emerges retroactively in the gap in the causal order to provide that stable explanatory mechanism. Samuelson's employment of "incentive" is as "objective" as one can get, and yet it remains locked within a tautology. The language of twentieth-century neoclassical economics is the best attempt to positivize the nonempirical quality of "incentive," but it is no better than a placeholder.

But overall, the reduction of economics to a science of individual decision-makers acting in accordance with their preferences hinges upon the prior acceptance of the immutability of the perfect laws of capitalism—the individualizing reversal depends upon the externalization of "incentives" as expressions of market mechanisms. The system is rational because it is capable of processing all desires instantaneously; it is the only representational mechanism devised to translate private, idiosyncratic desires into a legible form.[61] It is not simply that humans are incentive-driven animals; it is that capitalism best articulates a system of rewards and penalties for behavior. McCloskey, in her highly influential *The Rhetoric of Economics*, says of Samuelson's 1947 *Foundations of Economic Analysis*: "It reduced economics to the mathematics of nineteenth-century physics, and is brilliant reading even now. And it laid down an official rhetoric."[62] That rhetoric is the language of mathematical proof. Whereas Marshall's method relied upon empirical observation and instinctive inferences about the "ordinary business of life," Samuelson's work transformed economics into a deductive mathematical science. In that work, Samuelson notes the shift from an analysis of "utility" away from the satisfactions of desires of individuals toward the scientific postulates of mathematical equilibrium: "One clearly delineated drift in the literature has been a steady tendency towards the rejection of utilitarian, ethical, and welfare connotations of the Bentham, Sidgwick, Edgeworth variety . . . Concomitantly, there has been a shift in emphasis away from the physiological and psychological hedonistic, introspective aspects of utility."[63] The shift in economics' object of study entails a subjective elision—desire and satisfaction drop out from consideration and are replaced with notions of market clearing. (In scientific economic thought, individuals do not enjoy on their own; the market enjoys when there is efficiency and clearing, and by extension, by discovering the preconditions therefor, the economist enjoys.) McCloskey identifies five stylistic strategies that Samuelson employs to aid his mathematical focus from two randomly selected pages of *Foundations of Economic Analysis*: appeal to an impersonal mathematical proof, six appeals to authority, appeals to "*relaxation of assumptions*," appeals to hypersimplified economies with only two products for sale, and multiple arguments by analogy and dead metaphor (references to "friction," "yield," and so on).[64] For McCloskey, each of these individual rhetorical strategies works in the service of Samuelson's organizing mathematical metaphor.

From the perspective of the economist, commodity markets themselves are perfectly efficient—absent interference, they clear automatically; thus, mathematical proofs are the ideal way to represent this seemingly incontrovertible proof. The three foundational postulates of neoclassical economics that Arnsperger and Varoufakis identified (methodological equilibration, methodological individualism, and methodological maximization) overlap in Samuelson's work and are united by the externalization of "incentive" therein. Desire and motive are displaced onto the objective features of market society (as signs of reward) rather than as measurements of internal or subjective motivation (or signifiers of desire). For Samuelson, "incentive" names what is latent within his work as a whole: the market system is self-evidently motivational—the existence of prices and competitive market conditions compel rational activity, and as such, the system is perfectly self-regulating. Given a certain ordinal preference structure, he postulates that "an increase in one good's price will, *ceteris paribus*, result in a decrease in its quantity."[65] And if one switches the viewpoint from the consumer to the capitalist, the behavioral postulates remain the same: Samuelson assumes that because people maximize their preferences, people in market societies will behave competitively for profits. Samuelson writes, "Profits are the carrots held out as an incentive to efficiency, and losses are the kicks that penalize using inefficient methods or devoting resources to uses not desired by spending customers."[66] And as he asserts elsewhere: "Profits and high factor returns are the bait, the carrots dangled before us enterprising donkeys. Losses are our penalty kicks. Profits go to those who have been efficient in the past—efficient in making things, in selling things, in foreseeing things. Profits are the report card of the past, the incentive gold star for the future, and also the grubstake for your new venture."[67] With Samuelson, "incentives" become disarticulated from internal motivation and exist "out there"—because there is a profit opportunity to be had, people are logically drawn to them. Market mechanisms provide the sole motive for gain-seeking behavior.

When the laws of capital accumulation are this handsomely laid out, anything that impedes them must be taken as demotivational. Samuelson, like other neoclassical economists, reserves skepticism and disdain for the other side of the incentive coin, the power that states have to tax. Once the laws of free market economics are affirmed, with their concomitant behavioral postulates, state activity inevitably *distorts* incentives. This does not just mean that resources are redistributed in a way Samuelson opposes (although this is certainly part of the story) but because tax policy alters the incentive structures of individuals and firms to comport to new external rewards. In other words, Samuelson is suspicious that states can "set the tune" of individual behavior outside of market precepts. In the 2010 version of *Economics*, Samuelson introduces the notion of incentives in reference to government policy prior to referencing how markets themselves provide them: "To maintain a healthy economy, governments must preserve incentives for people to work and to save."[68] Samuelson notes the paradox inherent in capitalist democracies. When the economic system appears to be unfair, citizens will seek political redress outside of this system: "Where a democracy doesn't like the For Whom pattern that results from *laissez faire*, it puts in tax changes, school and other expenditures, fiats and subsidies, to change the pattern. This helps some incomes, hurts others. These redistributions are acquired at a cost. What cost? The cost of distortions of incentives, distortions which may somewhat lessen the efficiency of the most efficient market system."[69] Samuelson thwarts ways of thinking about how social policy works (including the decision of what and how to tax) because the postulate of maximizing behavior within the confines of a free-market system provides all the incentive one needs to act. In *Economics*, Samuelson waxes on how taxes "often distort" behaviors by providing the story of a hypothetical innovator who takes a civil service or bank vice president job rather than become an inventor if innovators' profits are highly taxed.[70]

This point is borne out by later economists: Mankiw, in his *Macroeconomics* textbook, adopts a deductive rhetorical stance in describing how incentives work; firms and individuals either have more or less of an incentive to save, invest, work hard, etc., depending on the relevant incentives at hand. For instance, in a discussion of taxes, Mankiw writes the following: "When people are taxed on their labor earnings, they have less incentive to work hard. When people are taxed on the income from owning capital, they have less incentive to save and invest in capital. As a result, when taxes change, incentives change, and this can have macroeconomic effects."[71] Incentives appear to be a multidirectional motivational mechanism—it can be applied to labor and capital, and both toward and away from activity. Yet its apparent universality as an explanatory mechanism has unidirectional effects: taxation only ever causes a reduction in the incentive to work, invest, or save. By contrast, economic policymakers gave "incentive" a positive connotation when coupled with financial reward. The post–World War II era brought about the rise of "incentive pay" as a way to describe extra rewards for both industrial workers and middle managers, in an operationalization of the economic insights Samuelson and others devised.[72] In this conjunctural moment, a question faced economists, policymakers, and business leaders: how do we stimulate labor (and increasingly, management) to produce surplus value for capital accumulation?[73] Henry Wallich, an early member of the Council of Economic Advisors (itself a mid-twentieth-century creation, formed in 1946 at the behest of President Dwight D. Eisenhower) had an answer, and foregrounded financial incentives in his 1960 book *The Cost of Freedom*.[74] An "incentive economy" solves a motivational problem for the capitalist mode of production: to motivate people to work one must offer them tangible rewards for their effort. Wallich's notion of an "incentive economy" essentially takes as given Marshall's concept of incentive as a marker of desire and operationalizes it. Incentives are not simply an analytical tool but are also a practical way to stimulate rational action.[75] Wallich writes that "a free economy means a decentralized economy. A system so constituted will work poorly unless the actors display a high order of initiative and drive. Its sponsors are committed, therefore, to a strategy of powerful incentives. To be successful, a free economy must be an incentive economy."[76]

Incentives, not commands, characterize this vision of a proper twentieth-century economy. Workers and managers alike must be incentivized through material gain. If the natural inclination of workers is leisure, then this inclination must be fought by the protectors and sponsors of the system itself. Wallich's contention that the capitalist mode of production is not an innate part of human nature but must be stimulated and safeguarded bespeaks his historical moment in a way that the present moment does not. In other words, the presence of existing alternatives to the capitalist mode of production, however incomplete or fictive, necessitated rhetorical labor on the part of those promulgating "free enterprise." This sentiment contains a necessary Cold War *petitio principii*: economies with private accumulation of wealth foreground material rewards for hard work, whereas socialized economies do not. The freedom to materially gain relies upon price signals (both high and low) to stimulate rational economic action, and since price signals exist in the absence of central planning, decentralized economies are prima facie freer. This is also the borrowed-kettle logic of those who defend income inequality: It is not simply that income inequality is an inevitable outcome of a private property–based economic system but that income inequality is necessary to stimulate those on the bottom of society to adopt the values of the wealthy. The fact of inequality itself is enough incentive for those to pursue wealth.

For Wallich, an incentive can be "noneconomic" (such as prestige, a private office, an award of recognition) but ultimately comes down on the side of financial reward as a modern society's primary incentive structure: "Even the incentives cannot be wholly economic. All forms of power and prestige, of sense of accomplishment, teamwork and service enter in, probably more importantly in the upper reaches of hierarchy. And there are all the lesser trappings for the younger set—the office rug, the desk placed catty corner, the private water pitcher, and whatever invidious distinctions an up-to-date personnel department can devise."[77] Here, "incentives" function as the Lacanian *objet a*: Monetary reward is both surplus and necessary, but that necessity is retroactively consti-tuted—monetary incentives are not the only way to motivate people. But once they are taken away, each of the other motives lose their consistency. He writes: "But the moral that seems to follow is perhaps less wellworn: if non-economic incentives are powerful, how essential are the purely financial? . . . To perform well economically, a society must appreciate worldly goods. Once it has acquired the taste, it will be receptive to and demand economic incentives."[78] Even investment in the stock market is "not exclusively wedded to the profit motive. It is related to other moti-vations—competition, sheer expansionism, prestige. . . . But remove profit and enough of the motive force probably will be gone to slow down the rest."[79] Wallich's position exemplifies the circular nature of incentives. They are both surplus and necessary; an "immaterial" incentive only works after material incentives have been satisfied. The insight to which Wallich arrives points to the nature of desire itself and the tendentious relationship it has with the money commodity. Money ceases to be "it," the "true" measure of desire, when money is a part of everyday social reality.[80]

The AMC television show *Mad Men* provides a useful, albeit fiction-alized, example of the dialectic of desire inherent in salaried work in the 1960s.[81] Peggy Olson, a junior creative director demands recognition from her superior, Don Draper, for an idea that became a Clio award–winning commercial. "You never say 'thank you'!" Olson tearfully says, to which Draper retorts, "That's what the money is for!" To those sympathetic to Olson's plight, the idea of monetary reward as an unsatisfying reward for their creativity points to the alienated nature of labor in the capitalist mode of production. To an economist, or to an employer, this insight is mobilized in the opposite direction: if a salary does not satisfy the desire of a worker, it can be minimized, or threatened with elimination, until proper action is restored. A twentieth-century "incentive economy" is an economy that centralizes monetary rewards for behavior—to motivate both "blue collar" and "white collar" workers to produce more output, they must be materially incentivized, lest they freeload off others. And any fully incentive-compatible economy requires coercion, for if one ceases to be intrinsically motivated to produce output, one must be extrinsically motivated to do so.

The "shareholder value revolution," which occurred in the late 1970s and early 1980s, intensified this tendency by shifting the locus of power from the manager to the stockholder by making the firm's stock price the primary aim (instead of a company's "fundamentals").[82] This "revolution" turned the focus of profit maximization and rational activity inward and outward simultaneously. Outward, toward the pursuit of share price above all, and inward, to cutting the "fat" of middle managers who were insufficiently incentivized by their salaries to relentlessly pursue profit. In fact, the prophets of the shareholder value revolution condemned exactly what the *Mad Men* characters orbited around—white-collar professionals were insufficiently incentivized to continue to produce, and instead, were incentivized by stability. Dominant today is a sublation of the two tendencies. Shareholder value and private equity foreground the solipsistic pursuit of raising stock prices for the firm, while individual workers are materially incentivized (through threats of coercion) to produce value. What we call "neoliberalism" today entails the atomization of even seemingly stable concepts within economic theory, such as the firm: all empirically observable entities (teams, groups, companies, individuals) can be stripped down into discrete analytic nodules called "agents" and must be assumed to act, or otherwise, compelled to act, economically rationally. The foregrounding of material incentives by policymakers is then turned inward: "Incentives" would no longer be set by policymakers, business owners, or managers but by "the market" itself—the ruthless application of supply and demand logic entails that every interaction becomes a race to the bottom to find the absolute minimum it would take to stimulate rational economic activity. But in the mid-twentieth century, these tendencies are only latent, but the coordinates will have been charted.

To summarize: Samuelson's professionalization and mathematization of the discipline of economics externalize Alfred Marshall's characterization of motivated economic activity. For Marshall, an incentive is a signifier of desire, and economics is the best-placed discipline to study human beings in the "ordinary business of life." Samuelson externalizes motive by averring the immutable, and perfect, laws of supply and demand, rendering an incentive a univocal sign of reward. Profit opportunities produce objective, unquestionable signs that utility-maximizing subjects are mechanically drawn toward. One can deductively postulate rules of behavior for individual economic actors only against the backdrop of a mathematically stable system. Yet in order for economics to become the scientific study of incentives, economics must produce an object called "an incentive" to be studied in the first place. Economics needed a vocabulary to translate desire into science, an enigmatic object that links together cause and effect, "the thing" that causes an individual to undertake economic activity, the nonempirical object that must be added to any interpretation of social reality to demonstrate a cause of desire that led to a tangible economic outcome. Ironically, the neoclassical constriction of "incentive" to a tangible financial reward as the proper object of a decision-making science ends up missing the very thing it attempts to study and instead confirms a basic Lacanian insight: to aim directly at satisfaction is to miss it entirely. The metonymic nature of desire, ever-referring to a "something else" virtually requires that monetary reward will miss the mark and instead provokes a different circuit of desire.

Conclusion: Incentives in the Water Now

In this chapter, I have traced a great compression in the sense of the term "incentive," from its origins in the right hand of an aulos pipe, to its use as a metaphor for mesmerizing (and erotic) speech. Within the discipline of economics, this compression is even more dramatic. Incentive describes an objective feature of a market society, a signal that must be obeyed, both to justify theoretical assumptions about the capacity for markets to reach equilibrium naturally and to explain how individuals undertake competitive behavior to maximize their utility. At this moment, incentive is not "everything," it is an objectively measurable signal presented by market economy—and a market economy is venerated precisely because of its ability to generate incentives for productive activity. If Marshall is describing a desire, Samuelson uses it to describe a reward. Yet this next move is absolutely pivotal. In order for "incentives" to metastasize into an explanatory mechanism for *all* human interaction, not just commodity-based ones, it must be disarticulated from "the price signal" narrowly conceived and given an autonomous status. A contemporary incentive is no longer simply a price signal but reestablished as a free-floating signifier of desire. The inversion from signifier to sign is sublimated—transferred—into a new signifier. Economics correctly identifies that not all desires can be made legible in the money commodity; in a Hegelian manner, this was a necessary error that led to a blossoming of inquiry. Once mathematics can demonstrate deductively that human beings have clearly defined preferences (desires that are circularly generated), they work tirelessly to maximize their utility (however defined) and do so within a perfectly self-regulating market system (as long as no taxation distorts their incentives), no problem cannot be solved from within these bounds. The messy language of desire can be entirely excised—cut off—from consideration.

Economics solves the problem of desire through a transfer, a metastasis: not by doing away with, or severely modifying the axioms of methodological individualism, maximization, and equilibration but to greatly expand them precisely onto the noncommodity realm. As I discuss in the following chapter, to centralize incentives centralizes the economist as the primary interpreter of social phenomena because the underlying laws of rational action are prima facie "economical." In the "neoliberal" era, "incentive" becomes reindividualized, resubjectified as a way to account for the market mechanisms active at every level of social life. If for Marshall and Samuelson what makes any action "economic" is that it can be registered as a market desire, for later economists, what makes any action "economic" is that it can be studied using the tools of economics. While this tendency is latent within neoclassical thought, Becker simply worked the most doggedly to ensure its metastasis. The style of analysis is retained even for things that are not commodities or not strictly organized in markets. Incentives thus come to the fore as the central substance of economics, for they are the clearest expression of individuals behaving rationally according to stimuli that cause their actions.

As the story goes, Marsyas's hubris cost him his life, and Apollonian social order won the day when the satyr was flayed alive, his skin left on the entrance of a cave in Phrygia. Yet in a delicious historical irony, Marsyas's incentive pipe did not truly remain banished to the countryside. According to myth, Marsyas's blood, flowing from his dying body, became the source of an eponymous river in what is now modern-day Turkey. In a similar vein, Apollonian social harmony no longer constitutes the dominant structure of feeling—no patrician warnings about the dangers of compelling charms can stop them from working on their listeners. By losing (his life), the Marsyan truth won, and today incentives have "bled into" culture from the discourse of neoclassical economics. In the following chapter, I attribute this cultural metastasis to a singular figure in the discipline, Chicago-school economist Gary Becker.

Chapter 3

Gary Becker, the Godfather of Incentives

In a 2003 episode of the animated television show *The Simpsons*, Homer Simpson purchases a talking astrolabe instead of presents for his family at Christmastime. When confronted with this fact, Homer explains, "There's a trickle-down theory here. If I'm happy, I'm less abusive to the rest of you!"[1] This joke is, with very little modification, economist Gary Becker's theory of love: The head of a household distributes love to the other members in such a way that maximizes the family's total social output and ideally (either through altruism or manipulation) sufficiently incentivizes the child to care for the parent once they become elderly.[2]

The previous chapter demonstrates an enormous discursive constriction of the proper object of study for economics: money, for better or worse, solves a representational problem for the discipline, and in so doing, it elevates "incentive" to a load-bearing term and insists that market-based economies are best organized to capture, represent, and articulate desires. Once an incentive is yoked primarily to the money commodity, albeit with some limitations, it becomes the closest approximation to human effort possible. However, the subject of this chapter reverses this metaphorical relationship: it is no longer that any human motivation can find expression within a commodity market; rather, all human motivation obeys the behavioral principles of commodity market activity. In Becker, it is the *style* of economic analysis that metastasizes across the social field—not the monetary object itself. In the words of one of his contemporaries, economics is the "one and only" social science precisely because of this universal applicability. Gary S. Becker, a tremendously influential economist from the University of Chicago, was honored with a Bank of Sweden

Prize in Economic Sciences in 1992 due directly to his drastic expansion of the field of economic inquiry. The prize committee wrote of his work: "Gary Becker's research contribution consists primarily of having extended the domain of economic theory to aspects of human behavior which had previously been dealt with—if at all—by other social science disciplines such as sociology, demography and criminology."[3] By adopting the style of economic analysis to interpret nonmarket, noncommodity interactions, economics' purview expands and centralizes the figure of the economist in any analysis—in society, culture, politics, and law. This move is what makes him the pivotal figure of this inquiry, and in my estimation the pivotal figure of Chicago school economics, even above Milton Friedman, George Stigler, or Richard Posner. Becker is *the* paradigmatic figure in the expansion of incentive logic from the narrow ambit of monetary logics to an all-encompassing description of the social field. When economists, noneconomists, politicians, influencers, journalists, and media figures use some variation of Mankiw's axiom, "people respond to incentives. The rest is commentary," they walk a trail blazed by Gary Becker. To answer the question "Why are incentives *everywhere* now?" a critical reading of Becker's work is indispensable.

What Becker calls the "economic approach to human behavior" treats any social field as if it were a market and any being therein as a rational market actor; incentives become the keystone of his method. As Becker and his wife, Guity Nashat Becker, wrote in a compilation of some of his works, "In this approach, behavior crucially depends on incentives."[4] This common theme, central to his entire oeuvre, both constricts the assumptions one makes (around the postulates of rational economic behavior) and drastically expands what economics can reasonably study. Economics becomes anything an economist studies, to paraphrase Gordon Tullock, not the strictly defined domain of commodity interactions, and economic methods become a governing metaphor for any human inquiry. The following is Becker's circular methodological anadiplosis: if economics is the study of incentives, and an incentive can be literally anything, then there is nothing that economics cannot reasonably touch. Becker's economic framework is a way to analyze any conceivable situation; his work openly metastasizes the neoclassical economic vocabulary of "incentives" onto choice of marriage partner, the number of children couples should have, proper penalties for crimes, the distribution of "love" in a household, and what sort of political system the United States ought to have. By postulating that people are always and already incentive driven, and that markets already organize social interactions at a stable equilibrium, the vocabulary of the incentive provides a retroactive justification for inequalities of all sorts.

In his *Speaking of Economics*, economist Arjo Klamer uses the framework "economics as a . . ." to discuss varying ways to think about the field: as a conversation, research program, social process, ideology, and so on.[5] Becker's contribution was to reverse the direction: any "thing," process, assemblage, or structure in the world is fundamentally economic in a strictly defined manner. His genius is that more than any economist of his era, he took the precepts of his field seriously; he was a "true believer" in the principles of neoclassical economics, and indeed, he used these firm principles to argue against his fellow travelers. Becker was also politically influential. He advised the 1996 Bob Dole presidential campaign on economic policy, was personally acquainted with former secretary of defense Donald Rumsfeld through the University of Chicago Price Theory Workshop, and gave talks to governments in Europe, Asia, and South America on taxation and economic policy. As a proud member of the infamous Mont Pelerin society (a key component of what Mirowski calls the "neoliberal thought collective"), Becker organized conferences in Chile and Hong Kong; in short, he was a nexus of an internationally coordinated group of economists who shared a common political project. Becker was also publicly influential within the United States and had a column in *BusinessWeek* for almost two decades in which he answered all manner of political, social, and legal questions explicitly using the "incentives" framework.

Becker's immense influence also epitomizes what Stuart Hall called "discursive struggle," in two ways. First, he was a builder of alternative institutions within the academy. At the University of Chicago, the eponymous Becker Center, and the Chicago Price Theory Workshop combined in 2011 to become the Becker Friedman Institute for Research in Economics. Becker was also a fellow associated with the Hoover Institution, a think tank housed at Stanford University. These institutions provided a durable font of "common sense" that could be authorized theoretically through the circulation of white papers, working papers, and peer-reviewed academic work. Second, Becker's public writing aimed directly at changing the conversation around the role of economics in human life by delivering a series of discursive body blows to liberalism. As he and Guity Nashat Becker write in *The Economics of Life*: "The long-term importance of ideas is the motivation behind the sometimes new and frequently 'unrealistic'

proposals advocated in this book. We do not believe that sharp alterations in the directions of policies are adopted quickly or easily, even if
the case for change is strong. But political power and intellectual fashion
could change, and the time become ripe for radical alternatives to present
policies."[6] With institutional backing from multiple private institutions,
and private funds, Becker's work could play the long game and become
a fertile rhetorical ground upon which the rapid political and economic
changes in the 1980s and 1990s could blossom.

In what follows, I elucidate Becker's work, both academic and
public-facing, and the application of the "economic approach to human
behavior" he maintains throughout. As he contended throughout his career,
the unflinching application of his three concepts (utility maximization,
stable preferences, and market mechanisms) provides a coherent explanation for literally all human behavior. In so doing, Becker metastasizes
the discipline of economics by shifting what it purports to explain: the
problem-space of economic inquiry shifts away from the movements of
commodities to the discovery of the unseen forces that motivate any and
all actions. The logic of the incentive is literally and rhetorically metastatic
(a stasis outside of the original) when applied ruthlessly to noneconomic
domains. The concept of the "incentive" acquires totemic status in his
work, for it functions as the "special stuff" that fills in any explanatory
gap. If a business owner discriminates against a Black worker, they are
merely incentivized by a "taste for discrimination"; if a person dies waiting for a kidney transplant, insufficient incentives have been introduced
into the organ transplant market, and so on. At various moments in his
oeuvre, Becker employs concepts like "shadow price," "psychic cost," or
even "energy" as a form of dark matter that can be input into any utility
function or supply and demand curve to produce the desired result. For
example, in a 1985 article, Becker purports to explain the gender pay gap
by positing a difference between "high" and "low" energy partners. He
speculates that "high energy" men tend to marry "low energy" women
whose energy levels make them better suited for domestic labor and
child-rearing, since those require a great deal more energy than leisure.
Married women thus earn less in the workforce because they rationally
expend their "energy" with children and are thus too exhausted to become
high earners.[7]

This is the value of the incentive—a symbolic representation of a
nonempirical quantity, something Alfred Marshall, one of Becker's primary
influences, attempted to depict as a measure of effort through money.

"The incentive" produces a mode of representation beyond the money commodity—as close as analytically possible for an economist to calculate the enjoyment of any economic decision. For Marshall, "money" is the representational vehicle to best measure effort—one can see how dear a product is to a person by evaluating how much they will pay for it, or how little they value their own labor by reducing their wages to a breaking point. For Becker, "incentive" transcends the meager representational capacity of money by attaching it to the decision-making processes that involve nearly everything—whom to marry, how many children to have, whether to be racist, whether to become addicted to cigarettes, whether to listen to music or read a book at night, and so on. There are some cases in which Becker directly advocates for the introduction of monetary relations into noncommodified social relations, but his system functions rhetorically whether money intervenes or not. Key to understanding Becker's work is how it consistently ascribes the precepts of market behavior onto nonmarket domains. Once this is achieved, Becker engages in the process of retroactive economic causality, attributing the cause of any outcome to a previously unseen market force, whether it be a cost or a preference. Once retroactive causality is established as the proper order of things, the discipline of economics can then proactively insert these economic assumptions into policy recommendations.

Economics has generated a complex methodology for interpreting the needs, demands, and desires of others, largely via their consumer choices. Lacanian psychoanalysis offers us this diagonal route into the same issues, with the added value of careful attention to the modes of representation that are deliberately overlooked by the discipline of economics. To better understand the rhetorical tenacity of Becker's work, I propose that we view the "incentive" as a Lacanian *objet a*: a virtual object, at times explicitly nonempirical, that joins together cause and effect, an unseen force that retroactively renders all action taken by any actor as prima facie "rational," expressive of the immutable laws of neoclassical economics. In a series of lectures at the Sainte-Anne Hospital in Paris, Lacan defined the *objet a* as "certainly an object, but only in the sense that it definitively supersedes any notion of the object as supported by a subject"—its value is its capacity to structure the desire of a subject, not to name it specifically.[8] In this setting, the *objet a* has attributive value: the fixity of something like "an incentive" (and incentive to discriminate, an incentive to sell a kidney, an incentive to marry) is meant to offer epistemic closure within the discourse of economics. However, a critical approach draws attention to the fact that "incentive" identifies not a fixity but the naming of a gap in the causal order. Gunn explains that the *objet a* is the subject's furtive apparatus for understanding psychical causality—the unknowability of the Other's desire provokes a question in the subject, which the *objet a* then fills as the attempt to answer the Other's call.[9] Thus, a psychoanalytic approach seeks out the explanation in language as an accounting of oneself, a redescription of a chaotic social reality as obeying simple immutable laws. Attributing someone's enjoyment to an unseen incentive gives tremendous license for the economist's unconscious to operate, to bend toward a desire for the market to always have been present, and to always have been the proper mode of social organization. Keeping the *objet a* in the register of language, rather than some enigmatic "thing," helps critical scholars guard against the very thing of which economics is guilty: finding a hidden "thing" present in the world that mysteriously coordinates the behavior of a subject.

Becker's "economic approach to human behavior" partakes in the logic of fantasy, as the production of a whole world within discourse that simply does not resemble that of "empirical reality" outside that of a small group of academic economists. To see a child as a durable good, or a family as a firm, or racism as a psychic cost is to produce a "whole" discourse, and depends entirely upon a strident indifference to empirical, or historical context. As Heidegger might have put it, language worlds a world.[10] While the word "object" may appear to give fixity to the concept, Lacan intended for the *objet a* to signify a relationship (in speech) with desire—it is not a tangible thing but rather that which organizes and orients the subject. It is not semiotic closure, or consummation, which the *objet a* offers, but rather, something that keeps desire alive. As Lacan writes, "What constitutes its force . . . is that the object *a* is utterly foreign to the question of meaning. Meaning is a little paint roughly daubed on this object *a*, to which each of you has your own particular attachment."[11] The incentive for Becker (and those in his wake) organizes the complexity of life into a knowable, stable conduit, and transforms all existence into a single substance—"incentive" summarizes all desires, actions, and structures and likens it to the behaviors of markets. Becker's centralization of incentives transforms economics into the study of enjoyment, and he discovers enjoyment in every possible social and interpersonal crevice.

This present chapter proceeds as follows. First, I elucidate Becker's "economic approach to human behavior," for which he won his Bank of Sweden Prize in Economic Sciences, and make the case that it involves a series of rhetorical challenges to his discipline that authorize the "economics imperialism" craved by many of its practitioners. The three components of the "economic approach to human behavior" coalesce around the concept of the incentive, and it becomes synonymous with the approach overall, even supplanting its other principles. Next, I evaluate how Becker deployed incentive rhetoric into various fields as a way to retroactively justify outcomes that favor the status quo. In Becker's work, the incentive functions as a neoclassical alibi for any and all behavior: by presupposing in advance the structure of desire and the nature of causality, the "incentive-based" approach finds what it seeks. The circularity of this explanation results from Becker's peculiar understanding of causality, which offers rhetorical (and mathematical) cover for the outcomes that politically Becker happened to support. The economic approach to human behavior transforms contingency into necessity by positing the hidden incentive structure that ultimately guides rational economic behavior. Becker's project is not simply to provide a retroactive account of all human behavior as obeying the principles of efficient markets and utility-maximizing atomistic actors. His project was explicitly aimed at extending the domain of economics into social formations and offering proactive (and provocative) policy recommendations to politicians and the public. To close this section, I employ two specific examples—the libidinal surplus that someone receives from listening to classical music and the hidden rationality of long queues at restaurants—to explore how Becker locates an economy of enjoyment that subsists beneath even commodity relations.

I conclude the chapter by phrasing Becker's unflinching employment of the "economic approach" as both a fulfillment of the promise of neoclassical economics, as well as a rhetorical challenge to its practitioners. Becker essentially drags economics toward his methods by asking his fellow economists to commit to their own professed principles and beliefs in the properties of markets and rational behavior. Becker's rhetorical strategies within his discipline, both restating and reformulating its basic principles, are a Janus-faced challenge, to the discipline of economics itself as well as to the trembling world outside. Much of Becker's strength derives from a method that claims to incorporate all context while explicitly indifferent thereto—economics, once framed in this mode, is a fully transcontextual discourse. Thus, I draw attention to how Becker's metastatic rhetorical strategy poses a challenge to the domain of rhetoric proper. His rhetoric answers, in its own way, how to view the relationship of structure, context, and contingency, a persistent problem for rhetorical studies. In its stead,

I propose that reading Becker from the perspective of the unconscious offers rhetoric its best hope of providing an alternative account to that of the discipline of economics.

Gary Becker's "Economic Approach to Human Behavior"

Becker's work rests on three, and only three components: "The combined assumptions of maximizing behavior, market equilibrium, and stable preferences, used relentlessly and unflinchingly, form the heart of the economic approach as I see it."[12] The story he crafts appears convincing because its alleged simplicity nods to a complexity in disguise—the idea that hidden forces operate below the level of social phenomena that condition them and that a single universal grammar can detect them if we look closely enough. He continues, writing that his approach is a "comprehensive one that is applicable to all human behavior, be it behavior involving . . . rich or poor persons, men or women, adults or children, brilliant or stupid persons, patients or therapists, businessmen or politicians, teachers or students."[13] The apparent simplicity of any given situation signals a deeper registrar of complex activity—that of the market. The simplifying assumptions that Becker makes end up truncating any context to render it under a neoclassical production function—the elegance he proffers is a Trojan horse for neoclassical truisms of behavior. In order to demonstrate the power of the economic approach, Becker argues that it simultaneously subsumes and dismisses all other forms of analysis: "Indeed, many kinds of behavior fall within the subject matter of several disciplines: for example, fertility behavior is considered part of sociology, anthropology, economics, history, and perhaps even politics. I contend that the economic approach is uniquely powerful because it can integrate a wide range of human behavior."[14] These three elements—utility maximization, equilibrium, and stable preferences—appear to supplement and mutually reinforce the others like a Borromean knot—if preferences are not assumed to be stable, then shadow prices do not explain changes in behavior, if people do not maximize, then markets do not reach equilibrium, if market mechanisms do not provide pricing information to inform consumer behavior, then actors cannot order their preferences or act accordingly. Becker's axioms can account for so much because they purport to be content-free, a mere set of heuristics that can convincingly explain every single human behavior, interaction, or structure. As noted,

Hirshleifer's enthusiasm for economics' "imperialist invasive power" is based on the "universal applicability" of its analytical categories: "scarcity, cost, preferences, [and] opportunities."[15] Within this statement one can detect an economic metastasis in action: Hirshleifer advocates for the mutual interpenetration of all social inquiries and economics, but the subject matter of other disciplines is simply the raw material for economic inquiry since nothing about their methods is worth retaining. The economic categories are not forms without content but rather entail specific contents and commitments to the "economic" point of view.

What authorizes the presumption that economics is better suited to analysis than any other mode of inquiry? Becker's response begs that very question with the first of his three pillars, utility maximization: "Everyone recognizes that the economic approach assumes maximizing behavior more explicitly and extensively than other approaches do, be it the utility or wealth function of the household, firm, union, or government bureau that is maximized."[16] Utility maximization at root entails the pursuit of satisfaction that comes from the purchase of a commodity. Utility can be modeled, in what is called a utility function, in order to derive meaningful postulates about one's behavior, and Becker drastically expands the notion of "utility maximization" to account for even noneconomic goods and influences. In *Accounting for Tastes*, Becker writes: "This extension of the utility-maximizing approach to include endogenous preferences is remarkably successful in unifying a wide class of behavior, including habitual, social, and political behavior. I do not believe that any alternative approach—be it founded on "cultural," "biological," or "psychological" forces—comes close to providing comparable insights and explanatory power."[17] Much like Hirshleifer, Becker transposes the assumption that individuals are utility maximizing within market contexts onto other contexts as a warrant for his assertion. For Becker, the individual utility function scales upward with no qualitative differences among unions, families, firms, and political organizations. In other words, because some people view altruistic behavior as utility-maximizing, altruistic behavior obeys the principle of rational choice.[18] Families operate like firms because the "head" distributes "love" like a capital good and seeks to maximize the family's output (i.e., utility).[19]

Becker's Bank of Sweden lecture begins with the claim that while "Marxian analysis" assumes "that individuals are motivated solely by selfishness or material gain," his approach is much broader than that. He states, "I have tried to pry economists away from narrow assumptions about self-interest. Behavior is driven by a much richer set of values and preferences. The analysis assumes that individuals maximize welfare *as they conceive it*."[20] Schlefer rightly notes that this is a conceptual sleight of hand, "a colorful way of stating accepted theory. The problem comes in the next step, when supposedly practical economists turn around and impose their own conception of utility on the agents in their models."[21] Once again, a circularity imbues the concept with libidinal force: people are motivated by their goals to obtain satisfaction, and they act. If a person acts, then they, ipso facto, are maximizing their utility, whether it be joining a protest march or laying off an employee. Utility maximization seems like an intuitive simplification: people who are motivated by their desires will act in accordance with them, and the inference is that they desired whatever outcome. However, economists the world over (Becker is not unique in this respect) combine the principle of utility with the presumption of the perfection of markets to ascribe rationality, and thus responsibility, to any potential outcome. If one is unemployed, it stands to reason that one derives greater utility from leisure time than gainful employment.[22] An economist must make one simple assumption: somewhere, someone out there is enjoying. This is the heart of what Becker and his colleague George Stigler call the "*de gustibus non est disputandum*" approach.

The "*de gustibus*" approach represents the first rhetorical push-back to Becker's discipline, in which he implicitly claims that economists who do not share his methodological rigor transpose assumptions about what motivates people (either selfishness or altruism) onto their behavior, which unnecessarily impedes their power of analysis. "*De gustibus*" roughly means there is no point in disputing tastes—if someone acts, that action satisfies their "utility function." Becker and Stigler write, in a lengthy passage:

> It is a thesis that does not permit of direct proof because it is an assertion about the world, not a proposition in logic. Moreover, it is possible almost at random to throw up examples of phenomena that presently defy explanation by this hypothesis: Why do we have inflation? Why are there so few Jews in farming? Why are societies with polygynous families so rare in the modern world? Why aren't blood banks responsible for the quality of their product? If we could answer these questions to your satisfaction, you would quickly produce a dozen more. What we assert is not that we are clever enough to make illuminating applications of utility-maximizing theory

to all important phenomena . . . [T]his traditional approach of
the economist offers guidance in tackling these problems—and
that no other approach of remotely comparable generality and
power is available.[23]

The argument is offered paradoxically. Direct proof of this assertion is
not available because the claim is being made about empirical reality, not
via formal logic. And although it is a generalization, individual examples
ought not suffice. The point remains, however, that the economic approach
simply assumes *that* people have preferences and act to achieve them, and
therefore economists can evade *what* the content of these preferences are,
or evaluate them in some meaningful sense.

Next, Becker supplements the principle of utility maximization with
his second pillar: that of stable preferences. Typically, a preference is understood to be a desire for a commodity—one prefers a certain brand of cola,
or car, over others, all of which are generally assumed to be substitutable
for one another. After all, they are "preferences" and not "ultimatums":
the classic question, "Is Pepsi okay?" when one orders a Coca-Cola at
a restaurant, is the best example of a preference. Becker refashions the
notion of preference in two ways. First, he metonymizes "preference" to be
something much deeper than the preference for a type of cola and links it
instead to an abstract quality, something like enjoyment: "The preferences
that are assumed to be stable do not refer to market goods and services,
like oranges, automobiles, or medical care, but to underlying objects of
choice that are produced by each household using market goods and
services, their own time, and other inputs. These underlying preferences
are defined over fundamental aspects of life, such as health, prestige,
sensual pleasure, benevolence, or envy, that do not always bear a stable
relation to market goods and services."[24] Becker's position mirrors that of
utilitarian philosopher Jeremy Bentham, and indeed borrowed his list of
affectations from Bentham himself. In his *Introduction to the Principles
of Morals and Legislation*, Bentham identifies fourteen different "simple
pleasures" (among them benevolence, amity, skill, and imagination), and
fourteen "simple pains," which are simply the contraries of the pleasures
(thus, the pain of benevolence, the pain of amity, the pain of awkwardness,
and so on).[25] But, ultimately, the philosopher subordinates these specific
pleasures and pains to the dyad pleasure/pain, and posits that the aim of
human experience is to pursue pleasure and avoid pain, and thus reduces
even further the dyad to the single substance of pleasure (or, as an econ-

omist would put it, utility). Becker's goal here is to be able to interpret the underlying rationality of a consumer choice and detect an economy of enjoyment circulating beneath, beyond, and within a commodity purchase. It is impossible to delink "preference" from "utility-maximizing" as Becker defines them since the underlying meaning of any preference or commodity purchase is ultimately to satisfy one's utility.

Becker offers a paradoxical case, regarding the price of heating fuel to demonstrate his assertion that individuals have stable preferences. Instead of applying a universally applicable theory of purposive behavior, Becker posits a universally applicable theory of economic causality to explain essentially identical outcomes. He asserts that "changes in tastes" cannot account for why households purchase different commodities to regulate their dwelling's temperature in different seasons: "If a household's utility function has heating fuel as an argument then its tastes must change seasonally to explain why it purchases more fuel in the winter (when the price of fuel is usually higher)."[26] Becker accuses, but does not cite, economists who rely on ad hoc shifts in values or tastes to explain why consumers purchase different commodities at different times, particularly when their prices would encourage consumers to do the opposite. In a 1988 interview, Becker claims, "Economists and others are very prone to do that. When one can't explain something, it is tempting to say that preferences changed or are different between groups. Yes, I do think it is a cop-out."[27] Because it is economically irrational to purchase a good (like heating oil) when its price is high, the economically rational agent must be satisfying a preference that is different from purchasing the commodity with the cheapest price. As Becker frames this example, a truly "rational" economic agent should purchase heating oil in the summer when it is demanded the least. Instead, the economic agent desires a noncommodity quality, something akin to "comfort," that they satisfy with a variety of commodities depending on the tilt of the earth's axis qua the sun. In psychoanalytic terms, Becker metonymizes commodity purchases by placing each in a series of equivalents that never fully catch up to satisfaction but momentarily capture it. As Lacan writes, metonymy is the structure of desire and "desire . . . is caught in the rails of metonymy, eternally extending toward the *desire for something else*."[28] Becker contends that every commodity purchase, every rational action taken by an actor, is done in the service of a noncommodity preference—the underlying values that motivate action in the first place. And because of this metonymic sliding, Becker is always able to defer (or better, to displace) the "meaning" of a commodity purchase into one he finds analytically palatable.

Later in his career, Becker redefines preferences to include the choices of others that meaningfully condition or constrain the actions of individuals, in what he calls a "metapreference." He writes, "What *de gustibus* assumes is that *metapreferences* are stable. Metapreferences include past choices and choices by others as arguments in a person's current utility function."[29] Becker uses the examples of a parent's decision to smoke while pregnant and raising a child, or a woman's past experiences with sexual abuse as "metapreferences": this is because, while not consciously chosen, they meaningfully constrain the future choices of an individual. In this case, a metapreference is not, as fellow economist Amartya Sen defines them, a rank-ordering of preferences that allows economics to broaden its too-narrow focus on individuals and their seemingly selfish consumer choices. Sen writes, "Economic theory has been much preoccupied with this rational fool decked in the glory of his *one* all-purpose preference ordering. To make room for the different concepts related to his behavior we need a more elaborate structure."[30] Sen's system allows for ideals, principles, values, and the contingent ordering thereof; however, Becker rhetorically immobilizes Sen's theoretical advance by enfolding those broader categories of motivation into the concept of "utility maximization"—one can include altruism, selflessness, and cooperation into one's individual utility function, just as much as one can include atavism, selfishness, and avarice. But more importantly, Becker's "metapreferences" concept exceeds even his own concept of "stable preferences," if they are taken to mean deep, underlying, noncommodity desires (like comfort or prestige). If a stable preference is an "underlying object of choice," by definition, a metapreference cannot be since it entails almost entirely the choices of others. As late as 2013, Becker was refining this concept, and advocated for parents to "influence their children's preferences in order to make the children willing to help them out when [they] are elderly."[31] As Becker and his coauthors argue, "It may pay for parents to spend resources to 'manipulate' the preferences of children in order to induce them to support their parents in old age."[32]

One should interpret this agentic reversal symptomatically. To defend against the demand for thinking about the determining role that context plays in the decisions that ordinary people make, Becker offers an alibi for these inequalities by saying it is economically (and psychologically) rational for people to accept that which has oppressed them:

In effect, they *wish* their actual preferences over good and other activities were different. But they do not act on this wish because actual capital stocks constrain their utility-maximizing choices, no matter how much they may regret the amount and kind of capital they inherited from the past. . . . Even though a person may greatly regret he acquired a taste for crack because both his parents took crack, he might be miserable if he ignored his background and abstained from taking the drug.[33]

Thus, Becker rhetorically navigates around both a plea for thinking contextually about how individuals' choices are constrained as well as how people are capable of a broader, noneconomical method of adjudicating competing values and beliefs. Since it is prima facie rational for a crack addict to remain a crack user ("metapreferences"), and economists can make no judgments about the decisions individuals make ("*de gustibus*"), economics ought not have anything to say about the pernicious results of drug addiction.

With this, the concept of "metapreference" yokes the concept of "stable preferences" to the final component of the economic approach: price mechanisms. For Becker, the assumption of stable preferences and utility maximization is completed by the preeminence of market mechanisms in determining behavior. For Becker, supply and demand dictate even interpersonal (and intrapersonal) activity—this means that all action is guided by the "prices" of certain outcomes, and one's purchasing power to satisfy one's preferences is expanded to incorporate all of one's privileges, experiences, and choices. Becker writes, "Prices and other market instruments allocate the scarce resources within a society and thereby constrain the desires of participants and coordinate their actions. In the economic approach, these market instruments perform most, if not all, of the functions assigned to 'structure' in sociological theories."[34] In other words, we can be agnostic about what motivates people and what they desire if we assume that in the final analysis, the supply, demand, and cost of certain behaviors is what matters. The eminent sociologist Talcott Parsons defines structure as a "relatively stable patterning of the relationships of the . . . component actors or as the roles in terms of which they participate in social relationships," so it is reasonable to infer that for Becker, price exerts a determining effect on individual actors, absent conscious direction or coercion.[35] The difficulty here is that Becker insists on two different, potentially incompatible phenomena simultaneously, which is the difference between "price" and "income." On the one hand,

Becker's assumption of stable preferences, and that stable preferences can be essentially reduced to utility/pleasure/enjoyment, means that *only* differences in income explain people's choices.[36]

The aforementioned example of crack addiction displays this perfectly. While it may be beneficial for someone to no longer be addicted to a harmful drug, the "cost" of doing so is simply too high. This concept further includes things like a "taste for discrimination," or the racist desire for an employer to hire only people of the same race or ethnic group; it also provides the basis for the concept of "human capital." Only income—the ability to pay for a given outcome—determines differences in outcomes.[37] Becker writes, akin to the concept of *"de gustibus,"* "Since economists generally have had little to contribute, especially in recent times, to the understanding of how preferences are formed, preferences are assumed not to change substantially over time, nor to be very different between wealthy and poor persons, or even between persons in different societies and cultures."[38] Because economics as a discipline cannot speak to the formation of individual preferences, it is better to assume that people are fundamentally the same across all contexts, classes, and temporalities and that only differences in income affect people's behavior. As Hirshleifer and others point out, the universal applicability of economic principles is economics' only defining feature; so more than a methodological simplification, it is also an assertion about the fundamental structure of reality itself.

Becker's foregrounding of price mechanisms as the primary cause of any action requires some unknown quantity to fill the causal gap when typical economic expectations are violated. He writes in a lengthy passage:

> When an apparently profitable opportunity to a firm, worker, or household, is not exploited, the economic approach does not take refuge in assertions about irrationality, contentment with wealth already acquired, or convenient ad hoc shifts in values (i.e., preferences). Rather it postulates the existence of costs, monetary or psychic, of taking advantage of these opportunities that eliminate their profitability—costs that may not be easily 'seen' by outside observers. Of course, postulating the existence of costs closes or 'completes' the economic approach in the same, almost tautological, way that postulating the existence of (sometimes unobserved) uses of energy completes the energy system, and preserves the law of the conservation of energy.[39]

In order to rescue economic causality from an explanation of behavior that lies outside the boundaries of economics proper, Becker posits a measurable but unseen force that coordinates behavior. The "psychic cost" of hiring a Black person, or the "psychic benefits" of having better children, entail that market rationality has penetrated more deeply into individuals' decisional structures than even economists heretofore imagined.

These assertions function as rhetorical salvos against Becker's own discipline, for his argument is strictly with how his contemporaries interpret the behavior of the people they purport to understand. His contention is that when faced with contradictory information, a change over time, or the beginnings and ends of fads, economists "hide the ball" by appealing to a noneconomic factor: the idea that people's tastes change. For Becker, this is simply not good enough: an economist must be able to derive changes endogenously from market principles, so any changes in consumption patterns must be the result of changes in income. If something other than changes in utility or changes in the "price" of an activity cause an outcome, then it was not caused by the market at all but merely registered by it. By foregrounding the mechanisms of price as causal, Becker upends the traditional way of viewing what a "market" is for. Markets do not register activity; they cause activity. From this perspective, wars, trends, and social movements do not cause outcomes on their own, they cause changes in the supply or demand of a given outcome and thus alter the structure of reality. It is not that a historical, contextual cause is inevitably registered by a market: it is that the very act of registration is the cause of the event that follows it. By accusing economists of hiding the ball in something like naïve humanism, or attentiveness to context as the cause of change, Becker hides the ball himself by appealing to a strict definition of economic causality.

To summarize, if one holds to the idea that the only preference one has is to pursue pleasure and avoid pain, then one does not need "stable preferences" as a pillar, since that idea is already incorporated in the principle of utility maximization. If one holds to the idea that market features cause rational economic activity by instantaneously conveying the "cost" of a behavior and actors instantaneously calculate the "benefit" they will receive therefrom, then one does not need "utility maximization" or "stable preferences" as standalone concepts, since they emerge only against the backdrop of economic causality. Particularly once Becker adds "meta-preferences" to his system, if one cannot "afford" ones preferences due to factors outside of one's control—he uses the example of a woman who is molested as a child and thus develops a "preference" for hating men—one's preferences take a back seat to the market mechanisms that more overtly condition one's behavior.[40] (One can resist or resent one's metapreferences, but it is more expensive to do so, hence, it becomes economically rational to follow one's initial outlays to satisfy one's preferences.) The tripartite system—stable preferences, utility maximization, market mechanisms—frays upon closer inspection not because of internal inconsistency, but because the parts betray a more fundamental unity. The components are tautologically linked via the logic of the incentive.

The Centrality of the Incentive

In his 2004 farewell column for *BusinessWeek*, Becker reflected on his nineteen-year tenure as a guest columnist for the magazine, noting that "there was a vacuum in discussions of public policies and events that affected the incentives of individuals, families, companies and governments. Since I have spent my career teaching and researching how incentives affect behavior, it seemed natural for me to help fill this vacuum."[41] However, in a 1997 compilation of his columns, Becker admits that he "did not start the columns with any statement of purpose, but practically all of them have in fact emphasized this link between incentives and public policies and other events."[42] That is, the absolute priority of incentives emerged from his columns after the fact—Becker discovered in his own work what had been latently there all along. The incentive acquires totemic value because it summarizes each of the three components of the economic approach to human behavior: The incentive causes action, it exists both inside and outside of the individual in question, and it relies on an incipient calculative rationality. With the incentive as the organizing principle of economic inquiry, and economic inquiry being a metastatic vocabulary to interpret all of human reality, there is nothing that Becker cannot touch, and ascribe economic rationality thereto. The incentive fills the causal gap in any "economic" explanation of behavior by presupposing, at some deep level, a quintessentially economic motivation (albeit not one specifically motivated by the money commodity) for an individual's actions. Although Becker claims that his approach is merely a method, and thus has no presuppositions, by presupposing that markets exist for all behaviors and that humans act rationally therein, his conclusions are irrevocably circumscribed thereby. What appears as openness is channeled into necessity: For Becker, economic causality could not be otherwise, hence my introduction of the *objet a* as a way to view the incentive in Becker's work.

Lacanian psychoanalysis uses topological models, such as the Borromean knot and the Klein bottle, to demonstrate the contradictory status of its object of study, the unconscious. The Borromean knot indicates the mutual necessity of multiple separate components: Cut one link in the knot, and the entire structure separates. It is impossible to separate the Imaginary from the Symbolic, the Symbolic from the Real, and so on. The Klein jug, by contrast, designates the unitary surface of the unconscious, but troubles our notions of what is "inside" and what is "outside." Becker's tripartite schema rhetorically presents itself as a Borromean knot, but in action, it functions as a Klein bottle: The rigorous application of one principle demands the passage into another, "stable preferences" metonymically substitute for "market mechanisms" since market mechanisms presuppose individuals have stable preferences and maximize their utility, "utility maximization" substitutes for stable preferences since Becker assumes that individuals maximize their utility as they see it, so they determine their own response to the market price of their behaviors, given their preferences. Thus the synthesis of these three components allows Becker to define the proper object of economic study, the incentive—the causal mechanism of human action.

As mentioned, the *objet a* offers not closure, but organization for a subject—it exists in a relationship of meaning with the subject's unconscious, and therefore can be transferred among objects. Since it is a virtual object, or as Lacan puts it, it is *"in you something more than you,"* rhetorical critics are uniquely equipped to evaluate how the *objet a* participates in a discursive economy.[43] It is not reducible to a "thing"—a beloved's feature, the roar of the crowd, a career-making promotion—but rather it is found in the desire it elicits and organizes for the subject. The word "incentive" functions to cover over a gap in the causal order—an interjection into reality but without positive consistency on its own. As Žižek puts it, the *objet a* is "an objectification of a void," but with a useful theoretical twist.[44] The positive consistency it offers is *"the retroactive act of naming itself,"* so what we call self-identity is itself already a discursive surplus imputed into the signifier.[45] For Becker, an "incentive" is merely the name given to whatever market force that cannot be discovered elsewhere, and its existence merely continually refers to the market structures that condition our social reality. The word "incentive" stands in, and positivizes, a lack in being, and rhetorically centers the economist as the key interpreter of social reality.

In his notes to a 2007 talk to the Becker Center, Becker wrote, "My view is that ~~rational choice~~ theory is by far the most powerful tool available for understanding human behavior."[46] Above the crossed out "rational choice" is the phrase "Chicago econ," and future references to "RCT" (rational choice theory) throughout the talk are crossed out and replaced with "econ th." The symbolic combination of "Chicago" economics and economic theory, and the replacement of "rational choice" testifies to the narrow band of economics Becker counted as economic theory. The slimness of the pediment contrasts with the expansiveness of the approach, since it only requires a minimal set of assumptions in order to draw vast conclusions. In this talk, Becker mentions three major implications of his approach, which are variants of those already mentioned. He indicates that behavior is "forward-looking," meaning that consumers are rational actors who seek to maximize their utility, and that "market equilibrium **enormously** [bold in original] affects the choices that individual decision-makers are faced with," meaning that price mechanisms and meta-preferences affect individual decision-makers.[47] But Becker positions incentives as the keystone of his intellectual edifice. He states: "Perhaps the most important is that consumers, producers, and government officials respond to INCENTIVES [capitalized in original]. The greater the benefit from an action, the more likely people are to take it, while they are less likely the greater the cost."[48] This is another mild restatement of the principle of price mechanisms—people respond to the "costs" of behaviors just as much as they follow their own desires. Rhetorically, the centrality of the "incentive" means that individual decision-makers are sovereign but that they act within constraints from the outside; and methodologically, to be incentive driven is to subscribe to the specific mode of retroactive economic causality that sustains the economic approach.

For Becker, an incentive can be anything: it can be something like the profit motive, a belief in one's innate racial superiority, or a predilection for a certain restaurant. By and large, politically, Becker's political recommendations are nearly uniformly right-wing, and in *The Economics of Life*, he suggests that Republicans are more attentive to the power of incentives than Democrats are, with few exceptions. (This statement may have been true at the time, but as I explore in subsequent chapters, the Democratic Party has caught up, if not surpassed, the Republican Party in organizing its political interventions according to the logic of the incentive.) Becker states that he is opposed to: "big government and central planning, illegal immigration, employment quotas and set-asides for minorities, union exemption from antitrust laws, highly subsidized tuition for middle-class and rich students at state universities, the NCAA restrictions on pay to college athletes, term limits for members of Congress, ESOPs and other subsidies to employee ownership of companies, and tariffs and quotas."[49] By contrast, Becker is in favor of "advocate selling the right to immigrate legally, extensive privatization of public enterprises, introduction of school vouchers primarily to poor children, legalizing many drugs, [and] substituting an individual-account system for pay-as-you-go social security."[50] For anyone familiar with "Chicago school" economics, Becker's political positions should come as no surprise. Yet what interests me more than Becker's political commitments is the way that the concept of the incentive organizes these commitments—it functions as an alibi such that his policy proposals appear to be led by incentive-based causality, rather than conservative political commitments.

Becker's advocacy for incentives in the public realm is largely organized around a prohibition: people are properly incentivized when markets are "free," they can only ever be improperly (or perversely) incentivized when unions, social movements, and governments get in the way. As Cooper puts it, "While individual preferences are always 'rational' and never 'perverse' within a law and economics perspective, incentives themselves can sometimes be considered 'perverse,' particularly when they approximate those of the welfare state."[51] Even if the ontological structure of reality resembles a market, and Becker foregrounds the assumptions of market equilibrium and "*de gustibus*," policies must be designed around the explicit organization of market relations in society. Thus Becker simultaneously advocates for a severe and violent crackdown on illegal immigration into the United States from Mexico alongside an auction system by which well-off immigrants could purchase their way into the country legally—such a system would reveal the desire (or incentive) that migrants have to enter the United States and reveals what kinds of contributions they would be able to make as workers within this country.[52] By formalizing market relations where there previously were none, human beings' activities become calculable, predictable, and especially manipulable toward the preferred political ends of its advocates. Governments, if they are to do anything besides enforce a regime of violent protection of private property and physical space, are to provide incentives (largely monetary) to citizens to behave in an economically rational manner.

Take for instance columns that Becker wrote in 1997 and 1999, which advocated for a system to, in his words, "bribe" families in "Third-World" countries to prevent them from sending their children to work in factories and sweatshops.[53] From the perspective of a political progressive, child labor represents an invidious scourge, the failure of a system to adequately provide substantial wages for its able-bodied members to provide for their children. Becker's position parallels a moral disgust about child labor, but his major concern is safeguarding the human capital of the children in places where sweatshops proliferate. His proposal: "Give parents a financial incentive to keep their children in school longer."[54] To finance this monetary incentive, Becker advocates for reduced spending on universities, rather than an increase in taxes on the corporations that operate sweatshops in these countries. Critics of child labor miss the mark when they seek to outlaw child labor in countries where it proliferates, because "the fundamental cause of child labor is poverty, not greedy foreign and domestic employers."[55] He adds that in the case of the United States, "Although legislation, unions, and other factors contributed to this decline [in child labor], studies indicate that greater prosperity was essential."[56] Becker's theory of causality reduces the "stuff" of history—labor unions pushing for higher wages, campaigns to outlaw or limit child labor—to the fringes, and foregrounds the causality of the economic. In brief, this example demonstrates Becker's method for implementing an incentive program: Hypostasize social reality as a series of economic inputs, isolate a manipulable causal feature, deliberately background any others as irrelevant, refigure existing programs perverse incentives or distortions of the market, slip the "proper" incentive into the context, and wait for the change to occur. This is how the metastasis of incentive rhetoric occurs—cause is displaced from one order (context, history, politics, the unconscious, and so on) onto the economic order, since it is the only thing capable of registering the change, once social reality is reorganized as a market.

The rhetorical strategy of deliberately and openly foregrounding incentives also sanctions Becker a trump card: the accusation that any alternative proposals are inattentive to the absolute causal priority of incentives. To outlaw child labor would distort the incentives of sweatshop owners and destitute families, to have public utilities distorts the incentives of energy companies and consumers, and so on. This strategy also allows Becker, and the discipline of economics, to be the primary arbiter of what counts as a proper incentive. When a family sends a small child to work in a sweatshop, they are improperly incentivized, when a head of household refuses to sign up for social welfare benefits, they are properly incentivized. When a white business owner refuses to hire a Black worker, their preferences, however misguided, are sovereign; when a heterosexual married couple evenly splits domestic duties, their household output will be inefficient. Because markets, and markets alone, are capable of registering human effort and desire, and dialectically produce reactions when alterations to inputs occur (like the claim that raising the minimum wage hydraulically causes an increase in unemployment, for example), nothing outside of market forces are capable of producing change. Aune points out that rhetorics of free markets frequently invoke "the perversity thesis," the idea that, following Hirschman, "the attempt to push society in a certain direction will result in its moving all right, but in the opposite direction."[57] The supposed law of unintended consequences disables any alternative modes of thinking since the "economic" approach demonstrates amply how futile any exercise in ameliorating social iniquities can be, unless done through the introduction of even more market relations. And this is the key discovery that Melinda Cooper and Philip Mirowski, among others, make: at a certain point, the neoliberal order, despite an almost religious faith in the power of markets, relies upon a non-market structure (like a government) to implement proper incentive structures.

This sweatshop example further demonstrates that the logic of the incentive is necessarily partial, since two of Becker's three operating principles, the presumption of market equilibrium and "*de gustibus*" fail to hold when the rubber meets the proverbial road for concrete policy proposals. Perverse as it may seem, what prevents us from interpreting the existence of child labor in the Global South as an example of a market at equilibrium, with parents satisfying their own preferences for their children to work in sweatshops? What prevents an individual worker from following their stable preference for working-class solidarity, and rationally maximizing their utility by joining a union? In his concrete policy proposals and public-facing work, the "incentive" rhetorically dominates Becker's other components of the economic approach to human behavior, and makes rhetorical questions like these moot. If the "economic approach" is to be a universal description of all human behavior, it must remain an empty vessel, and thus must be capable of explaining nothing, merely re-describing the structure of social reality as always-already subject to the causal priority of incentives (whatever they may be) and the structuring power of markets that stretch far beyond and below commodity markets.

Becker's policy proposals steadfastly refuse this challenge in favor of the introduction of market relations into social reality.

Incentives as Hidden Rationality

In the previous section, I have laid out how "incentive" in Becker's work rhetorically metastasizes even within his own corpus, and becomes interchangeable with "the economic approach to human behavior" writ large. The rhetorical power of "incentives," and careful attention thereto, allows for a nonneutral redescription of social reality in accordance with the postulates of neoclassical economics. In this section, I explore the rhetorical mechanisms that Becker employed to solidify the metastasis of incentive logic, and the deep market rationality of all human behavior. Two key examples suffice for how this hidden economic cause offers an alibi for the rectitude of the status quo. The first example returns "incentive" to its origins in antiquity, as the "playing of the tune" features as Becker reformulates some foundational neoclassical tenets to make room for enjoyment; the second concerns the hidden rationality of market actors beneath even commodity interactions. Becker's task is to locate the *objet a* in these studies that orbits extant social reality—it is the trait, or feature, that explains (away) the present as deeply expressive of economic logic. The twist is that Becker must contend with his own discipline's precepts in order to metastasize it into new fields. The incentive is both a cudgel and a Trojan horse for a quintessentially economic explanation for human life. What emerges in each example is an economy—not of money—but of *jouissance*, that economics alone promises it can count, measure, and judge.

To be fair, the central role that monetary incentives play in some of Becker's public-facing work, as techniques of governing the actions of individuals does make Becker proximate to Marshall's conceptualization of the incentive. Money is the closest representational approximation to effort and desire, and thus one can gauge the value that someone places on an outcome by witnessing the price they would be willing to pay for it. But Becker's appeals to non-monetary structures would be his strongest case for metastasizing the logic of the incentive into all social realms. As Becker himself admits, to presume something like an unseen "market force" that causes any outcome is to engage in tautological reasoning.[58] This is, however, precisely the point at which Becker finds his greatest strength, since a tautology (like A = A, or "God is God") is never an empty signifying gesture. To borrow Žižek's Hegelian insight, a tautology unconsciously conveys a hidden generative opposition—one fills the empty vessel of the first word with the symbolic power of the second.[59] As Bates puts it, "*Difference* in tautology is *power*."[60] The tautology "Law is Law" depends on seeing "the law" as an empty or powerless device unless tautologically "filled" with a power beneath or beyond it, which never quite lives up to, or adequates, to the signifier. In this case, the tautology launders the market into a description of social reality, thus confirming the basic tenets of market behavior as retroactively having caused all action. "Incentive" holds together the economic approach's edifice, and closes the causal loop by continuously pointing to the unseen, hidden incentive by which all market actors are motivated.

According to an interview, Becker claims that his theory of preferences and his "*de gustibus*" position emerged from an attempt to retroactively reconstruct the truth value of an offhand statement by Alfred Marshall about the value of classical music to a listener: "[George] Stigler came to me one day and said, 'Look at this quote by Alfred Marshall.' Alfred Marshall had said something like 'With respect to classical music it's not true that the more you hear the lower the marginal utility. The more you hear, the higher the marginal utility.' How do we explain that?"[61] From an analytic standpoint, Becker's admission is propitious. Not only does Becker use music as his entry point for how incentives can "set the tune" of behavior, he deliberately notes that his project was to reconstruct a rationale in the present from a comment made by Marshall in the past, thus allowing Marshall's insight to give credence to future expansions and modifications of his method. In so doing, Becker and Stigler must gently reformulate the "law of diminishing marginal utility," something central to the field of neoclassical economics. The concept suggests that "the marginal utility of a good declines as more of that good is consumed."[62] Classic examples involve the purchase of an ice cream cone or some other frivolity: Having one ice cream cone is delicious, two is extravagant, and beyond that, the acquisition becomes gluttonous. One's enjoyment of the third ice cream cone is less than that of the first, thus one's utility has diminished.

How, then, can economics explain the increase in utility one gains from listening to a classical music album, learning to play piano, taking up tennis, etc., if one presumes the law of diminishing marginal utility? Becker answers this challenge with a remarkable rhetorical elision: Becker metaphorizes the consumption of the product—classical music, in this case—as a capital investment instead of a commodity purchase. For Becker, consumption of a product never exists on its own—*consumption* is instead the *production* of satisfaction. Becker evades entirely what "diminishing marginal utility" is designed to explain, which is the purchase of multiple substitutable commodities, and instead locates his inquiry in the enjoyment of the product already procured. Michel Foucault, in one of his *Birth of Biopolitics* lectures, characterizes Becker's innovation thusly: "The man of consumption, insofar as he consumes, is a producer. What does he produce? Well, quite simply, he produces his own satisfaction. And we should think of consumption as an enterprise activity by which the individual, precisely on the basis of the capital he has at his disposal, will produce something that will be his own satisfaction."[63] This consumption-as-production reversal is Becker's argument for the concept of "human capital," or the notion that human beings make "investments" in themselves with habits, training, education, and good choices.[64] Brown's 2015 *Undoing the Demos* involves a critical inquiry on "human capital" in the neoliberal age by pointing out how it largely renders individuals responsible for their choices, and eviscerates the positive role that collective political action can do for individuals.[65] I supplement Brown's analysis by highlighting Becker's methodological innovation: He locates within the field of economics a way to account for enjoyment beyond commodity consumption, and calls that mode of enjoyment "capital."

As Lacan puts it in his twentieth seminar, to "usufruct" is to enjoy the property of others; for Becker's version of economics, one's human capital investments allow one to "enjoy oneself," or to put oneself to work.[66] By shifting the inquiry entirely into how a subject puts their enjoyment to work, away from the purchase and sale of empirical goods, the discipline can stretch without forgoing any of its principles. However, the point regarding diminishing marginal utility for neoclassical economics is not specifically reducible to some abstract qualia called utility: simply put, the price of an item is derived from the amount one would be willing to pay for the last ice cream cone before your "utility" diminishes, in this example. Becker reverses this presumption entirely: "Music" becomes a capital good—an investment that generates surplus—rather than a consumption good. Further, the consumption of a good that is "good" for one's earnings allows Becker to impute retroactive causality upon the choices of consumers by calling them human capital investments: smoking crack is an unwise human capital investment, while becoming a member of an art museum is a wise one. In this view, it is not a commodity that consumers purchase, it is enjoyment.

Becker's 1991 article, "A Note on Restaurant Pricing and Other Examples of Social Influences on Price," accomplishes a parallel set of rhetorical and methodological tasks. First, it corroborates the economy of enjoyment found in his other works, and retroactively confers stability on a given situation. And second, it, like his pushback against the concept of diminishing marginal utility, reframes "rational action" as that which even contravenes the profit motive. If an incentive no longer must obey the tenets of even market forces, there is no limit to its ability to metastasize as an explanation for social relations. Becker begins by witnessing an apparent contradiction in received neoclassical economic theory: "A popular seafood restaurant in Palo Alto, California, does not take reservations, and every day it has long queues for tables during prime hours. Almost directly across the street is another seafood restaurant with comparable food, slightly higher prices, and similar service and other amenities. Yet this restaurant has many empty seats most of the time. Why doesn't the popular restaurant raise prices, which would reduce the queue for seats but expand profits?"[67] The supply/demand relationship, a hallmark of what Noah Smith calls "101ism," is an ostensible truism for the discipline of economics, so much so that a published article can begin by commenting upon its apparent flagrant violation by a rational economic actor.[68] A restaurant with a long queue to seat customers should, in theory, raise its prices until the demand finds its equilibrium level. In fact, Becker argues, to act otherwise is economically irrational—a restaurant leaves money on the table each time a customer pays the standard price rather than one representative of the excess demand that the product elicits.[69] Becker solves this problem by transitioning into the language of desire: The customers are not consuming a *meal* at the popular restaurant, they are consuming its *popularity*. He writes, "[A] consumer's demand for some goods depends on the demands by other consumers . . . [T]he pleasure from a good is greater when many people want to consume it."[70] This explains why consumers remain in long lines to enter nightclubs, restaurants, Broadway theaters, and the like, since exclusivity is built into the product.

But Becker's problem-space is something else entirely: Why does the restaurant in question not raise their prices to capture the excess demand in profits? Becker posits that businesses are capable of discerning the utility functions of the customers whose demands fluctuate according to the demands of others, and set their prices accordingly. Becker's mathematical proof for this claim is that consumers are capable of cognizing the demand functions of other customers, and when fewer customers demand the same product, their own demand attenuates. Becker's rational consumer resembles the Lacanian neurotic subject, whose desires are never fully self-transparent, but rather are organized by the question "What am I for the Other?" Or perhaps more colloquially, resembles the Marx Brothers routine in *Duck Soup* in which Groucho and Harpo mimic one another across an empty mirror pane, with neither of them knowing whether what they recognize is their own reflection or an imposter. Because the subject can never fully know how they appear from the outside, the misrecognition/resemblance effect is structurally uncanny; when Groucho moves, he can never be sure if what he sees is his own desire to be seen moving, or the desire of an other to match his movements. Becker makes no attempt to resolve the problem of representation in this mathematical proof—how one's demands for an exclusive restaurant are communicated to others in the marketplace outside of a refusal to patronize the restaurant is left unacknowledged.

But Becker's point is a fairly standard neoclassical economic argument, contorted through the position of the hyperrational consumer, and the restaurant capable of anticipating potential demand fluctuations in advance. Becker's argument is that if a business raises its prices to sweet up surplus profits due to excess demand, fewer people will demand that business' product (their demand becomes "discontinuous" at a certain point in the demand curve). As a result, customers who derive utility from these "hot" businesses (the ones that engender excess demand beyond capacity) will no longer desire their products. In short, the fewer people who desire the product, the less attractive it becomes to others, thereby driving demand downward. But this is merely a restatement of the standard neoclassical relationship between price and demand: If a firm increases the price of a product, fewer people should be able to purchase it, thereby driving down demand. Becker adds a layer of self-conscious, reflexive rationality to this standard formulation and lodges the intersubjective nature of desire firmly within commodity interactions. The twist is that this centers the rectitude of the market at a deeper level—consumers and capital owners are *more rational* than we give them credit for, they feel the pull of economic truisms even more deeply than even economics as a discipline does.

As it should be clear, this example strictly resides in the realm of parable, or myth: Becker did not seek out data from the aforementioned Palo Alto seafood restaurants to inquire about their prices, production factors (labor costs, rent, raw materials), average customer wait time, or their proprietary market research data about what customers would pay, nor did he corroborate his hunch about the latter restaurant having "many empty seats most of the time" with data. Becker derived the mathematical postulates of what must be the case if his hunch were true. This, and other economic parables, should thus be read as symbol systems that function as internally consistent stories according to the discursive communities in which they are located. This is not work for public consumption but rather an academic article. What Becker in particular is skilled at is the relentless application of economics axioms to put on display within the domain of economics—he forces his discipline to reckon with the things that are supposedly foundational. So at first glance, Becker's argument strategy appears to be a direct challenge to the fundamental precepts of neoclassical economics but in actuality represents its fulfillment. Economic rationality can be observed beneath commodity interactions; an economy of enjoyment underwrites the activities of consumers, and some businesses are perceptive enough to discern the immaterial demand qualia and set their prices accordingly. The principle of presuming equilibrium—while appearing perplexed at an evident disequilibrium—is tremendously effective, for it allows an economist to discern the unseen market forces at work that the untrained eye cannot.

Becker also rhetorically accomplishes his goal by employing fairly standard persuasive appeals. Perhaps his conclusions are exceedingly simple, even simplistic, partaking in what McCloskey called the "3x5 card" problem in economics.[71] But in this case at least, his audience actually are academic economists who are trained to follow the enthymematic proof of his demand curve model. At the formal level, Becker employs fairly straightforward enthymematic deduction. The simplicity of his arguments, in which causes neatly match effects and where supply and demand work perfectly dialectically in harmony with one another, invites assent in his audience. Hauser writes that an enthymeme must begin with some common ground, combined with a linking premise between that common ground and the point the speaker wishes to make; this allows for a co-constitution of meaning in which the audience member is an active participant.[72] A good enthymeme lives up to its namesake—it occurs *in the thymus* of the audience member being persuaded, not in the head of the speaker. Becker's work also adheres to McCloskey's judgment that the dominant trope of economic writing is irony, for it revels in the neat reversals that its conclusions proffer. For instance, arguments that affirmative action causes racial discrimination, that increasing the minimum wage causes job loss, or that species protection laws kill animals are part of the repertoire of economic thinking. The economic enthymeme, inviting its audience to visualize the impending reversal, works in Becker's favor. "Language, in its very notion, involves a minimal distance towards its literal meaning—not in the sense of a some irreducible ambiguity or multiple dispersion of meanings, but in the more precise sense of 'he said X, but what if he *really meant* the opposite.'"[73] This mode of ironic deduction operationalizes the binary force of language. Hazlitt calls economics a "science of deductions," and Becker is simply asking that his audience of academic economists live up to their own professed principles.[74] In fact, this is Becker's great methodological innovation: the relentless application of economic theory to every conceivable context.

But the provocation Becker advances remains a controversial one, and the strategy he adopts employs a more sophisticated persuasive technique. Becker's challenge to academic economics actually asks something very simple of academic economists: to apply the previously agreed-to principles of markets (price functions, equilibrium) and individual market behavior (utility maximization, defined preferences) to new or overlooked contexts. In a sense, these parables and thought experiments that pepper economics textbooks and economists' blogs are merely asking readers to agree to something they have already tacitly endorsed. This concept is what persuasion theorist Robert Cialdini called "consistency," or "the drive to be (and look) consistent" in public, looped together with a parallel concept, "commitment," meaning when people "take a stand or position . . . [they] are more willing to agree to requests that are in keeping with the prior commitment."[75] Because appearing to have unwavering beliefs is considered socially beneficial, persuaders can induce agreement in their audiences by yoking their end goal (for instance, donating to an immigrants' rights legal fund) to an affirmative answer to the question "Isn't it shameful that asylum seekers are being denied legal counsel in deportation hearings?" Commitments involve publicly living out values, and refusing to donate after publicly committing to the moral rectitude of the cause induces the appearance of inconsistency.

In this case, Becker formalizes what appears on its face as irrational behavior by a restaurant, and swiftly re-figures it as ultra-rational. If an economist is presumed to adhere to the axiom that markets are naturally inclined to reach equilibrium, then Becker's discovery of an instance in which a stable equilibrium is located at a level other than one strictly based on supply and demand should invite the reader to concur. As mentioned, Becker frequently chastises economists who, in his view, invoke "ad hoc shifts in preferences" to explain economic outcomes.[76] Rather than appealing to context, time, or empirical events, Becker insists that only changes in the prices of commodities ever affect consumer behavior.[77] His appeal to his readers, to have consistent beliefs regarding the properties of markets, behooves them to make a commitment to this limit case. Like the sophist Protagoras, whose boast that he could "make the weaker argument the stronger," Becker made the consideration of limit cases central to his work; for instance, on numerous occasions, he proposed the introduction of markets in human organs.[78] Alongside fellow Chicago school thinker Richard Posner, Becker also proposed using economic theory as a tool for weighing the rationality of suicide.[79] Becker spreads economic theory, and the "economic approach to human behavior," over the world not by refashioning it to make it appear more palatable and realistic but instead by the exact opposite strategy: forcing economics as a discipline to adhere to its own professed concepts.

Conclusion: Becker's Rhetorical Challenges

The work of Gary Becker is tremendously influential in the field of economics, and by extension, contributed greatly to the drastic expansion of economic methods onto the social field. It is my contention that "the incentive" is his key discovery, for it provides neoclassical economics with an explanation of cause that is stably kept within its own stated boundaries. In this way, Becker builds on the concepts discussed in the previous chapter: Economics as a deductive science posits that market signals automatically motivate individuals to act according to their utility functions. Becker simply metastasizes the definition of markets and market behavior to presume that this occurs in all settings, not just commodity-based ones. And yet, as demonstrated, Becker posed a series of serious rhetorical and methodological challenges to his field, even as he heralded the rectitude of its foundational assumptions. Instead of deploying a discourse sensitive to context, Becker organized his discursive edifice around indifference thereto. This is, indeed, its greatest rhetorical strength: By laundering context through a market structure, it renders actors responsible for their choices, no matter the context or setting. If someone cannot afford the monetary, "human capital," or psychic cost of an outcome, this is an expression of their preference, a variation in their utility function, or simply a problem of past income. The incentive binds these components and becomes a generalized explanation for individuals' behaviors. Using incentives as the proper object of economic analysis, Becker explained the existence and, indeed, the rationality of why women earn less than men, why people commit suicide, why women have the number of children they do, why people remain addicted to cigarettes, and why some restaurant queues remain long. Once a given incentive functions as the retroactive explanation for an outcome, it can be then used as data to proactively contour future contexts: Becker challenged the stable equilibria of social welfare in the United States, sweatshop workers in Latin America, nearly all public utilities, and the human organ "market."

To conclude, I meditate on the tremendous rhetorical challenges Becker levels against both his own discipline, and that of rhetorical study. Becker's genius was to essentially force his discipline to adhere to its own professed principles about the power and properties of markets. Given the many discursive struggles Becker embarked upon, his rhetorical successes are undeniable: His concept of the incentive metastatically shifts what economics purports to study, and authorizes its insertion into culture and politics as a backward- and forward-facing vocabulary for explaining the enigma of cause. This is what makes economics such a difficult discipline to counter-argue—its proper order of signification is not "real" or in "reality," but in the Symbolic order. Its proper object, once Becker completes his work, is the *objet a*. Economics can symbolically attribute an economic cause—the incentive—into any given setting in an auto-eidetic manner: What remains true no matter what are the principles of prices, preferences, and utility maximization. In other words, the economic approach to human behavior functions as a description of context without context: Its greatest strength is not its flexibility, but its rigidity, and the forcible bending of social reality to adhere to market principles, not the other way round.

This poses a methodological, political, and ethical challenge to the discipline of rhetorical studies within the humanities. Since antiquity, rhetoric's foundational concerns and methodological uniqueness depend upon a proper appreciation of context both for the production and critique of rhetorical artifacts. One's successes as a speaker, Aristotle reminds us, depend upon the display of practical wisdom (*phronesis*) just as much as the knowledge of formal argument.[80] Nancy Streuver calls Renaissance rhetoric thoroughly "contextualist" and calls rhetorical decorum "the ideology of contextualism."[81] As Victoria Kahn thoroughly demonstrates, throughout the Middle Ages, and the Renaissance, rhetoric's concern with the trans-contextual power of language (specifically the generative power of trope) was equaled by its concern with decorum, and prudence, particularly from the Latin translations of Aristotle's *Rhetoric* and *Nicomachean Ethics*.[82] Patricia Spence locates within the philosophy of Adam Smith (classical economist and nascent rhetorical theorist) propriety as a controlling factor, which arouses a "social self" that sympathetically connects an individual to an other.[83] Mark Longaker links Smith's lectures on rhetoric to his economic theory, and cuts against the supposed bifurcation between the two: "Smith's lectures on rhetoric and belles lettres theorized and taught a mode of practical judgment (phronesis) that he later applied to commutative justice and commercial transactions."[84] Even when contemporary rhetorical theory foregrounds openness to an encounter with an Other—whether that Other is a concrete body or alterity-as-such, the open palm as opposed to the pointing finger is an ethical relation that rhetorical theory aims to establish.

Rhetorical criticism also labors with the millstone of context upon it—the "fitting response" of Bitzer's rhetorical situation involves retroactively isolating the key rhetorical feature that made a speech adequate to the exigent demands upon the speaker.[85] Hauser summarizes Bitzer's approach as both "functional" and "situational," which despite significant advances in the field, Lundberg contends that much critical rhetoric remains in thrall to its basic presuppositions.[86] While contemporary rhetorical criticism is not naïve about the strictly instrumentalist vision of rhetoric, Lundberg, following Gaonkar, argues that an overreliance on "context" in rhetorical studies entails losing the specific value of a rhetorical approach in the first place; any discourse so conditioned by its historical, social, national, context renders the context itself the object of study.[87] The notion of a "fitting response" to a "rhetorical situation" is ultimately tautological, since from the perspective of the present, the response could not have been otherwise—any one speech that is imagined as a "fitting response" becomes a vanishing mediator, or a Lacanian *objet a* for rhetorical study itself. Rhetorical criticism that looks for the specific rhetorical choices that produced an effect ultimately means to find what it seeks, and bind contingency into necessity: A chaotic past is retroactively narrated as the necessary expression of prior *kairotic* rhetorical choices. This is, paradoxically, the mirror image of what Becker's incentive-based rhetoric accomplishes: the economic approach to human behavior flagrantly violates the presumption that context ought to have a controlling interest in how to assess a situation. Becker's work promises a transcontextual, transhistorical mode of analysis that, ironically, appears to have produced outsized rhetorical, political, cultural, and economic effects.

A strictly contextualist vision of the rhetorical situation Becker found himself in may allow for alternative interpretations of how his work found purchase. While Becker's work undoubtedly contributed to the expansion of the domain of economics rhetorically, this expansion happened alongside movements in the economy worldwide—the breakdown of the Bretton Woods Agreement, the turn toward financialization as a response to downturns in profitability, the use of central bank lending rates to combat inflation and protect bondholders over workers, and an intense focus on destroying organized labor within the United States. Becker's conjuncture at the University of Chicago is inextricable from fierce political actions by those in power: the Trilateral Commission, the Central Intelligence Agency's attempts to disrupt leftist movements and left-leaning governments worldwide, the FBI's COINTELPRO actions, as well as debates within the labor movement about how best to respond to the threat of globalization all constrained available rhetorical activities. The adoption of economic methods in emerging fields like law and economics, rational choice theory, public choice theory, and game theory all have a material (both political and economic substrate). Among others, Amadae and Mirowski detail the relationships between the national security community and the discipline of economics that fostered the turn to rational choice and game theoretic methods in foreign and domestic policy.[88] In sum, Becker was unquestionably rhetorically situated within a specific conjunctural moment, and was simultaneously engaged in an act of strategic rhetorical action aimed at securing advantage for his approach both within his discipline and far beyond it. Yet the incentive-based *indifference* to context is precisely what is the proximate cause of his rhetorical "effectiveness."

As currently formulated, my assessment may appear contradictory: Becker's trans-contextual method exerted tremendous instrumental effects. The first violates the spirit of rhetorical theory and criticism, the second violates the aforementioned critique of contextualism. In other words, his rigidity, not his attunement to context, guaranteed his success. Therefore, I propose that the metaphor of the unconscious better describes the rhetorical effectivity of Becker's work and posit that one proper object of rhetorical inquiry ought to be the Lacanian *objet a*. The concept allows rhetorical inquiry to negotiate how it is that speakers, writers, and those in power symbolically negotiate their own relationship to the social totality as they interpret it. One need not weigh Becker's rhetorical choices against a contextual reality, or examine the "truth-value" of his statements—as mentioned, Becker professed that his work was more about opening discursive space for the discipline of economics than faithfully representing a world outside. And as established above, Becker's rhetorical choices dwell in the realm of fantasy: they produce a vision of the whole absent contradiction, and without fail, obey the iron laws of economics. What Becker's work achieved was to provide a governing logic for the discipline of economics itself—his work revealed what was latent—unconscious—in the field all along. It is not instrumentality, but an articulation, that Becker offered to economics. This is not context, propriety, or a "fitting response" in the traditionally understood manner. It is, rather, the promise of an explanation of cause. As Lacan's famous dictum, "the unconscious is structured like a language," goes, Becker's rhetorical invention was to provide the necessary coordinates for economics to metastasize over the social field, to give it a vocabulary for expressing the rationality of markets and the rationality of market actors despite being faced with contradictory information. To locate the hidden incentive is to retroactively locate the specific causal mechanisms to which market actors respond; beyond even the money commodity, economics can instead measure the movements of enjoyment that affect the decisions of individuals. By foregrounding the non-commodity incentive behind the commodity interaction, Becker produces a universe in which there is no "energy" lost, all enjoyment is constantly reincorporated into a utility function; there is no unspoken or unenjoyed remainder.

A Lacanian approach allows the critic to locate how a specific speaker productively (mis)perceived their given context in order to render a judgment about their context. In the terms of American rhetorician Kenneth Burke, in claiming to produce a "chart" of reality, he in effect produced both a "dream" and a "prayer" thereabout.[89] The concept of the unconscious, as a mechanism for understanding how a speaker symbolically interprets their own given conjuncture allows us to see how in this case, Becker instantiated a mode of inquiry that transports itself beyond context despite being deeply bound within. What is "instrumental" about Becker's language is what it symbolically unlocked for the discipline of economics, and how it provided an alibi for the rectitude of its animating postulates. The key feature of analysis, then, is the *objet a*, what a Lacanian analyst must discern in the analysand's speech, as a tic, or signifier back to which the speaker consistently loops. The object, as Lacan puts it, sets desire into motion through an enigmatic cause, and this is precisely what Becker purports to offer to his field.[90] As Ernesto Laclau describes, the *objet a* is a "retrospective illusion deprived, as a result, of access to a direct representation. So it is both an impossible and a necessary object. Its representation is thus only possible if a partial object, without ceasing to be partial, is invested with the role of representing that impossible totality."[91] This summarizes the incentive: an alibi constructed around the edifice of the economic subject, the hidden force that joins cause and effect and renders the world knowable, and stable, under the auspices of neoclassical economics. The incentive-based approach metastasizes through both the discipline of economics as well as the world outside precisely through this mechanism of ascribing economic causality to all actions. It simultaneously satisfies the desire to know, offers a set of techniques for intervening into contexts in the future, and, as an unseen, immaterial force, keeps desire alive to ever elude the grasp of its seeker. As Becker wrote in his final column for *BusinessWeek*, he feared running out of topics, but "events continue to serve up new economic issues, or old issues in new clothing, that push and pull incentives in different directions."[92] The universal applicability of a method means that there will always be new worlds to discursively conquer, more incentives to discern, more equilibria to explain. In the next chapter, I evaluate how the introduction of incentive rhetoric in matters of political importance is used to justify women's continued oppression and unequal treatment, both privately and in the workforce.

Chapter 4

"What Does Woman Want?"

Equal Pay and "Women's Incentives"

When Senator Barbara Mikulski announced her retirement from the US Senate in 2015, it is no exaggeration to say that the possibility for women's equal pay legislation also left the legislative body for the foreseeable future. The senator from Maryland left the Senate having introduced some version of the Paycheck Fairness Act in nearly every legislative session since 1997. The Act is a tame piece of legislation; it is designed to constrict the legal defenses employers have to pay women at a discriminatory rate around a "bona fide factor," and provided for the collection of information for salary pay databases to improve individual women's abilities to bargain for higher wages. Despite how incremental and noninterventionist the text of the bill was, opponents mobilized arguments about its danger for the free enterprise system itself and invoked fears of government wage-setting. The bill was first ratified by the US House in 2009 but failed to pass with a filibuster-proof majority in the Senate, despite having fifty-three "aye" votes, and as of 2021, had not passed the Senate. Yet around the time of the Act's original passage in the House, Congress had ratified the Lilly Ledbetter Fair Pay Restoration Act; indeed, it was the first bill President Barack Obama signed in January of 2009. The Lilly Ledbetter Act amended the Civil Rights Act of 1964, and guaranteed a worker's right to sue for damages after receiving discriminatory paychecks, effectively reversing a 2007 Supreme Court decision that curtailed this right. These two bills were the only significant legislation dealing directly with women's equal pay during the Obama administration and had divergent legislative fates.

The passage of the Lilly Ledbetter Act and failure of the Paycheck Fairness Act are not strictly reducible to the partisan politics of the era. It is not persuasion per se that is at issue but enjoyment. The fights over these bills reveal an epistemological conundrum that is produced from within the Symbolic order and the sexed nature of the capitalist mode of production itself. That is, the easy partisan answer, that the Democratic Party could not overcome a threat of a filibuster by the Republican Party, belies a more fundamental question: what is it that politicized the issue of "equal pay for equal work" to make the Paycheck Fairness Act nearly impossible to pass? The epistemic resources of incentive-based rhetoric, I contend, were mobilized in order to make any potential reform on the basis of sex impossible. The issue of equal pay legislation offers a clear insight into how the logic of the incentive metastasizes into the public domain and directly attributes economic causality onto the choices of individuals. Incentive-based rhetoric did not cause the Paycheck Fairness Act to fail, but it promoted a fertile discursive ground for those who required a rhetorical alibi to justify the continued underpayment and systematic oppression of women. While the wage system, and the capitalist mode of production more broadly, involves a complex assemblage of bodies, ideologies, signifiers, laws, and institutions, a politically engaged psychoanalytic reading practice allows us to see how opponents of equal pay for women manufactured a symbolic irresolvability out of a political controversy. Given Freud's political pessimism (an understandable position to take after one is exiled from one's home country by the Nazis), and Lacan's ostensible detachment from political struggles in his own era, it is fair to conclude that psychoanalysis as a reading practice does not have a political program on its own. Yet McGowan concludes that is its greatest strength as a mode of critique of our existing society: "Psychoanalytic theory never preaches, and it cannot help us to construct a better society. But it can help us to subtract the illusion of the good from our own society."[1] The problem of equal treatment for men and women in the capitalist mode of production did not emerge from speech itself, and it certainly cannot be resolved by speech; however, through this case study, we may be able to see how the problem of equal pay becomes irresolvable within speech.

Working through the legislative missed encounter and the discourse surrounding these two bills serves two purposes. First, their divergent legislative fates offer a useful comparison point. As I argue, the Lilly Ledbetter Act, while named for a woman, concerned a desexed liberal juridical subject, and the Paycheck Fairness Act revealed anxieties concerning the hidden abode of women's work within the capitalist mode of production. Second, these bills provide an auspicious test case for the discourse of incentives and reveal the extent to which incentive rhetoric has metastasized into the field of the political, and what the consequences are upon its arrival. Overall, those opposed to the bills invoked "women's incentives" as the source of the gender pay gap, and the reason why any public policy aimed at reducing this gap is counterintuitive. According to this view, women have natural, or trained, preferences to care for children and the elderly, and thus they make choices to leave the workforce or to take lower-paying jobs that emphasize care work. The Federal Reserve Bank of St. Louis calculated women's unpaid domestic work within the United States at nearly 1.2 trillion dollars per year, if domestic labor were paid at the federal minimum wage of $7.25 an hour.[2] Because women are socialized to perform domestic labor, from within the incentive-based position, they have greater "human capital" investments in these activities. For these reasons, "equal pay" would be unequal for men and women, but in the opposite direction, for women would gain recompense from both their "women's incentives" as well as their wages. The surplus value that women create through domestic labor exemplifies Marx's concept of "productive consumption," for they both engage in valuable social reproduction and earn back their specifically "female" enjoyment from their human capital investments. The circumstances that lead to systematic gender inequality emerge as either gender-neutral or the result of women's preexisting incentives and preferences. Incentive logics represent a domesticated and digestible way to infer people's choices, beliefs, and behaviors—a rationality without interiority.

I make three key Lacanian diagnoses of opposition to these bills, concerning verbal negation, the Real, and the twin statuses of *jouissance*. I first employ Freud's concept of negation as a way to explain how opponents of the Paycheck Fairness Act resisted the implementation of a "bona fide factor" (such as training, education, or experience) as a justification for salary discrepancies between men and women. Previously, courts ruled that the language of "any factor other than sex" in the Equal Pay Act of 1938 could be interpreted literally, thus giving businesses virtually any alibi for underpaying women. Because the Paycheck Fairness Act would force the signifier of "sex" into the libidinal and discursive economy of employment law, those opposed to the bill demanded that "any factor" remain the law of the land, that is, a woman can be underpaid for any reason, as long as her not-sex is used as the reason. Second, I employ the Lacanian concept of the Real, or the anamorphic stain upon "reality" that prevents a full picture of reality appearing as such. The gender pay gap is Real in the

Lacanian sense, for it allows no neutral ground upon which to adjudicate claims of underpayment—women are both systematically underpaid and paid exactly at their marginal contribution to society. This epistemological deadlock can best be explained by the two competing orders of knowledge Lacan identifies in his late seminars: that of masculine and feminine *jouissance*. Much like the fantasy of "woman" itself, "women's incentives" are a fantasy construction of masculine *jouissance* that domesticates and stabilizes women's unrepresentable desires in a calculable form. Gherovici writes, "Masculine and feminine positions are predicated on contradictory systems; they follow dissymmetrical logics that are two ways of exemplifying how language fails to signify sex."[3] This structural dissimilarity, based on the unrepresentability of sexual difference, functions as an allegory for the political subject of the capitalist mode of production. Within capitalism, the implied subject is formally "un-sexed"—as long as that figure does not need to raise children or perform household labor. This debate reveals that the neutral subject of capital covers over the fact of sexual difference and how it disproportionately harms women.[4] Women cannot "have it all" as long as a wage system that favors men remains intact.

Ultimately, this issue concerns the overlap of two gaps. First, the gender pay gap, calculated by the National Women's Law Center as an 18 percent difference between women's and men's earnings (a figure that is exacerbated for Black and Brown women).[5] The second gap is that of rhetoric itself. As Gérard Genette describes, a rhetorical figure names a gap: "[B]etween the letter and the meaning . . . there is a gap, a space, and like all space, it possesses a form. This form is called a *figure*, and there will be as many figures as one can find forms in the space that is created on each occasion between the line of the signifier . . . and that of the signified."[6] The gender pay gap is Real, for it appears as an anamorphic stain on reality itself and is structurally impossible within language to adequately represent. Yet despite its impossible status, those invested in maintaining it cover over this gap with language. Those who opposed these tame reform bills employed displacements, negations, and crucially, the trope of "women's incentives" in order to manage this 18 percent gap, and explain it away.

The Lilly Ledbetter Fair Pay Restoration Act of 2009

The Lilly Ledbetter Act updated the Civil Rights Act of 1964, and in so doing, reversed a 2007 Supreme Court ruling against the namesake of the law, Ledbetter, who had successfully sued for back pay and damages from her employment at a Goodyear tire plant in Alabama. Although Ledbetter was underpaid relative to her male peers for years, the Supreme Court ruled that "employees cannot challenge ongoing pay discrimination if the employer's original discriminatory pay decision occurred more than 180 days earlier, even when the employee continues to receive paychecks that have been discriminatorily reduced."[7] The Supreme Court's ruling meant that a worker who believes she is discriminatorily compensated has only 180 days from her first unfair paycheck to challenge it.[8] This narrow interpretation of the Civil Rights Act would have effectively insulated corporations from litigation regarding any discriminatory pay of any kind, provided a worker does not challenge their paycheck within six months—upon one's 181st day of employment, the Court ruled that one forfeits their right to challenge their compensation. The law instead: "Allows liability to accrue, and allows an aggrieved person to obtain relief, including recovery of back pay, for up to two years preceding the filing of the charge, where the unlawful employment practices that have occurred during the charge filing period are similar or related to practices that occurred outside the time for filing a charge."[9] This type of wage discrimination is prevalent in many industries: Wal-Mart, Merrill Lynch, and other major American corporations have had class-action lawsuits brought against them for their discriminatory wage practices, with varying results for plaintiffs.[10]

In this section, I briefly interpret the arguments made for and against the Lilly Ledbetter Act in Congressional testimony, from 2007 to 2009, to provide a comparison point between this and the Paycheck Fairness Act.[11] The bill failed initially in 2007, under a Republican-controlled congress, but after its reintroduction in 2009 under a majority-Democratic congress, it passed with newly inaugurated President Barack Obama's support.[12] Several themes emerge from testimony: proponents of the bill employed the language of fairness and justice, and linked the bill directly to its predecessor, the Civil Rights Act of 1964. However, proponents also employed the rhetoric of incentives, particularly those generated by the legal system itself, to argue for the bill's passage. Opponents, unsurprisingly, also relied upon incentive rhetoric, but that of greedy trial lawyers and self-interested litigants so as to profit from the law. Yet the bill's passage hinged upon what is left unstated by its opponents: that a fundamental civil right of a liberal juridical subject would be imperiled by the precedent set by the Supreme Court, regardless of their sex.

In his five-minute opening statement in favor of the Fair Pay Restoration Act, Senator Edward Kennedy uses the term "civil rights" five times, explicitly linking the issue of fair pay to American civil rights:

"Equal pay for equal work is a fundamental civil right in our society."[13] He mentions the terms "fair" or "fairness" seven times, both in reference to the proposed law being fair to workers and employers and also the social bond implied in a contract for work.[14] Senator Patty Murray, in her remarks, mentions the notions of "justice" and "injustice" thrice, and needing to remedy paycheck "unfairness" twice.[15] Senator Mikulski gestured in two directions. First, she links the health of the nation's economy to the power of women to earn equal pay: "If you want to get the economy going, let us start paying women what they are worth."[16] Second, Mikulski emphasizes that women struggle with genuine discrimination at work and quotes Justice Ruth Bader Ginsburg: "The court does not comprehend or is indifferent to the insidious way in which women can be victims of pay discrimination."[17] This rhetorical strategy—paying heed to the realities of gender-based workplace discrimination—is embodied by the testimony of Lilly Ledbetter herself, who wove together her discriminatory treatment at work with the unfair ruling delivered by the Supreme Court. Ledbetter called her discriminatory paychecks an "insult to [her] dignity," and despite the Court ruling that what she received was not illegal discrimination, "It doesn't feel like any less like discrimination because it started a long time ago. Quite the opposite, in fact. But according to the court, if you don't figure things out right away, the company can treat you like a second-class citizen for the rest of your career, and that is not right."[18] At the end of her testimony, Ledbetter renounces her own self-interest, and because the Supreme Court rescinded her damages, offers that the beneficiaries of the bill will be other women: "Goodyear may never have to pay me what it cheated me out of, but if this bill passes, I will have an even richer reward because I will know that our daughters, our grand-daughters, and all workers will get a better deal. That's what makes this fight worth fighting and it's what makes this fight one we have to win."[19] The rhetorical weight of fairness, justice, and civil rights by Ledbetter and elected officials was supplemented by the invocation of "incentives" by Margot Dorfman, CEO of the US Women's Chamber of Commerce.

Dorfman indicates that because the Supreme Court decided to only allow 180 days for women to make a claim about a discriminatory paycheck, workers must act hastily with their civil rights claims: "The 180-day time limit also creates incentives for business practices that will be detrimental to both business owners and workers. Rather than take the time necessary to evaluate their situation and confirm they have been subject to discrimination before filing a claim, the new deadline puts pressure on employees to file complaints as quickly as possible."[20] By contrast, Dorfman indicates that businesses now have an incentive to head off or stall claims: "And while the previous system promoted voluntary employer compliance, this new interpretation provides an entirely different incentive . . . Under this decision, employers instead have a reason to be less vigilant about pay discrimination, knowing that after 180 days, they will be insulated from future challenges."[21] To be clear, Dorfman's comments are not exclusively limited to the "incentive-based" approach, for she also links the Act to the tradition of American civil rights and references the particular struggles with poverty that women experience; however, her comments are illustrative of the metastatic nature of the incentive-based approach. She argues that by closing off avenues for redress after six months, the Supreme Court inadvertently distorts the playing field against businesses that voluntarily comply with the law. Because women-owned businesses "frequently provide stronger employee benefits than their male counterparts," the Court's interpretation doubly discriminates against women—both female workers in male-dominated industries and female business owners.[22] Dorfman adequately characterizes the symbolic logic of the incentive developed in chapter 2: market structures incentivize rational economic action, so businesses have a reasonable basis for exploiting the loophole that the Supreme Court's ruling created. Yet she posits a gendered exception to the law of markets: women-owned businesses would not exploit this rule and would refuse to illegally underpay female employees.

Those opposed to the Lilly Ledbetter Act deploy several arguments against the bill based largely on a slippery slope they impute into the bill's language and the incentives that workers have to delay their discrimination lawsuits for a large payoff. The bill as written only allows for back pay for up to two years and damages of up to $300,000, but opponents of the bill rely solely on the threat of large payoffs and infinite liability for the businesses involved. But it is no matter: since the bill constitutes a regulation of *jouissance*, it must be categorically opposed. Senator Johnny Isakson explicitly condemns the bill for going "overboard in favor of trial lawyers" and that "the bill is ripe for abuse and amounts to nothing more than a gift to trial lawyers eager for a frivolous lawsuit."[23] (Opponents of this bill, and later, the Paycheck Fairness Act, consistently refer to the threat of greedy trial lawyers as the primary beneficiaries of bills aimed at ameliorating discriminatory pay. In 2019, Representatives Liz Cheney of Wyoming, and Vicky Hartzler of Missouri used nearly identical language to oppose the Paycheck Fairness Act, calling it the "Pay the Trial Lawyers

Act," and Representative Kim Foxx of North Carolina called it a "bill that will help trial lawyers, plain and simple"[24]).

Eric Dreiband, former general counsel for the Equal Employment Opportunity Commission, and opponent of the bill, asserts, "By eviscerating the charge-filing period, the Fair Pay Restoration Act would require the EEOC to conduct investigations into events that happened decades before anyone filed a charge despite the absence of records. Witnesses' memories will be faded. Some witnesses will be missing. Others, as in the *Ledbetter* case, may be dead."[25] The US Chamber of Commerce's statement similarly argued, "An employer's ability to tell its story dissipates sharply as time passes. Memories fade; managers quit, retire, or die, business units are reorganized, disassembled or sold; tasks are centralized, dispersed, or abandoned altogether."[26] In this testimony, the living body of the worker is opposed to the incorporeal essence of the corporation, but it is the corporation in this instance that is disadvantaged because of the finite existence of its component parts. A worker's discriminatory treatment is held corporeally (and this becomes her advantage) whereas a business is presumptively infinitely liable and unable to defend itself as a result. Dreiband continues: "The Fair Pay Restoration Act would also require anyone accused of discrimination to make a dreadful choice—preserve records in perpetuity or lose the ability to mount a defense to a charge that challenges decades-old employment decisions. The cost of perpetual recordkeeping would be enormous and, in the cause of public employers, would add to the taxpayers' burden."[27] The deliberate obfuscation of the bill's provisions cannot simply be reduced to *mauvais foi* by those testifying; there must be some psychoanalytically revealing rationale behind this argumentation strategy. The essence of law, as Lacan reminds us, is to "divide up, distribute, or reattribute everything that counts as *jouissance*," so one can detect in testimony the properly ethical opposition to this (or any) regulation.[28] To be held responsible at all for mistreating a worker is to subject the corporation to infinite liability, and any burden whatsoever (to keep payroll records, to render back pay) is framed as unjust.

However, what is missing from opposition to the Lilly Ledbetter Act is, surprisingly, the status of women (and discrimination against them) as such. During a Senate floor debate in 2008, Senator Isakson claims that his opposition to the bill is the open-ended time for a worker to file a discrimination claim (calling the statute of limitations "one of the bedrock principles of all Judeo-Christian jurisprudence") and that opponents of the bill are placed in the "false light of being unsympathetic to victims

of pay discrimination."[29] That is, opposition to the bill is framed proce-
durally, which allows for the idea that women may indeed be victims of
discrimination at work but that this specific bill is the improper method
to rectify it.[30] Whether opponents of the bill are forthright about their
opposition to discrimination or not is tangential, for I choose to read this
opposition to the letter, momentarily, and return to the precedent that
the Supreme Court set with its 2007 ruling. Lacan reminds us that verbal
resistances are key to analytic understanding, and one should read the
opposing testimony both in what it denies, as well as what it does not say.
By eliminating Ledbetter's ability to bring a challenge to a discriminatory
paycheck after the first 180-day period (with few exceptions), the ruling
imperiled the possibility for any worker to ever challenge their compensation: hesitating to bring a federal Civil Rights Act challenge would have
constituted tacit acceptance of their discriminatory pay rate.

Such a ruling poses a problem for more than Ledbetter herself,
or even all women—the ruling poses a problem for the liberal juridical
subject writ large, to be barred from having a day in court on the merits
of one's case. Therefore, the Ledbetter Act ceased to be a "women's issue,"
and became an issue concerning the (supposedly) desexed liberal juridical subject; arguments opposing the bill had to rest upon this stasis and
not the stasis of sex. Isakson's comments defending the ruling from the
perspective of the law's statute of limitations exemplify this strategy: since
even opponents of the bill did not deny the specific discrimination that
Ledbetter and other women experienced, they had to concede the reality
of sexist discrimination and resort to this narrow procedural argument.
By arguing at the level of procedure, opponents unconsciously admitted
that the stakes of the bill both could not be argued on the merits of
the Ledbetter case (and the women similarly affected) and instead must
concern the status of the desexed juridical subject's right to claim redress.
Yet if the legislature could grant an employer immunity from any Title
VII accusations of pay discrimination after 180 days, workers would be
deprived of that basic constitutional right beyond even that of the existing
Civil Rights Act, and potentially could have set up another constitutional
challenge.

In the end, the narrow proceduralist argument lost out, Congress
passed the Lilly Ledbetter Fair Pay Act, and the newly inaugurated president, Barack Obama, signed his first bill into law on January 29, 2009.
In his remarks, Obama synthesized the strands of argument generated by
its advocates, arguing for equal pay as good business sense, an issue of

fairness, as well as a moral test for the United States: "Ultimately, equal pay isn't just an economic issue for millions of Americans and their families, it's a question of who we are—and whether we're truly living up to our fundamental ideals."[31] On the other hand, we may read the verbal resistances to the bill symptomatically—that those opposed to the Lilly Ledbetter Act were cornered into making a narrow proceduralist argument against the bill's legitimacy, in effect, conceding the determining force that gender may have in the workplace, to the bill's supporters. The bill was de-sexed not by its supporters to gain legitimacy, but by its opponents, precisely because it concerned the liberal juridical subject writ large and only upon that basis could it be contended. Secondarily, opponents unsurprisingly deferred to market logics and the specter of self-interested trial lawyers as the primary beneficiaries of the bill, in effect confirming the determining power that market structures have upon individuals: If a law opens the possibility for money to be made, rational actors (both aggrieved workers and greedy lawyers) will automatically be incentivized thereby, and act. The bill on its own is of minor analytic value, but its major value is that it offers a contemporaneous counterpoint to testimony surrounding the Paycheck Fairness Act, and the differences that made a difference in its failure to pass in similar political circumstances.

Paycheck Fairness Act

I now turn to testimony for and against the Paycheck Fairness Act (hereafter referred to as PFA, or "the Act"). For this section, I reviewed every mention of the Act in the United States Congress from 1997 to 2019, including congressional reports, committee hearing testimony, as well as floor debates and speeches. I have also included relevant opinion pieces published in major news sources during this period to apprise the stakes that were constructed by the amassed rhetorical forces. Overall, opposition to PFA was organized around the habituated repetition of "women's incentives": the nonmonetary rewards that fill in the gap between what women and men make, such as the joy of caring for the elderly, or the desire to become pregnant. Circumstances that lead to systematic gender inequality emerge as either gender-neutral, or the result of women's pre-existing preferences. Gender inequality is expressly unfixable with public policy because women voluntarily choose options other than high-earning jobs, including raising children, doing domestic work, and doing "care work" with children or the elderly. These low-paying jobs typically gendered "feminine" carry with them their own rewards that resonate with the "essentially" feminine qualities of women. Female-gendered jobs often hover around the legal minimum because they involve less training or have more flexible hours. However, careful attention to this argument reveals that the logic of "incentives" works retroactively to justify their choices stemming from their innate preferences for care work. Women are both incentivized by child-rearing (thereby accounting for cultural and biological influences), and their time out of the workforce accounts for their lower wages, thus providing an elegant justification for inequality. That is, women's preferences are retroactively posited as the cause of their low wages rather than an effect of constrained choices. Claiming that women follow their preferences retroactively symbolizes this as a straightforward supply-and-demand problem.

This bill provides a clear expression of how the metastatic rhetoric of incentives guarantees a rearguard justification of the status quo; opponents of the bill give no possible alternative explanation for the systematic underpayment of women, nor do they offer any contravening ameliorative force that would solve said underpayment outside of market forces. The rhetorical strategies employed by public figures opposed to equal pay laws largely mirror the positions of economists who employ the incentive-based approach. Gary Becker, previously discussed, argued that women are incentivized by child-rearing instead of high earnings, and therefore they do not invest in "education and training that improve earnings and job skills."[32] William K. Black writes that according to Becker, "women and men are genetically predisposed to *desire* to work, respectively, in the household and paid labor sectors."[33] Becker similarly argued that two-sex households that split domestic labor equally between men and women are inefficiently allocating their resources, since men tend to have greater human capital investments in wage-earning, whereas women have higher human capital investments in domestic labor, therefore "fully sharing household tasks would lead to an inefficient allocation of resources."[34] Using Becker's argument from efficiency, it is always too late to alter the ratios of human capital toward a more egalitarian society, since these investments occur prior to the conscious choice of the child.

Levitt and Dubner, authors of the Freakonomics book series and self-professed inheritors of Becker's "economic approach to human behavior" legacy, adhere to Becker's conclusions about what women truly desire: "Rather than interpreting women's lower wages as a failure, perhaps it should be seen as a sign that a higher wage simply isn't as meaningful an incentive for women as it is for men. Could it be that men have a weakness for money just as women have a weakness for children?"[35] List and Gneezy make a similar argument, positing that "men and women have different preferences for competitiveness, and at least part of the wage gaps we see are a result of men and women responding differently to incentives."[36] During an address in which she admitted the existence of the gendered wage gap, Claudia Goldin, onetime president of the American Economic Association, holds that the wage gap is a numerical problem: "The gender gap in pay would be considerably reduced and might even vanish if firms did not have an incentive to disproportionately reward individuals who worked long hours and who worked particular hours."[37] Occupations like lawyers, doctors, and pharmacists are associated with high wages because their practitioners are rewarded for long hours, or recompensed for unusual hours. Employees who pick up children from school, care for young ones, and perform domestic labor in the evenings will inevitably earn less—hence, a gender gap in pay. From this perspective, any robust debate about fairness in compensation is disfigured in advance, since opponents defer to "women's incentives," their "human capital" investments, and their individual rational action to explain why women take home smaller paychecks than men. The rhetoric of incentives functioned as a positivization of the gap between what women and men make; for the bill's opponents, women are already incentivized by nonmonetary rewards. Thus, to pay women equally for equal work is to function as a disproportionate double reward: any action a woman takes, be it caregiving or leaving the workforce, is retroactively narrated as an expression of her underlying incentives, and she is paid at exactly the rate she deserves.

I interpret opposition to the bill using three interlocking psychoanalytic concepts: the Real, verbal negation, and women's *jouissance*. First, testimony surrounding PFA demonstrates that there is no "neutral ground" upon which one could determine the existence of unequal pay, the source thereof, or any possible remedies. Thus the gender pay gap is Real because of its anamorphic status: on one hand, no one seriously disputes the existence of a demonstrable difference in pay between women and men. Yet those who oppose equal pay legislation claim that the gap has perfectly good reasons for existing—which implies there is no "gap" whatsoever, only a coherent social reality that abides different rewards for different genders. Second, in closing the "factor other than sex" loophole, opponents employ the concept of verbal negation. Because the bill would have forced employers to name a "bona fide factor" (such as training, experience, or education) to justify pay disparities between men and women, I argue that "sex" operates as the forbidden keyword in this discursive economy: literally any feature can be named to justify pay inequality, as long as the signifier "woman" is disavowed. Thus, the fact of sexual difference is verbally negated: the positive feature (a bona fide factor) replaces this open set (her not-sex), which presented a bridge too far for those testifying against it. Finally, those opposed to the bill posit that a woman has calculable, but unwaged *jouissance* (or enjoyment); a woman's love of children and domestic labor are nonmonetary rewards that must not be doubly registered with equivalent wages to men. To do so would constitute a disproportionate double reward for women, who would enjoy both their waged and unwaged (or underpaid) labor. Here, I contrast Lacan's concepts of masculine and feminine *jouissance* to explore how opponents of equal pay legislation attempt to answer the question, "What does woman want?" with an affirmative figuration, a feminine essence that justifies their unequal treatment.

The Act was designed to supplement the existing Fair Labor Standards Act of 1938 (otherwise known as the Equal Pay Act). It was ratified in the US House in 2009 but failed to pass with a filibuster-proof majority in the US Senate. Senator Mikulski introduced the bill in April 2014, but it once again failed in September of the same year for the same reason.[38] As of 2021, it has been introduced but has not passed the Senate. The bill has three major provisions.[39] First, it tightens up the language in the Fair Labor Standards Act of 1938: whereas the current law allows for differences in pay based on seniority, merit, quantity and quality of goods produced, and "a differential based on any other factor other than sex," the bill specifies "a bona fide factor other than sex, such as education, training, or experience" as the heretofore unnamed "any factor other than sex."[40] As Mikulski argued on the Senate floor in 2010, "The law would clarify that gender difference alone is not adequate pay differential must be based on legitimate, job-related requirements," and that it "would create incentives for good behavior by providing technical assistance and employer recognition awards."[41] Next, it prohibits "retaliation for inquiring about, discussing, or disclosing the wages of the employee or another employee in response to a complaint or charge, or in furtherance of a sex discrimination investigation, proceeding, hearing, or action, or an investigation conducted by the employer."[42] Finally, the bill would compel the federal government to gather data on gender pay gaps and provide such information to aid in enforcing already existing discrimination statutes.[43]

These three provisions—a demand that private businesses give an account of their pay disparities in writing, some enhanced protection for workers who bring discrimination claims, and the collection of information for salary databases—are tame, painfully so, and adhere largely to the modern Democratic Party's ethos of contouring laws around the will of corporations and nibbling at their edges. The bill does not mandate equal pay, make it easier for workers to organize their workplaces, nor provide for paid childcare, paid maternity leave, a higher minimum wage, or a host of other provisions that would collectively increase women's wealth and earnings. And yet, the bill provoked vociferous opposition: opponents predicted the collapse of the American free enterprise system and the introduction of government-mandated wage setting. The simple political answer, that the Democratic Party could not overcome a filibuster threat, is an unsatisfying one, for it merely begs the question of why equal pay legislation is a nakedly partisan issue in the first place. Albeit unconsciously, it is the question of sex as such, and the relationship of sex to the capitalist mode of production, that is at issue in the PFA debate. The virulence of opposition to the Act betrays an unconscious truth, that the subject of the capitalist mode of production is indeed sexed, and that to account for an alternative way of being is impossible within the framework of wage labor and unwaged social reproduction.

Closing the "Factor other than Sex" Loophole via Verbal Negation

I begin with the provision of PFA, which specifies that only "a bona fide factor other than sex, such as education, training or experience" can justify a pay gap between a man and a woman for equivalent work. The original Equal Pay Act allowed employers to justify gender pay disparities with four affirmative defenses: seniority, merit, quantity/quality of produced goods, and "any factor other than sex," the latter of which functioned as a catch-all term to hide any gendered underpayment. According to Congressional testimony, courts have used this "any factor" to include virtually anything that would justify a difference in compensation, including height and weight requirements, and the higher prior salaries of men (since salary-matching to attract an employee is considered a gender-neutral business tactic).[44]

Marcia Greenberger further points out that "at least two circuits have accepted the argument that 'any' factor other than sex should be interpreted literally and that employers need not show that those factors are in any way related to a legitimate business purpose."[45] The extreme textualism on display by appeals courts render "any factor" a password for literally anything to be invoked to justify pay discrimination; thus "sex" becomes the keyword that must be disavowed within this discursive economy. It is the one factor that must not be named.

In a 1925 paper, Freud describes a patient who says during analysis, "You ask who this person in the dream can be. It's *not* my mother."[46] When faced with uncomfortable truths, Freud finds that "[n]egation is a way of taking cognizance of what is repressed; indeed, it is already a lifting of the repression, though not, of course, an acceptance of what is repressed . . . The outcome of this is a kind of intellectual acceptance of the repressed, while at the same time what is essential to the repression persists."[47] Negation is a verbal denial of a truth that is nevertheless unconsciously admitted. This works as a cognizing strategy for people in analysis, as Fink writes, "As long as it is denied, it *can* be mentioned . . . for they do not see anything fishy in such denials; in other words, they do not believe that they are revealing anything in particular by making a negative claim."[48] This rhetorical strategy is not strictly reducible to the analytic framework—when someone says "I'm not mad, just disappointed," the signifier "mad" is raised in order to place into the other's unconscious the negated truth of the statement. While for Freud, negation was a verbal strategy "introduced by the process of repression," it is effective at the level of the idea, not simply at the level of affect.[49] As McGowan points out, the subject's entrance into language produces the possibility for negation.[50] The binary system of male/female, analogized to the fact of sexual difference, and the anxiety it elicits in men and women, is managed through symbolic negations and displacements or functional negations through appeals to positive features.

Since according to courts "any factor other than sex" means just that, the negation of sex acquires a positive existence in the form of height/weight requirements, existing salary disparities, competitive forces, and so on. Negation is more than simple verbal denial, or the addition of "not" to an utterance, although Freud acknowledges this strategy by patients who wish to tacitly reveal ill will toward a parent.[51] The concept conjoins the complex relations between simple verbal negation and something more vehement—disavowal. For Laplanche and Pontalis, in "the specifically Freudian usage, there seems to be a justification for distinguishing between '*verneinen*' [negation proper] and '*verleugnen*' [denial, disavowal]," and that Freud reserved "disavowal" for when a patient denies an external fact.[52] "*Verneinen*" refers to statements like "I do not like pomegranates," whereas "*verleugnen*" would involve the parent of a gay child saying, "My child is *not* gay," or most vehemently, "I have no (gay) child." Negation works precisely because of the indeterminacy between "logical" negation and "rejection" (or "disavowal") in wage discrimination cases. Because employers have recourse to external features (height requirements, equivalent positions' pay, etc.) that justify unequal pay, they become rhetorical resources, as they serve as displacements for the more fundamental fact of sex. Experiments, surveys, and lawsuits have demonstrated that women are systematically paid less after controlling for "factors other than sex"; hence "sex" is the singular piece of the discursive economy that must remain unsaid.[53] That is, the "external fact" that must be disavowed is the worker's sex, and this is accomplished through invoking "any factor other than sex." Like the previous verbal resistance, it works retroactively, wherein a minimal, accidental feature (like weight) acquires a positive value in order to cover for the maximal feature—that of sexual difference.

Camille Olson, representing the United States Chamber of Commerce, predicts that companies will be unduly burdened by the requirement to justify pay inequality with a bona fide factor, claiming that it would be "nearly impossible for an employer to defend against a claim that a wage differential existed by explaining that the differential was based on a factor other than sex."[54] She further objects to the provision that "the factor responsible for a wage differential not only is something other than sex, but also meets a higher standard of 'job relatedness' or 'legitimate business purpose.'"[55] That is, businesses must be freed from the burden of proving that a man's higher salary represents a legitimate business purpose. Google has deployed this tactic to defend itself against accusations of extreme, systematic wage discrimination. According to a legal filing, "The process of compiling data for the DoL [Department of Labor] has required engineers, lawyers and employees across departments to build new systems, conduct extensive quality reviews of files, redact documents and complete other complex tasks."[56] For the world's largest search engine corporation, it is possible to accurately assess a worker's marginal contribution to determine their wage but not when assessing whether that wage is attached to a man or a woman.

Instead of Betty Friedan's "problem that has no name," the problem of unequal pay has a name—it simply cannot be uttered by employers.

The gender pay gap appears through the symbolization of "any factor"—and can thus be legally disavowed. To paraphrase Freud's analysis, under current law, employers may say in court, "I do not know why I paid this woman less—all I know is that it was *not* because she is a woman!" The burden of applying a positive feature is too onerous—better to negate the single external fact of a woman's sex. The law renders "woman's" sex, the mark of her unequal treatment, as "not-woman," so both the existence of ill treatment and the only mark that would prove it as such—her sex—is disavowed. Negation works as the disavowal of the Real of sexual difference, and PFA encountered verbal resistances precisely because the language crowded out the rhetorical resource of negation. By substituting an open set ("any factor other than sex") for a closed one ("a bona fide factor"), employers could no longer adopt this legal strategy. Paradoxically, the existing legal framework demands such a strategy, such that a woman's existence is rendered inconsistent, merely a set of negative features (not tall enough, not making enough money already, not in an equivalent position).[57] What is repressed in the symbolic of the legal realm returns in the Real of salary data.

"Women's Incentives" Fill the Gender Pay Gap . . .

Opposition to the PFA further sublimated traditionalist arguments about women's enjoyment into the language of economic incentives: Gender inequality is natural (and expressly unfixable with public policy) because women voluntarily choose options other than high-earning jobs, including raising children, doing domestic work, and doing "care work" with children or the elderly. In her testimony, Olson argued that "personal choice; women's disproportionate responsibilities as caregivers and other family obligations; education; self-selection for promotions and the attendant status and monetary awards; and other 'human capital' factors" are the primary contributors to the gender pay gap, and contended that both labor economists and feminist scholars agree that intentional discrimination does not cause this gap.[58] Olson's comment is correct, in a narrow sense, for PFA does not presume that wage discrimination is intentional, or the result of individual malice, but rather the inevitable result of structural factors that give rise to discriminatory outcomes. In an editorial, expressing opposition to the Act, Sabrina Schaeffer from the Independent Women's Forum (a right-wing think tank) writes, "The differences in pay between men and women come down to choices. Choices women—and men—make have costs. More women than men choose to take time off to raise a family, but that's a far cry from discrimination. And costs are the result of a woman's freedom, not an injustice imposed on her by society."[59] Incentive-based language is almost always "responsibility-oriented," meaning that because any choice is assumed to be voluntary (a choice is an expression of a preference that satisfies one's utility function), those who act take sole responsibility for the consequences thereof. And because they are inferred retroactively as the result of stable preferences, we can only conclude that women who choose something other than a high-paying job have simply followed their existing incentive structures.

"Women were more likely than men to leave the workforce with intentions to sacrifice their paychecks for the sake of caring for their families," writes Penny Nance, of Concerned Women for America.[60] Jennifer Colosi corroborates this claim with anecdotal data from her own firm, that Silicon Valley firms wish to hire women, but women turn them down because of family commitments: "They say 'no thanks' because they are unable to travel or commit the hours for the job that would move their careers further upward."[61] She concludes, "Women and men are different . . . and it should stay that way!"[62] Within an incentive-driven vocabulary, it is always too late to talk about change. The idea that women have innate incentives for care work and domestic labor also works in reverse, that men (through either innate desire, training, or compulsion) take on work that women will simply not do. Representative Foxx submitted the column "Feminists Meddle with the Market" from the *National Review* in the Congressional Record on July 31, 2008, which argued that "men are the ones working in our sewers, guarding our prisons, laying concrete in the scorching sun, and catching and gutting our fish," while women "disproportionately work indoors, in safe, climate controlled buildings, with regular, or even flexible, hours. More people are interested in working in libraries and school buildings than on the fishing boats featured in Deadliest Catch."[63] That is the gender pay gap persists because women are believed to find safer work more innately rewarding, while men are rewarded for dangerous work.

Each person who argued against PFA employed the notion of choice but yoke women's choices to something either trained or innate in women's experiences that prevent them from becoming high earners and contributing to an equalization of the gender pay gap. In so doing, they reverse cause and effect, by positing women's constrained choices (to have families, to take lower-paying jobs) as the cause of the outcomes they accept, rather than the effect of the constraints that are put upon women as a whole. By contrast, PFA supporters invoke how contexts constrain women's choices to indicate possible opportunities for action and redress. Incentives (like "women's choices," "disproportionate housework responsibilities," or "raising children") operate as displacements of a fundamental antagonism that slips away when equal pay opponents invoke them in a metonymic chain. Philip Cohen, testifying in favor of PFA, notes this reversal in causal attribution: "Women do make choices that have negative effects on their long-term earnings but the choices they make are highly constrained and a lot of the times, those choices are constrained by factors at their places of work."[64] Jocelyn Samuels of the National Women's Law Center directly impugns the capitalist mode of production as the cause of the wage gap, not the individual choices that women make: "Market forces themselves not only cannot alone solve these inequities but, in fact, are based on the kinds of prior barriers and discrimination that have prevented people like women, like minorities, like people with disabilities from reaching the same level playing fields that men have occupied."[65] Because a market can only register extant preferences through the commodity form, women who are systematically underpaid cannot express a preference for a higher-paying job without the power to obtain one. Certainly, contemporary social relations make it economically "rational" for a woman to leave her job to raise children, or to take lower-paying jobs that afford flexibility. There is no economic feedback mechanism to alter existing incentive structures, since every action by a woman is then taken as evidence for the sustenance of gender inequality. A woman's underpaid work becomes a justification for continued unequal treatment of her gender, and the retroactive symbolization of her actions as "incentivized" by low-paying work is thrown forward to determine her future.

The autonomist feminist author Silvia Federici notes how deferring to women's "innate" qualities to perform unwaged domestic labor is an ideological tool of the capitalist class: "Not only has it been imposed on women, but it has been transformed into a natural attribute of our female physique and personality, an internal need, an aspiration, supposedly coming from the depth of our female character. . . . Capital had to convince us that it is a natural, unavoidable, and even fulfilling activity to make us accept working without a wage."[66] In this debate, economists infer, and pundits extrapolate, that women must have been incentivized by their culturally agreed-upon role because they have performed it—the "selfish behavior axiom." Thus it is not that capitalism is inherently sexist—men simply happen to develop better wage-earning potential, and women invest their human capital in domestic chores and raising children. Women are held responsible for this historical accretion as well as the contemporaneous practices that contour their lives; their available menu of choices can never be unencumbered by gender. Such is the analytic value of reading such verbal opposition as displacements rather than lies or obfuscations. All of the factors ("personal choice," "disproportionate household responsibilities," and so on) are unquestionably reasons why women are underpaid relative to men. But Federici points out that they are effects, not causes, of the wage gap.

. . . and Reveal the Real

This is where the concept of the Lacanian Real enters: The gender pay gap offers no "neutral ground" upon which to adjudicate claims of underpayment or discriminatory treatment, since opponents can explain that (controlling for certain measures) women are not underpaid at all, and if they are, it is for entirely explicable chosen reasons. On the one hand, no one seriously disputes that the gender pay gap exists. Yet those who oppose equal pay legislation claim that the gap has perfectly good reasons for existing—which then implies that there is no "gap" at all, only a coherent social reality that abides different returns for different genders. This "borrowed kettle" logic allows for women to be paid less not because of discriminatory practices but because they (are free to) choose things other than high wages, including child-rearing and affective labor. The gender pay gap is Real precisely because it resists adequate symbolization and synthesis—there is no one signifier that negotiates the incompatibility between these two regimes of knowledge. What is revealed instead, then, is the sexed nature of the capitalist mode of production itself: "Sexual difference" is allegorical for the privatized responsibility of social reproduction, what prevents women from earning equivalent wages to men. The antagonism that rests at the heart of the gender pay gap exists not between "women" and "men," but between sexed beings and those who are not.

Lacan's concept of the Real is not some inaccessible, nonfigural, Kantian *ding-an-sich* but a gap that opens up within the Symbolic order itself: "The Real is first there as the anamorphic stain, the anamorphic distortion of the direct image of reality—as a distorted image, a pure semblance that 'subjectivizes' objective reality."[67] This sense of the Real differs from an "objective reality" to which one could appeal as "really out there"—it is rather the thing that prevents "reality" from appearing as such. Matheson approaches the Lacanian Real from a diagonal perspective and argues that the Real is rather the condition for the Symbolic order: there is an unsymbolizable excess, a residue, in "reality," which language can never capture.[68] Despite this structural antagonism, speech persists as a mechanism for attempting to account for this excess and reintegrate it into a subject's symbolic universe. From either starting position (the Real as the condition/limit of the Symbolic, the Real as the failure of the Symbolic), what matters is that speech, the proper domain of the rhetorical tradition, is the site of how this abyssal gap is managed. Other rhetorical scholars have noted that diverse concepts of the Real appear as productive resources to interrogate how speakers manage the gap between competing orders of reality. Johnson & Asenas note that in rhetorical studies, scholars have appealed to the Real as a void, a return, a source of enjoyment, a recalcitrance to symbolization, and materiality itself.[69] In my usage of the term, the Real operates in between what they describe as a source of enjoyment, as well as a recalcitrance which resists symbolization.[70] The Real appears as an anamorphic stain on reality—that which prevents the full appearance of "reality" as self-identical due to the undecidable split between the signifier and the signified. In this setting, the Real functions as a simultaneity, or a both/and-ness that renders a judgment about "reality" impossible. When it comes to equal pay, there is no neutral ground upon which to stand to discover whether or not there is discrimination, or what to do about it. Women are simultaneously underpaid and adequately paid, and to disturb the natural equilibrium at which American society has arrived is to interfere at the level of the Real.

In recent years, scholars have extended Lacan's development of the Real and his lectures on feminine and masculine *jouissance* to read them as allegorical for one another. Within Lacan's provocative claim of "sexual difference is Real," is not simply that there are definable traits of the female and male sex (that these differences ex-sist), but that between the male and female sexual organs, there is no "neutral" or objective ground that organizes them. Rather, the sexes are defined as pure difference from one another—there is no "human as such." Fink writes: "There is, according to Lacan, *no direct relationship* between men and women insofar as they are men and women. In other words, they do not 'interact' with each other as man to woman and woman to man. Something gets in the way of their having any such relationship; something skews their interactions."[71] We may view sex itself as the name of the Real, as the hard rock, or hitch, which prevents the achievement of complementarity between men and women. Lacanian theorist Alenka Zupančič uses this framework to consider sexuality and the erotic as compensation mechanisms for this unbridgeable chasm between two incompatible positions. As Zupančič puts it, "The something produced by the signifier, in addition to what it produces as its field, curves or magnetizes this field in a certain way. It is responsible for the fact that the symbolic field, or the field of the Other, is never neutral (or structured by pure differentiality), but conflictual, asymmetrical, 'not all,' ridden by a fundamental antagonism.[72] Speech itself emerges from the necessity to cover this gap, to manage or discipline it, yet any attempt to speak it out of (or indeed into) existence is impossible. Gunn, concurs, naming the link between speech and the unconscious 'sexual,' as both an electric charge of enjoyment and a space of habitual, insatiable repetition."[73]

Thus the Real reveals the two absolutely incompatible orders of knowledge, to which Lacan gives the names "masculine" and "feminine" *jouissance*. While it is reasonable to distrust the purported phallogocentrism of Lacan's thought, a possibility Biesecker raises, Lacan's adoption of these terms is meant to defamiliarize the seemingly necessary qualities that contemporary culture associates with each category.[74] Gherovici writes that "what Lacan calls the 'male side' and 'female side' are not determined by biology but by the logic of unconscious investments."[75] Masculine *jouissance* entails a process of objectification, or "the reduction of the Other to an object," as Lundberg writes.[76] By contrast, Lacan's feminine *jouissance* exceeds that of the signifying order—it is supplementary, non-All, on the side of the infinite.[77] Rather than being strictly reducible to an object, Lacan claims that "there is always something in her that escapes discourse."[78] If the "masculine" enjoyment of objects is ultimately masturbatory, with the phallus standing in as analogue for any object, then feminine *jouissance* involves enjoyment outside of this idiotic nonrelation. The conflict between these two orders of knowledge is on display during the PFA debate, but just as Lacan indicates that the Real emerges from the cracks within the Symbolic order, these two regimes of knowledge emerge from within the opposition to the bill. Opponents of PFA rely on feminine *jouissance* as a rhetorical resource, to be the "great outdoors," or unsymbolizable Real that cannot be captured by economic analysis, at the same time that they hold a place open for it to be accounted for within the framework of women's incentives. Masculine *jouissance* (the reduction of "woman" to an object) attempts to incorporate feminine *jouissance* (enjoyment without reduction to calculation) as a way to justify the continued systematic underpayment of women.

This elision occurs primarily through opposition to the third major provision of PFA: the gathering of salary data across industries and geographic locations. Whereas sunshine has historically worked in favor of laissez-faire positions, in what Poovey calls the creation of "epistemological facts," contemporary objectors to PFA resisted the collection of salary data stemming from the fear that plaintiffs would misuse it.[79] The production of numerical proof that women are systematically underpaid would, in Senator Tom Harkin's words, "give women the information they need to identify discriminatory pay practices negotiate better for themselves—which, in the end, could reduce the need for costly litigation in the first place."[80] This provision was designed to delicately avoid actual wage-equalization practices or mandates and to allow women to individually bargain for better wages. Yet those who opposed the bill located a challenge to the capitalist mode of production and the ability for an owner to set the wage of a worker. Diana Furchtgott-Roth writes: "The Paycheck Fairness Act would require practically all employers to give the government information on workers' pay, by race and sex, with the goal of equalizing wages of men and women in different job classifications. This would represent a substantial intrusion of government into wage-setting and would discourage hiring."[81] Senator Mike Enzi of Wyoming complained that were this bill to pass, women would "make highly selective use of statistical data reported by the Department of Labor's Bureau of Labor Statistics to support their position."[82] Nance reverses Harkin's position and claims that were the Act to pass, there would be more frivolous lawsuits brought by women and that the only way to improve women's economic well-being is to "nix excessive government regulations and taxation."[83]

In particular, opposition to the PFA from women—Olson, Schaeffer, Nance, Colosi, Foxx, Furchtgott-Roth—reveals how the split between "man" and "woman" must be safeguarded from intrusion by women as a historical collectivity. Soler identifies that the universalization of scientific discourse, which "knows nothing of sexual difference," impels women into the market, to be one worker among many.[84] The extensions of market relations and feminist political movements ensure that "virtually no domain" remains inaccessible to women, provided that they partake in phallic *jouissance*, which she defines as that which "can be capitalized upon" and "available to everyone."[85] Lacan identifies the paradox of phallic *jouissance* by differentiating between "being" and "having" the phallus—women are presumed to "lack" something and thus must gain access to it through a symbolic detour, while men are presumed to "have" it (but crucially, cannot simultaneously "be" it). The historical correlate of having been historically deprived of political and economic power appears in the unconscious as lacking some "thing." Women who give up something in order to rise in the corporate ranks must necessarily calculate their choices through the logic of phallic enjoyment—one sacrifices one's being (in whatever form that may take) in order to possess something (in this case, to possess the kind of disproportionate economic power that men have typically enjoyed).

We tend to think of money as the common denominator of social interactions, but the rhetoric of the incentive—and in this particular case, "women's incentives" both supplants and supplements monetary recompense for women who oppose equal pay legislation. The women who oppose the PFA highlight the value of "choice" or "women's choices" to either become mothers or to remain in the workforce and earn what they deserve as a result. This is the lure of phallic *jouissance* as yoked to the capitalist mode of production. If one is willing to submit to its sway, not simply as a mode of production but as a mode of explanation, then one does earn what one deserves. Lacan's distinction between masculine and feminine *jouissance* is precisely what allows antifeminist, antiequal pay positions to retain a veneer of equality and meritocracy: the dividing line for women who oppose the PFA is not, and has never been "man/woman" but between masculine and feminine *jouissance*—only one of which appears as a desirable wage. This dividing line between must remain intact. Women who do not do the kind of work that makes them equal or high-wage earners must retain their "women's incentives" for low-paying care work and remain figured "as women"; a woman who sacrifices this historical destiny is free to earn what she can in the labor market.

Furthermore, the false dividing line between "man" and "woman," rebuked by opponents who presume that any discrimination must be intentional to be legislated against, hides in plain sight the more fundamental binary of "woman" and "women." Consider that the statement "I am systematically underpaid" is both true and meaningless: "Women" as a whole are systematically underpaid, while "a woman" earns the value of her marginal product, according to neoclassical economic theory. Opposition to any legislation, even as tame as the PFA, evinces the libidinal investment in retaining this binary. "Women" as a historically situated class cannot earn collectively what any one "woman" has earned through partaking in phallic *jouissance*. The PFA would, in the eyes of its opponents, encourage individual women to misuse data that proves that women are systematically underpaid precisely because they assert that women are already recompensed at a rate consonant with their marginal productivity. To demonstrate the epistemological fact of women's underpayment is to in fact misread the texture of social reality and reward women disproportionately for their work. Publicly available wage information cannot adequately represent women's incentives and is thus untrustworthy—women's incentives are embodied in the durable goods of children and tidy homes and to pay them equally for their work while at work constitutes a double reward.

The solution is then to bar this knowledge from coming into being, in effect regulating (by prohibition) the self-interested activity of female workers. Zupančič uses sexual difference as allegorical for social antagonism writ large: "The political explosiveness of 'the woman question' does not lie in any specificity or positive characteristics of women, but it in its capacity to inscribe the problem of division and difference into the world the homogeneity of which is based on exclusion . . . of *the split* (social antagonism) *as such*."[86] The split Zupančič identifies is within the regime of masculine knowledge, based on the binary logic of the One and the Other, which cannot recognize genuine alterity (and hence, must adopt a fantasy to offer some minimal conceptual stability). This Real split, the split of sexual difference is not reducible to "women" and "men" but to sexed beings and the fantasy that there is a not-sexed being. A gender pay database itself would constitute an intrusion into the Real, into the two incompatible regimes of knowledge that virtually guarantee women's underpayment relative to men by revealing this divergence among gendered lines. The fact that women do disproportionately handle domestic responsibilities and raise children is transformed into a logical necessity, an outgrowth from a historical contingency. It is simply that the capitalist mode of production rewards labor that grows capital, and those who do not or cannot partake in this activity cannot ever become equal, regardless of their gender.

In sum, the opponents of PFA mobilized three major defenses against the bill's provisions. To counteract the provision that employers must name a "bona fide factor" to justify pay discrepancies, opponents relied upon the verbal negation of the signifier "woman" within the discursive economy of employment. If employers were forced to symbolize a justification for paying a woman less than a man, then the free-market system itself would be imperiled; the Act would have forced the concept of sex directly into discussions of compensation. To counteract the creation of a salary pay database, opponents invoked two arguments: First, women are not systematically underpaid but have incentives innate to their gender that make them more amenable to lower-paying jobs and to leaving the workforce to raise children. "Women's incentives" fills the gender pay gap and renders women's constrained outcomes as the effect of their free choices. Second, women cannot be trusted to appropriately use a database that would empirically demonstrate their systematic underpayment. The gender pay gap is Real, for there is no way to reconcile these incompatible findings, and those opposed to the bill unconsciously revealed the stakes of any debate over equal pay in the capitalist mode of production. Sexual difference must not be accounted for in a way that would adequately compensate women for their unwaged work.

Conclusion: What Does ~~Woman~~ Want?

In his twentieth seminar, on feminine sexuality, Lacan takes up Freud's infamous question, "What does woman want?" via a detour into masculine *jouissance*. He declaims that embedded within this question is already a figuration, a reduction of "woman" to a fantasy substance around which the masculine position can cognize. Instead of enjoying the body of the woman as such, "precisely what he enjoys is the *jouissance* of the organ," the phallus.[87] In other words, masculine *jouissance* is ultimately masturbatory, for the aim and object of pleasure is not "woman," but rather, the phallic object already possessed by the man. This has a direct analogue to debates about equal pay. According to those who oppose equal pay legislation, life is a set of trade-offs, and women rationally trade economic equality for rewards innate to their gender. In the hands of economists, "women's incentives" are commensurable with a wage; when masculine *jouissance* objectifies a woman, they reduce their culturally constrained choices into an innate expression of their economic preferences. In answering the question "What does woman want?" they reduce women to beings of pure autotelic enjoyment, basking in their innate qualities of care work and domestic labor. "Women's incentives" become rhetorical resources: The gap of intelligibility, of being able to definitively account for all of human interactions, is precisely how opponents of equal pay can posit that "women's incentives" exist, and they are calculable at the same ontological level as wage earning.

In public debates such as these, Lacan's categories are not static or abstract: one regime of knowledge dominates the other. Suzanne Barnard reminds readers to set Lacan's categories into dynamic motion in the act of interpretation.[88] The absolute incompatibility of the two forms of *jouissance* mark the difference as Real: there is no neutral ground to adjudicate this issue; the two regimes cannot communicate with one another. As Zupančič insists, the Real is not one side of an antagonism or another: it is the split or antagonism itself. Both masculine and feminine *jouissance* are attempts to speak the same phenomena—women's choices are either objects of calculation ("masculine") or inaccessible thereto ("feminine"). I supplement Matheson's claim that "silence, interruption, awe, and terror" are hallmarks of the Real with the extant discursive fact of incompatible regimes of knowledge; the Real is found in the hitch that makes solving the equal pay issue with speech alone.[89] What makes this rhetorical strategy pernicious is that this purported agnosticism about "woman" is in fact an alibi for the persistence of stereotypes that surround all women. The split between masculine and feminine *jouissance* helps configure how antiequality actors essentialize "women" as caregivers and childbearing vessels, these selfsame actors' arguments are effective precisely because they attribute an inaccessible *jouissance* to women, an enjoyment that does not partake in (masculine enjoyment within) the marketplace.

Lacan's radical point is that *jouissance* is split by an internal contradiction: There is no "woman-as-such," no "concept of woman" that would fulfill an ultimate fantasy of wholeness for man. There are only concrete, individual women, each making hard choices bound by context. But it is each individual's incompleteness that provides the foundation of masculine *jouissance*'s reduction of "woman" to "object." Masculine knowledge at its root operationalizes this disavowal, so that women's *jouissance* appears inaccessible to legislators, barred precisely because of the reduction of "woman" to "object." "Woman" is a fantasy-structure within a signifying economy that reduces concrete Others to objects of control. The concept of woman, much like the wage gap itself, is both/and, not either/or: women have both the nonmonetary incentives inaccessible to capitalism as well as the figuration as "woman" that guarantees their unequal treatment thereby. That is, if we attribute to her the predictable essentialist predicates, "woman" does have a substance: they are caregivers, raise children, and desire to do housework. And because economists posit her enjoyment as instantaneously calculable, and resulting from innate preference structures, woman's work must never be valued monetarily as highly as the work done by men. It is an act of attribution that occurs here, not one of substance. The masculine *jouissance* of the economist, the politician, and the testifier is the real object of circulation in these debates—"women's incentives" is where meaning resides for the speaker, not for the women who are the objects of speech. Both types of *jouissance* work in tandem to cloak discriminatory treatment: the inaccessibility of "feminine *jouissance*" lends itself to the assumption that those who have access to it (those who are not-men) enjoy it equivalently to a wage.

Thus it is no surprise that "sex" becomes for the opponents of PFA the singular deadlock. If only women were not "women" (that is, if only women were not the gender that gives birth, which has disproportionate cultural expectations to be caregivers, etc.) they would earn a wage equivalent to men. Opponents to the legislation want women's *jouissance* to be countable but not waged. As long as a woman is not a "real woman," she can achieve anything she wants in the capitalist mode of production. In the end, it is not that women cannot "have it all" because to be sexed is to be treated unequally. It is instead that the capitalist mode of production cannot have "it all," a universality without remainder—a system of sexed beings and those that are not. Here is the alliance between Lacan's masculine *jouissance* and Marx's reading of the capitalist mode of production. Masculine *jouissance* is a universality grounded in an exception; Marx defines capital as that which generates its own unstable excesses while continually reabsorbing them.[90] Reproducing the worker and reinscribing market equilibrium both necessitate labor power's relation to its supplement, "woman." She is the part of no part, generated precisely to be incalculable by a wage. Such is the nature of the Real—the stain that prevents the whole from relating to itself, a hitch that generates an anamorphic reality. When legislators attack equal pay legislation, they point to this supplementary enjoyment, contending that both women and firms already calculate it. "Incentive" becomes the discursive signal of this attributive enjoyment and its alibi for nonremuneration. The capitalist mode of production would be imperiled if this enjoyment were doubly registered—if women close the wage gap legislatively, it means they would enjoy their nonmonetary incentives (housework) and their monetary incentives (wages) too.

Between the legislative fights over these two equal pay bills, one comes across a conceptual contradiction: the Lilly Ledbetter Act, despite being named for a woman, was effectively desexed and testimony hinged upon the status of the liberal juridical subject writ large. By contrast, the Paycheck Fairness Act, despite its seemingly neutral moniker, became a referendum on the sexed nature of the capitalist mode of production, and whether equivalent monetary recompense could ever be possible as long as there is a sexed division of labor (both within the household and among industries more broadly). Such is the value of reading Congressional testimony symptomatically, and to the letter—through the trope of hyperbole, through the invocation of the slippery slope, and especially through the trope of metastasis, cultural anxieties about the place of "woman" are elicited by those who opposed these miniscule reform bills. The metastatic logic of the incentive, once introduced into public policy debates, entails that nothing that cannot be expressed thereas, which ultimately means that women are always already barred from equal treatment by the capitalist mode of production. Existing social relations will always make it "economically rational" in the aggregate for women to leave the workforce, accept lower-paying jobs, and remain underpaid; their choices will inevitably appear as if they are following innate incentives to do so. "What a woman (really) wants" is inaccessible to the wage relation, and structurally incalculable. The same signs ("care-work," "domestic responsibilities," "raising children") function for both models of *jouissance* since opposition to PFA gestures to this supposedly feminine *jouissance* as a way to prevent the bill's passage. Within this signifying regime, these signs are characterized by an internal split, so women's own actions and desires can be used against them to retroactively justify their continued mistreatment.

Chapter 5

Nudge Theory and the Politics of Neurosis

In September 2015, President Barack Obama released an executive order
to create a team that would advise federal agencies to use insights from
behavioral economics in policymaking, named the Social and Behavioral
Sciences Team (or SBST) since a "growing body of evidence demonstrates
that behavioral science insights . . . can be used to design government
policies to better serve the American people."[1] In so doing, Obama continued his own trend of relying on behavioral economists to influence
government policy, such as Cass R. Sunstein, one of the authors of the
popular 2008 book *Nudge: Improving Decisions in Health, Wealth, and
Happiness* who served in the administration from 2009 to 2012 at the
Office of Information and Regulatory Affairs. Similarly, before leaving
for a position at Citigroup, economist Peter R. Orszag headed the Office
of Management and Budget from 2009 to 2010; *Bloomberg News* credited
Orszag with implementing incentive-based schemes within the Affordable
Care Act and the Dodd-Frank financial reforms, noting that his team's
"handiwork can be seen in proposed rules ranging from mine safety to
retirement savings, tire durability, and food labels."[2] Throughout its time
in power, the Obama administration explicitly opposed outright regulation
of industries (even after direct financial rescue) and preferred instead to
contour individual behavioral choices around predetermined political
outcomes in virtually all of its initiatives: the "incentive-based" behavioral
economic policies exemplified by the SBST, the ACA (the administration's
signature legislative achievement) as well as a variety of educational, nutri-
tional, and environmental policies. Among its publicized achievements,
the Social and Behavioral Sciences Team used nudges to encourage 5.7

percent more eligible high school students to enroll in college and nudged government employees to use less paper when printing from a computer by encouraging them to switch from single- to double-sided printing.[3] (According to *Time* magazine, "Double-sided printing when up about 6%."[4])

In 2010, *Bloomberg* heralded the proactive approach taken by the Obama administration in its initiatives as a return of the "regulatory state," which was "poised for a dramatic comeback following decades of retrenchment."[5] Yet the policies the Obama administration advocated for were self-professedly not regulatory; rather, its agents contrasted what they called "command and control" regulation with incentive-based regulations. *Bloomberg*'s prognostication failed to materialize in any meaningful sense, and the specter of the regulatory state invoked by the press and Obama administration officials is long dead, with its utility primarily as a rhetorical resource, a fear that must be avoided via prudent tailoring of market-based policies. After the Obama administration left power, the SBST was shut down, and the National Science and Technology Council, which housed the team, delivered no public work once the Trump administration took power in January 2017.[6] As the *New York Times* reported, after news of Trump's election arrived at the Obama White House, "Barack Obama slumped in his chair in the Oval Office and addressed an aide standing near a conspicuously placed bowl of apples, emblem of a healthy-snacking policy soon to be swept aside, along with so much else."[7] During the Trump administration, the SBST's reports, fact sheets, event agendas, as well as the executive order authorizing its creation mentioned above, were deleted entirely from the White House's official website. In April 2022, the Joe Biden administration announced the Subcommittee on Social, Behavioral and Economic Sciences would return, tasking the group with crafting a "'blueprint' for the use of social and behavioral science research to advance evidence-based policymaking," due one calendar year after its rechartering.[8]

Within the United States, nudges and incentive-based policies appear largely to be the domain of the Democratic Party, yet they are a global phenomenon and entrenched in multiple countries as well as multinational agencies: According to the World Bank, "nudge units" have been set up in more than ten countries, as well as at the World Bank itself, the United Nations, and European Union.[9] While conservatives in the United States tend to prefer the "real thing" of monetary inducement over the soft-pedaled indirection of liberal ones, conservative governments, such as that of the United Kingdom, have made "nudge theory" a component of statecraft even into 2020. Peter Self, of the London School of Economics, as early as the 1970s used the term "Econocracy" to describe the overreliance on cost-benefit analysis as the primary rubric for political decision-makers.[10] Clive Barnett notes governments that foreground cost-benefit analysis lead "to a search for incentive structures that will encourage agents to align their own self-interests with forms of action which will also be of benefit to their clients. It also recasts the role of elected officials as champions of the interests of public service users, seeking to rein in and discipline indifferent and inflexible 'producer' interests in bureaucracies and expert professions."[11] As Richard Thaler, Sunstein's coauthor of *Nudge* is quoted as saying, nudges use "rightwing means to achieve progressive ends."[12]

The turn toward nudges in statecraft, away from what economists derisively call "command and control" policies, represents the culmination of an incentive-based vision of the social bond, in which policymakers take as given the market principles of stable preferences, pricing mechanisms, and utility maximization. Nudge theory mobilizes the basic presumption of incentives as behavioral motivation—and crucially the necessity of indirection—to achieve any goal: states cannot directly provide social goods but must incentivize businesses and nongovernmental organizations to provide them and for citizens to choose beneficial outcomes freely. On the one hand, nudges are organized by the logic of prohibition: on universal public goods, the possibility of directly guaranteeing any political outcome, and indeed, on the possibility of representation at all. Yet simultaneously, nudges operate as a disavowal of this very belief. Nudges self-consciously accept market frameworks, yet their existence nevertheless presupposes that well-meaning government actors actually can direct the choices of individuals toward socially beneficial ends. This performative contradiction is the source of much debate around the value of nudges, and the approach called "libertarian paternalism," for it operates according to the logic of the fetishistic disavowal, or "I know full well [that market principles structure all human interactions], but nevertheless [I can design a policy that improves upon them]."

The previous chapter demonstrated how the invocation of "incentives" works as a *retroactive* justification for existing gender inequalities; opponents to social change have an inexhaustible rhetorical alibi for the status quo by appealing to the underlying incentive structures that brought it about. Nudges act as the *proactive* implementation of this retroactive technique—the insertion of incentive schemes into social reality in order to contour it toward a predetermined end. Whereas within a strictly incentive-based framework, the status quo is organized like a market and therefore at "equilibrium," the nudge framework presupposes that market conditions must be introduced into social reality for individuals to begin acting rationally. Faced with an apparent inexistence of neoclassical theory in reality, the behavioral economist forces it to become true through state action. The nudge is the highest expression of the incentive-driven program, as it is a self-conscious actualization of economic theory—it treats the postulates of market behavior as true, but what is found lacking is reality itself. Whereas incentives are presumed to directly cause behaviors within markets, nudges portray themselves as allowing maximum freedom for the chooser, while still encouraging them to make the economically rational (and in the nudger's eyes, socially beneficial) decision. The widespread presence of nudges in politics exemplifies how the style of neoclassical analysis has metastasized; thus it is not simply the content of the nudge that must be treated with skepticism, but its form, which stems directly from its theoretical genesis in neoclassical economic theory. Nudges have very little to do with "the economy," broadly understood, and everything to do with the powerful discourses of economics, narrowly so.

Nudge theory instantiates a political neurosis through the introduction of ultimately false binary choices for individual(ized) choosing subjects; nudges force the subject to ask the neurotic's question, "What does the Other want of me?" in all manner of social and political settings. In a nudge, the choosing subject is typically offered a choice between two options but with the "choice architecture" contoured toward the "choice architect's" preferred end. Consider the "nudge" of a website asking you to either "Accept All" tracking and marketing cookies rather than the lengthier process of refusing them. The nudge is designed to elicit the true desire of the subject at the lowest cost, but because the intended result is prescribed in advance, the subject's desire is proscribed. The binary choice is not one at all; the obligation to choose masks something that is more fundamentally relinquished within a symbol system. The introduction of a "two" represses that a "one" is closed off by the domain of politics. Neurosis, properly understood, acts as a solution, albeit an incomplete one, that allows a subject to manage their relationship to the signifying order and to their own desires. Nudges do not deliver socially beneficial outcomes, nor are they designed to; instead, they are designed to repress the provision of universal public goods, like housing, healthcare, and education through mechanisms of forced choice.

This chapter and the following one form a dyad: to understand nudges, the hold they have on the contemporary political order, and how it both functions and falters. First, I define the key terms that surround nudge theory, beginning with "libertarian paternalism," coined by economists Richard Thaler and Cass R. Sunstein, who have formally and informally advised the Obama administration as well as the United Kingdom's Tory government under David Cameron. I elucidate "choice architecture," "behavioral market failure," the all-important "nudge," and explore what distinguishes it from different modes of state action, like regulations and bans. I then offer a Lacanian critique of the nudge, with a particular focus on the role the signifier plays. Nudges, as mentioned, "work" because they implement the neurotic's question into the political field; they defer satisfaction for any unarticulated desire for a political good by placing it under a regime of signification mediated through the economist's desire. Neurosis is a political response to guard against the kind of satisfaction economists call the dreaded "perverse incentive," in which subjects enjoy without proper payment. I draw attention to how nudges, despite attempting to bypass the role representation plays in politics (bypassing legislatures, prohibitions, regulations, etc., in favor of executive action), they fail even in this regard, adding a layer of indirection that further defers the achievement of any preferred political end. In the following chapter, I evaluate the way incentives were mobilized in policy to mitigate and recover from the COVID-19 pandemic, to explore how incentives, in crucial moments, fail to work when set up against a generalized social crisis. The apparent failure of two policies—ending supplemental unemployment benefits and incentivizing vaccinations—speaks to the success of the incentive-based vision of society as a whole, which figures all people as individual choosers with no way to mediate their relation to others. I also evaluate the "decline of symbolic efficiency" hypothesis, and how the metastasis of the nudge form in politics virtually guarantees that no mass, univocal, public action can be implemented.

To be fair to their advocates, the elimination of needless physical waste, a greater number of organ donors, healthier food options, and the other aims of nudges are undeniably laudable. And it is worth acknowledging that nudges arrive in liberal democracies at a certain moment in cycles of capital accumulation and electoral polarization, such that they appear as the only way to address any public problems whatsoever. Yet as I demonstrate, nudges do not merely fall prey to the same individualizing, responsibilizing logic that incentives do overall; they interdict upon the very concept of universal public goods because all decisions must be laundered through marketlike apparatuses. Nudges index not merely a profound symbolic exhaustion in the political realm but also a symbolic impotence: the kind of approach that prevents large-scale solutions from being attempted at all.

Libertarian Paternalism, Choice Architecture, and the Nudge

Libertarian paternalism encapsulates the metastatic logic of incentives by folding the market-based approach to human behavior into a technocratic tailoring of social reality. Behavioral economics, upon which nudges are based, does not reject the neoclassical framework but rather expands its scope directly into the political field: "[Behavioral economics] is not based on a proposed paradigm shift in the basic approach of our field, but rather is a natural broadening of the field of economics . . . built on the premise that not only mainstream *methods* are great, but so too are mainstream economic *assumptions*."[13] While behavioral economics asserts innovations upon the standard account, its alterations are largely cosmetic and supplementary to the underlying neoclassical models of behavior. Since these economists adhere to the meta-structuring capacities of the market and to the behavioral postulates embedded therein, "nudges" will inevitably fall prey to what all market-based approaches to social change do. Like all incentive-based policies, nudges individualize the responsibility for a given choice by offering a "choice architecture," which reveals the preferences of that choosing individual. Because nudges are designed to be cheap (if not "free"), and unobtrusive (if not invisible), they depend upon not only the postulates of market behavior but also the structuring agency of existing laws and social norms to function as their backdrop.

Crucially, the nudge model uses the neoclassical economic assumption of "competitive conditions" as its theoretical justification for introducing market conditions into social reality, a social inequity or iniquity is not a sufficient criterion for a "behavioral market failure" on its own; a nudge is only justifiable when individuals lack a meaningful choice to make to rationally improve their own lives. Essential to the nudge model is a prohibition on systematic, universal, and collective change; it is the singular axiom around which the rest of these interventions must bend. The term "choice" resides symptomatically in the discourse of Thaler and Sunstein, it possesses an outsized value within a libertarian paternalist approach, above even that of the content of what is chosen. According to neoclassical theory, markets can only exist if multiple options are available to consumers, so the presence of a "one" and an "Other" guarantees that the more efficient outcome will occur by virtue of this act of choice. In practice, this entails governments deliberately introducing choice into "markets" for schools, healthcare, utilities, and public services in order to generate efficient outcomes, rather than offering robust public services on their own.

Here, I define three terms: libertarian paternalism, choice architecture, and the all-important "nudge." Libertarian paternalism, authors Thaler and Sunstein admit, is a term that will satisfy virtually no one but themselves; they ask their audience to hold both terms in tension. The pair approvingly cite Milton Friedman as their libertarian of choice, citing his axiom that people should be "free to choose," and good policies are "liberty-preserving."[14] As Sunstein puts it, this type of paternalism refers to *"actions of government that attempt to improve people's welfare by influencing their choices without imposing material costs on those choices."*[15] From now on, I use "paternalism" in lieu of "libertarian paternalism"; Sunstein drops the adjective in *Why Nudge?* owing to the fact that any behavioral governmental intervention could never be genuinely "libertarian." However, the term remains latent in the unconscious of its proponents, largely because what "libertarian" refers to is not "liberty" in the abstract sense but a commitment to the inviolability of private property.[16] By suppressing the term itself but retaining its features, nudge theorists disguise one of the key components of their discursive edifice.

Paternalism begins with the conceit that a neurological basis exists for dividing a person into two subject positions: "Humans" and "Econs."[17] A "Human" is an emotional, impulsive, Homer Simpson type, acting without thinking.[18] An "Econ," is deliberative, a Mr. Spock type who contemplates rationally and "insists on the importance of self-control."[19] Because in some contexts human beings make unreflective choices and occasionally fail to match their means with their ends—despite aiming at a satisfying choice, they err. Rebonato summarizes this assessment: "According to libertarian paternalists, what individuals freely choose is not only not always good for society, but even for them."[20] If these errors are systematic and widespread, they result in a "behavioral market failure," which authorizes a paternalistic solution.[21] Although he quibbles at the edges of the definition, Sunstein approvingly quotes Rebonato's definition of libertarian paternalism as "the set of interventions aimed at overcoming the unavoidable cognitive biases and decisional inadequacies of an individual by exploiting them in such a way as to influence her decisions (in an easily reversible manner) towards choices that she herself would make if she had at her disposal unlimited time and information, and the analytic abilities of a rational decision-maker (more precisely, of *Homo Economicus*)."[22] That is, if it is possible to indirectly turn a "Human" into more of an "Econ," a choice architect will take that action. To wit, Sunstein argues that public figures should frame environmental or security regulations in terms of cost/benefit calculations to "weaken the effect of intuitions" and improve decision-making by members of the public.[23]

A "choice architect," according to Thaler and Sunstein, "has the responsibility for organizing the context in which people make decisions."[24] Those who design ballots, doctors who choose treatments, professionals who design health-care enrollment forms, parents, and salespeople are all choice architects because they exercise some meaningful control of how other people make their own choices; good architects "realize that although they can't build the perfect building, they can make some design choices that will have beneficial effects."[25] Because of—not despite—the fact that individuals have systematic biases (toward defaults, anchoring points, overconfidence, false optimism, and so on), their choices can still be interpreted using traditional economic models of behavior. A "default," for instance, acts as a systematic bias toward a given outcome; the authors use an example of experimental participants being asked to provide their phone numbers, add two hundred, and then answer the question, "When did the Huns sack Europe?" According to the results, "People's answers differ by a few hundred years depending on whether they have a low or a high anchor."[26] Because these biases are systematic, they can be modeled and mitigated—with new defaults encouraging individuals to act in accordance with a given "choice architecture." Thus, the same basic assumptions about individuals from the "economic approach to human behavior" are adopted by paternalists: individuals (1) act to maximize their utility (2) in accordance with their selfish preferences, and (3) they respond to the "prices" of behaviors, financial or otherwise. Therefore, the best social policy is not to prohibit any behaviors but rather to raise the cost of behaviors and appeal to people's rationalities. The *Nudge* authors aver that if people want to smoke, paternalists will not force them to quit, "or even make things hard for them."[27] In this framework, everything is permitted, as long as you are willing to pay—one is not prohibited from smoking, one simply pays a penalty, either monetary or social. The coercion implied by outright regulation makes way for a soft entreaty for better behavior. For Thaler and Sunstein, a good choice architect is aware that "everything matters," meaning that every signifier a subject emits can be potentially interpreted by the choice architect in a manner consonant with their expectations.[28]

A choice architect is cognizant of the power of incentives: "Choice architects must think about incentives when they design a system. Sensible architects will put the right incentives on the right people. One way to start to think about incentives is to ask four questions about a particular choice architecture: Who uses? Who chooses? Who pays? Who profits?"[29] So committed to the incentive-driven approach are the authors that they place it first in their mnemonic device for "nudges" by creatively fudging the terminological arrangement. Choice architects should adhere to the following acronymic checklist:

iNcentives
Understand mappings
Defaults
Give feedback
Expect error
Structure complex choices[30]

A nudge is the implementation of the paternalist approach; as they define it, it is "any aspect of the choice architecture that alters people's behavior in a predictable way without forbidding any options or significantly changing their economic incentives."[31] This means, as mentioned, retaining the theory of the subject borrowed from neoclassical economics, and making changes "cheap" or "free" (either psychologically or symbolically, and rarely monetarily). But this definition demonstrates that the authors retain an expansive view of what an incentive is, for "incentives can come in different forms."[32] Any change that alters the "cost" of a behavior, whether monetary, psychic, symbolic, or cognitive, qualifies as an incentive; so while monetary incentive alterations are off the table for political reasons, choice architects are at liberty to alter incentive structures through nudges as they see fit. Sunstein employs the metastatic version of both the definition and scope of incentives by characterizing all interventions by paternalists on a continuum from "hard" (which entails material costs like fines, imprisonment, regulations) to "soft" (which entails imposing "psychic costs" and social pressure).[33]

This is the sequence of a nudge, from the perspective of the choice architect:

$$\frac{Choice\ (signifier)}{Preference\ (signified)} \nearrow \begin{matrix} Nudge \\ \overline{} \\ Desire \end{matrix}$$

On the left is a Saussurean signifier/signified dyad. When someone makes a choice—say, a candy bar in a workplace cafeteria—it is assumed they have expressed their preference for some satisfaction that the candy bar offers. While the "meaning" of that choice can be polyvalent or contradictory, the choice architect isolates the key signifying feature as the raw material for the nudge. In the case of a candy bar, it may be proximity to the register, attractive packaging, the satisfaction of the oral drive, or even its placement at eye level; other potential signifieds (subduing hunger, a childhood memory, its taste) drop out in favor of that which can be technocratically tweaked. The choice architect then produces a substitute object based on that chosen signified: in this case, fresh fruit replaces the candy bar. The object occupies the same position in the network of signifiers but is the "better" choice from the perspective of the architect. Thus, the "desire" beneath the nudge is intended to be the "true" desire of the chooser whether they are conscious of it or not, with the implicit understanding that desire is functionally metonymic and can be substituted with no loss of enjoyment. For the paternalist, the desire is also simultaneously the economically "rational" decision as well as the socially beneficial one, so all parties benefit, and most importantly, no one's liberty is violated.[34]

Nudges, in an inverted manner to psychoanalytic practice, seek out the unconscious libidinal quotient of any signifier and bend it toward the policymaker's preferred end. The nudge elicits not the desire of the nudged person but that of the "choice architect." Such a strategy is a mirror image of Becker's metonymy of desire: The policymaker is at liberty to say, "You chose X, but what you *really* chose was Y." The nudge approach makes this sleight of hand explicit by announcing that individuals are frequently unaware of their underlying preferences, or even that their choice will satisfy their desires. By presuming that individuals have unconscious desires, inaccessible except through consumer choices, choice architects rearticulate their actions as expressive of a different unconscious desire, in line with the policymaker's priorities. Nudges reveal the stable preferences of utility-maximizing individuals by altering the external prices of their available choices. While no action should ever be prohibited by a choice architect, they can inflict "psychic costs" upon choosers to alter their actions, in much the same way Becker indicated that psychic costs function as revelatory of behavior.[35]

The incentive-based model stands in contrast to what Thaler and Sunstein call "command and control" policies, in which activities are directly regulated or prohibited by states. Sunstein identifies several reasons why regulations fail: statutory failure (meaning that those writing legislation fail to capture the actual source of the problem) and implementation failure (meaning a failure to properly police, enforce, design response mechanisms, and so on). Specifically, Sunstein places the responsibility for regulatory problems on "poor diagnosis on the part of Congress, of interest-group power, of changing conditions, or of inadequate strategies for implementation."[36] Among others, he blames unions, government bureaucracies, and politically connected industrial interests for stifling change, even if the regulations themselves are well intended. The ascent of an economist like Sunstein into the executive branch under the Obama administration offers a clue for how he envisioned overcoming these problems. An empowered executive branch can act, and react, much more quickly to a perceived problem than a legislative body can. Sunstein and Thaler oppose "command and control" regulations not simply because they are poorly implemented or devised by slothful organizations but because they reduce freedom, and from within the perspective of paternalism, this reduction is as bad, if not worse, than a pernicious outcome of a poor choice.

Nudge and incentive-based policies represent a departure from not only a mode of governance and policy but also a model of representation that authorizes it. Typically, governments collect tax revenues progressively based on earnings as well as on certain activities (like investments, estates, or wage-earning) then redistribute that surplus toward programs and agencies that work toward the political goals of whoever is in power. In addition, state agencies enforce regulations for businesses and individuals, such as environmental protections, food safety standards, or building codes in order to maintain the health and well-being of the populace. For instance, between 1879 and 1906, "nearly 100 bills had been introduced in Congress to regulate food and drugs," according to the Food and Drug Administration, despite each one of them failing to become law.[37] The publication of Upton Sinclair's *The Jungle*, first published in serial form in *Appeal to Reason*, and later on its own as a novel, galvanized public support for safety standards, and contributed to President Roosevelt signing the Food and Drugs Act in 1906. This law instituted a set of regulatory agencies and regimes for insuring food safety through inspections and standards and represents one of the high points of the Progressive Era in the United States. While the novel did not necessarily advance the rights of workers despite Sinclair calling attention to their plight, it did introduce regulations on food quality, meaning strict safety specifications with financial and criminal penalties for noncompliance.

Similarly, after the passage of the 1970 Clean Air Act that established the Environmental Protection Agency, the United States federal government has implemented standards specifically designed to reduce automobile pollutants.[38] In addition, the EPA has legal limits on the contaminants allowed in drinking water thanks to the Safe Drinking Water Act.[39] These actions—taxation, regulation oversight—are the complex expressions of social priorities, legislative compromise, interest group power, and political will, among many other factors, but the animating belief is that a state can cause, via injunction and penalty, its preferred outcomes once an electoral majority has expressed a desire for that outcome. The twentieth-century environmental movement exemplifies how the direct appeal of a social movement to governments and states could prevent ecological catastrophe through publicity (as in the publication of Rachel Carson's *Silent Spring*, credited by the Environmental Protection Agency's own publication, *EPA Journal*, as a direct cause of the agency's existence) or through demonstration and lobbying.[40] Yet since the 1970s, what one might broadly call the "neoliberal" era, governments have substituted the expressions of state power in favor of strictly "economic" approaches due to an acceptance of the critique that neoclassical economics poses to statecraft in general. In particular, the Democratic Party has instead enthusiastically embraced the logic of the incentive in social policy as part of the uptake of "public choice"–based policies writ large.[41]

Although many environmental regulations have had dramatic and positive environmental effects, their enormous cost makes implementing "incentive systems in the place of command and control regulation" much more efficient.[42] Sunstein also claims that emissions standards on automobiles are both too costly to justify and produce unintended consequences: owners of fuel-inefficient vehicles retain their cars for longer, while simultaneously standards have "caused significant losses in lives" because newer, fuel-efficient cars are lighter, smaller, faster, and therefore more prone to fatal collisions.[43] These arguments against emissions standards deploy the retroactive causality of the incentive to embody an ideological investment in antiregulatory politics. Emissions standards raise the price of vehicles, therefore people retain less fuel-efficient ones; when people do purchase new vehicles, the EPA's program "indeed has caused significant losses in lives as a result of producing more dangerous vehicles."[44] Sunstein offers no evidence for these claims; they operate as deductive conclusions from the data point that vehicles are now more expensive thanks to better emissions standards. Sunstein's argument sinks below even that of a *cum hoc, ergo propter hoc* fallacy since traffic-related fatalities have largely declined in both absolute terms and terms relative to population from 1970 onward. Rather, it partakes in the libidinal strategy of guarding against alternative interpretations of social reality.

Lacan's insight, that law is essentially libidinal, and concerned with the channeling, organization and distribution of *jouissance*, explains the economic resistance to "command and control" regulation. One should read the surplus of explanations against regulation as borrowed kettle logic, protecting the unassailable belief in markets at all costs: not only are environmental regulations costly and inefficient, they harm the environment, and worse yet, they claim more lives than they save. The discursive justification for nudges, alongside the concomitant argument against top-down regulation, is the rejection of a "no," of any inhibition to the free flow of capital. In the place of a "no," the nudge model prohibits behaviors only if the "cost" (monetary, symbolic, psychic) is too high: rather than making it illegal to pollute protected lands, polluters should be nudged to avoid it due to the high cost of noncompliance. This is the inversion of Anatole France's definition of freedom within the capitalist mode of production: both the rich man and poor man are free to purchase anything, assuming they can afford it.

The rejection of the "no" of regulation is supplemented by the positive claim for incentive-based regulations, that the presence of "choice" itself is an unmitigated good.[45] Choice functions for the paternalist as that which axiomatically guarantees better outcomes since competition entails the victory of a more efficient actor/program/policy/institution over the inefficient one. Indeed, a "behavioral market failure" in the first place bespeaks the necessity of a choice architect to implement a nudge into a given setting—if competitive conditions do not exist, a government's job is to instantiate them. One outcome of this axiom is that no universal social good can ever be endorsed if a dual system can be implemented instead. Competitive conditions can be applied to any political issue—healthcare, education, energy sources, and so on, since by definition, a monopoly will always be less efficient than the presence of alternatives. In no uncertain terms, this entails a government ought to deliberately empower actors that are hostile to the aims thereof, such as for-profit charter schools, in the name of introducing competitive conditions. As Dardot and Laval write, competition is the "relationship that best corresponds both to economic efficiency and to the moral requirements expected of human beings, in as much as it enables them to assert themselves as autonomous beings, who are free and responsible for their acts."[46] Unsurprisingly, as OIRA head, Sunstein trumpeted executive orders that emphasized reducing the burdens on businesses "to promote flexibility and freedom of choice, and to make sure that the benefits justify the costs."[47] Competition is both described as the natural state of things, as well as a command—within a neoliberal framework, Milton Friedman's "freedom to choose" becomes instead an obligation to choose.[48]

The paternalist's obligation to install competitive conditions has an antecedent in neoclassical economic theory; the assumption of "competitive conditions" tautologically authorizes the superiority of market approaches in economics. From the neoclassical framework, one assumes competitive conditions to draw meaningful conclusions about behavior—if economics is an inquisition into the choices that rational actors make, they must be presumed to have choices before them in the first place. Competition is one of the primary social justifications for capitalism engendering the best possible outcomes; it presumes that rational individuals are presented with two substitutable products and make a choice between them, usually based on price. The presence of an "other" that can provide the same enjoyment for a lower cost ensures an efficient result. Formally, competitive conditions stem from the assumption of "perfect competition," popularized by Frank Knight in his *Risk, Uncertainty and Profit*. In order to model a "pure enterprise economy," the following axioms must be obeyed: individuals must have complete rationality (including knowing the consequences of their actions once taken), no transaction costs whatsoever, all elements (including commodities and labor) must be infinitely divisible, and there must be "*perfect competition.*"[49] Perfect competition entails the equal distribution of all information in a market (so no one can make decisions based on things information of which their competitors are unaware) and all actors are "price takers," meaning that no market participant is powerful enough to affect the price of the good in any direction.

For instance, insider trading is frowned upon for it breaks the presumption of equal information (since knowledge can be exploited for profit); the "price taker" requirement means that no one actor, such as Amazon or Wal-Mart, could alter the price of a good using monopoly power (by selling it at an unusually high price) or a monopsony power (by purchasing enough of it to put competitors out of business). Schlefler notes that publishing in the discipline of economics often depends upon relaxing some assumptions (it "is a good way to win a Nobel Prize"), and that information and competition imperfections may lead to practical solutions to real-world problems, such as unemployment and price-fixing.[50] However, these relaxations should be interpreted as supplementary to, not critical of, the assumptions of neoclassical economics writ large—individuals will remain rational, forward-thinking, utility-maximizing and so on. McDermott avers that virtually every major figure in neoclassical economics—Kenneth Arrow, Milton Friedman, Lionel Robbins, John Hicks, Paul Samuelson, Herbert Simon, Gerard Debreu, Joseph Schumpeter, John Maynard Keynes and Léon Walras—endorse "perfect competition" as a formal assumption.[51] According to Knight, although these assumptions are idealizations, they *"hold good more or less in reality."*[52]

The presence of the adjective "perfect" to modify "competition" gives a clue for how to interpret this neoclassical axiom. The Lacanian approach entails attention to the letter of the analysand's speech; not simply the "meaning" of what is said, but the "what" that is said in order to discover the analytic truth of the statement. Much like the (dis)appearance of "libertarian" in "libertarian paternalism," the presence of adjectives in the speech of the analysand indicates an affective resonance, a surplus that both attempts to fix the "true" meaning of the word modified and yet is not physically present, but symbolically so. Despite the *Oxford Dictionary of Economics* calling perfect competition an "outdated concept," it is outdated only insofar as it is an unnecessary adjective to term the assumptions necessary in order to derive meaningful conclusions.[53] As long as market participants have symmetric information and act as if they were price-takers, then the same outcome will occur whether perfection is presumed or not. That is, as long as market participants act as if there is perfect competition, the outcomes will be indistinguishable from perfectly competitive conditions. In Lacanian terms, the assumption of "perfect competition" in neoclassical theory partakes in phallic logic: it both organizes a given field and yet is physically absent when called upon to account for itself. Perfect competition is the assumption from which all neoclassical theory derives its behavioral postulates but becomes unnecessary once instantiated; it functions as a vanishing mediator to aver that perfect or not, markets still function perfectly. In other words, "perfect" need not modify competition because "competition" entails all of the specific behavioral postulates embedded within "perfect competition" already. Once again, neoclassical economics offers a retroactive causal loop even from within the theory itself—although "perfect competition" does not empirically exist, it must be posited in order to authorize the theory. Thereafter, "perfection" can be discarded since empirically verifiable competition meets the minimal conditions of "perfect competition" already.

This circumlocution is necessary to demonstrate how the behavioral-economic foundations of paternalism inherit these basic neoclassical assumptions about behavior. As economists Loewenstein and Ubel put it in an editorial for the *New York Times*, "Behavioral economics should complement, not substitute for, more substantive economic interventions [of] traditional economics."[54] Hence, both for neoclassical economic scholarship and for paternalists, any relaxation of assumptions is always ever supplementary to the basic axioms of market behavior. In the case of nudges, the assumption of perfect competition, metonymized into competitive conditions (without losing any of its postulates) is taken as fact, so when a choice architect discovers a lack of choice in a given setting, it is prima facie a "behavioral market failure." The solution is to then instantiate competitive market conditions through the introduction of nudges. Whereas Becker discerned the hidden incentive structures within a given social setting (and unsurprisingly discovered a stable equilibrium no matter what) by assuming that the "economic approach" is universally true, the paternalist's approach is to force the economic approach to become true through the introduction of a choice architecture. The nominal presence of competition is thus one rhetorical resource that authorizes incentive-based politics, for it becomes a mediating device in and of itself. The presence of an "other" allows for a consumer to make a better choice than they would have without one. In the best-case scenario, mediating desires through choices, a paternalist can reveal what preferences the utility-maximizing subject has had all along.

To summarize, libertarian paternalism owes a great deal to its foundations in neoclassical economics; by and large, its modifications of the standard model are supplementary to the basic assumptions that individuals are selfish, utility-maximizing individuals acting within market structures. The differences, whether they are defaults, anchoring points, and so on, are cosmetic, largely because they take on the same problem-space as neoclassical economics itself. One derives meaningful conclusions by assuming perfect competition and rational market behavior and then works backward to find the meaningful incentive that temporarily upsets the equilibrium point. When individuals fail to act in their own best interests and the interests of society as a whole, paternalists are empowered to make subtle course corrections without necessarily violating the freedom of an individual to make a choice. "Choice" functions symptomatically within the discourse of paternalism, for it is derived from a theoretical assumption of competitive conditions and introduces the presumption of efficiency into the delivery of social services. Paternalism authorizes nudges by appealing to "behavioral market failures" when rational economic choices cannot be made, resulting in the metastasis of market-style relations into social reality, outside of the framework of the political, and into the domain of the economic. The behavioral-economic approach to policymaking by and large accepts the meta-structuring capacity of the market and only aims to temporarily and unobtrusively act therein; any action more drastic than individual-level personal changes may in fact distort individual incentives for rational economic behavior. Rhetorically, nudges are defined in opposition to "command and control" policies, which are seen as both economically inefficient and a drain on individual freedom. Seen from this perspective, a nudge is not simply designed to engineer the best social outcome but meant to incentivize economically rational behavior.

Nudges as Political Neurosis

Straightforwardly, nudges "work" because they replicate a basic feature of life in the capitalist mode of production: We are offered a menu of choices, tacitly accept that some persuasion is at work, and perform as if the choice we make is both unencumbered and reflective of our underlying desires. And to their credit, nudge theorists use this insight as part of their rationale: corporations, organizations, and individuals nudge people at every possible turn, we exist in networks of signification that attempt to alter our behavior, from punch cards at automobile repair shops to team-building exercises at our workplaces. The sheer preponderance of commodity-adjacent interactions in our everyday lives authorizes choice architects to set up similar marketlike structures to provision political and social goods. But psychoanalytically, the structure of nudges has appeal because it replicates a basic condition of subject-formation, following Lacan's concepts of alienation and separation. These terms refer to the "forced choice" that subjects enter into when they partake in the symbolic order—we sacrifice a zone of our being in order to obtain intelligibility and enjoyment for, and from, the other. But nudges are also difficult to dislodge because they instantiate a regime of political neurosis, forcing individuals to address the question, "What does the Other want of me?" in each nudge interaction. Nudges are structured around an unspoken prohibition, or repression. By introducing the appearance of choice in a setting (like signing up for life insurance, health savings plans, the school your child attends), they interdict on the universal political good that could be provisioned. Choosing subjects are addressed solely as individuals (and not collectivities, communities, polities, or classes) and forced to discern what is being asked of them, without ever being certain that this choice architecture is designed to channel their desires, or the desires of its creator. Political outcomes like health care, education, or a habitable environment cease to be the responsibility of states to deliver to their subjects but the responsibility of individuals to desire properly. In what follows, I advance a psychoanalytic critique of nudges, first by discussing what Lacan calls the "forced choice" (or *vel* of alienation) and the subject's subsequent separation from their desire. Next, I argue that we should think of nudges as an engine for organizing political neurosis, a way of repressing the desire for universal public goods and locking subjects into questioning their own desires and whether they are enjoying properly. My invocation of neurosis describes not simply a clinical condition but a political one—it functions as a structure of discourse, not a diagnosis of an individual, and is designed to draw attention to the individualization of outcomes and the attribution of unconscious desires by those in power to those outside of it.

For Lacan, what one calls a subject is never given in advance but is rather a logical space implied by the cut that the symbolic order introduces into being; he employs the term "alienation" to describe a part of this process of subjectification. Alienation constitutes a basic human experience at multiple levels: the ontological, the symbolic, and the political. Analogously, Marx identified that in a system of privately held wealth, human beings are alienated from the product of their labor and control over the labor process; as a result, human beings are estranged from their "species being" (they are disconnected from something both human and more-than-human, or connected to the totality of the universe), as well as from each other.[55] These levels, in some form, are mirrored in Lacan's approach. Consider any of the many origin stories that psychoanalysis tells of the ontogenesis of the human subject, that when babies are born, they enter into a system of meaning that over-codes their relation to the "real" world—one may have an infinite desire to suckle or eat but is cut off by a "no" (of the mother, of the father, or of culture itself).

Lacan employs a both/and approach: The literal, biological level marks a "real lack" that is then compensated for by a signifying regime, or the introduction of "lack" at a conceptual level. What Lacan calls a "real lack" is akin to the splits between masculine and feminine *jouissance* developed in chapter 4: there is no "human as such," every being is marked by a real difference, not just from one another but from the world as a whole.[56] To be sexed is to bear witness to an ontological antagonism with the world. Even if it is possible to pro-create, it is impossible to re-create (oneself) in an infinite play of repetition.[57] One's very being testifies to one's difference with reality itself in its infinite diversity, no human is either autogenic or autochthonous. The facticity of sex is not to be read in a complementarian manner, that "male" and "female" are mutually incomplete and must couple in order to find a unity—for Lacan, it is the precise opposite.[58] Desire, Lacan contends, must be articulated, or learned, via the symbolic order. "Sexuality" is the name of what emerges in this gap; it "is established in the field of the subject by a way that is that of lack."[59] As Žižek reiterates, we are not born with an innate understanding of what to desire; it must be taught. This is the role of fantasy.[60]

To be alienated, then, is to encounter the second lack, that of the signifying order. Laurent writes that alienation represents "the fact that the subject, having no identity, has to identify with something"; alienation functions as the name for a compensatory action by the speaking being to ascertain some certainty once introduced into a regime of presences and absences.[61] Alienation is what Lacan calls a "forced choice," or the obligation to enter into the field of language. When one becomes a "speaking being," one must forgo an imagined oneness with the world (which was already fictive, in Lacan's estimation) and make this "forced choice" into the symbolic order. As Fink writes, "*Alienation represents the instituting of the symbolic order—which must be realized anew for each new subject— and the subject's assignation of a place therein.*"[62] Lacan uses the mugger's classic line "your money or your life!," which indicates that this choice is always a false one. If one clings too hard to one's money, one loses one's life (and subsequently one's money).[63] If one clings to life and loses one's money, one loses what is worth living for.[64] Lacan contends that this is not simply true in lethal matters but a result of being confronted by the signifying order itself, which presents itself as an enigma to the subject.[65]

Nudges claim to offer a binary choice, despite this being an obvious obfuscation of the matter. In a nudge, the field is titled toward the policymaker's preferred goal, so the binary choice masks a more fundamental lack of choice. Lacan's concept of the signifier is more radical than a simple either-or, for it is elementally nonidentical; it has no essence on its own but takes on an essence as a result of its circulation in an economy of presences and absences. When Lacan uses the formulation, "the signifier is that which represents a subject for another signifier," he is gesturing at this fundamental nonidentity.[66] Any signifier emerges out of the withdrawal of its own absence, it signifies difference in itself (regardless of what it signifies at a symbolic level). As Žižek puts it, "'Differentiality' designates a more precise relationship: in it, the opposite of one term, of its *presence*, is not immediately the other term but the *absence* of the first term, the *void* at the place of its inscription."[67] A signifier *is not* its void: that is its first "presence." It is only against this backdrop that the possibility for play emerges, for a signifier to mean something other than itself. Misunderstanding, subterfuge, irony, and rhetoric emerge as compensatory actions from within the gap of nonidentity. For the choice architect, A = B (an unhealthy choice really is a desire for something else, the object chosen can be replaced with no "cost" to the subject). For the psychoanalyst, A = not-A: If a choice is anything, it is not (reducible to) itself.[68] The sign is internally split—a signifier and a signified, a relation of nonidentity, which means that representation can never be as fixed as either the libertarian fantasizes or the paternalist believes they can modify.

What Lacan calls "separation" occurs at this moment, a recognition by the subject that the Other possesses a lack. Fink writes that separation begins "from a barred Other, that is, a parent who is him or herself divided," and that the subject attempts to address the gap, the interval, that answers their unarticulated desire.[69] The symbolic order's postulate of nonidentity mentioned above suggests that to offer a choice is to ask the question of desire, not simply about what I want but what the Other wants (of me). "Man learns to desire *as an other*," Fink writes, "as if he were some other person."[70] For the nudge, this means acting as if one is a "rational economic subject," in lieu of—separated from—one's own idiosyncratic, inexpressible desires. The nudge's obligation to choose represents the alienation and separation that forces the question of meaning onto the subject. As Lacan writes, "The subject as such is uncertain because he is divided by the effects of language. . . . He will simply find his desire more divided, pulverized in the circumscribable metonymy of speech."[71]

The presence of a (signifying) nudge is the introduction of a choice: does it mean this, or that? Lacan puts the problem plainly: *"He is saying this to me, but what does he want?"*[72] Freud describes this possibility within language with an old Jewish joke, the punchline of which is "you say you're going to Cracow, you want me to believe you're going to Lemberg. But I know that in fact you're going to Cracow. So why are you lying to me?"[73] The purpose of the joke is not to make a person or institution the butt of the joke but rather "the certainty of our knowledge itself, one of our speculative possessions."[74]

In a nudge, the opacity of knowledge on the side of the Other leaves the individual chooser uncertain. Is the "default setting" what the Other wants of me, or am I being asked to click a different option in the dialog box? Is the presence of fresh fruit meant to direct my eye elsewhere? Is the encouragement to sign up for a retirement plan what my employer *really* wants of me? These choices, in the long run, are ultimately false, and why critiques of nudges that complain about a loss of individual choice can only go so far. It is not that individuals are unfree because their choices are constrained, individuals are unfree because they are forced to choose and are thus barred from communion with "the thing itself." (This is especially true with nudges that eschew the pretense of structuring a complex choice, or even eschew visibility altogether. Hill writes that "some nudges may be invisible," or "covert," rendering both the experience of a nudge and any retrospective accountability impossible to judge.[75] The form of the mediating object—not just the content—stands in the way and diverts a subject into a choice that by its very design is a false one. The theoretical postulation of competitive conditions has a knock-on effect, for it breaks the back of a universal good and postulates an even better outcome—an "efficient" one. Each major political issue addressed by nudges is organized around the prohibition on a universal good: decommodified health care, adequate action to address climate change, universal public education. In a market society, the only desire one cannot express is a nonmarket desire.

Alienation and separation describe a structural process of subject-formation, a symbolic exchange through which speaking beings go. Nudges, however, represent an intensification of this process, such that a neurotic structure results. There is, of course, no such thing as a "typical" subject; each of us partake in various differential structures in various ratios. Neurosis, perversion, and psychosis represent the three most common structures for a Lacanian intervention, with neurosis being the most prevalent. As with a clinical diagnosis, one should think of neurosis as a question that addresses a genuine problem, which besets the unconscious of the subject.[76] Neurosis is characterized by "a certain degree of uncertainty about what it is that turns one on, [and] considerable difficulty pursuing it even when one does know."[77] The classic joke, "The food here is terrible—and in such small portions!" exemplifies the neurotic's approach, wherein one is beset by the question of how to enjoy properly; neurotics fail to enjoy even as they are enjoying because they are unsure of how this enjoyment will be registered by the Other. Lacan, following Freud, argues that repression is the source of neurotic behavior, that neurotics have an encounter that is not foreclosed, or rejected outright, but accepted (however minimally) around which they organize their unconscious.[78] Lacan, testifying to the prevalence of neurosis, contends that repression of a binary signifier is the necessary condition for the formation of the unconscious itself. When we enter into the symbolic order, we sacrifice a unity, and some aspect of us is carved out: "In neurosis, the mechanism of repression implies the loss of the object. Total satisfaction becomes impossible because the object that could satisfy the drive has been lost."[79] Each of us carries this neurotic tendency and manage it to varying degrees; a developed neurosis entails organizing one's own life circling this impossibility, never knowing for certain whether one's enjoyment is truly one's own.

Lacan describes the "drama of the neurotic" as one made of an already-existing otherness; the neurotic "sees appearing beside himself a figure. . . . It is not really himself: he feels excluded, outside of his own experience, he cannot assume its particularities, he feels discordant with his own existence."[80] This lack of self-identity stems from the repression of a binary signifier, which Fink describes as a signifier that transforms desire into signifiers.[81] This signifier, which Lacan calls the "Name-of-the-Father" (also phonetically translatable to "No-of-the-Father") has two important features for our purposes. First, the Name-of-the-Father instantiates a dialectic of desire into the subject: it is the signifier that cuts into pure being and inaugurates, or "means," a field of meaning. The withdrawal of the Void, in Žižek's parlance, to mark a field as meaningful is one way to think of this signifier's function. Second, this signifier always functions retroactively: the "name" or "no" is always substantialized in the subject's unconscious *après-coup*, as that which quilted the field of meaning.[82] This retroaction entails that the neurotic (nudged) subject bends their desires backward toward the Name-of-the-Father; as Fink writes, "Nothing is innocent," all speech "implies a subject position with respect to the Other."[83] This signifier "freezes" the subject into all signifiers bearing witness thereto—in common conversation, the conversational phrase "You know what that reminds me of?" is a neurotic gesture, bending each instance of the new back to the neurotic's chosen signifier.

Neurotic behavior can be further characterized as a failure to negotiate the discordance between the desire of the Other and the demand of the Other. Lacan writes that the neurotic "identifies the Other's lack with the Other's demand" and rewrites the subject's fundamental fantasy ($\$\Diamond a$) as $\$\Diamond D$, or the subject set in motion to, and by, the Other's demand.[84] Put straightforwardly, to approach the desire of the Other is to presume a minimal distance, an admission of the lack in the Other (described above as the process of separation). The neurotic subject attempts to satisfy the desire of the Other by attempting to satisfy their demands—to fastidiously follow rules in school, or the speed limit to avoid punishment, to give to a romantic partner exactly what they say they want is the neurotic's strategy—not for enjoying but for guarding against the absence of enjoyment. By interpreting all enigmatic signification from the Other as an explicit statement of demand, the neurotic can never truly transgress or be held responsible for "not getting it," thus maintaining their position for the Other. Lacan describes the neurotic's journey thusly: "In his desiring function, the subject elects a substitute. This is the crux of neurosis. Consider what actually happens at the end of the obsessive's complicated maneuvers—he is not the one who enjoys."[85] The same process occurs by choice architects in nudge situations: although nudge theorists attempt accessing the subject's unconscious desires (albeit clumsily) by presuming that individuals are not self-present or fully capable of satisfying themselves with their choices, nudge theorists miss the mark entirely precisely because they lock subjects into choice architectures with "competitive conditions," meaning they will only ever be locked into binary, marketlike choices. This forces nudged subjects to only ever address the signifiers of demand rather than approach their unarticulated desires. "Am I being asked to choose this charter school, or that public school?" is not a question that adequately approaches desire, except for the desire of the choice architect themselves (who desire the efficient, decided-in-advance outcome).

The neurotic subject is barred from the enjoyment that would truly satisfy them and orbits a series of substitute enjoyments (what Lacan reiterates is a metonymy); they "take a pathway about which we can say that it consists in *devoting himself to satisfying*—as much as he can here—all of the other's demands, even though he knows that those demands constitute a perpetual object to his own desire. in other words, in his devotion to the other, he blinds himself to his own lack of satisfaction."[86] Nudges instantiate this enigmatic structure upon subjects in specific discursive settings, wherever choice architects hold sway; we are neuroticized by nudge theory and its meaningful signifiers and forced to ask questions about the other's demands and unable to access desires outside of this framework. De Kesel writes, "The obsessional idea that it is he, rather than the Other, who falls short is a way of avoiding the fact that it is in the first place the Other who is marked by lack."[87] The imposition of choice forces subjects to be neurotic, barred from accessing the unpleasant truths inaccessible to both them and the choice architects that refuse them something more meaningful. McGowan's characterization of capitalism as inducing a neurotic relation, albeit for different reasons than theorists like Karen Horney and Herbert Marcuse, is apropos here: the neurotic clings "to the Other's demand rather than confront the abyss of its own subjectivity."[88] I part ways with McGowan's assessment of the subject's abyssal form by locating the displaced lack elsewhere, upward. Rather than interdicting on what is unspeakable in the subject, nudges repress the potential for the construction and provision of universal public goods—by introducing competitive conditions, the fiction of choice, presuming an irrationality in subjects who contravene neoclassical assumptions, nudge theory disavows the very possibility that things like health care, education, a habitable environment, and so on, are deliverable by political actors at all.

Take, for instance the dozens of incentives and nudges in the Affordable Care Act's provisions.[89] At its heart, the ACA aimed to incentivize health insurance companies to provide higher-quality, lower-cost care to American citizens through a vast array of agencies, programs, organizations, rewards, penalties, regulations, and exchanges. Instead of directly guaranteeing care to Americans, the bill used the mediating agency of the incentive (largely monetary, occasionally regulatory) to induce health insurance companies to offer health insurance plans; in areas of what Thaler and Sunstein would call behavioral market failure, the federal government promoted health insurance exchanges designed to stimulate rational action by for-profit insurance companies. "Choice" once again resides symptomatically in the bill's text; the section that deals with these exchanges is titled "Consumer Choices and Insurance Competition through Health Benefit Exchanges."[90] On the coercive end of the incentive spectrum, the bill also contained a highly contentious "individual mandate" that required Americans to purchase some form of health insurance, lest they be hit with a $695 maximum fine.[91] Whether penalty or reward, nudges were built into the

ACA as the only way to alter individual behaviors toward the goal that its crafters and implementers set out to achieve. A historical irony deserves note: although the "individual mandate" penalty was repealed (and in 2020 its constitutionality was challenged in the Supreme Court) and the ACA's Medicare expansion has been incompletely implemented, some of the most durable parts of the ACA, which have not yet been ruled unconstitutional by the Supreme Court or legislatively repealed, are classically regulatory. For instance, the law eliminates lifetime caps on certain forms of coverage, prevents insurers from dropping their customers if they become ill, prevents gender discrimination in premium rates, and prohibits insurers from denying health insurance to people with preexisting conditions.

The bill's "nudges," rather, included provisions for better food nutrition labels and smoking cessation programs included in health insurance plans. For instance, the "HealthQuest Rewards Program" at the University of Kansas incentivizes employees to drink water, lose weight, quit smoking, and get regular checkups with the reward of a reduction in monthly premiums.[92] For certain workers, handing over sensitive health information and agreeing to corporate surveillance is worth a $480 reduction in one's yearly premiums, but for employees at other institutions, the injunction to be surveilled for one's health was accompanied by a penalty if one did not partake. According to Katie Endicott, a West Virginia public school teacher, her district forced her to download an app, called Go365, which would track her steps, and if she did not earn enough "points," she would be penalized $500 at the end of the year: "People felt that was very invasive, to have to download that app and to be forced into turning over sensitive information."[93]

Conclusion: The Return of the Repressed

When choosing our health-care plans, whether to eat fresh fruit, or to become an organ donor, choosers are only ever situated at the level of demand—what is demanded of them by the choice architects in positions of power, largely through the introduction of marketlike spaces where we are "free to choose" but always unconsciously aware that we are being subtly persuaded to choose the efficient outcome. In the capitalist mode of production, we can only ever address the other in terms of supply and demand, not in terms of supply and desire. In this chapter I have offered, in a Lacanian vein, how the neurotic's question organizes the structure of nudges and how this question makes nudges "work." I have argued that the structure of the nudge neuroticizes subjects, forcing their choices to connect to the desire of the policymaker, their preferred end, not the subject's own unspeakable, idiosyncratic desire. Yet neurosis is organized by a repressed element, that of the binary signifier, and it is necessary to address what precisely is repressed here. Albeit not by choice, what is fundamentally repressed in this nudge structure is the aforementioned provision of actual universal public goods in the political system. Because the structure of the incentive functions as a mediating device, that which depends on a symbolic curve around desire, no public good can be promised and delivered therein, lest the system set up a "perverse incentive" or enjoyment without payment. As De Kesel puts it, "Obsessional neurosis . . . protects one against an *excess* of pleasure coming from the 'thing.'"[94] This neurotic structure guards against the potential for free riders, or those who unthinkingly make the inefficient choice; instead of guaranteeing health care, nudges guarantee that people are forced to make individual decisions that may ensure that their health is an eventual outcome. To play the role of the fool momentarily, to nudge individuals, forcing them to make better choices within market structures inside of a cafeteria, means one never is forced to address underlying causes of unhealthiness in what Marx called the "hidden abode" of production. Nudge theory presumes that since one could never bar, ban, or regulate an industry better than it can itself, one can never touch the processes that precede the moment of consumer choice.

Thus, in the next chapter, I address why, in crucial scenarios, nudges *do not work*—the repressed returns. The COVID-19 pandemic, beginning in early 2020, provided a test case for nudge theory and incentive-driven statecraft writ large; the universality of a deadly pandemic asked serious questions about the capitalist mode of production's capacity for organizing behavior differently, in both mitigation strategies, treatment strategies, as well as the strategies to "get back to work." Nudges failed precisely because of a moment of symbolic exhaustion and a tacit admission of impotence by this political form.

Chapter 6

Nudging Ourselves to Death

The previous chapter concluded with a provocation: nudges, as practiced by governments, are both a formal interdiction on the provision of universal public goods (through the postulate of "competitive conditions" and presuming a "behavioral market failure" exists when individuals choose an outcome that contravenes the assumptions of neoclassical economic theory), as well as a profound figure of symbolic exhaustion. This prohibition on the provision of universal public goods is part of the charm of nudges writ large—one must only ever incentivize proper behavior to obtain a good. (The command to work, the elementary injunction of the capitalist mode of production, is predicated on this very "incentive": one has no right to shelter, food, education, or health; one must work for these ends.) A state must never provide public goods on their own, for such a practice leads to the dreaded "perverse incentive," in which individuals enjoy without payment (also known as the "free rider" problem).[1] Such an insight aligns with the psychoanalytic conceptualization of desire. Lacan, in his eleventh seminar, introduces a distinction between the subject's "aim" and their "goal."[2] The nature of desire is such that aiming directly at an object and attaining it is impossible—it must go through some swerve or *clinamen* in order to achieve satisfaction and, indeed, enjoyment depends on the circulation around one's satisfaction rather than obtaining it directly. As Laurent writes, "In psychoanalysis you cannot grab hold of an object. You can, however, aim at it. Using signifiers, you have to target that point. You cannot hit it directly."[3]

Yet this psychoanalytic reminder of the unstable relation between signifier and signified, made trickier by the nonrelation between desire and demand, is not an alibi for the economic approach but its conscience, its internal limit. Social policy in the capitalist mode of production must always be mediated through the money commodity; any short-circuit that offers a glimpse of a noncommodity interaction is seen as dangerous or potentially iniquitous. (McCloskey pointing to the "ironies of social engineering" and economics' function as a discipline is to warn the public away from such mistakes.[4]) Incentives derail desire precisely because they fall prey to the assumption that they are a more direct medium of representing an economic, social, or political desire and not a network of signifiers on their own with their own pathways organized around the desire of economists and policymakers. Political neurosis is the result. Individual choosers—always addressed as individuals—are caught in a deadlock of demand, contoured to choose between options that are organized around that repressed signifier and that states in the capitalist mode of production cannot directly provision goods without being mediated through some marketlike interaction. Yet, as the Freudian phrase reminds us, the repressed returns—albeit in unexpected ways.

This chapter evaluates the sites wherein incentives approach their limits, where this repressed signifier returns. Thus far, this work has argued for the prevalence and the power of incentives, not simply in their effects but in their inescapability. Because incentives are designed to retroactively reveal the underlying economic preferences of individuals addressed by them, they can never truly fail; they claim to reside in the domain of suasion and not coercion. With careful attention to two sites adjacent to the COVID-19 pandemic, this chapter makes the opposite argument: beneath the regime of incentives resides the threat of coercion, executed through privation. In particular, the language of "incentive" was deployed as a rhetorical strategy to entice individuals back into the labor force and was tied directly to a causal mechanism: the ending of supplemental federal unemployment benefits in September 2021. Alongside the quotidian lament, "No one wants to work anymore," economists, business owners, and policymakers invoked monetary deprivation as the primary incentive to return the labor market to "normal." Whereas in other settings, "incentive" is a token of symbolic exchange, a signifier that fills a gap by revealing a preference (such as when Gary Becker argues that racist business owners have a "taste for discrimination," such that they are willing to underpay Black workers). The symptomatic utterance of "incentive" here reveals that labor discipline, via the removal of even minuscule benefits to working people, is the symptom's true addressee. The unemployment policy change failed at the professed aim of stimulating the labor market, but that was not its goal; being able to discern between these two is the key task of a psychoanalytically engaged politics.

Simultaneously, the COVID-19 pandemic, which began for the United States in early 2020, provided a natural experiment for incentives and nudges to contour social behavior toward a socially beneficial direction; cities enacted masking and distancing policies, states undertook public information campaigns, and the federal government accelerated a vaccine development program to mitigate the impact of the virus as soon as possible.[5] Yet the widespread refusal of individuals to protect not only others but themselves by taking certain behavioral modifications appeared to be tailor-made proof of a "behavioral market failure," with nearly a half million deaths in the United States occurring after vaccines became widely available in early 2021 (after many explicit safety provisions were eliminated or attenuated).[6] Nudges, in the form of voluntary requests to wear masks, wash hands, and avoid contact with others, failed to fill the gap entirely and were instead met with derision, resistance, and dismissal (alongside, to be clear, acquiescence by much of the American public). Meanwhile, "incentives" to get a vaccination, including cash rewards, failed to achieve their purpose, while coercion by employers and governments was revealed to be far more effective at increasing the vaccination rate. Public nudges surrounding the COVID-19 pandemic were victimized by the success of incentive rhetoric writ large; with a focus on individual decisions, individual cost-benefit assessment, and an insistence on low-cost measures meant that nudges could be ignored without severe penalty. Nudge theorists in the United Kingdom developed a phrase for it, "nudge fatigue," which we may characterize as the "decline of symbolic efficiency," understood by Dean as when "circulation has eclipsed meaning."[7] Nudges, perhaps more than any other signifying regime in the contemporary moment, epitomize the decline of symbolic efficiency: this is not because individuals themselves no longer "believe" in the efficacy of the Symbolic order but because the Symbolic order fails to believe in itself. Nudges only emerge when policymakers admit that political priorities can no longer be represented from a political will and toward a political end. With a nudge, failure is always an option, especially in a pandemic that claimed millions of lives worldwide. By examining how incentives and nudges failed to achieve their announced ends in these key sites, we can reveal the limits of discourse as a whole and what it portends for future signifying regimes.

Deprivation as Incentive:
Ending Supplemental Unemployment Benefits

The United States government implemented a series of measures to mitigate the scope of the social crisis brought on by the pandemic, beginning in 2020 with the Families First Coronavirus Response Act, followed by the Coronavirus Aid, Relief, and Economic Security Act (otherwise known as the CARES Act), and the American Rescue Plan Act. The scope and sheer size of these bills were enormous, dwarfing even the "bailout" bills and recovery acts surrounding the 2008 financial crisis; sections of each bill increased unemployment benefits and expanded eligibility for those displaced by the pandemic.[8] The CARES Act introduced supplemental benefits totaling $600 per week for unemployed workers until July 2020, and the American Rescue Plan Act reduced the amount from $600 to $300 (with an added $100 to be added from state budgets) and extended the relief until September 6, 2021. On that date, the remaining federal supplemental unemployment insurance benefits ended, with roughly eight million workers removed from the rolls. *Bloomberg News* greeted the expiration of the benefits by writing, "Economists and companies expected a wave of interest from workers as the financial lifeline was pulled away, hoping it would provide the incentive to get back into the workplace."[9] The language of the incentive—in news coverage, by business leaders, and by political actors—acted as the vehicle to express a desire to return to "normal" in the labor market. According to received theory (as elucidated in chapter 2), incentives—especially monetary incentives—exert causal power upon individuals, so the opposite, hydraulically, ought to be true. Individuals should "rationally" choose to return to work once benefits dip below their previous wage.

Even prior to the reduction in benefits, in July 2020, Representative Greg Steube of Florida sent a letter to then-president Donald Trump to end the $600/week unemployment benefits, writing that the program would "create disincentives for returning to work."[10] In June 2021, Representative James Meijer of Michigan introduced a bill that aimed to "incentivize Americans to return to work," since the Biden administration's benefits program (which began under the Trump administration) was too "lucrative" and would "incentivize Americans to stay at home."[11] Representative Chip Roy of Texas also introduced a bill that, unlike Meijer's bill that provided "incentive payments" for workers who did take jobs, ended the $300 supplemental benefits entirely because, in his words, they "incentivize Americans not to return to work."[12] During an interview with Fox News, Ohio Senator Rob Portman insisted that the unemployment benefits create "a disincentive to work," pointing to "small businesses and from larger and mid-size businesses and from nonprofits."[13] Also on Fox News, Jon Taffer, host of the CNBC show *Bar Rescue*, likened those receiving unemployment benefits to dogs, saying "they only feed a military dog at night because a hungry dog is an obedient dog . . . Well if we're not causing people to be hungry to work, then we're providing them with all the meals they need sitting at home."[14]

This acute moment offers a test case for the logic of the incentive: Does the incentive of privation exert causal power? The policy's results, even by the standards of the business press, were resoundingly mixed. Even prior to the official lapse of the $300 per week supplemental benefits in mid-2021, after more than half of US states ended their programs early, Morgan Stanley analysts suggested that there was "mixed evidence" that the unemployment situation was any better in the states that refused federal money.[15] Indeed.com reported that job searches in states that ended benefits early did not increase, while UKG, a payroll firm, revealed that states that ended benefits early had, ironically, slower growth in shifts than states that maintained them.[16] Below, I evaluate why the logic of the incentive "sticks around," as libidinal quotient, despite the obviousness of its inadequacy, but for now, it is worth considering, even as back-of-the-envelope calculations, who was concretely affected by these policy changes. According to the Bureau of Labor Statistics, labor force participation remained steady at 61.7 percent from July to October of 2021, then rose to 61.9 percent starting in November; the unemployment rate dropped from 5.2 percent to 4.2 in the same time period, indicating roughly 1.8 million people returned to the workforce in that time.[17] That is, after the COVID-19 pandemic spiked the unemployment rate at around 15 percent nationwide, the rate returned to roughly the same level (around 4 percent) prior to the pandemic; the downward slope of the unemployment rate can be interpreted less as a success of the policy change and more what economists would call a "secular" change, with some form of "normality" returning to the labor market. Politicians, journalists, and media figures clamoring for the end to supplemental unemployment benefits, repeating the phrase "no one wants to work anymore," aimed to affect 0.2 percent of the country's working-age population. According to the US Small Business Administration, there are roughly 5.5 million "small businesses" that employ at least one other person, so even if every single remaining unemployed worker in the country took a job at a "small business" (and not at large firms, which currently employ over half of the current workers in the United States), each business would have gained fewer than two workers in total.[18]

The claim that unemployment benefits remove the "incentive to work" has been an arrow in the rhetorical quiver of conservatives for as long as the benefits have existed but arise in acute moments not because of their dubious truth value but because they provide a causal explanation for why the world does not appear to spontaneously adhere to the principles of economic theory. As Chang puts it, "Conservatives have often criticized [unemployment insurance] for a moral hazard problem that creates a work disincentive and perpetuates long-term unemployment."[19] The fact that these benefits were designed to be temporary (lasting less than a year for even the largest amount) and supplementary rendered the vociferousness of the opposition more acute—not only do all unemployment benefits disincentivize hard work, but these benefits represented, in Lacanian terms, surplus enjoyment, more generous than generous, and thus more threatening to the social order. Ironically, right-wing figures were right on the details of the policy, if not on the merits: full-time workers who earned the federal minimum wage actually did receive more from the supplemental unemployment benefits than they would have from a minimum wage job. It cannot be overstated how paltry the typical benefits for unemployed people are: the New York Times reported that on average, unemployment benefits cover only 38 percent of a worker's salary, but with the supplemental $600, the average worker is made whole.[20] According to the Missouri Department of Labor, a laid-off full-time minimum wage worker in the state would earn around $214 per week in unemployment benefits.[21] With the supplemental $600 per week, an unemployed worker in Missouri would (temporarily) earn the equivalent of $38,000 per year; with the $300 supplemental benefit, they would earn roughly $24,000 per year, or less than $12 per hour.[22] Those arguing for an end to the supplemental benefits demanded, by presuming that workers are solely motivated by take-home pay, that workers ought to return to jobs that recompense them for less than $12 per hour. Thus the statement "no one wants to work anymore" suppresses a supplementary clause: "for the wages that the capitalist class offers."

The business press expressed both befuddlement and resolution about the causal power of incentives. The Economist, labeled by Marx as "the European organ of the aristocracy of finance," addressed the conundrum head-on: why did the end of the supplemental unemployment benefits fail to achieve their goal? As the *Economist* put it, "Economic theory says that UI deters jobseeking—a prediction supported, at least to some degree, by most studies of its effects before 2020. Yet this relationship has not been apparent during the pandemic."[23] The article points to the United States' lack of guaranteed health care as a reason why workers rationally ought to return to the workforce, and that since wages had not demonstrably soared, the only reasonable explanation was a "lack of jobs, not an unwillingness to work." The *Economist* also found that any differences in job seeking were negligible between states that ended their benefits early and found instead that those in states with Republican governors had greater difficulty in paying bills, and lower spending levels.[24] The *Wall Street Journal*, by contrast, constructed a funhouse mirror version of the *Economist*'s perplexity, arguing: "There also continue to be strong government-made disincentives to work even in GOP-leaning states, including free health care, an eviction moratorium and the child tax credit that amounts to a guaranteed monthly income."[25] Even if the policy change was not as effective as originally intended, more hardship can be dealt to working people to induce a behavioral change. (Ironically, by having an explicit class allegiance, the *Economist* is more honest than even the bourgeoisie's ideologists—pointing out when economic theory is wrong spurs a search for a solution, not simply to point at the model and fulminate.) For the *Wall Street Journal*'s editorial board, coercion represents a legitimate incentive for policymakers to use; the only problem with the American workforce is that it is insufficiently incentivized to accept less.

Yet if incentives are the primary force for human motivation, then the *Journal*'s recommendations appear as reasonable and is testament to the seductiveness of the framework, if even a global social and economic crisis reinforces, rather than undercuts, its explanatory power. The business press follows the lead of the prophets of incentives: mainstream economists, who also had recourse only to incentives to explain (away) this epistemological conundrum. Economists at some of the nation's leading programs (MIT, Yale, Chicago, Harvard, Berkeley, etc.) were surveyed by the University of Chicago's Initiative on Global Markets on the issue of unemployment benefits; 72 percent agreed or strongly agreed with the following statement: "Employment growth is currently constrained more by firms' lack of interest in hiring than people's willingness to work at prevailing wages." Yet in a follow-up question, 80 percent of the same group agreed that states should reduce supplemental unemployment benefits

172 | Works like a Charm

to below the worker's previous wage rate to incentivize them to return to work.[26] Although the surveyed experts nearly uniformly suggest that capital, not labor, bears greater responsibility for the unemployment rate, the only solution thereto is to deprive labor of unemployment benefits to "balance incentives."

The "great resignation," the cries of "no one wants to work anymore," and that the "government creates disincentives to work" all confront the conundrum of an absent cause—this cause is not merely death on a massive scale but the absent cause of complexity. David Robinson, a professor of finance at Duke University, suggests that "sharp, easy" answers are not forthcoming: "Yes, removing benefits sharpens the incentive to find work immediately, but it does little to smooth over the complexity of child care issues. It doesn't make used cars cheaper so that people can get a second set of wheels to get to work."[27] Absent a robust explanation for why things did not go "back to normal," incentives to work (or lack thereof) symbolically filled the gap. When incentives are the primary way of narrating human activity, they crowd out alternative explanations and force all participants into a language game that economists are always capable of winning. "Incentives" to work (or not) stick out, and stick around, in the rhetorical repertoire of political figures and policymakers because they are a natural outgrowth of a fundamentally economic way of viewing human life.

Yet in this case, the libidinal investment in incentives appears to be a dead end—the proclamations in the future tense failed to materialize a statistically significant change in the unemployment rate. Further, the amount of dollars at issue, and the amount of people who would have been affected by these policy changes, represented a drop in the bucket and nowhere near the size of the relief bills as a whole or the American working population. So in this specific case, the rhetoric of incentives appears to fail, even on its own terms. Yet the failure is more analytically propitious than its success because it reminds us of the basic Lacanian insight that communication is always indirect, addressed to both a concrete other and a "big Other."[28] The gap in explanatory power testifies to speech's power to supplement an inconsistent reality—in this case, the persistence of "incentives" in speech is less of a reminder of what latently motivates all human beings but a coercive reminder that working people are beholden to class struggle. If the intended effect was to increase the labor supply in the United States, it was relatively unsuccessful. If, instead, the intended effect was to proclaim the widespread agreement that labor must be disciplined to accept less, then the policy was a success. The "absent third," or material support of the policy's unarticulated desire, is stationed, sentrylike, outside of the labor-capital relation to remind workers that it could always be worse. The downward-facing, individualizing nature of all incentive rhetoric also prevents an alternative case—the government refuses to "incentivize" businesses to pay their workers more, its role as mediator only functions in one direction.

Lacan describes the distance between the "aim" and the "goal" of a subject as evidence of the partiality of drive; sexuality is polymorphous and perverse, so all acts only ever incidentally reach their intended target. Consider that even for sexual reproduction, a temporal gap of around nine months exists between the act and (the goal of) reproduction. Lacan writes, "No drive represents . . . the totality of the *Sexualstrebung*, of the sexual tendency, as it might be conceived of as making present . . . the function of *Fortpflanzung*, of reproduction."[29] What emerges between the sexual drive and its fulfillment is what we call sexuality. Between these two moments, secondarily, emerges signification, an entry point wherein language attempts to bond the two together—prior to paternity tests, for instance, "fatherhood" was an imaginary relation, subsequently assigned to the order of the signifier for the purposes of patrilineality. As mentioned, the psychoanalytic impossibility of fully equating "aim" and "goal" closely mirrors that of neoclassical economics: one cannot aim directly at a desired object and achieve it without inducing the possibility of "perverse incentives," "free riders," or "moral hazard." The interceding object—typically the money commodity—must exist to account for this gravitational curve, thereby ensuring that the goal remains shrouded behind layers of desire.

Lacan's point is far more penetrative than this, for he insists that something fundamentally changes when language enters the scene. The presence of the signifier is what swerves desire from its aim, which then becomes the point of investment itself. As he puts it, "What the drive integrates at the outset in its very existence is a dialectic of the bow, I would even say of archery."[30] Lacan illustrates this point by playing off two senses of the term "*but*" in French, translatable as both "aim" and "goal": "In archery, the *goal* is not the *but* either, it is not the bird you shoot, it is having scored a hit and thereby attained your *but*. If the drive may be satisfied without attaining what, from the point of view of a biological totalization of function, would be the satisfaction of its end of reproduction, it is because it is a partial drive, and its aim is simply this return into circuit."[31] In archery as in other sporting events, there is no way to aim at "the score" directly: one must aim at "the bird" and achieve satisfaction thereby. Lacan's point is that the satisfaction behind the object is thus not "the real thing" either—it is not copulation, or bodily satisfaction (or even the bird), but the signifier, the trophy, or the target, that retroactively names the act of achievement.[32] The real impossibility of achieving one's goal (of copulation, of satisfaction, of wholeness) introduces the need for signification to step in to fill this gap, yet the introduction of signification inevitably distorts even this furtive attempt. Castoriadis, synthesizing some Freudian insights, calls this "the *domination of representational pleasure over organ pleasure.*"[33]

For Lacan, drive is fundamentally partitioned by the signifier (the order of the Other); this turns the impossibility of closure (or communion) into an engine for desire, or what he calls the "metonymic remainder."[34] We can mobilize this insight when interpreting the persistence of "incentives" surrounding unemployment and bring it closer to the neurotic's circuit of desire: an aim is satisfied precisely to avoid an unspoken, unspeakable goal. In this case, "incentive" intercedes in public discourse on employment to guard against what cannot be countenanced in the capitalist mode of production: enjoyment without labor. The supplemental unemployment benefits temporarily pointed to alternative possibilities for millions of working people to consider something other than their prior occupation and briefly short-circuited the wage labor process, skipping the mediating step of labor. As blogger Matthew Yglesias pointed out, the program "set aside normal concerns about incentives" to simply distribute the equivalent of $15 an hour to unemployed workers, plus their state's unemployment benefits.[35] This potentiality, to momentarily purchase space and time outside of an exploitative wage relation, had to be eliminated not simply because of the dollars and cents at issue but because the system's imperatives cannot countenance it. In the capitalist mode of production, it is perverse for a working person to enjoy without laboring, despite it being an ideological fantasy to live off of passive income, interest-bearing capital, or wise investment. The disciplining force of chatter around "disincentives to work" is not aimed only at the policy's recipients but also at the labor force as a whole.

The attempt to attribute the lack of incentive to work during the COVID-19 pandemic as the cause of a labor shortage failed not only because it ran up against the hard rock of several simultaneous crises but because the discursive limits of an incentive-based vocabulary were put on display. The repression of an economic signifier took place on two levels:

First, politicians and policymakers refused to countenance the possibility that low wages, unsafe working conditions, or a reassessment of one's place in the world were legitimate reasons to refuse to wait tables or process snack foods. Second, and more fundamentally, speakers were obligated to repress the presumed economic truism that a decrease in supply of labor without a decrease in demand for goods ought to hydraulically increase wages. The framework of incentives as an explanatory framework for all behavior—ostensibly a neutral framework for interpreting, rather than dictating, outcomes—serves only to distribute responsibility, and coercion, downward. The libidinal force of these messages far outlasted the policies that sparked them: in mid-2022, with a national unemployment rate of 3.6 percent, and nearly a year after the supplemental unemployment benefits lapsed, and two years after stimulus checks were distributed to Americans, Senator Mitch McConnell claimed that Americans were "flush for the moment" and expressed hope that "once they run out of money, they'll start concluding it's better to work than not to work."[36] It is impossible to discount how powerful repetition is as a libidinal motor force; Chaput argues that the way economists who ideologize on behalf of the capitalist mode of production latch on to affects that engender repetition, thereby shaping ideological context.[37] By habitually repeating that the issue depends on workers being willing to work for less than they had before, any structural issues regarding the organization of the economy writ large can safely be avoided—the aim avoids the goal, and the cycle of enjoyment repeats. The proactive implementation of an incentive masks their purpose as tools to retroactively reveal the preference that workers had for alternatives to their occupations, and the business class's preference for labor discipline. By "failing" on their own terms as a causal mechanism, the incentive of ending unemployment benefits revealed that yet more of the paltry social safety net in the United States needed to be dismantled and that workers would need to return for less money.

To conclude, the prevalence of "incentives to work" surrounding the pandemic displays the coercive threat lurking beneath labor policy, and the essentially classed nature of the way that "incentivization" is mobilized downward, rendering individual people responsible not only for their own fates but that of the economy as a whole. The fact that economists and policymakers could "play the hits" of incentives despite ensuring a near-total political victory of returning most waged workers back to the labor market (and after having dismantled most coronavirus precautions) indicates that the addressee of these policy changes was not the unemployed but the working class as a whole. Following the diagnosis of (political) neurosis, which depends upon a repressed signifier, "incentive" represses signifiers in two directions. First, depending on individual "incentives to work" represses the unstated conclusion to the phrase, "for the wages that the capitalist class offers," meaning less than what was offered temporarily through unemployment benefits.[38] Second, "incentive" guards against the perverse idea (at least for the capitalist class) that someone can temporarily bypass the mediation of labor and yet earn a living. A perspectival shift in the structure of desire and perversion reveals the classed nature of these statements: Lacan indicates that perversion inverts the "normal" subject position of the barred subject set in motion by the *objet a*, turning $\$\Diamond a$ into $a\Diamond\$$. This is, of course, the same structure viewed from two opposing perspectives: what appears as perverse to a business owner is a worker following a different path of desire.

Incentives in American Statecraft

After vaccines for the COVID-19 virus were approved for emergency use authorization by the Food and Drug Administration in the United States in December 2020, hundreds of millions of doses were distributed and disbursed to a public eager to get "back to normal" and end the various (albeit incomplete and contentious) states of social distancing, "lockdowns" and masking that had beset the world the previous year.[39] Yet according to the Centers for Disease Control and Prevention, it took until August 2021 for 50 percent of the population to be considered fully vaccinated (at the time, the equivalent of two doses).[40] In predictably neurotic fashion, millions of people, for a variety of reasons (both political and unconscious), refused to become vaccinated, prolonging the pandemic and various strategies of mitigation; soon after, well-funded, coordinated efforts to end mask mandates in public places, initiate lawsuits against vaccination requirements, and pass laws to shield businesses from liability ensured that any large-scale pandemic defense strategies would be curtailed in advance by an individualist approach. Large-scale testing (and even tracking) of cases, hospitalizations, and deaths attenuated in 2021, while vaccination was promoted by the Biden administration as the primary tool to prevent mass deaths as well as "economic and educational shutdowns."[41]

The COVID-19 pandemic offered a fertile test case for the power of incentives to address a matter of life and death and offered a possibility to bridge the horizons of individualism and social well-being, doubly so because, as health officials from both major political parties decided that individual decisions to become vaccinated would be the only large-scale campaign worth pursuing. The United States government's refusal to require vaccines for interstate travel, its halfhearted attempt to require vaccines for employment (withdrawn after the Supreme Court struck down a federal rule), combined with a pivot to individual responsibility and corporate prerogatives to dictate decisions for workers and consumers, turned incentives and nudges into the tools for guarding against the ravages of a pandemic. Scientific assessment of the efficacy of incentives and nudges found that they had little significant effect on generating mass vaccinations, and even into 2022, the United States remained below the threshold that would constitute "herd immunity" from the virus.

The failures of incentives and nudges to demonstrably increase vaccination rates on their own terms is a victory for the logic of the incentive writ large. The length and breadth of the COVID-19 pandemic stem from a society thoroughly inculcated in a discourse that prioritizes both methodological and possessive individualism, combined with governing strategies that explicitly downplay or dismiss the capacity for governments to materially affect the well-being of their residents through executive action. Ironically, incentives in this particular case are victimized by the success of incentives metastasizing across the social field; at a moment when the governing metaphor of "the economic way of looking at behavior" has taken hold, individuals responded in ways that contravened even economists' assumptions about behavior and refused to be incentivized to take protective action. Below, I frame these lethal failures primarily as emblematic of the "decline of symbolic efficiency." Yet the decline of symbolic efficiency, I argue, is no natural outgrowth of a symbolic regime but rather has an antecedent in the shift toward incentive-based policies, for they testify to a profound—and structural—impotence at the heart of statecraft. Because even governments fail to believe in their own efficacy, and subjects have been conditioned to prioritize their own idiosyncratic expressions of freedom (using the model of consumer choice) over collective action, regimes of incentives fail precisely at the moment of triumph when they are most widespread.

The idea that states ought to avoid coercive action to achieve political goals (in favor of incentives and rewards) has been a part of American statecraft for decades, in what Dardot and Laval call a "rationalization of existence" through market apparatuses.[42] This rationality finds clear expression in the United States in the 1992 book *Reinventing Government* by David Osborne and Ted Gaebler, which describes an "entrepreneurial government" whose task is to "promote competition between service providers," "take power away from the bureaucracy," and encourage "market mechanisms" to solve social problems.[43] While the specific language of behavioral economics and nudges is a fairly recent development, the use of incentive-based programs in lieu of social-democratic or redistributive ones within the Democratic Party spans at least as far back as the Carter administration, which inaugurated the centrality of economists and their use of microeconomic tools and cost-benefit analysis in federal policy.[44] While the Clinton administration was outwardly enthusiastic about the role of government in regulatory issues, when guidelines arrived in 1993, the "regulatory" nature of regulation was either absent or severely attenuated in lieu of incentive-based policies. Cooper writes that the Clinton administration outlined "a focus on policy that emphasized the creation of policies that relied as much as possible on incentives and other market dynamics and not primarily on implementation and administration by public administrators."[45] Take the September 1993 Executive Order #12866: "Each agency shall identify and assess available alternatives to direct regulation, including providing economic incentives to encourage the desired behavior, such as user fees or marketable permits, or providing information upon which choices can be made by the public."[46]

Vice President Al Gore partook in this strategy as a policy endeavor: In an overview of the entire American government in a commissioned "National Performance Review," two of the vice president's suggestions to "invent a government that puts people first" are: "Replace regulations with incentives" and "Search for market, not administrative solutions."[47] The language of the "performance review" was explicitly borrowed from corporate management—Gore simply applied this logic of a "performance review" to the federal government itself. Debates over "welfare reform" in the mid-1990s also turned on incentives—the government must shift from incentivizing receiving public assistance toward incentivizing wage labor. As then–First Lady Hillary Clinton wrote of President Bill Clinton's welfare reform bill, "Bill and I, along with members of Congress who wanted productive reform, believed that people able to work should work. But we recognize that assistance and incentives were necessary to help people move permanently from welfare to employment."[48] Foucault identified this as a neoliberal strategy to get as many people to play the "economic game" as possible and for the state to facilitate and officiate.[49]

The Personal Responsibility and Work Opportunity Act imposed lifetime limits on receiving social welfare benefits and required individuals seeking assistance to partake in "federally recognized work activities."[50] For the Clinton administration, when governments give needy people the "ends" of a social welfare system—housing, food, money—they blunt the poor's incentive to work. Instead, an incentive must mediate, and just like the ending of supplemental unemployment benefits decades later, that incentive was privation.[51]

The issue of public education has long been a struggle between the forces defending public education as a universal good and those in support of a privatized or mixed system, especially within the forces typically aligned with the Democratic Party, in the late twentieth and early twenty-first century. (Unsurprisingly the authors of *Nudge* use "school choice" as a prime example of the unalloyed value of "choice" in and of itself: the mere existence of alternatives to public schools can prevent a behavioral market failure from occurring.[52]) In a 1990 Progressive Policy Institute paper authored by Ted Kolderie entitled "Beyond Choice to New Public Schools: Withdrawing the Exclusive Franchise in Public Education" (a working paper that, apocryphally, then-governor Bill Clinton carried on his person while running for president), the PPI makes an argument for states to *"simply withdraw the local districts' exclusive franchise to own and operate public schools."*[53] This would involve the explicit introduction of market forces into public education, transforming it entirely to be subject to the initiative of wealthy individuals, businesses, or institutions to provide education to children: "The school district's monopoly on public education is the heart of the problem."[54] Kolderie's argument, in line with what would become a nudge approach in the Obama administration, is that states alone are "the critical actor"[55] and thus the impediment—in forcing systemic change, so they must both abdicate their role (as a monopoly) and fulfill it (by instituting sweeping change). The $4 billion Race to the Top program devised by the Obama administration, although less explicit than the PPI's attempt to fundamentally alter public education, introduced a series of "policy competitions" to state education boards, including incentive schemes into teacher compensation. As Obama proclaimed in a speech in 2009, Race to the Top aimed to "incentivize excellence and spur reform and launch a race to the top in America's public schools."[56] As Levine and Levine note, many of the reforms in Race to the Top are borrowed from the "school reform" movement aimed at introducing a rationale for charter schools to compete with public schools.[57]

For Race to the Top, incentives are built into the very structure of the program itself; it is a nesting doll of incentive structures. The program implemented incentive schemes into teacher compensation, school funding, and so on but was also predicated upon the idea of a nudge in the first place: It remained an entirely voluntary program. Howell and Magazinnik write that if "states opted not to participate in the competition, they suffered no penalty. To win federal funding, states only needed to demonstrate their willingness to adopt policies that conformed to the president's education agenda."[58] State education agencies, stimulated by the promise of financial reward, would spur competition in school districts by incentivizing high achievement on statistical benchmarks.[59] Since from this point of view it is difficult to locate the cause of educational high achievement, it must be indirectly stimulated by introducing incentives. Chait approvingly notes how the Race to the Top initiative exemplified a political triangulation by the Obama administration: by designing its monetary incentives to appeal to state education agencies, the administration could achieve a series of political victories while counteracting any potential political rebukes in advance. Race to the Top would avoid the appearance of interfering in local school districts' education while simultaneously weakening teachers' unions. Conservatives concerned with local control of school districts and working-class progressives in unions made "strange bedfellows" and a political coalition too weak and diffuse to successfully fight the reforms.[60] As Chait notes, under the Obama administration "charter school attendance grew rapidly," thus indirectly achieving the preferred policy goal of the administration (weakening the public school system and its organized workforce, particularly in Democrat-controlled "blue" states) through the incentives embedded in Race to the Top.[61]

In 2019, then-senator Kamala Harris introduced a bill, the Maternal CARE Act, designed to "incentivize maternal health care providers" to reduce maternal deaths and attenuate racial health disparities.[62] Despite specifically citing a North Carolina state program that reduced racial disparities in maternal mortality rates, $125 million of the bill's $150 million budget request would go toward funding five-year studies across ten states in order to discover the "best practices" to reduce the racialized maternal mortality gap.[63] In other words, the bill was not designed to reduce the maternal mortality rate, rather, it would have provided monetary incentives to study what might contribute to better health outcomes for Black women. Despite having evidence that an existing state program had successfully addressed the issue already, Harris's bill relies upon competitive action between states to be incentivized to discover how best to address the problem, much in the same way the Obama administration's initiatives presupposed that competitive outcomes would automatically generate better outcomes. Also in 2019, the former mayor of South Bend, Indiana, Pete Buttigieg advocated for a "public option" supplement to the ACA, but accompanied it with an even fiercer penalty for failure to partake in the individual mandate, central to the ACA's rationale. Instead of being penalized a proportional fine, under Buttigieg's plan, someone who failed to purchase health insurance would be fined the total of the premiums they would have paid had they been enrolled in a plan, characterized as "retroactive enrollment."[64] In an interview with the *Washington Post*, Jared Bernstein, a Democratic Party operative, maintained that "without the retroactive penalty, consumers would have no incentive to sign up rather than to simply wait to become sick before seeking care."[65] Buttigieg's incentive to purchase health insurance echoed a 2017 attempt by the Republican Party to replace the ACA entirely with the American Health Care Act. Contained within the bill was a "continuous-coverage incentive" that penalized anyone who remained uninsured for sixty-four days a "30-percent late-enrollment surcharge on top of their base premium."[66] This provision would perhaps discourage individuals from signing up for a health insurance program, knowing they would be legally overcharged hundreds, perhaps thousands, of dollars. But the rationale between both proposals remains the same: instead of providing health care to American citizens, the role of government is to incentivize rational activity and force consumers to purchase health insurance from a provider.[67]

Finally, in a particularly gruesome example of the Obama administration's insistence on mainstream economics as its guiding metaphor, the administration performed a cost-benefit analysis to gauge measures to limit prison rape and abuse. The 2003 Prison Rape Elimination Act set standards to prevent sexual violence within federal, state, and local facilities, provided it did not impose "substantial additional costs" on the facilities to achieve these standards. In order to adhere to this legislative guideline, the Obama administration commissioned a study that assigned a monetary value to prison rape and abuse but not from the perspective of a penalty for committing such a crime but instead looked at the amount someone would pay to avoid a sexual assault. As Lisa Heinzerling of Georgetown Law School described it, "Never mind that the law under which DOJ was acting is the Prison Rape Elimination Act, not the Prison Rape Optimization Act. In the topsy-turvy world of cost-benefit analysis, DOJ was compelled to treat rape as just another market exchange, coercion as a side note, and the elimination of prison rape as a good idea only if the economic numbers happened to come out that way."[68] That is, the law is designed for incarceration facilities to eliminate prison rape through concrete actions, not to merely incentivize rational behavior to discourage prison rape. Although this is an extreme demonstration of what a cost-benefit analysis aims to clarify for a government, it partakes in the same logical universe as Sunstein's castigation of onerous environmental regulations and, most importantly, Becker's threefold "economic approach to human behavior." Once a government inaugurates the presumption that individuals have stable preferences around which they structure their utility-maximizing actions, the only possible method to spur change is by contouring the "market" for those choices and raising or lowering the costs of behaviors.[69]

To summarize, incentive programs, particularly around the issue of health, arose at a precise moment within liberal democracies wherein executive bodies are empowered to implement policy when legislatures fail to do so. Recall, Thaler and Sunstein argued in 2009's *Nudge* that choice architects are not only nimbler than legislatures but nimbler than even other regulatory agencies in implementing executive priorities. The self-reported agility of nudge units comes at a cost—by instituting nudge policies writ large, governments testify to a symbolic impotence in implementing any vision of "the good" through large-scale or regulatory action. Public-facing incentives are the victim of the success of the "incentive-driven" discursive regime writ large; only once the metaphor of market interaction has metastasized over the social field, behavioral nudges lose their effectiveness. To be clear, the decline of symbolic efficiency does not mean that individuals believe in meaningful signifiers any less—far from it. Indeed, belief is stronger than ever, in the form of cults, religious feelings, intensities of affect, passionate attachments, and so on. Decline in symbolic efficiency refers to the institution's belief in itself, the big Other's own capacity for registering symbolic activity as meaningful.[70] The intensity of belief that persists in individuals is in fact proof of the decline in symbolic efficiency, for individuals are now tasked with believing (in) themselves when the big Other seems incapable of doing so.

Vaccination Incentives, Nudges, and the Decline of Symbolic Efficiency

American policymakers in 2021 faced a conundrum: vaccines were free and plentiful, but tens of millions of adults remained unvaccinated. Absent any political will to enforce a national mandatory vaccination program (and precluded by several state legislatures passing laws forbidding public institutions from mandating vaccines), conditions for a national experiment arose: could incentives and nudges move the needle on coronavirus vaccinations? The answer: a qualified no. Offerings ranged from free amusement park tickets, to small cash rewards, all the way up to the chance to win $1 million in Ohio. (The CDC also released guidelines suggesting that private businesses ought to incentivize their workforce, suggesting cash bonuses, gift cards, and food, although the CDC also reported that only 24 percent of businesses employed these tactics.[71]) A review of vaccine incentive programs from 1980 to 2012 found that they tended to work, even with minuscule cash payments.[72] Researchers in Sweden found that a modest $24 incentive increased the likelihood of vaccination by 3.9 percentage points, up to 87.1 percent, although they similarly found that communicative nudges to entice vaccination did not increase uptake.[73] Survey data collected throughout the COVID-19 pandemic suggested that incentives would work: a UCLA study suggested that $100 cash payments, or the end to masking requirements, caused an increase in those likely to receive a vaccination.[74] Survey data from the University of Kansas also suggested that students would be willing to test for COVID-19 if they were entered into a lottery to win $100.[75] National survey data gathered by management and business scholars in 2020 suggested that people reluctant to take the vaccine would relent if they were offered $1,000.[76] The guiding principles of incentive-driven behavior had theoretical and survey-based support to spur health officials into action, yet in practice, these efforts fell short of expectations.

Anecdotal, state-level data was similarly inconclusive. *ABC News* reported that in Louisiana, vaccination numbers remained level, while in Arkansas, rates actually decreased following the announcement of a lottery.[77] While Ohio reported a jump immediately following the announcement of a $1 million lottery prize, the increase tailed off; officials in Missouri suggested that the incentives played a role in raising the statewide rate from 40 to 48 percent.[78] Research published in the *Journal of American Medical Association* later found no evidence of an increase in vaccinations in Ohio following the lottery incentive, and that the brief increase may have been attributable to younger age groups becoming eligible for injections.[79] Several studies found that incentive programs at the state and city level had no significant effects.[80] Not only did cash incentives and messaging nudges not increase vaccination rates, they may have backfired, with economist Tom Chang admitting that offering a cash reward may have in fact made people distrustful of the vaccination, as if they were being bribed: "I was just completely wrong, in the sense that we looked at the data. And nothing seemed to work."[81] Instead, the researchers advocated for "much stronger policy levers, such as employer rules and government mandates," to reach high levels of vaccination.[82]

One of the study's coauthors, Kevin Volpp, head of the Center for Health Incentives and Behavioral Economics at the University of Pennsylvania, expressed an anxiety that offers a clue as to why these incentives failed to hit their targets. The introduction of an incentive program may, in a delicious "irony of social engineering," affect how people will act in the next public health crisis. Volpp writes, "People might learn that if you wait, you'll get an incentive next time."[83] This anxiety emerges from the structure of a nudge itself: individuals (and always individuals) are addressed as rational economic actors in need of a nudge and offered a binary choice that is presumably cheap ("if not free") but tilted in a socially beneficial decided by a policymaker. From the economist's perspective, if a rational person expects a reward for behaving in a socially beneficial manner, waiting until they are rewarded increases their utility (and, following the principle of methodological individualism, the total utility of society as a whole). Once marketlike apparatuses are introduced into social relations, it is impossible to dislodge them, even if one tries. This is because these apparatuses do not lodge themselves merely into the available repertoire of policymakers but into the unconscious of every acted-upon subject. Incentives function as ineluctable phallic signifiers, inaugurating a regime of punishment and reward retroactively intagliating all prior behavior as having operated under its purview. By presuming that individuals are always and everywhere incentive-driven, economically minded policymakers ensure that individuals will begin to think of themselves as existing under that signifier.

By introducing an incentive structure to an act of social solidarity, the obligation to choose *even the right decision* becomes the retroactive question: "By what was I incentivized?" which is another way of framing the neurotic's question, "What does the Other want of me?" By lodging an unavoidable signifier into the unconscious of the choosing subject, they are now obligated, from now on, to consider whether they are altruistic or willing to be bribed. When subsequent pandemics or public health disasters arise, the contemporary presence of incentives will inevitably morph the terrain upon which individuals are forced to stand. To ask why incentives and nudges failed during the COVID-19 pandemic obligates us to consider that this failure owes much to the success of the "incentive-driven" program writ large. Incentives to return to work, and to become vaccinated, reside in a world in which the obligation to choose, and to think of oneself as a rational economic decision-maker, has metastasized over the social field. To assess one's own capacity for risk (and the risk one is willing to subject others to) in a pandemic is merely a restatement of the tenets of neoclassical economic theory: we have stable preferences, act to satisfy our desires, and choose according to the prices of the available options.

Nudges also seemed to be ineffective in stopping the spread of the disease in the first place. In spring 2020, as various national governments responded to the global pandemic with varying degrees of coercive measures, the Tory government in the United Kingdom began not with lockdowns (as they employed after the disease had already reached uncontrolled spread throughout the country) but with a series of behavioral nudges. According to the *Guardian*, the government's March 12, 2020 coronavirus action plan explicitly refused to ban large gatherings and place a "lockdown" on social activity out of a fear of inefficacy: "Anything too onerous suggested by the government—such as a two-week isolation period for a whole household—might be adopted enthusiastically for a few weeks but then people get bored and leave their homes."[84] Tony Yates, a former professor of economics at University of Birmingham, criticized the government's approach at the time for relying on nudges to reduce disease spread—individualized messages to "wash your hands, don't touch your face, don't shake hands with others," and so on, when other measures could be taken.[85] The UK government's aversion to inducing "fatigue" testifies to a failure of imagination intrinsic to nudges as a governing metaphor. If coercive policies, such as lockdowns or mask mandates, can be safely ignored, then nudges can be, too. Yates writes, "The state lives with this 'fatigue' in the design of the laws and norms that permanently regulate our lives."[86] To ignore a polite handwashing sign, or tune out a friendly announcement to socially distance while on the tube, is the democratic promise of the nudge, built into their very structure and pitched specifically as an improvement upon coercive policies.[87] Baldwin calls this phenomenon "nudge fatigue," or the exhaustion that publics have when they are aware of the fact that they are being nudged and behave accordingly.[88] Nudges subsist, parasitically, upon social intercourse and cannot substitute for guiding principles on their own; there must be an equilibrium already in existence that requires disruption. Thus, in a Hegelian manner, wherein essence and appearance coincide, "fatigue" bespeaks an unpleasant truth, that the appearance of not directly exerting effects ends up failing to exert an effect.

The possibility for a nudge to be refused is one of the nudge's fundamental tenets, and the persistence of this binary yes/no opposition offers a clue for why opposition thereto, especially from political conservatives, is so unyielding. Mark D. White, from a libertarian perspective, levels two major complaints at nudges, which when read from a psychoanalytic perspective reveal the libidinal engine that makes them objects of scorn and fascination. White argues that any state's attempt to alter someone's behavior through a nudge represents a violation of private property; even nudging someone away from a donut and toward a healthy snack is iniquitous. He writes, "Policymakers have no way to know whether a particular choice made by a person is good or bad—only that person can make that judgment because only that person knows his or her true interests and motivations for that choice."[89] That is, even if an unhealthy baked good is chosen for the "wrong" reason (or because they have a childhood memory, or because they aim to satisfy the oral drive), there is no justification for a nudge. The mere presence of a "choice architecture" is a reminder to the chooser that their social interactions are exposed to the gaze of others and that there are other interpretive frameworks into which their polyvalent signifiers can be classified. This represents a metastasis of private property beyond a commodity or a choice but to the signifiers that emanate therefrom. Since, according to White, only an individual is capable of knowing their true interests, only they can own the proper interpretation of their choices.[90] For the libertarian, a signifier must be barred from representing the subject for another signifier.

Resistance to nudges is a strategy for protecting the property owner from the unpleasurable, repressed knowledge that they exist in social relations with others. Diane Davis, synthesizing the work of Emmanuel Levinas, Jean-Luc Nancy, and Maurice Blanchot, points to the "exposedness" of being that preexists any symbolic relation whatsoever as a condition for rhetoric. Such a framework allows us to see what the libertarian rejects by expanding private property into the aftereffects of one's choices. Davis frames rhetoric as the call to an ethical response to the presence of the other, even if that other embodies a "surplus of alterity" that exceeds every attempt at figuration.[91] In searching for a non-Hegelian, nondialectical account of recognition, Davis points to the logical indiscernibility of the relation between Others, constituted by the relation and yet exceeding it; in this framework, rhetoric is not what is said, but the pure saying thereof:

"The responsive address *says* the surplus of sociality, a shared exposedness, a 'we' that precedes and exceeds hermeneutic understanding."[92] One need not wholeheartedly endorse Davis's adoption of Levinasian ethics in order to see the value of rhetoric as an encounter among bodies who exceed one another's capacity for interpretation. What the libertarian fantasizes is more than the fantasy that they can possess their own bodies (as private property) but that they can possess the signifiers that exceed them, which shoot off in all directions through interaction with the world and with others.

The libertarian rejection of "exposedness" can be explained through reference to a classic psychoanalytic concept, what Freud called the "anal stage" of psychological development. Using Freud's insight that children migrate from the "oral" to the "anal," then "genital stage" of development as a metaphor is helpful in understanding how human beings relate to objects beyond their childhood development; in this case, it demonstrates how the libertarian approach aims to hold on to what Lacan calls a "yieldable object" in their social relations.[93] Freud uses the example of a child being toilet trained as exemplary of anal erotism: because the Other (a nurse in this case) demands something from the child, some children will willingly "hold back their stool till its accumulation bring about violent muscular contractions."[94] Gunn identifies the anal stage as a site of enjoyment for the child, who is now in possession of a "gift" they can disburse or withhold, and thus, becomes an object that acquires autonomous value.[95] Once it becomes an object, it can participate in relationships of meaning for the human subject. Matheson writes that Lacan situates the anal stage within "part of the broader economy of the Symbolic: the Other's apparent demand for defecation, the scorn exhibited by the Other when it is done inappropriately, and the sense that one is therefore both giving a gift and taking a risk."[96] The libertarian's objection stems from this risk of loss, since the inauguration of a regime of nudges means that an individual subject will no longer have the capacity to know whether their desires are their own, or an other's. The libertarian solution to the eternal question, "What does the Other want of me?" is to double down on the grip one has on their products.

The characteristics associated with anality, in the colloquial way we think of it (as Freud put it, "especially *orderly, parsimonious,* and *obstinate*") is a reaction to subjective exposedness, of which libertarian thought is an especially acute case.[97] For Davis, to be in the world is to be exposed to the infinite demand of an other; for Freud and others in

188 | Works like a Charm

the psychoanalytic tradition, one response is to neurotically exert some control over this demand by holding tightly to one's own "property." The anality of the libertarian is a rebuke to the call of the other, a vigorous reassertion that certain things ought not be owned by anyone else. Put simply, White wants to own both the donut and the interpretation thereof; put crudely, White wants to consume the donut and consume its "end result" as well. (And as Matheson points out, Freud's symbolic equation of the fecal object with gold makes the contemporary right-wing obsession with gold as a store of value in a rapidly changing world all the more explicable.[98]) For the choice architect, the choice of a donut reveals the consumer's preference for an unhealthy snack, so using the framework developed above, will aim to metonymically substitute the donut for an object that is nutritionally healthier, like fresh fruit, by assuming that what the chooser desires is "satisfaction" rather than the thing itself.[99] The libertarian's objection follows Ayn Rand's theory of identity, that A = A: The donut means only what the person who chose it intended for it to mean; it cannot metonymically slide into nonidentity or become something other than the expression of the individual's univocal interest. By metastasizing the logic of private property, the libertarian metonymically equates the individual, their interests, those interests expressed as choices, and how those choices are meant to be interpreted. The binary choice, yes/no, becomes an opportunity to resist yielding one's desire to exposure to the Other, resist admitting that despite one's best efforts, it is impossible to not be exposed to alterity.

The second major objection to nudges similarly stems from this inflation of the concept of private property: not only should a government be disallowed from the interpretation of the choices (or signifiers) of individuals but also something structural in the logic of signification itself prevents it from occurring at all. The libertarian's strict reliance on methodological individualism and ontological sovereignty means that a state's functionaries are structurally incapable of representing anything beyond their own individual biases and thus will only ever contour the choices of individuals toward preplanned outcomes. Despite the appearance of free choice, choice architects nudge individuals into choices they would not have made otherwise. White writes that libertarian paternalism "falls victim to the same flaw as does any type of paternalism: rather than serve people's own interests, as it claims, it serves the interests that policymakers think people do or should have."[100] Because "nudge units" purport to be capable of interpreting the behaviors of individuals and then contouring their future behavior, the libertarian can argue that any such action remains a proverbial "thumb on the scale," which only corporations and other individuals should be allowed to do. As Shane Ryan puts it, "The project . . . is to make certain outcomes that may benefit their targets more likely."[101] Nudges may be designed to make "humans" act more like "Econs," but in a way that presumes they will make the choice that has already been deemed socially beneficial by the choice architect.

This objection to state intervention has an antecedent in Friedrich Hayek, who argued for a nonconscious, evolutionary, imitative apparatus in the human mind, what he calls a "mechanism of sensory pattern transfer" that allows individuals to spontaneously organize themselves; this spontaneous organization inevitably leads to hierarchies, the public nature of which displays to individuals how to recognize successful patterns of behavior and emulate them.[102] Chaput contends that the "concrete neurological evidence" that Hayek cites provides the "scientific backing to support what [Adam] Smith understood yet could not adequately explain": proof of the existence of the invisible hand.[103] To nudge someone is to manipulate their ignorance, but for Hayek, ignorance is a virtue that only the capitalist mode of production can reward. As Mirowski put it: "For Hayek, the conscious attempt to conceive of the nature of public interest is the ultimate hubris, and to concoct stratagems to achieve it is to fall into Original Sin. True organic solidarity can obtain only when everyone believes (correctly or not) that they are just following their own selfish idiosyncratic ends."[104] Because of the enormous complexity of social life that "no individual can completely survey," markets must be the only way to organize society outside of state manipulation.[105]

It is easy to see what makes nudges so particularly iniquitous to a devotee of the capitalist mode of production: they self-consciously accept that market mechanisms are the primary fasteners of social order, even attempting to be as unobtrusive as possible.[106] Yet the unobtrusive, occasionally covert status of nudges is doubly unjust because it disallows the capacity for someone to learn from their choice and decide differently the next time. Nudges combine both market mechanisms with the belief that markets (or poor market design) occasionally lead to suboptimal outcomes, placing a technocratic tweak upon the ignorant behavior of an individual, which is, for Hayek at least, the only genuine evidence of human freedom. From this perspective, it is the status of knowledge (and its counterpart, ignorance) that provides the backbone of a critique of nudges. At the individual level, no one can know their own desires, and nudges prevent meaningful choices from which one can learn; this aggregated lack of knowledge heaped together is what we call "society," so there is no vantage point to view, much less manipulate, this aggregated totality without deforming it somehow. By emphasizing knowledge (and who has access to it), the Hayekian position can be safely insulated from what is at stake. A position from which one cannot see the totality, while insisting on a spontaneous order to the totality that must not be touched, doubly guards against both the nudge and any attempt to overcome the rule of capital by working people.

The complaint leveled against nudges, and to be clear, any challenge to the market whatsoever, can be unwrapped by triangulating knowledge (or ignorance, since for Hayek they are only relational terms and have no absolute status) with two others: representation and private property. To oppose nudges is to believe that a state both *cannot* and *must not* know what the Other desires because even individuals cannot always know what they have desired. This seems like a basic psychoanalytic insight, at first glance. The signifier of the lack in the Other testifies to this conundrum; no state actor (or economist) is self-present, so any attempt to impute their desire onto an Other will inevitably be diverted. Yet the Lacanian point is that the strict setting up of limits in knowledge is already a tacit admission that the Other "knows too much," the state cannot know that it lacks, it cannot violate the "private property" of the individual's choices (as above) or their lack-of-knowledge. The libertarian's objection to political representation is paralleled in the objection to symbolic representation: my choices have meaning only for myself; they cannot be seen as signifiers that act as the subject for another signifier. Furthermore, the right-wing objection to nudges is an objection to the state's self-conscious metastasis of economic reasoning and tools into social reality, not the use of private property to achieve one's chosen ends. White makes this point explicit, arguing that only governments should be barred from nudging people, while corporations should be free to do so: "Is there manipulation in these business practices? Of course there is . . . we expect businesses to do it, *but we expect more from our government.*"[107] This refusal, characterized previously as anality, and this refusal to partake in sociality except on the proverbial "on one's own terms," is not only all-encompassing: because both privilege markets and property as organizing metaphors they cannot but impotently alert us that the tools of economics are simply being used by the wrong people. The lack of objection to private property and its use by corporations is the signal that it is not knowledge that must be defended but that knowledge must be foreclosed from the Other in a private property regime, and no choice, learning, knowledge, or ignorance can be transmitted representationally to anyone else. That is, the proper objection to any Hayekian diagnosis, and indeed any attempt to reconcile Hayek with, or claim him for a critical intellectual project, is to point to the absolute limit that private property puts on thought—and to resist representation as a concept out of hand risks granting credence thereto.

The nudge's standing as a critique of representation exists not merely at the conceptual level but also at the political level, despite being representational vehicles in their own right. And the choice architect's purported ability to assign meaning to a polyvalent signifier that brings it in line with their political priorities means there is a grain of truth in the conservative objection to nudges. Yet it is one thing to object to (potentially) naïve attempts to nudge people to make better consumer decisions but quite another to refuse a potentially life-saving vaccine. Tens of millions of people refused to be vaccinated, no matter the positive reward (the chance at one million dollars) or the negative cost (of dying, of infecting and endangering others). The structure of the nudge remains identical, however, which accounts for resistance thereto: one's inability to truly imagine one's own death, one's noninclusion into the world (itself a binary opposition), means the logic that governs "should I choose an apple or a donut?" is the same one as "should I take a vaccine?" The Freudian term "death drive" seems apropos to explain the unexplainable during the COVID-19 pandemic. Why were so many people commit-ted to endangering the lives of others, risk one's livelihood and health, in order to "return to normal"? Incentive schemes to bribe recalcitrant individuals found only what they could seek—if nothing else, subjects in a capitalist society ought to be motivated by money, according to public health officials. Yet this presumption became demonstrably untrue for tens of millions of people who refused to become vaccinated against the COVID-19 virus. The precision of the death drive refers not to a "desire to die," or the intentional sacrifice of others for the profit system (although this iniquitous practice is a key component of the social expression of the death drive) but refers to goal-inhibited self-destructive behavior. The death drive is a conservative force, a drive toward a continuity of the past and present, a "return to normal" that indirectly ensures that this goal is never reached.[108] The death drive is evident in the refusal to vaccination not because people had a willingness to die for their beliefs, but that the compulsion to "return to normal" over and above any health advisory would in fact mean that the pandemic would continue to claim lives, delaying "normal" in attempting to achieve it.

The presence of the death drive makes the challenge of ending a pandemic appear insurmountable. Yet the death drive should be thought of as a failure of mediation: as mentioned, in the final analysis, we cannot imagine our own deaths, our noninclusion in the world. Any self-destructive behavior that we undertake depends upon not reaching our goal. The missing signifier of death is the missing signifier of sociality and our incapacity to mediate between "the individual" and "the collective." Incentives, predicated on methodological individualism, refuse to mediate this binary opposition, presupposing that society is composed exclusively of individuals making rational economic choices; pandemics make this binary opposition even more difficult because in conditions of political neurosis we are never sure what difference makes a difference. Is wearing a mask going to save the life of a stranger? Did I catch the coronavirus at work, or in flight? Did getting vaccinated save my life, or would I have weathered the disease on my own? The lack of a guarantee is the question of mediation, of representation, of guarantee, par excellence. Neoliberal conditions of existence suggest that we are always on our own, with no guarantee (even from the big Other) of whether we are making the correct decision or not. Nudge theory suggests, in a mirror image of psychoanalytic practice, that we are never fully self-transparent, our existence is expressed through our revealed preferences: who we are is the momentarily out of joint set of decisions we have made; one is what one is revealed to have been.

Thus, to conclude, we should interpret both the successes and failures of nudges and incentives as emblematic of the decline of symbolic efficiency—but to such a degree that it is not merely inefficiency but symbolic impotence. Symbolic efficiency requires *not* that signifiers and signifieds have specific meanings, or that the big Other presides over a relationship of symbolic certainty. But rather, as Žižek argues, symbolic efficiency depends on acknowledging a minimal *gap* between signifiers, the capacity for signification to function not as psychosis (with a refusal to acknowledge a nonidentity of signifier and signified) but in its "normal" functioning of connection and disconnection. Symbolic efficiency depends on the sincere lying of the big Other, of the public performance of semiotic closure, and the private acknowledgment of its absence.[109] Consider the behavioral oddities one encountered during the pandemic—one was never sure whether one's actions were appropriate, there was no "final guarantee" of whether one had successfully avoided infection, one could congregate at bars and coffee shops with friends and decry how unsafe others were being, and so on. Pandemic conditions depended upon the enforcement of effective symbolic fictions in order to maintain a fiction of sociality, which indirectly produces the behavioral outcomes aimed for. Yet the operative theory of incentives, that coercion, and "command and control" regulations are not simply ineffective, but "anti-liberty" and potentially induces the opposite result, is the precise inverse of this fiction: governments no longer appear to believe in their own potency to represent the will of a public, or to exert an effect on them whatsoever.

Incentives fill the gap that stems from the decline of symbolic efficiency; they act as the momentary, provisional attempt to offer solidity to a choosing subject but, in so doing, render them neurotic through the obligation to choose the proper outcome. Mark Fisher, in *Capitalist Realism*, identifies this experience as "reflexive impotence," or "they know things are bad, but more than that, they know they can't do anything about it."[110] As with nudges writ large, rewards and punishments offered throughout the COVID-19 pandemic depended upon refusing to either coerce or persuade, despite experts and researchers concluding that these methods would have the highest chance of success. Although the CDC suggested that businesses offer incentives to workers, the organization's own chosen success stories, from meatpacking factories to private universities, did not include any of the recommended incentives (aside from paid time off to receive and recover from injections). The successful efforts instead relied upon multilingual outreach, union representation, mobile vaccination clinics, and, in the case of Duke University, a mandate.[111] By laundering a social interaction through a marketlike space, a nudge cannot be conceived of as persuasion in the classic sense, even if they ultimately are persuasive, in that they exert effects. Since the structure of a nudge relies on introducing the possibility of choice, and the choice then taken is revelatory of the individual's underlying preferences, there is a fundamental difference in the conditions of addressivity between persuasive discourse and "nudges." Researchers writing in the *New England Journal of Medicine* suggested that a marketing strategy, rather than rewards, ought to guide vaccine promotion, suggesting essentially old-school persuasive techniques to increase uptake (including finding a common enemy, suggesting the threat of scarcity, and using analogy and metaphor).[112]

The symbolic impotence of governments to represent a political will, or the desires of their subjects, is part and parcel of the incentive-driven program writ large, and an insistence on mediating a desire only through an incentive structure that directs desires away from universal political goods and toward "good" and rational economic choices. Nudges are the inculcation of the idea that state action is only ever dyadic and vertical: states can only ever limit freedom of free individuals and exert pressure downward.[113] Yet an alternative possibility must be countenanced: state action, coercive as it may be, ensures conditions for justice to emerge between horizontally located subjects. Sunstein argues against mandates in government activity unless "it can be shown that a mandate will clearly improve people's lives," but these conditions are limited and provisional, and Sunstein spent much of his time at the White House generating road-blocks to mandates and regulations.[114] Rules—from speed limits, to bans on pollutants, and indeed, mask mandates—are doubtlessly coercive. But to presume that they are *only* coercive and *only* vertical is to miss the role that mediation plays in ensuring a minor relationship of sociality among lateral relations (to borrow a concept from Juliet Mitchell).[115] If a customer is obligated to wear a mask inside a store, certainly they are being coerced but primarily in order to prevent a stranger from being infected with an incurable disease. Similarly, a speed limit coerces a fast driver with threat of a ticket but also prevents that driver from endangering others on the road. The indirection of the signifiers of mandates, coercions, rules, and regulations is downplayed in incentive-based discursive regimes, virtually guaranteeing that they will miss their mark.

Conclusion: Failure through Success

In this chapter, I have assessed two major social crises—unemployment and vaccinations—from the perspective of the incentive-driven discursive regimes that attempted to intervene upon them. In order to return the labor market "back to normal," economists and policymakers attempted to incentivize a return to work by eliminating temporary supplemental unemployment benefits. This policy and the habitual invocation of "incentives to work" reveals that latent in all incentive-based discourse is the threat of privation: workers must be willing to return to work for less if the priorities of the system are to be satisfied. If the end of the supplemental benefits was designed to exert a macroeconomic effect, this policy failed, even according to economists and policymakers enthusiastic about the causal power of incentives.[116] Yet the failure is more auspicious than success: "incentives" acted as a shibboleth to remind working people the extent to which policymakers and businesses would attempt to enforce labor discipline. The momentary minimal freedom that some unemployed workers enjoyed was cut off not simply for base economic reasons but because a signifier had to be repressed: that one cannot have enjoyment in the capitalist mode of production without toiling. Hence, to guard against this "perverse" idea required an attack on temporary unemployment benefits. Similarly, incentives and nudges designed to increase vaccination rates failed, with experts suggesting that the introduction of choice and reward either failed to convince subjects, or worse, induced a neurotic condition. The symbolic impotence of governments to induce universal acquiescence was on full display in the United States. Vaccine incentives emulate the Freudian "Why are you telling me you are going to Cracow" joke structure, with "Why are you telling me to take the vaccine, when the vaccine is good?" Or put more bluntly, "Why are you bribing me to take the vaccine, when the vaccine is free?"

In both cases, the success of "incentives" as a governing metaphor for social interactions writ large meant that incentives designed for public health and labor discipline would fail. These failures are instructive because they point to the internal discursive limits of the vocabulary when set against a social crisis. The difference between the coercion within the labor market and the refusal to coerce to vaccinate should be clear: under the rules of an incentive-driven society, *only* the market can coerce. Yet from a psychoanalytic perspective, the role that incentives played in the unconscious of both populations points us to the centrality of desire. Incentive schemes—because they emerge from conditions of signification—address only the question of the subject's demand, not their unspoken desire. In other words, you cannot spell "incentive" without two "I"s: that of the methodologically derived individual and that of the policymaker that implements them, neither of whom have transparent desires to the other. Incentives and nudges are too clever for their own good, believing one could outsmart the unconscious by pegging idiosyncratic choices to the subject's unarticulated preferences, locking them in as expressive of some underlying economic rationale. Ironically, by reminding both unemployed people and vaccine skeptics of the imperative of the capitalist system—to produce surplus value—means that their unspoken desires were indirected toward refusal.

There is, to be clear, no honor in adhering to one's drives at the expense of the well-being of others, the psychoanalytic explanation for why people refused to vaccinate does not excuse the behavior. But it identifies the critical conscience that psychoanalysis can bring to these public questions and why liberal, progressive nudges fail and seem baffled at that failure. McGowan writes that psychoanalysis must abandon the concept of "the good" as a normative political idea, for "the good" is precisely what engenders the gap between a state's professed values and what they are capable of actualizing.[117] I part ways with McGowan, not because his assessment is incorrect but because "the good" arises outside of anyone's conscious control and that kneecapping this potential in advance is precisely the move that incentive-based politics asks us to make as well. Mediation happens, and the abandonment of mediation or representation as a category abandons it to the wolves of neoliberalism. By attempting to address the unspoken remainder of behavior, the desire unexpressed in other forms of social or political choices, yet insisting on doing so through the mechanisms of markets and with the assumptions of market behavior as foundational, nudges ironically end up further from the desires of their acted-upon subjects. A politically engaged psychoanalysis is not a naïve plea for an "unmediated" existence; it is in fact the opposite—mediation matters. The psychoanalytic critique functions as a conscience, the cosmic background radiation of all political urgencies, but the concrete political outcome today means that any program that even attempts to achieve a universal public good is barred in advance because the dominant model of mediation for contemporary politics is mediation through market structures. The COVID-19 pandemic revealed the limits of incentive rhetoric; the concluding chapter assesses what options are available with the epistemic door momentarily cracked open.

Conclusion

Breaking the Spell

> Before my first album came out, I wanted people to like me, and to realize that I had good intentions. Then I realized that no one has good intentions—we all just have incentives.
>
> —Donald Glover[1]

In this work, I have addressed the deceptively simple question, "Why are incentives everywhere now?" with a three-part answer. First, *incentives* (as opposed to any other word) are everywhere now due to neoclassical economics' uptake of the term as a way to summarize the heretofore unquantifiable motivating forces that guide human action. "Incentive" sutures desire and effort, and at least theoretically, was metonymically reduced to market-based structures. The term is not one among others but holds a privileged status as a governing metaphor for fundamentally economized social relations. In neoclassical economic theory, markets generate incentives—desires and responses—that automatically motivate individuals and cause rational activity. Next, incentives are *everywhere* now because the term partakes in the trope of metastasis: it is capable of spreading through the body politic (and the body social, the body cultural) by displacing the cause of any action onto the stasis of the economic. Incentives promise a coherent explanation of causality, and metastasis is its tropic vehicle. The constriction of incentive around financial motivation is an intermediate step, and its drastic expansion is due to the influence of economist Gary Becker, whose monumental academic and public presence made incentives a part of both policymaking and ordinary discourse. Thus to understand why incentives are everywhere *now*, one must look to how

197

198 | Works like a Charm

Becker and those in his wake deliberately foregrounded the application of incentives to noncommodity interactions.

I have further demonstrated what the consequences are of its metastasis into political life, both when retrospectively applied to issues of justice and when proactively applied to state policy. When introduced into issues of persistent, systemic, and historical inequalities, the language of "incentives" retroactively becomes an alibi for these very inequalities—women freely choose lower-paying jobs or to leave the workforce entirely because of their incentives for caregiving and domestic labor. And when incentives become the organizing framework for governmental policy, then nudges are its end result: a gentle contouring of individual, minute decisions organized around a prohibition on the delivery of public goods. By rhetorically privileging irrationality while holding to a theoretical framework that assumes rational behavior, libertarian paternalism gives a wide berth to choice architects to contour decisions toward their predetermined outcomes while simultaneously using "choice" as the theoretical warrant for the introduction of market-style relations. In each of these cases, incentives individualize outcomes and render individuals responsible for their choices. The discursive edifice of incentives acts as a rhetorical buffer zone for inequality, since every outcome, both retroactive and proactive, can be expressed as the result of an individual freely choosing from an available set of market outcomes.

In addition, I have offered how a psychoanalytic framework makes the discourse of incentives so powerful. As incentive rhetoric, and neoclassical economics writ large, offers a coherent explanatory framework for all matters market and nonmarket, Lacanian psychoanalysis works deliberately the opposite way; it looks for the slips, the breaks, the hand wavings, and august silences that any rhetoric relies upon to make itself make sense. Therefore, I have offered how to view "the incentive" as neoclassical economics' *objet a*, the nonempirical, fantasmic object that organizes its endeavors. The incentive is economics' privileged object because it presumes a theory of motivation, the concept of an acting subject, and, most importantly, an unseen force that binds outcomes together. (And as economists are happy to proclaim, their methods are better suited for this charge than any other discipline or mode of inquiry.) I have also forwarded the psychoanalytic concepts of masculine and feminine *jouissance* and the Real to interpret the rhetorical behaviors of interested parties. Specifically, the Real emerges in debates about equal pay because the sexed division of labor in the capitalist mode of production renders women's work structurally un(ac)countable, so it is impossible to provide a "neutral ground" to adjudicate proper recompense for women, hence why debates over this issue hyperbolically, but truthfully, point at capitalism's inability to provide equal pay or equal justice to workers. I have also demonstrated how the psychoanalytic distinction between the "aim" and the "goal" of a subject, and the concept of the forced choice, to explain why nudges are both structurally incapable of reaching their targets and coerce individuals into making constrained choices within these market frameworks. To reverse Milton Friedman's famous dictum: incentivized subjects are unfree to choose.

"Incentive" is a magic word, and its spell must be broken. To that end, this concluding chapter has two tasks. The first is to emphasize what makes incentive rhetoric so difficult to dislodge, precisely because incentives act as an interdiction on social desire. Although incentives act as a mediating device, in that they fill in the gap of causality when alternative accounts fail, they perform a sleight of hand by figuratively displacing cause from one realm into the domain of the economic. From this position, only markets are capable of registering human desires, and no moment of self-reflection, democratic deliberation, or nonmarket desire can achieve a comparable effect. The prophets of incentives insist on a gap between a desire and its fulfillment, then mobilize that gap by naming it an "incentive" and rendering it subject to the ironclad, irresistible laws of neoclassical economics. Incentive rhetoric does not channel desire to a "truer" outcome than any other one, it merely re-displaces it onto the stasis of the economic by returning to the seemingly quaint issue of representation, I explore what a politically engaged psychoanalysis can offer to resist regimes of incentivization. The only way out is through (not around) the critique of representation that neoclassical economics levels against alternative visions of sociality. Therefore, I conclude the chapter, and the book, by offering some concrete, if heavily caveated, advice about how to fight against these charms. Here I call attention to the democratic consequences of incentives in public and why they must be relentlessly scrutinized: as Kenneth Burke phrases it, we use words, but words also use us. Its appearance in discursive formations is never a neutral term, whether deployed consciously or unconsciously, and I draw upon lessons from psychoanalytic practice for how to interpret, and hopefully resist, the lure.

Resisting the Charm

If incentives truly are the cornerstone of modern life, that they operate both beneath and beyond commodity interactions, and are the proper way to organize an economy, a society, and a political system, then literally every outcome is explicable with a few simple assumptions about people's behavior. The incentive summarizes the three tenets of neoclassical economics (utility maximization, stable preferences, and market structures), and it is a totalizing theory of motivation that smuggles in a quintessentially economic perspective on the variety of human life. My criticism of incentives is not because they do not work. It is that, at some level, they do. In the capitalist mode of production, to induce a worker to produce more output, it is "economically rational" to tie their paycheck thereto; as a worker, it is economically rational to avoid starvation thereby. In a sense, the discourse of incentives gives expression to the purified concepts of market behavior by revealing what has been latent in market relations all along. The piecemeal pay that Marx described in *Capital* vol. 1 and the backbreaking labor of the migrant worker picking blackberries in the United States today both partake in the logic of the incentive. But its power is not total. Incentives must often be enforced within populations and workplaces; they are employed by powerful politicians, well-connected economists, and influential journalists. The discursive expression of incentives indicates not the actual introduction of market relations into all of human activity but the application of the style of market relations to interpret all of social reality. In each of the aforementioned postulates thereof, the centrality of signification shines through: incentives are not literally the structure of reality; they are a funhouse mirror of social reality, a fetishistic inversion of social intercourse organized around economic lines. In their attempt to short-circuit mediation, incentives find an unlikely analogue to the "critique of representation" in the critical humanities more broadly. Psychoanalysis, as a science of speech interpretation, is our best hope for releasing the stranglehold that economics has on public discourse.

My methodological plea is for attentiveness to the rhetorical mechanisms of representation that render incentives a coherent, prevalent, and consequential framework that conditions our capacity to imagine otherwise. The discourse of incentives is a discourse in a literal sense—it is a mode of address that must be interpreted according to a rhetorical framework; it is not an accurate depiction of the social bond but an image of the social bond as economists wish it to be. Representation may be a "long error," as Deleuze put it, but it is a socially efficacious one.[2] It may also seem like an unfashionable concept, for a "crisis of representation" has hung around the critical humanities for decades. Thinkers as varied as Deleuze, Derrida, and Foucault have levied accusations against the rule of the signifier in critical inquiry.[3] As Peter Hallward puts it, for Deleuze, it is not simply that representation "tends to get things wrong" but that the error of representation "lies in the presumption that such a relationship could have any sort of validity at all."[4] Bradford Vivian, following Deleuze's critique of representation in *Difference and Repetition*, posits that representation derives its power from the logic of identity—identity "holds an exclusive organizing value in traditional conceptions thereof."[5] Borrowing from Foucault, in *The Order of Things*, Vivian locates this movement of thought within the Enlightenment in which the relationship between a word and a thing "was organized by rigid and distinct categories."[6]

Yet rhetoric's relationship with critiques of representation are not idle musings on the play of signifiers; it is rhetoric's social charge that embroils it in these problems of whether representation is possible, or ethical. Rhetoric can be collectively mobilized toward a social good, such as in a social movement or political revolution but can also be employed by the powerful to enforce iniquitous social hierarchies—thus deserving of critical scrutiny. Being-with-others typically entails a bringing together around a collective identity or "strategic essentialism," to promote sociopolitical transformation, so any study thereof means wrestling with how speech is put into practice despite being always-already deconstructed.[7] Hanchey divides those addressing this problematic into two camps, those from an "immanentist" perspective who claim to have transcended the problem of representation altogether, and those who retain some semblance of representation despite its drawbacks in order to advocate for social change.[8] Hanchey's answer (relational politics) and Vivian's (a middle voice) are both compromises that acknowledge the enormous challenge that Deleuze, Derrida, Foucault, and others levy against rhetoric's own purview.

Incentives work, I have argued throughout this book, because they embody the trope of metastasis, the rhetorical transfer of cause from one domain to another; alternative explanations of cause are crowded out by the imperial power of the economic. Incentives function as both a critique of representation, broadly construed, and its fulfillment: only market structures can adequately convey the multitudinous desires, fantasies, and motives that people have, and any system of representation that is inattentive to incentives is doomed to fail from the outset. This is a two-

202 | Works like a Charm

step sleight of hand: first, there is no zero-degree of discourse, and yet incentive promises that at the level of the copula (the "there is"), human relations are market relations, which are themselves a mediating agency. Because the incentive is a rhetorical phenomenon, it follows and falls prey to the problem of language as a structure. That is, psychoanalysis gives an answer that involves a minimal perspectival shift from the "critique of representation." Žižek writes that "for Lacan, representation is never a mere screen or scene that mirrors the productive process in a limited and distorted way, it is rather the void or gap that splits the process of life from within, introducing subjectivity and death."[9] Rather than viewing the signifier, and speech by proxy, as an extension of the logic of identity, psychoanalysis views speech fundamentally as a relation of nonidentity: one speaks where being is not (A = not-A). Psychoanalysis is not alone in its position that language points to the nonbeing at the heart of every signifying moment, but it takes the persistent repetitious instantiation by speaking beings as a clue: speech was never the locus of truth, it is rather a technology of desire (itself a functionally metonymic process) that can never fully catch up to itself. For psychoanalysis, "presence" is a problem that speaking subjects negotiate. Split by the symbolic order, and beset by unconscious desires (and the desires of others), speech is rhetorical because it constantly negotiates the gap between signifier and signified. Representation is both impossible and the basic condition of language's functioning, and speech is the repetitious activity that functions despite this impossibility. We signify under conditions of a failed unicity, as Lundberg reminds us, and rhetoric is the social practice of feigning a unicity in its place. With no "zero degree" of discourse, rhetoric fills the lack. Ideological discourse, like that of the incentive, is a further distortion of this originary distortion. Or as Ernesto Laclau would put it, ideological discourse is the concealment of a distortion, which attempts to erase the original constitutive distortion in human reality.[10]

Thus it is true that speech is structured by the impossibility of communion, the lack of an im-mediate relation, but this is simply a structurally operant limitation. Representation happens. *Eppur si muove.* Incentive rhetoric takes a structural limitation of language and transforms it into an injunction at the level of the social: if the nature of language is that one *cannot* ever reach "the thing itself," incentive rhetoric says one *must not* ever reach "the thing itself." The introduction of an incentive scheme is an interdiction into social reality that does not bend desire closer to the desired goal but toward the signifier of the incentive itself. A change that the Clinton administration made to the income tax code exemplifies this phenomenon: American corporations are now at liberty to exploit a tax loophole in which they can deduct only $1 million from their tax bill toward CEO compensation unless the pay is designated as "incentive" or "performance" pay. According to Brian Hall of Harvard Business School, "The dramatic explosion in stock option grants during the past 15 years represents a major change in the financial incentives facing US top executives. CEOs of the largest US companies now receive annual stock option awards that are larger on average than their salaries and bonuses combined."[11] According to the Roosevelt Institute, this well-intentioned strategy to better tax executive pay has ended up completely inverting: it "has not only further driven the rise in average executive pay (while reducing tax revenues), but restructured it such that it has skewed economic incentives, arguably to the detriment of our economy."[12] Since their pay is tied directly to stock performance, CEOs are rationally incentivized to increase the stock price at the expense of other business functions. A greater focus on incentivization bends the desires of rational activity away from even the minimal responsibility corporations had to other parties (workers, the public writ large, the community, and so on) and toward the money commodity itself.

The right-wing critique of liberal democracies, that the incomplete application of market principles is the sole source of human misery, acknowledges the issue of mediation but compounds the error by presuming that market structures themselves are not also mediating agencies.[13] It is the system of representation embodied by the money commodity that interdicts upon human desires far more than a government's taxation or regulatory scheme could.[14] Lacan's claim that "nothing malfunctions more than human reality" is a plea for critical attention to how signification interdicts upon desires.[15] The rhetoric of incentives cannot channel desires in a "truer" direction. Incentives stand in between what is desired and what is present and operate as an alibi for any failure. If a public school system is failing, teachers are improperly incentivized; if a business goes under, the incentives of its workers and managers are misaligned; if a homeless person is given a home, their incentive to work is blunted. In a society organized around the commodity form, it is impossible to reach that which is desired directly: it must be channeled through some mediating agency. The introduction of monetary reward to act as social lubricant/ social mediation acts *in nuce* the M-C-M' circuit of capital that Marx identifies in *Capital* vol. 1. Money itself (in)directs human activity toward that which is—autotelically—profitable, even if it is not socially beneficial. The object of exchange (to acquire goods) becomes the object of desire (the end in itself) in the capitalist mode of production; this contradiction is displaced—metastasized—into the analysis of social phenomena within social relations that take place within the capitalist mode of production but are not strictly commodity-based themselves.

The application of this rubric onto noncommodity relations is merely a displacement of the original antagonism that is the unsurpassable horizon of capitalist society: the limits to capital is capital itself, there is no unmediated social relationship that produces surplus; the money commodity is the subject of capital because it presentizes this deadlock of social interactions. Money is both the closest and best approximation of human desire (as Alfred Marshall contended) and its absolute negation. This is the best case for why the incentive-based approach takes place under conditions of "neoliberalism," when it is not simply that market relations have taken hold but that the fully elaborated discursive edifice of economics has also taken hold: Social goods (like health care, education, a livable planet) cannot under any circumstances be guaranteed, much less promised, if the form of social relations is also organized by a prohibition on fulfillment. The structural indirection of language coincides with the capitalist mode of production's mode of objectification—the commodity form. Incentives metastasize as an explanatory matrix for the set of social relations that promise you anything, provided you can afford it.

To see the rhetoric of incentives from this perspective is to see the charm for what it is: speech that attempts to retroactively narrate the multitudinous, infinitely variegated desires of people as obeisant to the strict form of neoclassical decision-making. Even if incentives are the cornerstone of modern life, the edifice does not deconstruct itself: rhetoric's ambit must be to locate the mechanisms by which contingent signifiers are transformed into unavoidable signs. To that end, Gunn points out that despite the deconstructability of the speech/writing binary, speech nevertheless produces "presence effects," which are "affective and sexual in character," and that whether "real" or not, they exert effects on listeners.[16] Psychoanalysis takes the "crisis of representation" seriously, but from within the coordinates of representation itself—it is not enough to be done with language, signification, representation, or speech without attending to their outsized effects on speaking beings. Hence why Lacan argues that speech functions as an *objet a* for the subject, something without substance but nevertheless exerts real effects.[17] The prophets of incentives make a promise that all causes, all effects, all motives and outcomes are explicable if you say the magic words, but it is precisely because the signifier "incentives" must be inserted into workplaces, legislation, interpersonal relations, culture, and society, demonstrates that they partake in a language game and not a transparent representation of reality itself.

Five Dialectical Postulates of Incentive Rhetoric

The word-magic of incentives is a rhetorical phenomenon that yokes together the postulates of market dynamics and individual behavior to literally any setting or context. To assume that people are "incentive-driven" is to smuggle in virtually every necessary postulate of individual and market behavior necessary to retroactively justify the existence of all heretofore inequalities, and to proactively justify the introduction of market relations into a given setting. In this section, I present a set of five postulates of incentive rhetoric that summarize the inquiry as a whole, along with accompanying countervailing postulates that, in some minimal way, can help people resist their charms.

1. INCENTIVES TREAT INDIVIDUALS AS UTILITY MAXIMIZERS. REPLACE UTILITY WITH *JOUISSANCE*.

Incentive programs and nudges are presented to us as "liberty preserving" because they offer the illusion of choice within marketlike structures and replicate consumer models of choice in the capitalist mode of production. When an economist, politician, or journalist reduces the complexity of human life to a concept of the subject that is strictly incentive driven, they are not simply applying a narrow economic model onto every facet of social reality. Yet incentives are doubtlessly a technique of passivity: to economists, we are utility maximizers, constrained by our budgets, motivated by our preferences, and obedient to price signals. Our capacity for action in our concrete life activity is transferred to the mechanisms of the market. According to received theory, markets (through the price system) automatically generate rational activity in human beings. While the story is never as clean as it is presented in textbooks, the intellectual through-line is clear—the belief that "humans are incentive-driven" reduces human beings to reward-seeking machines or pleasure-seeking automatons who can be manipulated through the proper alterations of price signals around them.[18] Incentives, as the avatar of the market, are the true subjects of history, and individuals are their mere conduit. On this point, the libertarian complaint leveled at nudges is absolutely correct: incentives structure the desires of individuals in advance, circumscribing their ability to make meaningful choices. Yet because it is limited by its support for the rule of private property, the libertarian cannot extend this same skepticism to employers, corporations, and other private entities.

The critique, however, cannot begin with a simple reversal, to assert the necessity of freedom, or worse yet, "liberty," instead. The libertarian critique of nudges is doubly false, displacing the constrained optimization of economics for the negative freedom of possessive, property-based solitude, exposed to market forces and refusing the exposedness of our being in common. The activity/passivity binary is false and only serves impotent visions of freedom; instead, incentives should be resisted from the principle of utility maximization, replaced with the primacy of the unconscious, with our desires opaque to even ourselves. Unconscious compulsion has been embedded within the incentive since antiquity: the incentive pipe of Varro set the tune for its listeners, and Marsyas's pipe was so mesmeric that it threatened the Apollonian social order. Thus, the myth of Apollo slaying Marsyas was as much an allegory for the shape of the social bond—the temperance and harmony of the city-state momentarily triumphed over the ribaldry and singlemindedness of the countryside. But as described in chapter 2, Apollo's victory was doubly false. Marsyas's blood trickled from his body's final resting place and formed the Marsyas River—the lifeblood of the incentive piper literally got "in the water." In a neat historical irony, the Apollonian social vision has been successfully undermined from within by the spread of incentives throughout the body. Further, Apollo's victory was not on its own merits—the god resorted to violence to quell the satyr. That is, the allegory performs without conscious admission that Apollo was faced with a danger that could not be fought logically, or with a "better tune." There is something within the incentive that is infinite—and irresistible. We may interpret Apollo's vision of the social bond as analogous to what one might have termed a "mixed economy" in the twentieth century, with clear delineations of private and public activity, a space for trade unions, democratic accountability for politicians and a freedom from corporate influence at every level of society. Suffice it to say that there is no going back to Apollo's allegorical solution—a victory of temperance, harmony, etc., with many of what appeared to be commonsense portions of American society hollowed out by the prophets of incentives. Apollo's clement vision of the social bond is no match for the Marsyan pipe, especially not now.

Neoclassical economics authorizes its principle that price signals act upon individuals through reference to the idea that individuals are, at heart, utility maximizers. As introduced in chapter 3, utility maximization is one of Becker's three pillars that holds up the "economic approach to human behavior," as well as one of Arnsperger and Varoufakis's three critical axioms that organize the discipline as a whole.[19] Individuals satisfy their infinite desires by making choices within market structures given their resources, their appetite for risk, whether they think long or short term, and so on. The principle of utility maximization merely presupposes that individuals' choices are an immanent expression of their preferences (whatever their source might be); they satisfy these preferences within defined parameters. As Amadae points out, the uptake of game theory within neoclassical economics, itself a Cold War decision-making apparatus, encourages economists to presuppose that their subjects act as if they are participating in the "prisoner's dilemma" in every conceivable setting, from buying shoes to auctioning off natural resources.[20] In the economic worldview, individuals are simultaneously rational, forward-thinking actors who calculate their expected utility prior to any choice, but because they respond to price signals, they are compelled by their commitments to act in accordance with them. Although the economic subject is bound by their purchasing power, they encounter nothing but utility (satisfaction) through their individual choices.

Primarily, to resist the charm means rejecting outright the presumption that individuals are merely incentive-driven creatures, compelled by their own desires and the incentive structures that surround them. Because incentives foreground an image of the human as a recipient of price signals, one must instead foreground how human beings act (rather than being acted-upon) and make history, albeit in conditions not of their own choosing. This includes replacing this image with a collective framework, that of the union, the strike, the boycott, and the social movement, each of which on their own work beyond the limiting form of the incentive and beyond the commodity form itself. Rather than an organizing metaphor that foregrounds how individuals are manipulated, I encourage a vision of empowered collectivities changing their own circumstances. Human beings are constrained by the circumstances that surround them, but they are doubly circumscribed by a discursive edifice that frames them exclusively as compelled by their immutable desires. Such a vision means seeing a political desire articulated in excess of the confines of neoclassical economics. The individual freedom to act must be eclipsed by the obligation to act in concert and in conditions that demand collectivity not out of charity but necessity.

At the same time, the lessons of Lacanian psychoanalysis can be put to work as a critical conscience of the discourse of incentives, without necessarily constructing a competing vision of "the good" on its own. (Psychoanalysis merely aims to transform neurotic misery into ordinary human unhappiness; the unconscious will persist as a form no matter which mode of production people live under.) At first glance, there may seem to be a hidden alliance between psychoanalysis and economics; after all, both appear to endorse the idea that individuals are motivated by their desires and act to fulfill them, even beyond their conscious control. I suggest the exact opposite: the practical concern of psychoanalysis is primarily with how enjoyment is blocked, stunted, and kneecapped at every turn through conditions not of any individual's own making. Despite the best efforts of the mode of production to satisfy our every desire, something gets in the way. McGowan writes that any cultural critique of the capitalist mode of production should begin by noting that satisfaction itself bears the form of dissatisfaction, for there is always another commodity or experience that promises the "something more" that will satiate one's desire once and for all.[21] Psychoanalysis' discovery that desire is structurally metonymic is a methodological breakthrough, for it means discovering that the capitalist mode of production must both promise and withhold the satisfaction of desire. If for economics there is nothing but satisfaction, for psychoanalysis, human existence is structured by the impediments thereto.[22] Thus, by reversing the status of desire, one can see how each answer provided by neoclassical economic thought is a misplaced attribution of desiring subjects.

In this specific case, the materialist axiom that people make history albeit not in conditions of their own choosing is given a Lacanian accent through reference to *jouissance*. An enigmatic term throughout Lacan's oeuvre, I previously defined *jouissance* as the marker of a compulsion to repeat; for rhetoricians, *jouissance* names how particularly resonant tropes circulate within public discourses. Using the example of Christ's crucifixion in *The Passion of the Christ*, both Gunn and Lundberg contend that for Christians, there is something enjoyable but inexpressible in this on-screen representation.[23] The clue that we are in the realm of *jouissance* is the fact that audiences do not simply seek out the repetition of an execution but that in its on-screen depiction, the execution itself must be eroticized and must involve a libidinal surplus of suffering, penetration, and verbal aches, presented in slow motion. *Jouissance* is surplus enjoyment beyond simply the satisfaction of enjoyment; it is a too-muchness that compels a subject to repeat. It is more than the fact viewers "enjoyed" watching something tragic, discomforting, ugly; it is that these unpalatable aspects became the condition of their repetition. I propose that *jouissance* serves as the conceptual antithesis of utility maximization: human beings are not utility maximizers; they are *jouissance* maximizers.

Lacan, in his twentieth seminar, contends that *jouissance* is that which does not serve a purpose—it is functionally useless but also a surplus that stitches together the actions of the speaking subject.[24] (Like Marx's discussion of Senior's "Last Hour," the surplus built into the system is its basic condition for functioning, there is no dynamic relationship, either in labor or in signification, that produces an equivalence without remainder.[25]) In speech, *jouissance* emerges from the structural discontinuity between the signifier and the signified; it is the indication that what is said never fully captures what is intended (either one says too much, or too little). The rhetoric of incentives, which metastasizes market postulates onto nonmarket relations, eliminates the excuse that individuals are merely satisfying preferences within a commodity market and that the world outside may indeed be where individuals find satisfaction. Economics attempts to constantly reintegrate the unspoken remainder as part of a utility function—the concepts of shadow price, psychic costs, and even nonmonetary incentives are designed to reintegrate what cannot be fully counted or countenanced. In other words, the imperial ambit of economics as a totalizing system of decision-making requires the constant reintegration of seemingly unfulfillable desires. Recall the argument Gary Becker made about the deep rationality of households buying heating oil in the winter and air conditioning in the summer—it appears "irrational" only from the perspective of the commodity price, where it would be more rational to purchase heating oil in the winter when the price is low, and vice versa for air conditioning.[26] This example allows Becker to claim that consumer desire is functionally metonymic: we do not desire the commodity itself but the satisfaction behind the commodity, irrespective of its monetary price.

When Lacan writes that our "desire is the Other's desire," this means that we desire what the Other desires as well as the Other themselves.[27] Desire is socially constituted because it happens under conditions of signification and is structurally metonymic. Whereas Becker locates the final meaning of the "utility" gleaned from the commodity purchase as a way to justify the economic approach, a focus on *jouissance* rather than utility maximization focuses our critical attention on the role of signification. The economic approach to human behavior binds individuals to the signifiers of their choices as emblematic of what "truly" motivated them and reintegrates the surpluses of human activity into a strict neoclassical framework. Instead of leaving the question of desire open, "What does the Other want (of me)?" it has a ready-made answer: "You desired to satisfy your utility function." Thus, the critical questions to ask when faced with a regime of incentives are: What are the specific regimes of signification, regulation, accounting, and order that are designed to divert desires? And what remainders of enjoyment are being reintegrated into a rational utility function?

2. An incentive individualizes outcomes. Foreground the social existence of the individual.

Next, incentive rhetoric also encourages those ensnared by its charm to be held personally responsible for the results of their choices. One of economics' key methodological presumptions is that of methodological individualism, or the idea that only the actions of discrete individuals (making rational choices) can be studied, without reference to the social totality that gives rise to them. The term makes its first appearance in economics in a 1909 *Quarterly Journal of Economics* article by Joseph Schumpeter, in which he outlines methodological individualism as precisely that—an inference economists must make about their object of study, but not one necessarily endorsing this value in the world outside of it. Yet because economics' own purview entails that the desires of individuals determine market outcomes, the methodological simplification transforms an observation into an endorsement of ontological individualism. Schumpeter writes that since "only individuals can feel wants," and these wants "and the effects of satisfaction on their intensity give us our utility curves," the aggregation of individual demands into utility curves then "have a clear meaning only for individuals."[28] Schumpeter further argues that the marginal cost of any good bears no relationship to the supply of the good in total but only to the individual who personally decides its value, given their means.[29] Since society as such "cannot feel wants," it is impossible to represent the utility of a society as a whole; it is possible only from the perspective of individuals.[30] Methodological individualism acts as a justificatory inner loop for the discipline of economics: a utility curve is the representation of aggregated individual desires that only have meaning for individuals, whose perfectly independent wills determine the cost of desires that then become the data that make up utility curves. Because each individual calculates their utility individually and acts independently of one another, at no point does a suprahuman collectivity ever arise.

However, methodological individualism is, even from within neo-classical economic theory, a relationship of signification that produces circumscribed outcomes. Cloud writes that individualism is central to the ideology that supplements the capitalist mode of production: "Liberalism's core is its notion of the autonomous individual who is ostensibly free from structural or economic barriers to fortune."[31] Margaret Thatcher's policies in the 1980s foregrounded the sovereign individual, according to Harvey: "All forms of social solidarity were to be dissolved in favour of individualism, private property, personal responsibility, and family values . . . 'Economics are the method,' she said, 'but the object is to change the soul.'"[32] If "the individual" is the subject proper to the capitalist mode of production, incentive structures are the technique that accomplishes them. Because they are designed to reveal the stable preferences of the individual, how an individual responds to an incentive spur only reveals the subjective value that they have placed on the outcome. (These individualized choices are then aggregated into the utility functions of economic scholarship, but the larger point is not to be missed: the individual is *the sole* unit of account when examining a social phenomenon.) When a business motivates an individual to work harder through bonus payments, the business reveals the individual preference that a worker has for greater remuneration; when a health insurance company promises a reduction in premiums if a client agrees to smartphone surveillance, it is the client's pocketbook alone that is affected. Incentive regimes render historically constrained, situated individuals individually responsible for the choices that they have made; recall how in debates over equal pay legislation—since women have been historically underpaid and enjoined to join labor sectors that privilege caregiving and domestic labor—women in the present are presumed to have these innate incentives, and thus it is irrational to change their circumstances through minor labor market reforms. Through the incentive, Schumpeter's diagnosis of economic methodology is yoked to an "economic" explanation of outcomes: individuals are held personally responsible for their choices because only individuals can make choices.

Taking methodological individualism head-on seems a fruitless task. The empirical existence of individuals making choices within markets provides ample evidence for economics' methodological commitments, but the courtesy is never extended in reverse; organizations, ideologies, collective identities both exist and exert effects, but they cannot be the basis of a science of rational decision-making. Or as Mirowski sardonically puts it: "Collectivities can't think; and therefore they possess the same ontological status as the tooth fairy, full stop."[33] However, it is imperative to foreground the social existence of the individual, and its imbrication within social practices, for as long as the concept of "the individual" holds sway as a methodological assumption, real-world human beings will inevitably be held responsible for the choices they make within these market structures. Rhetoric is uniquely suited to this endeavor, for its starting point is the social individual caught up in a network of meanings, norms, operant tropes, and practices; as Gaonkar describes it, one image of rhetoric is a "globally pervasive constitutive agency."[34] Contemporary rhetorical theory no longer requires the image of the great individual speaking to a mass audience as its fundament, but even this traditionalist concept can be viewed from a social perspective. The work of any one speaker can be viewed as much an effect of their context and their social imaginary as their own individual creation, a node through which socially resonant tropes flow.[35] In an ironic way, Becker's own "economic approach to human behavior" provides an inverted mirror of sociality, in which the market acts as the avatar of the "social individual." Institutions, discourses, beliefs, groups, etc., all exert effects insofar as they are registered as market inputs—price signals within an individual's utility function. This rationale for the "economic approach" is an extreme contortion of the principles of empirically existing market structures as a way to authorize its metastasis into noncommodity relations. The concepts of the "shadow price" and "psychic cost" are retroactive stitchings-up of heretofore unseen forces that affect individuals' choices that do not necessarily register as actual prices, but rather, like black holes, exert gravitational effects on passing bodies.

By drawing attention to the role signification plays in human life, rhetoric denaturalizes what appears to be a relation of identity—the copula that economics yokes between social reality and market features is momentarily disrupted when interpreted from a rhetorical perspective. Marriage is not literally a market, children are not literally capital investments, and racism is not literally a preference: these are arguments "for the sake of which," grounded by a signifying practice. Methodological individualism is itself a signifying practice that grounds economic inquiry, a necessary mystification that sets limits on what can be inferred about the texture of human reality. It is here that Marx's concept of the commodity fetish can aid in a rhetorical approach. Marx's analysis of the commodity reveals not that the world of market exchange *is* society but that it is the necessary *image* of society that the mode of production presents to those within it.[36] Individuals—and only individuals—are met in the marketplace with a dazzling array of commodities, objects that bear the form of this reductive objectification. Such is a socially necessary mystification that arrives as a result of the commodity form; it is not a spontaneous feature of human life. The concept of commodity fetishism reveals how the social existence of a commodity (the labor process that brought it to being) is masked behind the commodity's identity as a thing "for us." Whereas the prophets of incentives see commodity relations as the stand-in for other relations, the commodity fetish denaturalizes this presumption. In a parallel tradition, Jodi Dean draws attention to the "collective desire" in the form of the Communist Party, which mobilizes positive affects of belonging in an existence outside of market or marketlike spaces.[37] Thus, the social existence of the individual—not the aggregated fiction of neoclassical economics—ought to guide inquiries about social phenomena, both because individuals are located within symbolic practices and because they are located within labor practices that individualize them.

3. AN INCENTIVE PRESUMES A DYADIC RELATION. FIND THE
UNSPOKEN ADDRESSEE.

In addition to incentives individualizing outcomes, they are also presumed to be dyadic: an economist, business owner, school superintendent, president, "choice architect," or a price signal emits an incentive that is acted upon by an ontologically sovereign, rational individual. (This is also what Schumpeter means when he argues that methodological individualism presupposes independent actors, which Knight followed to theoretically authorize the concept of "perfect competition.") However, signifiers sweat from every pore of the discourse of the incentive, and a way to break their spell is to look for an unacknowledged addressee thereof. The possibility of incentive indirection becomes socially operant in nudges, all of which contain an unspoken (true) addressee—not the person who is directly nudged, but the entity to whom the nudge's results are meant to address. Lacan's "Schema L" schematizes the insight that there is never a single addressee of speech (the concrete other person in a given setting) but also addresses the ego of the speaker, and what Lacan called the "big Other," or the supraindividual registrar of intelligibility.[38] Furthermore, because speech itself is a technology of indirection, it is structurally impossible to say exactly what one means—we must rely on figures of speech, elisions, allusions, and other tropes to convey meaning to our addressee. This is precisely why Lacanian psychoanalysis plays so nicely with rhetoric, for the theory agrees that there is no "zero degree" of discourse and that figuration is never simply excessive but integral to the human experience of communication. Rhetoric is simply the excess of signification over information, and psychoanalysis is the critical interpretation thereof.

It is here that Lacan's critique of intersubjectivity can be of political aid: there is no natural complementarity between the elements of a dyad because an absent third organizes it. All relationships involve some level of nonreciprocity or noncomplementarity, for "relation" implies the domain of speech and sociality (and not a mythic "immanence" or "relation without relation"). To exist within a symbolic network is to exist within a state of lack, for a signifier is a nonidentity in a dual sense: it is both by definition not the referent it names, and it is an object that refers to another signifier. Lacan gives the name "phallic signifier" to a signifier without a referent, that which marks difference as such: the pure difference between a one and a not-one. Lacan claims that the phallic signifier plays a central role in the organization of "male" and "female" positions within the symbolic order but argues that "men" do not naturally possess it. Rather, it stands between those symbolized as "men" and those symbolized as "women" as a constitutive distortion of intersubjective human relations.[39] Barnard writes that "this asymmetry marks the lack of reciprocity or harmony of structure between sexed subject positions and determines that masculine and feminine subjects relate to each *other* in terms of what they lack in relation to the *Other* (the Other here as the Other of the signifier)."[40] There is no such thing as a "proper" intersubjective relationship because all relationships of signification necessitate dwelling in this realm of overlapping lacks. So many of our ordinary binary oppositions operate as allegories for this original nonidentity within the signifier: Activity/passivity, presence/absence, subject/object, identity/difference, and particularly "male" and "female" all dramatize the deadlock. As Žižek puts it, "In the case of sexual identity, an anatomic difference is 'sublated,' turned into the medium of appearance or expression—more precisely into the material support—of a certain symbolic formation."[41] It is not the sexes that are insurmountably different, it is that sexual difference is the appearance of an idiotic material support that institutes value into difference.[42]

The unspoken addressee of an incentive can be general or specific. In the workplace, an incentive payment scheme can be read as addressed to a generalized "big Other" of the market: the more productive a worker is, the more productive the company—and the happier the stockholders and bondholders. (The bondholders in this case act as the concrete materialization of capital's drive toward realization.) Yet incentives can also be read as a message to a specific third (absent) other. As articulated in chapter 6, the aim of the Obama administration's Race to the Top program was ostensibly to improve achievement in public schools, but the vehicle for accomplishing that goal was to threaten teachers' unions with greater accountability and achievement metrics. The introduction of (voluntary) incentive programs for state education boards to compete for was an indirect method of putting downward pressure on the teachers' unions that then Education Secretary Arne Duncan saw as intransigent.[43] Similarly, Steve Kelman, the former administrator of the Office of Federal Procurement Policy under Bill Clinton (and one of the architects of Clinton's "Reinventing Government" endeavor) wrote that as a procurement officer, "Some of the worst experiences [he] had in what generally was a super job was dealing with efforts by the political people in the West Wing to use the government contracting system to promote Democratic Party goals using executive orders."[44]

Kelman's complaint was specifically that executive branch operatives would encourage him to avoid companies that "had 'bad' labor practices that the unions didn't like but were not prohibited by law."[45] That is, his goal was not to advance the political goals of influential constituencies supportive of the presidential administration or increase their material wealth but to do the opposite—refuse to add "additional requirements" to government contracting as a way to "attract more predominately commercial firms into the government marketplace."[46] Instead of satisfying the desires of organized labor, Kelman and the administration prioritized satisfying the law of economy: whatever good was cheapest in the marketplace would win the contract. The shift toward a "performance culture in government" with market- and incentive-based solutions ensures that the political priorities of workers' groups and anything that either does not register as a commodity price (or registers as part of a commodity's price but in the "wrong" direction) must be cast aside.[47] Unions function as the unspoken addressee in these recent examples, for they can rhetorically be framed as intransigent, reactionary forces precisely because they acted as an interdicting force against the political priorities of Clinton and Obama.

Thus to engage critically with any regime of incentives is to seek out this unspoken addressee and discern what unspoken desire is being satisfied if an incentive is successful. Thus the ideological question, "*Cui bono?*" can be supplemented by "Who desires?" The Affordable Care Act is a prime example of an incentive-based policy that, at a structural level, cannot lower health-care costs because its primary mechanism for incentivizing health insurance companies to cover more patients comes through financial subsidies passed through individual consumers. According to the Kaiser Family Foundation, family health insurance premiums have increased from about $13,000 per year in 2009 to around $20,000 per year in 2019.[48] As a result, UnitedHealth, the largest health insurance corporation in the United States, went from $87 billion in annual revenue in 2009 to $242 billion in 2019, with increases every single year.[49] Individuals, who up until 2019 were legally mandated to purchase insurance to avoid a financial penalty, acted as the vehicle for wealth transfer from government revenues into the health insurance industry. Because these dyads are noncomplementary, insurance companies can only be induced to provide coverage through a positive inducement (a financial reward), but individuals were induced to purchase coverage through a negative one (a financial penalty). The government, acting as a mediating agent, absorbed the cost of the effort without altering the terrain upon which health insurance operates. And of course, these mutually contradictory dyadic movements are organized around the prohibition on guaranteeing health care as a right. To summarize, because of the structural indirection of language itself, there is no "pure" relation between the incentivized and the incentivizer—any incentive is aimed at satisfying an unspoken third's desire.

4. An incentive is downward-facing. Look upward.

Fourth, it is not enough to simply recognize that individuals are held personally responsible for their choices and that an absent third is often the unspoken addressee of an incentive. It is also vital to recognize that aggregated individuals have an interest in locating a collectivity in this aggregated individuality and then turning that collectivity upward, recognizing that there is a vertical antagonism built into the structure of the incentive. Levitt and Dubner aver that with an expansive definition of incentives, markets do not create them alone: "Most incentives don't come about organically. Someone—an economist or a politician or a parent—has to invent them."[50] Although commodity markets themselves theoretically generate incentives to act rationally, social life is beset on all sides by hierarchies that are organized "like" commodity markets. As Thaler and Sunstein describe it, choice architecture is inevitable, for social life itself is organized (whether spontaneously or not) into contexts in which individuals must make choices.[51] In each instance of incentives seeping into new social formations, there must be someone creating an incentive, and someone who is assumed to react to it (like a parent incentivizing their child to run errands, or a college dean incentivizing peer mentorship). Hence why incentives and nudges take priority in technocratic visions of politics: if the masses do not know what they desire, and often make the "wrong" choice, they must be nudged by their social betters toward the proper one.

Contemporary American society is riddled with invitations to look downward, rather than upward, for solutions to collective problems. To attempt to address budgetary shortfalls, my institution, the University of Kansas, announced in June 2020 a "Voluntary Separation Incentive Program to encourage eligible staff and faculty to retire early. The administration's announcement that 147 workers would be leaving the university was accompanied by the news that "a majority of these positions will not be refilled."[52] To borrow (and invert) Margaret Thatcher's pithy phrase, the problem with capitalism is that eventually you run out of retirement-eligible people. A straightforward remedy to this problem is to turn our attention upward and once again ask what political desire is repressed when the responsibility for change is placed on the "price-takers" of social action, for the other name for human beings collectively endeavoring to change the priorities of the people in power is "mass politics." A solitary voter, union member, or protestor cannot "change the incentives" of politicians, political parties, or corporations without acting in concert toward a collective goal, in open defiance of the methodological individualism that is its economics' lifeblood. For those interested in progressive or leftward political change, the uptake of incentive-based language within the Democratic Party, for example, should be particularly worrying.

The logic of incentives is even lodged into politically inclusive endeavors: the American Civil Liberties Union's "Campaign for Smart Justice" identifies unaccountable prosecutors as one of the drivers of mass incarceration in the United States. The group's solution—voter education, litigation, and voter education—is designed "to change the incentives for prosecutors."[53] In each specific case, it is worth examining whether "incentive" is a miserly or spiteful sheath. The language of incentives is not merely redundant, but unnecessary, if the strategy for addressing actual inequalities comes from a collective perspective. On the other hand, if the logic of the incentive is deployed downward to motivate people without power into acting, then it is by definition not liberatory. It is that it is impossible to think outside of a downward-facing posture within the logic of the incentive. If an entity is in a position to create an incentive, that person, group, party, or corporation thinks they possess a determining power over your choices. Chapter 1 framed Quintilian's definition of metastasis as a transference of responsibility from one cause to another as a defensive posture, a trope to be employed only when under question. "Incentive" can today only be put on the defensive when responsibility is transferred upward within social hierarchies. This is no simple task. Looking upward, the way public school teachers did by striking in five states in 2018 and 2019, requires bravery, organization, and a refusal to be simply counted as molecular, discrete individuals, acted upon by decision-makers from above.

Once again, the ideological binding of incentives is a real danger, for their all-encompassing nature is that any choice is revelatory of one's individual preference; one can never simply choose the "other" side without participating in the regime of calculation that underwrites all incentive schemes. Refusing to sign up for bodily surveillance out of principle means one has valued one's personal autonomy over a premium reduction; refusing to work an overtime shift may transfer more work onto one's coworkers. And it should not be understated that in some cases, incentives are more coercive than suasive. States that implement "workfare" requirements incentivize indigent people to seek out low-paying jobs in exchange for medical care, but this choice often yokes people into low-paying jobs to meet the bare minimum standards. As the Urban Institute points out, over one hundred thousand people in Kentucky were at risk of losing their Medicaid enrollment thanks to a 2018 regulatory change despite the fact that they have severe illnesses, disabilities, or cannot physically access employment.[54] As Lacan writes, whenever faced with a binary choice, one must reject it as false—some sacrifice of enjoyment is ever-present. The "your money or your life!" binary is materialized in these pernicious workfare requirements. Once again, the danger of incentives is not that they do not work but that they work far too well.

Consider the Lacanian dictum, "The unconscious is the discourse of the Other": the discourse of incentives encourages adopting the rhetorical position of the technocrat, the economist, or the politician, looking downward at any incentive scheme. Incentives offer for people a perspective, from this position of the third, to imagine what motivates the other, and to enjoy whether they act or not. If one is not the direct addressee of an incentive—say, if one is not specifically demonized by campaigns decrying "Welfare Queens"—one can instead revel in the adoption of the technocrat's rhetorical position. If an individual succeeds in making the "rational" choice, or is socially irresponsible, the discourse of incentives is victorious coming and going: either the incentive scheme was successful (and changing individuals' incentives changed the outcome) or it was unsuccessful (thereby generating an alibi about the unacknowledged incentives that motivated people's behaviors). This downward-facing position is not imaginary—the absent third persists in every incentive, whether obvious or not. The pervasiveness of incentives as a catch-all explanation makes this position easier to adopt, for it directs enjoyment downward, upon the chooser who has failed to enjoy properly, who has chosen the suboptimal, aneconomic path. The greatest fear of any incentive regime is that somewhere, someone is out there, not optimizing; "incentives" provide mathematical proof of a moral or economic failure to behave rationally. The superegoic injunction "Enjoy!" contains a silent addition: "properly."

5. ALL INCENTIVES FUNCTION RETROACTIVELY. REFUSE THE TELEOLOGICAL BINDING.

Central to the incentive is the process by which all choices in the present are assumed to have been caused by an unseen market force in the past, effectively insulating a critical interpretation of the present. The psychoanalytic concept of retroactive causality (the retroactive attribution of cause) is the economic alibi for all manner of inequalities, both social and economic. From the mundane, such as attributing a football player's missed shot to their incentive for personal glory, to the consequential, such as attributing someone's failure to sign up for welfare benefits as evidence of the incentive for personal dignity, incentive rhetoric locks its interlocutors in a loop, in which the best one can do is neurotically chase down an alternative incentive. This process is not reversed or remedied when incentives are applied proactively onto a social field. Whether in a politically conservative direction (like Becker advocating for a market in human organs) or a politically neoliberal one (like the Obama adminis-tration incentivizing preventative health measures), the animating form remains the same: individuals are utility maximizers with stable preferences making choices within a market structure. This process is not natural (not even economic) but rhetorical. Incentive rhetoric bends the attribution of cause backward to insulate the status quo from criticism, inverting the Nietzschean axiom into "thus, *you* willed it." Each of these examples weds the new to the old, an eternal repetition of the same within the clear confines of neoclassical economic theory.

While economics works backward to retroactively justify the pres-ent, psychoanalysis looks for the signifiers that will unbind the action of retroactive causality. Retroactive causality is the keystone of incentive rhetoric, and the critical task is to unbind the metonymic chain that turns a contingent outcome into an inevitable one. One example illustrates the perfidy of retroaction that works on behalf of the powerful, with the unsymbolized gap between cause and effect hanging over its subjects like the sword of Damocles. According to an investigation into on-the-job injuries at Amazon, workers were offered pizza by the megacorporation "as a reward for a streak of injury-free shifts."[55] Yet the investigatory report would not be out of place in Marx's *Capital*, for it details how the increased mechanization at Amazon warehouses did not free workers from their toil, but instead, placed even greater pressure on them to fulfill orders at a much higher rate. (In some cases, once robotics were installed into warehouses, workers were asked to fulfill four times as many orders as before.) Crucially, there is a split between what is enunciated and what is conveyed in the offer of a pizza reward—this gap is the space of rhetoric. At the level of the enunciation, the pizza reward, offered by representatives of the world's wealthiest person, is an incentive to work safely to avoid injury. Yet Amazon workers were acutely aware of what the incentive meant to convey. The incentive was not designed to prevent an injury at work: it was designed for workers not to report injuries at work. According to *Reveal News*, "Some workers would push through the pain rather than be the person who cost their co-workers free pizza."[56] The incentive does not eliminate workplace injuries; it introduces a regime of signification between what is desired and what is achieved in order to insulate Amazon from paying worker's compensation to injured people.

If individuals have *an incentive to avoid reporting injuries*, then a regime of signifiers has interdicted upon the setting and exerts a causal force on the workers without changing the context of their actions. The workplace is not safer; workers are simply made aware of their safety by being promised a reward if they maintain it. It should go without saying that the value of the pizza is far, far less in monetary terms to Amazon than the orders delivered, but that of course is even beside the point. This particular incentive knots together solidaristic and monetary incentives and puts pressure on workers to avoid reporting injuries not for themselves but because doing so would take the reward away from others. Thus the incentive functions as an interdiction upon looking upward—if a worker is injured on the job, they are personally responsible for their entire workplace being denied a reward. Amazon workers have protested, petitioned, and begun the hard process of unionization to protect against the scapegoating of individual workers' injuries and mistreatment within warehouses, so any downward-facing blame is never guaranteed. However, incentives like these will always function as the managerial alibi for outcomes within a workplace; they are the socially operant fantasy that is imputed into social reality, not the texture of reality itself.

The ineluctability of the signifier is the cause of every outcome within a regime of incentives, whether that incentive is successful or not. There are four options available within this particular scheme:

a. Worker is more careful about their actions, earns pizza (which reveals that their own bodily safety can only be supplemented by material reward and the fear of letting down their colleagues).

b. Worker reports an injury (is revealed to not be motivated by pizza or their own safety, held personally responsible for their choices, and denies their coworkers a reward).

c. Worker suffers an injury at work but refuses to report it, in order to ensure coworkers receive reward.

d. The fourth option speaks to the hole at the heart of the incentive-based approach: a worker may be motivated to aid their colleagues and gain a material reward themselves, but is beset by their own self-consciousness about the injunction to be more careful, and makes an honest mistake.

Of course, what is barred from this decision matrix is the most obvious: it is the responsibility of the warehouse owner and manager to ensure the safety of their workforce with adequate equipment, protocols, standards, and so on. No incentive can reveal what it is deliberately designed to conceal. This incentive materializes the old proletarian slogan "An injury to one is an injury to all," but inverts its meaning through collective punishment.

It is because human beings are cursed with an unconscious that incentives cause a structural destabilization within them—the unconscious opens the space for retroactive causality to emerge. As Fink writes, "*The unconscious is full of other people's talk, other people's conversations, and other people's goals, aspirations, and fantasies.*"[57] This does not mean that individuals are entirely self-conscious or self-present about their own motives and action, rather the exact opposite: because we are ruled by our unconscious thoughts, we can never be sure whether what we do is what we desired. The inability for any person to have the final word and express the final cause of their action leaves a gap that is filled retroactively by the incentive. In each of the possible outcomes, the worker's actions and desires are bent around the unavoidable signifier "pizza," which is metonymically chained to other signifiers in the subject's unconscious (the names of coworkers, the image of their disappointment or happiness, and so on).[58] And like the injunction "do not think about an elephant," the incentive may even become the cause of the opposite outcome intended. The presence of an incentive turns the neurotic's unanswerable question, "What *did* I truly desire?" into a definitive answer: "You desired *that.*" We are never rid of the agency of the signifier: just because something is *called* an incentive does not mean that the so-called incentive itself more effectively captures the unarticulated desire; the self-conscious application *of* incentives to issues of public importance compounds the error by making incentives a part of our consideration (rather than merely the name we affix to the spontaneous actions of individuals within market society). Language's own "inner distance," its inability to fully signify what is intended, is the clue that we are working within circuits of desire around an impossibility.

To summarize, each of the five postulates of incentives must be met not simply by their negation but by action. Since incentives turn individuals into utility maximizers, one must locate the unspoken desire—the useless *jouissance* in people's activity. Since incentives render people individually responsible for their constrained choices, one must foreground the social existence of individuals and their situatedness within rhetorical contexts. Since incentives are presumed to be dyadic, working from one source onto an incentivized population, one must seek the unspoken addressee of any incentive. Since incentives are downward facing, it is absolutely essential to look upward and question a technocratic, top-down vision of the social bond. And finally, since incentives are organized by retroactive causality (which summarizes each of these prior commitments), one must look to the agency of the letter in the unconscious to unbind what appears to be an airtight explanation of the cause of all social reality. The game is, unsurprisingly, rigged on behalf of the powerful: those who use the data of the past as a justification for the present and who use the "economically rational" decision as proof of why the poor act the way they do or why the climate cannot be saved. Castoriadis's phrase, "causation by representation" summarizes the commitments of critical psychoanalytic work: human beings, in thrall to signifying regimes, are in an imaginary relationship with the signifiers that circulate around them.[59] The signifiers of neoclassical economics narrate cause back to us and render a chaotic, criminally unequal world as justifiable. Psychoanalysis alone cannot construct a new vision of "the good," but its concept of a rhetorical unconscious serves as a guiding principle for critical inquiries into the works of the powerful. The story economics tells us is never as airtight as it imagines, for it must occur within the coordinates of speech, a terrain I hope to not concede any further. Workers of the world, unite! You have nothing to lose but your metonymic chains.

Notes

Introduction

1. Philip Mirowski, *Never Let a Serious Crisis Go to Waste: How Neoliberalism Survived the Financial Meltdown* (New York: Verso, 2014), 222.

2. Steven D. Levitt and Stephen J. Dubner, *Freakonomics: A Rogue Economist Explores the Hidden Side of Everything* (New York: William Morrow, 2005), 13.

3. Quoted in Jeanne Lorraine Schroeder, *The Triumph of Venus: The Erotics of the Market* (Berkeley: University of California Press, 2004), 17.

4. Jonah Keri, "The Duncan Way: How Cardinals Pitchers Continue to Dominate by Exploiting Hitter Tendencies," *Grantland*, May 21, 2014, http://grantland.com/the-triangle/st-louis-cardinals-pitchers-dave-duncan-adam-wainwright-michael-wacha/.

5. Kevin D. Hoover, "Causality in Economics and Econometrics," in *The New Palgrave Dictionary of Economics*, ed. Steven N. Durlauf and Lawrence E. Blume. 2nd ed. (London: Palgrave Macmillan, 2008), https://doi.org/10.1057/978-1-349-95121-5_2227-1), 719–728.

6. Steven D. Levitt and Stephen J. Dubner, *SuperFreakonomics: Global Cooling, Patriotic Prostitutes, and Why Suicide Bombers Should Buy Life Insurance* (New York: William Morrow, 2009), 45.

7. "Incentives," in *Oxford Dictionary of Economics*, ed. John Black, Nigar Hashimzade & Gareth Myles, 3rd ed. (Oxford: Oxford University Press, 2009).

8. "Linking Staff Incentives with Frequent Reporting and Target Hitting," *Be the Business*, https://www.bethebusiness.com/productivity-insights/linking-staff-incentives-with-frequent-reporting-and-target-hitting (accessed September 9, 2020).

9. Wendy R. Boswell, Alexander J. S. Colvin, and Todd C. Darnold, "Organizational Systems and Employee Motivation," in *Work Motivation: Past, Present, and Future* eds. Ruth Kanfer, Gilad Chen, Robert D. Pritchard (New York: Routledge, 2008), 368.

10. Chidiebere Ogbonnaya, Kevin Daniels, and Karina Nielsen, "Research: How Incentive Pay Affects Employee Engagement, Satisfaction, and Trust," *Harvard Business Review*, March 15, 2017, https://hbr.org/2017/03/research-how-incentive-pay-affects-employee-engagement-satisfaction-and-trust.

11. Elizabeth Findell, "Debate over City Incentives Stirs Concern," *Austin-American Statesman*, September 25, 2017.

12. Aaron Mak, "Here Are the Outrageous Incentives that Losing Cities Offered Amazon for HQ2," *Slate*, November 14, 2018, https://slate.com/technology/2018/11/amazon-hq2-incredible-incentives-losing-cities-offered.html.

13. N. Gregory Mankiw, *Principles of Macroeconomics*, 5th ed. (Mason, OH: South-Western Cengage Learning, 2008), 7.

14. Gary S. Becker, *The Economic Approach to Human Behavior* (Chicago: University of Chicago Press, 1976), 14.

15. Christian Arnsperger and Yanis Varoufakis, "What Is Neoclassical Economics? The Three Axioms Responsible for its Theoretical Œuvre, Practical Irrelevance, and, thus, Discursive Power," *Panœconomicus* 1 (2006), 5–6. The authors rightly decry critics of neoclassical economics for directing their ire at "hyper-rational bargain hunters . . . *selfish* individualism or Pareto optimality," each of which are features but unnecessary for the enterprise to function as a whole.

16. Steven D. Levitt and Stephen J. Dubner, *Think Like a Freak: The Authors of* Freakonomics *Offer to Retrain your Brain* (New York: William Morrow, 2014), 106–7.

17. Benjamin Powell, "Private Property Rights, Economic Freedom, and Well Being," Mercatus Center, George Mason University, Working Paper 19, https://www.mercatus.org/system/files/Private-Property-Rights-Economic-Freedom-and-Well-Being.pdf (accessed September 10, 2020).

18. Gary S. Becker, *Accounting for Tastes* (Cambridge, MA: Harvard University Press, 1998), 4.

19. Robert H. Frank, *The Economic Naturalist: Why Economics Explains Almost Everything* (London: Virgin, 2008).

20. Jack Hirshleifer, "The Expanding Domain of Economics," *American Economic Review* 75 (1985): 53.

21. Hirshleifer, "The Expanding Domain of Economics," 53.

22. Maurice Allais, "Nobel Lecture," in *Nobel Lectures, Economics 1981–1990*, ed. Karl-Göran Mäler (Singapore: World Scientific Publishing Co., 1990), 243.

23. Ernest Fehr, interview in *European Economics at a Crossroads*, ed. J. Barkley Rosser Jr., Richard P. F. Holt, and David Colander (Northampton, UK: Edward Elgar, 2010), 72–73.

24. Ben Fine and Dimitris Milonakis, *From Economics Imperialism to Frea-*konomics: *The Shifting Boundaries between Economics and other Social Sciences* (New York: Routledge, 2009) 95.

25. Joe Earle, Cahal Moran, and Zach Ward-Perkins, *The Econocracy: The Perils of Leaving Economics to the Experts* (Manchester, UK: Manchester University Press, 2017).

26. Nancy MacLean, *Democracy in Chains: The Deep History of the Radical Right's Stealth Plan for America* (New York: Viking, 2017), 195.

27. See chapter 2, "The Other Doctor Shock: Milton Friedman and the Search for a Laissez-Faire Laboratory," in Naomi Klein, *The Shock Doctrine: The Rise of Disaster Capitalism* (New York: Picador, 2007).

28. Quoted in Becky Beaupre Gillespie, "Partnerships and Learning at the Mothership of Law and Economics," *Law School Communications*, July 27, 2017, http://www.law.uchicago.edu/news/partnerships-and-learning-mothership-law-and-economics.

29. H.R. 3590. "Patient Protection and Affordable Care Act." 2010.

30. Lawrence Grossberg, *Cultural Studies in the Future Tense* (Durham, NC: Duke University Press, 2010), 148.

31. Quoted in "Sorry Ma'am—We Just Didn't See it Coming," *Associated Press*, July 26, 2009, http://www.nbcnews.com/id/32156155/ns/business-world_business/t/sorry-maam-we-just-didnt-see-it-coming/#.X1Z5vnlKg2w.

32. Grossberg, *Cultural Studies in the Future Tense*, 110.

33. See Marshall Steinbaum, "Empiricism Alone Won't Save Us," *Boston Review*, March 26, 2019, https://bostonreview.net/forum_response/marshall-steinbaum-empiricism-wont-save-us.

34. Jacques Lacan, "Presentation on Psychical Causality," in *Écrits*, trans. Bruce Fink (New York: W. W. Norton, 2006), 139.

35. Adam Kotsko, *Neoliberalism's Demons: On the Political Theology of Late Capital* (Stanford, CA: Stanford University Press, 2018), 33.

36. From now on, I largely refer to "neoclassical economic theory," or to the discipline of economics, rather than to "neoliberalism" as my object of analysis and critique. This is not to say that neoliberalism is not worth studying as a periodizing concept or an adjective attached to specific practices—as Kotsko points out, the Affordable Care Act is a prime example of neoliberal policy. I agree with David Harvey's assessment of neoliberalism as a class project aimed at redistributing wealth upward. See David Harvey, *A Brief History of Neoliberalism* (Oxford: Oxford University Press, 2007), 16. The means by which this is achieved and theoretically justified is through the application of neoclassical principles, with some slight revisions, into noneconomic domains. Its signifying practices did not "cause" neoliberalism but rather act as a causal alibi for the implementation of neoliberal policies.

37. See G. Thomas Goodnight and Sandy Green, "Rhetoric, Risk and Markets: The Dot-Com Bubble," *Quarterly Journal of Speech* 96 (2010): 120; and Joshua S. Hanan, Indradeep Ghosh, and Kaleb W. Brooks, "Banking on the Present: The Ontological Rhetoric of Neoclassical Economics and its Relationship to the 2008 Financial Crisis," *Quarterly Journal of Speech* 100 (2014): 149.

38. Crystal Colombini, "Energeia, Kinesis, and the Neoliberal Rhetoric of Strategic Default," *Journal for the History of Rhetoric* 21, no. 2 (2018): 178–93.

39. Blake Abbott, "'A Widespread Loss of Confidence': TARP, Presidential Rhetoric, and the Crisis of Neoliberalism," *Communication Quarterly* 66, no. 5 (2018): 463–80.

40. Jacques Lacan, *The Ethics of Psychoanalysis, 1959–1960: The Seminar of Jacques Lacan, Book VII*, ed. Jacques-Alain Miller, trans. Dennis Porter (New York: W. W. Norton, 1988), 33.

41. Thomas Rickert, *Acts of Enjoyment: Rhetoric, Žižek, and the Return of the Subject* (Pittsburgh: University of Pittsburgh Press, 2007), 63.

42. See Jacques Lacan, "The Instance of the Letter in the Unconscious, or Reason since Freud," in *Écrits*, trans. Bruce Fink (New York: W. W. Norton, 2006).

43. Among others, see Joshua Gunn, "Refitting Fantasy: Psychoanalysis, Subjectivity, and Talking to the Dead," *Quarterly Journal of Speech* 90 (2004): 1–23; and Calum Matheson, "'What Does Obama Want of Me?' Anxiety and Jade Helm 15," *Quarterly Journal of Speech* 102 (2016): 133–49.

44. Fredric Jameson, *An American Utopia: Dual Power and the Universal Army*, ed. Slavoj Žižek (New York: Verso, 2016), 74.

Chapter 1

1. Jacques Lacan, *The Seminar of Jacques Lacan, Book V: Formations of the Unconscious*, ed. Jacques-Alain Miller, trans. Russell Grigg (Malden, MA: Polity, 2017), 12.

2. Lacan notes "metaphor, catachresis, antonomasis, allegory, [and] metonymy," among others. Lacan, "The Function and Field of Speech and Language in Psychoanalysis," 222.

3. Sigmund Freud, *The Interpretation of Dreams*, trans. James Strachey (New York: Avon Books, 1998), 601–2.

4. Derek Hook, "Toward an Erotics of Truth: Commentary on Session I," in *Reading Lacan's Seminar VIII: Transference*, ed. Gautam Basu Thakur and Jonathan Dickstein (Cham, Switzerland: Palgrave Macmillan, 2020), 9.

5. Ronald Walter Greene, "Another Materialist Rhetoric," *Critical Studies in Mass Communication* 15 (1998), 21–41.

6. Dan Mills, "'Set and Characters' and 'The Metaphor of Love: Phaedrus'— Commentary on Sessions II and III," in *Reading Lacan's Seminar VIII: Transference*, ed. Gautam Basu Thakur and Jonathan Dickstein (Cham, Switzerland: Palgrave Macmillan, 2020), 27.

7. Christian O. Lundberg, *Lacan in Public: Psychoanalysis and the Science of Rhetoric* (Tuscaloosa: University of Alabama Press, 2012), 3–4.

8. Lundberg, *Lacan in Public*, 2–3.

9. Lundberg, 4.

10. Rickert, *Acts of Enjoyment*, 64.

11. Néstor A. Braunstein, *Jouissance: A Lacanian Concept*, trans. Silvia Rosman (Albany: State University of New York Press, 2020), 13.

12. Silvia Rosman, "Introduction," in Néstor A. Braunstein, *Jouissance: A Lacanian Concept*, trans. Silvia Rosman (Albany: State University of New York Press, 2020), 4.

13. Christian O. Lundberg, "Revisiting the Future of Meaning," *Quarterly Journal of Speech* 101 (2015): 173–85.

14. Rickert, *Acts of Enjoyment*, 98.

15. Sigmund Freud, *Three Case Histories* (New York: Macmillan, 1996), 195, 215.

16. Jacques Lacan, "The Function and Field of Speech and Language in Psychoanalysis," in *Écrits*, trans. Bruce Fink (New York: W. W. Norton, 2006), 213.

17. Aristotle, *Aristotle's Physics*, revised by W. D. Ross (Oxford: Clarendon, 1955), 16.

18. Jacques Lacan, "Science and Truth," in *Écrits*, trans. Bruce Fink (New York: W. W. Norton, 2006), 741.

19. Aristotle, *Aristotle's Metaphysics*, trans. Hippocrates G. Apostle (Bloomington: Indiana University Press, 1966) 74.

20. Paul Humphrey, "Metaphysics of Mind: Hylomorphism and Eternality in Aristotle and Hegel" (PhD diss., State University of New York at Stony Brook, 2007), 71.

21. Lacan, *Anxiety*, 284.

22. Lacan, 284.

23. Jacques Lacan, *The Seminar of Jacques Lacan, Book X: Anxiety*, ed. Jacques-Alain Miller, trans. A. R. Price (Malden: Polity, 2014), 218.

24. The game "rock, paper, scissors" exemplifies the logic of the unconscious. The three terms entail that for each winning throw, there is one other option that would have changed the outcome. If one throws "rock," and loses to "paper," one need only have chosen the other signifier, "scissors," to win the hand. The truth of this missed encounter, however, only emerges retroactively and cannot have been known ahead of time; neurotically, and in any other similar situation, we look back at this failure and think, "If I had only used the other signifier . . ."

25. The psychoanalytic unconscious means not that people do not know the hidden truths about the depths of their psyche but that they do—and deploy psychological mechanisms to repress these truths.

26. Jacques Lacan, *The Seminar of Jacques Lacan, Book XI: The Four Fundamental Concepts of Psychoanalysis*, ed. Jacques-Alain Miller, trans. Alan Sheridan (New York: W.W. Norton, 1998), 128.

27. Philippe van Haute, *Against Adaptation: Lacan's "Subversion" of the Subject*, trans. Paul Crowe and Miranda Vankerk (New York: Other Press, 2002), 92–93.

28. Jacques Lacan, "The Subversion of the Subject and the Dialectic of Desire in the Freudian Unconscious," in *Écrits: A Selection* trans. Bruce Fink (New York: W. W. Norton, 2006), 294.

29. The persistence of "nominative determinism" in fiction, with soldiers named "Hunter," or reporters named "Scoop," is the deliberate instantiation of this phenomenon; outside of fiction, individuals named things "Winner," "King," or "Destiny" is the parental gamble that the signifier will exert agency on the child. In extreme cases of nominative determinism result in a married pair of pioneering sex researchers being named Masters and Johnson.

30. Cicero, *de Oratore* Book III, trans. H. Rackham (Cambridge. MA: Harvard University Press, 1942), 163.

31. Gary A. Remer, *Ethics and the Orator: The Ciceronian Tradition of Political Morality* (Chicago: University of Chicago Press, 2017), 27.

32. Quintilian, *Quintilian's Institutes of Oratory: or, Education of an Orator*, vol. 2. Trans. Rev. John Shelby Watson (London: George Bell & Sons, Ltd., 1891), 44–45.

33. Henry Peacham, *The Garden of Eloquence* 1577, 181–82, http://gateway.proquest.com.www2.lib.ku.edu/openurl?ctx_ver=Z39.88-2003&xri:pqil:res_ver=0.2&res_id=xri:lion&rft_id=xri:lion:ft:pr:Z200728358 (accessed February 1, 2016).

34. George Puttenham, *The Art of English Poesy, A Critical Edition*, ed. Frank Whigham and Wayne A. Rebhorn (Ithaca, NY: Cornell University Press, 2007), 318.

35. AgentShades, "Why I Hate *The Phantom Pain*'s Tranquilizer Gun," *Kotaku*, September 23, 2016, https://tay.kinja.com/why-i-hate-the-phantom-pains-tranquilizer-gun-1786994266.

36. Crime Prevention Research Center, "Updated: More Misleading Information from Bloomberg's Everytown for Gun Safety on Guns," September 1, 2014, https://crimeresearch.org/2014/09/more-misleading-information-from-bloombergs-everytown-for-gun-safety-on-guns-analysis-of-recent-mass-shootings/.

37. Richard H. Thaler and Cass R. Sunstein, *Nudge: Improving Decisions about Health, Wealth and Happiness* (New York: Penguin, 2009), 1.

38. Ezra Klein, https://twitter.com/ezraklein/status/1354134416377827328, January 26, 2021.

39. State of Kansas HealthQuest 2017 Incentive Guide.

40. Sajit Mehmood, https://twitter.com/smehmood/status/773596786434961408, September 7, 2016.

41. Kaushik Basu, *Beyond the Invisible Hand: Groundwork for a New Economics* (Princeton, NJ: Princeton University Press, 2011), 102.

42. Basu, *Beyond the Invisible Hand*, 139.

43. James M. Buchanan and Gordon Tullock, *The Calculus of Consent: Logical Foundations of Constitutional Democracy* (Ann Arbor: University of Michigan Press, 1962), 67.

44. Gary Becker and Guity Nashat Becker, *The Economics of Life: From Baseball to Affirmative Action to Immigration, How Real-World Issues Affect our Everyday Life* (New York: McGraw-Hill, 1997), 101.

45. Thaler and Sunstein, *Nudge*, 4.

46. Maurice Godelier, *Rationality and Irrationality in Economics* (New York: Verso, 2013), 12, 14.

47. Quamrul Ashraf and Oded Galor, "The 'Out of Africa' Hypothesis, Human Genetic Diversity, and Comparative Economic Development," *American Economic Review* 103 (2013), 43.

48. Ashraf and Galor, "The 'Out of Africa' Hypothesis," 2.

49. Ashraf and Galor, 43.

50. Ashraf and Galor, 43.

51. Luke Adams, "Players with Incentive Bonuses for 2016/7," *Hoops Rumors*, November 7, 2016, https://www.hoopsrumors.com/2016/11/players-with-incentive-bonuses-for-201617.html.

52. Derek Thompson, "The Economics of Penalty Kicks in Soccer," *Atlantic* June 10, 2010, http://www.theatlantic.com/business/archive/2010/06/the-economics-of-penalty-kicks-in-soccer/58001.

53. P. A. Chiappori, S. Levitt & T. Groseclose, "Testing Mixed-Strategy Equilibria When Players Are Heterogenous: The Case of Penalty Kicks in Soccer," *American Economic Review* 92 (2002), 1139, 1141. The authors also assume that one player's action does not affect the other and that shooters behave as if the goalkeepers are all identical.

54. Chiappori, Levitt, and Groseclose, "Testing Mixed-Strategy Equilibria," 1150. These simplifications nullify the analysis' predictive value: predictive models are ultimately self-defeating according to received economic theory, since markets resettle at new equilibria once new information enters the system. Once shooters habitually kick down the middle, rational keepers will remain still and swat away attempts until behavior changes.

55. Levitt and Dubner, *Think Like a Freak*, 6–7.

56. Catherine Chaput, "Popular Economics: Neoliberal Propaganda and Its Affectivity. In *Propaganda and Rhetoric in Democracy: History, Theory, Analysis*, ed. Gae Lyn Henderson and M. J. Braun (Carbondale: Southern Illinois University Press, 2016), 157–80.

57. Andy Hunter, "Ivory Coast Given Incentive to Transform Elephants' Forgettable Record," *Guardian*, June 23, 2014, http://www.theguardian.com/football/2014/jun/23/elephants-ivory-coast-world-cup-greece.

58. Jacques Lacan, *The Seminar of Jacques Lacan, Book III: The Psychoses*, trans. Russell Grigg (New York: W. W. Norton, 1993), 82.

232 | Notes to Chapter 2

Chapter 2

1. Hyun-Ah Kim, *The Renaissance Ethics of Music: Singing, Contemplation and* Musica Humana (New York: Routledge, 2015), 42.

2. Richard B. McKenzie and Dwight R. Lee, *Managing Through Incentives: How to Develop a More Collaborative, Productive, and Profitable Organization* (Oxford: Oxford University Press, 1998), 18.

3. Plato, *Phaedrus*, www.classics.mit.edu/Plato/phaedrus.html.

4. C. K. Ogden & I. A. Richards, *The Meaning of Meaning* (San Diego: Harcourt, 1927), 36, 24.

5. Gorgias, *Encomium of Helen*, in *Reading Rhetorical Theory*, ed. Barry Brummett (Fort Worth: Harcourt Brace, 2000), 32.

6. Plato, *Gorgias*, www.classics.mit.edu/Plato/gorgias.html.

7. Sigmund Freud, *New Introductory Lectures on Psycho-analysis*, trans. W.J.H. Sprott (New York: Norton, 1989).

8. Joshua Gunn, *Modern Occult Rhetoric: Mass Media and the Drama of Secrecy in the Twentieth Century* (Tuscaloosa: University of Alabama Press, 2005), 40.

9. John Durham Peters, *Speaking into the Air: A History of the Idea of Communication* (Chicago: University of Chicago Press, 1999), 13.

10. Deirdre McCloskey, *The Rhetoric of Economics* (Madison: University of Wisconsin Press, 1998.

11. Mankiw, *Principles of Macroeconomics*, 9. Clearly, he is nodding to Gary Becker, the subject of chapter 3.

12. As addressed in chapter 1, methodological equilibration as a foundational axiom for neoclassical economics presumes that markets clear, or have always-already cleared. The theoretical twist that Gary Becker (and others) make in the 1970s is that if a market appears at disequilibrium (such as widespread racial discrimination or income inequality), the desires of market participants are being satisfied in ways unseen or unthought by traditional economic analysis (and certainly unthought by other disciplines, such as sociology, anthropology, or history). The metaphor of financial motivation as the basis for all human action transforms into economics becoming a unified theory of all motivation, whether it be financial or not. Money becomes one signifier among many, and "the market" itself becomes the governing metaphoric apparatus.

13. Hanan, Ghosh and Brooks, "Banking on the Present."

14. In a conversation on Michel Foucault's interpretation of his work in 2013, Gary Becker tacitly agrees to this one criticism of his "economic approach to human behavior." When it becomes a proactive set of implementable techniques rather than an empirical account of behavior, knowing what incentives work on different people makes them liable to being influenced beyond their conscious control.

15. Marx's discovery of surplus value is that, in seemingly "equal" exchanges (like a worker offering labor power in exchange for a wage), an inequality arises. Incentive rhetoric provides ideological cover for the fundamental inequality that fuels the capitalist mode of production. Adding "the incentive" to social relationships forces them to obey the tenets of markets—if anything happens, it is because someone "was incentivized" to take that action freely, or was perversely incentivized by entities that neoclassical economists disdain: unions or governments. For instance, Becker supports a wide range of coercive state action (violent crackdowns on immigration, continuing the "war on drugs," the elimination of teacher tenure, bans on various consumer goods, etc.) that would alter the incentive structures of the relevant actors, but because they fit his chosen political proclivities, they are acceptable. The work of Gary Becker will be discussed in greater detail in the following chapter.

16. "Incentive," *Online Etymology Dictionary*, n.d., https://www.etymonline.com/word/incentive#etymonline_v_6305, accessed October 1, 2020.

17. "Incantation," *Online Etymology Dictionary*, n.d., https://www.etymonline.com/word/incantation#etymonline_v_6296, accessed October 1, 2020.

18. Varro, *On Agriculture*. Translated by W. D. Hooper (Harvard University Press, Loeb Classical Library, 1934), 177.

19. Plutarch, *The Philosophie, Commonlie Called, the Morals Written by the Learned Philosopher Plutarch of Charonea*. Translated by Philemon Holland (London, Arnold Hatfield, 1603).

20. Plutarch. *Plutarch's Morals*. Translated by Several Hands, corrected and revised by William W. Goodwin, vol. 2, Little, Brown, 1878. Holland translates the passage as "it pricketh, provoketh, and stirreth exceedingly," 308.

21. Plutarch. *Moralia*, trans. W. M. Helmbold (Cambridge, MA: Harvard University Press, 1939), 4:323, 325.

22. Johann Wolfgang von Goethe, "Der Rattenfänger," *Stade Hameln*, n.d., https://www.hameln.de/en/thepiedpiper/thepiedpiper/pied-piper-by-goethe (accessed October 1, 2020).

23. As I discuss in later chapters, the Lacanian interpretation of this is simple: any desire must be indirectly, asymptotically approached. Economics is not wrong in that regard. However, the lesson must be redoubled and folded back onto the language of "incentives" itself: to be incentivized by (indirect) incentives is itself a "perverse" outcome, and not any more "true" than the initial reward. The money commodity, moreover, is itself a mediating device and not a pure conduit of desire. In sum, not all desires are perverse, but all satisfactions are. A Lacanian distinguishes between desire and satisfaction, whereas the neoclassical economists suture them.

24. In the Latin: "In historico namque contextu chronographorum nobis diligentia delegato relucet clarius norma morum, forma vivendi, probitatis incentivum."

25. Michael Drayton, *Poly-olbion. or A chorographicall description of tracts, riuers, mountaines, forests, and other parts of this renowned isle of great britaine with intermixture of the most remarquable stories, antiquities, wonders, rarityes, pleasures, and commodities of the same: Digested in a poem by michael drayton, esq. with a table added, for direction to those occurrences of story and antiquitie, whereunto the course of the volume easily leades not.* London, Printed by Humphrey] Lownes] for Mathew Lownes: I. Browne: I. Helme, and I. Busbie. Retrieved from www2.lib.ku.edu/login?url=https://www.proquest.com/books/poly-olbion-chorographicall-description-tracts/docview/2248504116/se-2?accountid=14556, 96, 97.

26. Selden, *Poly-Olbion*, 164.

27. Selden, 164.

28. Higden, *Polychronicon Ranulphi Higden Monachi Cestrensis.* London, Longman & Co., 1865, 5.

29. John Milton, Elijah Fenton, and Samuel Johnson. *Paradise Lost.* Cambridge, Harvard University Press, 1821, 184.

30. Jacques Lacan, *The Seminar of Jacques Lacan, Book VIII: Transference* (Cambridge: Polity, 2015), 151.

31. Joshua Gunn, "For the Love of Rhetoric, with Continual Reference to Kenny and Dolly," *Quarterly Journal of Speech* 94 (2008), 131–155.

32. Plato, *Symposium of Plato*, trans. Tom Griffith, engraved by Peter Forster (Berkeley: University of California Press, 1989), 215c. Ironically, Alcibiades was murdered in Phrygia, the place where Marsyas was (mythologically) said to have been flayed by Apollo, his blood forming the source of the Phrygian River.

33. Quinet, *Lacan's Clinical Technique*, 32.

34. See Lacan, *The Seminar of Jacques Lacan, Book XI: The Four Fundamental Concepts of Psychoanalysis*, 258.

35. Lacan, *Transference*, 27.

36. Fink, *Lacan's Clinical Technique*, 32–33.

37. Antonio Quinet, *Lacan's Clinical Technique: Lack(a)nian Analysis* (London: Karnac, 2018), 93.

38. Quinet, *Lacan's Clinical Technique*, 92.

39. The *objet a* is, at root, a compromise formation that takes place from within the coordinates of masculine *jouissance*. It names, but does not solve, the problem of human desire as inevitably yoked to signifiers, whereas a more inclusive vision of *jouissance* would include that which resides wholly outside the law of the signifier. Lacan's concept of "feminine *jouissance*," or an enjoyment without reduction of the Other to an object, is this other *jouissance*, which I take up in chapter 4. The money commodity exemplifies masculine *jouissance*, for it promotes an articulation of desire condensed into an intelligible object. Money is never one's "own," as it partakes in a mystification by which it appears to be the "real thing" that indicates value despite taking part in an economy of desire. Others (Tomšič, Žižek, even Lacan to some extent) have propitiously interpreted

the relationship of money to castration, and their insights are useful here. To reduce one's own desires to money is to sacrifice some (inarticulable) portion to a dialectic of recognition; the supposedly "universal" standard of value depends on being recognizably worthwhile to others. The unstated supplement to the seemingly incontrovertible statement, "People respond to incentives" is "in accordance with the laws of neoclassical economics." But it is precisely this supplement that functions as symbolic castration and circumscribes (pun intended) any available answer in advance.

40. Robert Heilbroner. *The Worldly Philosophers: The Lives, Times, and Ideas of the Great Economic Thinkers*, 7th ed. (New York: Touchstone, 1999), 209.

41. Heilbroner, *The Worldly Philosophers*, 209.

42. Alfred Marshall, *Principles of Economics*, vol. 1 (New York: Macmillan & Co., 1895), 75.

43. See Philip Mirowski, *More Heat Than Light: Economics as Social Physics, Physics as Nature's Economics* (Cambridge: Cambridge University Press, 1991).

44. Marshall, *Principles of Economics*, 16.

45. Jeremy Bentham, *An Introduction to the Principles of Morals and Legislation* (London: Clarendon Press, 1789), http://oll.libertyfund.org/titles/278, 196–97 (accessed March 14, 2016).

46. Bentham, *An Introduction to the Principles of Morals and Legislation*, chap. 5, paragraphs II and III; and chap. 10, paragraph XXXI.

47. Marshall, *Principles of Economics*, 83.

48. Marshall, 77.

49. Maurice Godelier, *Rationality and Irrationality in Economics* (New York: Verso), 253.

50. James Arnt Aune, *Selling the Free Market: The Rhetoric of Economic Correctness* (New York: Guilford Press, 2001), 25. The "ceteris paribus" and "de gustibus non est disputandum" mantras appear to be a foolproof alibi for the discipline of economics avoiding normative assessments but contains a petitio principii because they presume that any action taken aids the utility function of the actor. One need not even be a hardcore, myopic Freudian to believe that people routinely invest in their own unhappiness, make ill-considered decisions, and choose poorly for a variety of reasons. The utility maximization principle presumes these to still be examples of rational, goal-directed behavior and therefore, unimpeachable as motives.

51. Marshall, *Principles of Economics*, 77.

52. Marshall, 83.

53. Samuelson, *Economics*, 430.

54. "Paul A. Samuelson—Facts." *Nobelprize.org*. Nobel Media AB 2014, accessed September 22, 2015. http://www.nobelprize.org/nobel_prizes/economic-sciences/laureates/1970/samuelson-facts.html. The generality of this endorsement is almost certainly a testament to the newness of that prize, first established in

1969, but also simply to Samuelson's widespread influence in the field, mainly thanks to his seminal *Foundations of Economic Analysis* and his textbook *Economics*.

55. Today, that synthesis is less important to the discipline of economics, since neoclassicism has largely superseded macroeconomic Keynesian dominance since the "marginalist revolution" of the 1970s. Samuelson is worth engaging with precisely because his problem-space is circumscribed to "economic" activity following Marshall, and stands upon the precipice of the "Chicago School" revolution that was soon to arrive. In fact, Samuelson decried the neoliberalization of economics and economies as late as 2010.

56. Deirdre McCloskey, *Knowledge and Persuasion in Economics* (Cambridge: Cambridge University Press, 1994), 82.

57. Samuelson, *Foundations of Economic Analysis*, 22.

58. S. M. Amadae, *Prisoners of Reason: Game Theory and Neoliberal Political Economy* (Cambridge: Cambridge University Press, 2016), 200.

59. Samuelson, *Economics*, 91.

60. See Joan Copjec, *Read My Desire: Lacan Against the Historicists* (New York: Verso, 2015).

61. This is why Ned O'Gorman, for instance, defines neoliberalism akin to a representational crisis—"the market" ceases to be a mechanism of articulating and representing desires once market mechanisms have taken the place of other social forms. "Market society," in the way that Polanyi would define it, relies upon the public/private/personal distinctions it nevertheless aims to eradicate. See Ned O'Gorman, *The Iconoclastic Imagination: Image, Catastrophe and Economy in America from the Kennedy Assassination to September 11* (Chicago: University of Chicago Press, 2015).

62. McCloskey, *The Rhetoric of Economics*, 35.

63. Paul Samuelson, *Foundations of Economic Analysis* Enlarged Edition (Cambridge: Harvard University Press, 1983), 90–91.

64. McCloskey, *Rhetoric of Economics*, 36–37.

65. Samuelson, *Foundations of Economic Analysis*, 97.

66. Paul Samuelson, *Economics: An Introductory Analysis*, 4th ed. (New York: McGraw-Hill, 1955), 605.

67. Samuelson, *Economics: An Introductory Analysis*, 610–11.

68. Paul Samuelson and William D. Nordhaus. *Economics*, 19th ed. (New York: Tata McGraw-Hill, 2010), 8.

69. Samuelson, *Economics: An Introductory Analysis*, 610.

70. Samuelson, 607.

71. Mankiw, *Macroeconomics*, 478.

72. "Incentive," *Oxford English Dictionary*, https://www-oed-com.www2.lib.ku.edu/view/Entry/93397?redirectedFrom=incentive#eid.

73. At this moment, prior to the priority of financial instruments and widespread, worldwide financialization, the onus is on worker productivity to

spur capital accumulation. If the labor theory of value appears outdated in both economics and critical theory, it is clear that at least within American manufacturing, productivity served as a useful approximation for both wages and profit.

74. The Council of Economic Advisors plays an important role, according to Harpham and Scotch, in forming the common sense of American capitalists and policymakers. They write: "The council has come to symbolize the crucial role that economists are expected to play in the formulation of public policy by the American state and the increasing legitimacy of economic reasoning as the mode of political discourse by policy experts in the state." See Harpham, Edward J. and Richard K. Scotch, "Economic Discourse, Policy Analysis, and the Problem of the Political," in *Handbook of Political Theory and Policy Science*, ed. Edward Bryan Portis and Michael B. Levy (New York: Greenwood, 1988), 224.

75. The extreme shift toward incentivization is an acceleration of what is latent within the capitalist mode of production—a coercive/objective supplement that contours individual action (as mentioned, incentive rhetoric bespeaks a technique of passivity, not action) but also the problem of "incentive alignment" in late capitalism. As Wallich will put it, without incentives, there is no capitalism. The recognition that incentives conflict between (and within) subjects, groups, and classes at least acknowledges the problems of resource and power distributions. However, to be attentive to incentives merely displaces the issue of power differentials onto the structuring ground of market relations.

76. Henry C. Wallich, *The Cost of Freedom: A New Look at Capitalism* (New York: Harper, 1960), 77.

77. Wallich, *The Cost of Freedom*, 87.

78. Wallich, 87.

79. Wallich, 126–27.

80. This hypothesis is stretched to its limit when economic policy involves the direct transfer of money to individuals: chapter 6 of this work investigates how supplemental unemployment benefits distributed during the COVID-19 pandemic were labeled as an "incentive not to work" or "disincentive." Here one must then point to the essentially *classed* nature of monetary incentives: capitalists and wealthy people are positively incentivized by monetary reward, while working people and the poor are negatively incentivized. As I argue, the purpose of ending the benefits was to force recently unemployed people to work for less, never to "incentivize" the capitalist class to pay workers more.

81. This scene dramatizes what happens when monetary reward is rendered commensurable with other orders of desire and why money cannot be "it" for the reasons that Marx enumerates in *Capital* vol. 1. Peggy desires love (or recognition) and receives money in return, and this structural incongruity is irresolvable. The contradictory character of money, as a store of value, as a general equivalent, as possessing both use and exchange value, entails that it dialectically condenses these orders into a single unit and, in so doing, castrates (and banishes) precisely

what it is meant to convey—a general marker of desire theoretically accessible to all members of a society. What *Mad Men* depicts is that monetary reward fails even at this, and masks the fact that while labor is inherently alienating, work does not have to be. Ironically, work that appears more rewarding is frequently invoked as a rationale for paying people less because enjoyment is theoretically incorporated into the wage. Indeed, this is the exact mode of argument marshaled against women who advocate for equal pay legislation and against the low wages of typically feminized occupations. The promise made by foregrounding monetary incentives is that one can satisfy their desire beyond the workplace.

82. A genuinely dialectical approach means that a focus on a qualitative "change" within the capitalist mode of production only retroactively sediments the meaning of what came before, as a capitalism within limits. Any harkening back to some "purer" or "humane" capitalism willfully ignores the role of class struggle that "settled" common sense around a social compact. The only "limit" to the capitalist mode of production is found in class struggle, not in discursive struggle: what is called "neoliberalism" is a tendency latent within neoclassical economics; the ability to implement it is a matter of politics.

Chapter 3

1. *The Simpsons*, "'Tis the Fifteenth Season," December 14, 2003, https://simpsons.fandom.com/wiki/%27Tis_the_Fifteenth_Season.

2. Gary S. Becker, Kevin M. Murphy, and Jörg Spenkuch. "The Manipulation of Children's Preferences, Old Age Support, and Investments in Children's Human Capital." Gary S. Becker Papers, University of Chicago, Special Collections Research Center, Box 1, 3.

3. "The Prize in Economics 1992—Press Release." *Nobelprize.org*. Nobel Media AB 2014, accessed December 12 2015. http://www.nobelprize.org/nobel_prizes/economic-sciences/laureates/1992/press.html.

4. Becker and Becker, *Economics of Life*, 4.

5. Arjo Klamer, *Speaking of Economics: How to Get into the Conversation* (New York: Routledge, 2007).

6. Gary S. Becker and Guity Nashat Becker, *The Economics of Life: From Baseball to Affirmative Action to Immigration, How Real-World Issues Affect our Everyday Life* (New York: McGraw-Hill, 1997), 8.

7. Gary S. Becker, "Human Capital, Effort, and the Sexual Division of Labor," *Journal of Labor Economics* 3 (1985): 33–58.

8. Jacques Lacan, *Talking to Brick Walls: A Series of Presentations in the Chapel at Sainte-Anne Hospital*, trans. A. R. Price (Medford, MA: Polity, 2017), 61–62.

9. Joshua Gunn, "Refitting Fantasy: Psychosis, Subjectivity, and Talking to the Dead," *Quarterly Journal of Speech* 90 (2004): 10.

10. This is especially true with Chicago school discourse and its associated terms. The terms themselves, like human capital, for instance, are not internally consistent: capital, in the economic literature, has various properties (it is transferrable, fungible, it depreciates), but "human capital" can refer to quite literally any experience, training, endowment, or choice. To be born a man, or to be born wealthy, is just as much one's "human capital" as whether one decides to jog or eat junk food. It constitutes an immanent plane of affirmations—one does not "lack" human capital, one simply has different investments. The fact remains that this is an entirely symbolic process—the term "human capital" performs rhetorical labor for an economist, it does not describe "reality" itself.

11. Lacan, *Talking to Brick Walls*, 87.

12. Becker, *Economic Approach*, 5.

13. Becker, 7–8.

14. Becker, 5.

15. Jack Hirshleifer, "The Expanding Domain of Economics," *American Economic Review* 75 (1985): 53.

16. Becker, *Economic Approach to Human Behavior*, 5.

17. Gary S. Becker, *Accounting for Tastes* (Cambridge, MA: Harvard University Press, 1998), 4. Becker has an ambivalent relationship with evolutionary biology in his work. As quoted, Becker contends that neoclassical economics subsumes every approach including biology, yet, in the same chapter, writes, "I believe the main reason habitual behavior permeates most aspects of life is that habits have an advantage in the biological evolution of human traits. For as long as habits are not too powerful they have social as well as personal advantages" (*Accounting for Tastes*, 9). Elsewhere, he writes,

To venture one further step, if genetical [sic] natural selection and rational behavior reinforce each other in producing speedier and more efficient responses to changes in the environment, perhaps that common preference function has evolved over time by natural selection and rational choice as that preference function best adopted to human society. That is, in the short run the preference function is fixed and households attempt to maximize the objective function subject to their resource and technology constraints. But in the very long run perhaps those preferences survive which are most suited to satisfaction given the broad technological constraints of human society (e.g., physical size, mental ability, et cetera). (Becker, *The Economic Approach to Human Behavior*, 145)

One could interpret these statements as indicating he believes that biology becomes a metaphor for economics, rather than the other way round, or that rational choice itself evolved as a preference over time (best suited for species survival). Yet if "rational choice" is only utility maximization as individuals see it, not a transcendent hyper-rationality, then his claim is entirely tautological: people acting in accordance with their own desires (utility functions) emerged as the best evolutionary way to ensure species survival. Mirowski, in *Never Let a Serious Crisis Go to Waste*, analyses the paradox of either arguing that market-thinking emerges from a market of choices (meaning it never emerged but was simply a transcendent principle) or that it arrived at a certain moment in evolutionary human history. For it to be the latter, the only intellectually coherent position is that we then retroactively transpose the rationality principle onto prehistoric formations for the purposes of simplicity, not because it bore any relation to reality at that time.

18. Gary S. Becker, "The Role of Altruism and Selfishness in Economic Life," George S. Eccles Distinguished Lecture Series, College of Business, Utah State University. Box 13.

19. Becker, *Economic Approach to Human Behavior*, 268.

20. Gary S. Becker, "The Economic Way of Looking at Life." *Prize Lecture*, 1992, www.nobelprize.org/prizes/economic-sciences/1992/becker/lecture, 1.

21. Jonathan Schlefer, *The Assumptions Economists Make* (Cambridge: Belknap, 2012), 263–64.

22. Debates over unemployment relief during the 2020 coronavirus crisis made this abstract academic conundrum front-page news: Senator Lindsey Graham, of South Carolina, decried the apparent generosity of unemployment benefits that were more lucrative than the wages of those laid off, calling it a "perverse incentive which needs to be fixed. Kayla Epstein, "'Over Our Dead Bodies': Lindsey Graham Vows Congress Won't Extend Additional $600 Coronavirus-Related Unemployment Benefits, as US Death Toll Crosses the 60,000 Mark," *Business Insider*, April 30, 2020, https://www.businessinsider.com/lindsey-graham-congress-coronavirus-un-employment-benefit-over-our-dead-bodies-2020-4.

23. Gary Becker and George Stigler, "*De Gustibus Non Est Disputandum*," in *The Essence of Becker*, 185.

24. Becker, *Economic Approach*, 5.

25. Bentham, Jeremy. *An Introduction to the Principles of Morals and Legislation*, chap. 5, paragraphs II and III.

26. Becker, *Economic Approach*, 133.

27. Gary S. Becker, phone interview with Roger Arnold, Department of Economics, University of Nevada, Las Vegas, March 16, 1988, 3–4, University of Chicago Special Collections Research Center, Box 22.

28. Lacan, "The Instance of the Letter in the Unconscious," 431.

29. Gary S. Becker, "Habits, Addictions, and Traditions," in *The Essence of Becker*, edited by Ramón Febrero and Pedro S. Schwarz (Stanford: Hoover Institution Press, 1995), 232.

30. Amartya K. Sen, "Rational Fools: A Critique of the Behavioral Foundations of Economic Theory." *Philosophy and Public Affairs* 6, no. 4 (1977): 336.

31. Becker, Murphy, and Spenkuch, "The Manipulation of Children's Preferences," 3.

32. Becker, Murphy, and Spenkuch, 3.

33. Becker, *Accounting for Tastes*, 21–22.

34. Becker, *Economic Approach to Human Behavior*, 5.

35. Talcott Parsons, "The Position of Sociological Theory," in *Classical Sociological Theory*, ed. Craig Calhoun, Joseph Gertels, James Moody, Steven Pfaff, and Indermohan Virk, 2nd ed. (Malden, MA: Blackwell, 2007), 409.

36. Becker, *Accounting for Tastes*, 24.

37. Gary S. Becker, "Changes in Tastes when Preferences Are Stable," in Gary S. Becker Papers, University of Chicago, Special Collections Research Center, Box 2, 5.

38. Becker, *Economic Approach*, 5.

39. Becker, 7.

40. Becker, *Accounting for Tastes*. 9.

41. Gary S. Becker, "A 19-Year Dialogue on the Power of Incentives," *BusinessWeek*, July 12, 2004, 28.

42. Becker and Becker, *The Economics of Life*, 4.

43. Jacques Lacan, *The Seminar of Jacques Lacan, Book XI: The Four Fundamental Concepts of Psychoanalysis*, ed. Jacques-Alain Miller, trans. Alan Sheridan (New York: W. W. Norton, 1998), 268.

44. Žižek, *The Sublime Object of Ideology*, 95. Lacan also calls this the "presence made of absence," see Jacques Lacan, "The Function and Field of Speech and Language in Psychoanalysis," 228.

45. Žižek, *The Sublime Object of Ideology*, 95.

46. Gary S. Becker, "Understanding Human Behavior," Conference by Becker Center, November 10, 2007. Gary S. Becker Papers, University of Chicago, Special Collections Research Center, Box 1, 1.

47. Becker, "Understanding Human Behavior," 2.

48. Becker, 2.

49. Becker and Becker, *The Economics of Life*, 6.

50. Becker and Becker, 6.

51. Melinda Cooper, *Family Values: Between Neoliberalism and the New Social Conservatism* (Brooklyn: Zone Books, 2017), 172.

52. Becker and Becker, *The Economics of Life*, 50.

53. Gary S. Becker, "Is There Any Way to Stop Child Labor Abuses?" *BusinessWeek*, May 12, 1997, 22.

54. Gary S. Becker, "'Bribe' Third World Parents to Keep Their Kids in School," *BusinessWeek*, November 22, 1999, 15.

55. Becker, "'Bribe' Third World Parents to Keep Their Kids in School," 15.

56. Becker, "Is There Any Way to Stop Child Labor Abuses?," 22.

57. James Arnt Aune, *Selling the Free Market: The Rhetoric of Economic Correctness* (New York: Guilford Press, 2001), 25.

58. Becker, *Economic Approach to Human Behavior*, 7.

59. Slavoj Žižek, *For They Know Not What They Do: Enjoyment as a Political Factor* (New York: Verso, 2002), 203.

60. Jennifer Bates, "Hegel's Inverted World, Cleopatra, and the Logic of the Crocodile," *Phenomenology and Life* 54 (2012), 431.

61. Gary S. Becker, "Interview with Gary Becker," n.d. University of Chicago Special Collections Research Center, 4.

62. John Black, Nigar Hashimzade and Gareth Myles, *A Dictionary of Economics*, 4th ed. (Oxford: Oxford University Press, 2012), 254.

63. Michel Foucault, *The Birth of Biopolitics: Lectures at the Collège de France*, ed. Michel Senellart, trans. Graham Burchell (New York: Palgrave Macmillan, 2008), 226.

64. Gary S. Becker, *Human Capital: A Theoretical and Empirical Analysis, with Special Reference to Education*, 3rd ed. (Chicago: University of Chicago Press, 1993).

65. Wendy Brown, *Undoing the Demos: Neoliberalism's Stealth Revolution* (Cambridge, MA: MIT Press, 2015).

66. Jacques Lacan, *The Seminar of Jacques Lacan, Book XX—On Feminine Sexuality: The Limits of Love and Knowledge (Encore, 1972–1973)* ed. Jacques-Alain Miller, trans. Bruce Fink (New York: W. W. Norton & Co., 1999), 3.

67. Gary Becker, "A Note on Restaurant Pricing and Other Examples of Social Influences on Price," *Journal of Political Economy* 99 (1991): 1109–16.

68. Noah Smith, "101ism," *Noahpinion*, www.noahpinionblog.blogspot.com/2016/01/101ism.html, January 21, 2016.

69. Becker, "A Note on Restaurant Pricing," 1112.

70. Becker, 1110.

71. The idea that all one needs as an academic economist is a three-by-five card of axioms to derive disciplinarily agreeable conclusions.

72. Gerard A. Hauser, *Introduction to Rhetorical Theory*, 2nd ed. (Long Grove, IL: Waveland Press, 2002), 125.

73. Žižek, *For They Know Not What They Do*, xiii.

74. Henry Hazlitt, *Economics in One Lesson* (New York: Pocket Books, 1952).

75. Robert B. Cialdini, *Influence: Science and Practice*, 4th ed. (Boston: Allyn and Bacon, 2001), 54, 96.

76. Becker, *Economic Approach*, 7.

77. Gary S. Becker, *According to Tastes* (Cambridge, MA: Harvard University Press, 1996), 18.

78. Gary S. Becker and Julio Jorge Elias, "Introducing Incentives in the Market for Live and Cadaveric Organ Donations," *Journal of Economic Perspectives* 21 (2007): 3–24. Becker, with various coauthors, presented similar arguments to

the Law & Economics Workshop at the University of Chicago's School of Law and the University of Chicago's Becker-Friedman Institute in 2012.

79. Gary S. Becker and Richard Posner, "Suicide: An Economic Approach." 2006. Unpublished. Gary S. Becker Papers, Special Collections Research Center, Box 14, University of Chicago.

80. Aristotle, *Rhetoric* Book II, www.classics.mit.edu/Aristotle/rhetoric.html.

81. Nancy S. Streuver, *Theory as Practice: Ethical Inquiry in the Renaissance* (Chicago: University of Chicago Press, 1992), 129. Streuver discerns within this obsession with contexualism the latent desire for its overcoming, that the power of language is not reducible to its situatedness but rather in its transcontextuality.

82. Victoria Ann Khan, *Rhetoric, Prudence, and Skepticism in the Renaissance* (Ithaca, NY: Cornell University Press, 1985), 29.

83. Patricia Spence, "Sympathy and Propriety in Adam Smith's Rhetoric," *Quarterly Journal of Speech* 60 (1974): 94. See also Stephen J. McKenna, *Adam Smith: The Rhetoric of Propriety* (Albany: State University of New York Press, 2006).

84. Mark Garrett Longaker, "Adam Smith on Rhetoric and Phronesis, Law and Economics," *Philosophy & Rhetoric* 47 (2014): 26.

85. Lloyd F. Bitzer, "The Rhetorical Situation," *Philosophy & Rhetoric* 1, no. 1 (1968): 1–14.

86. Gerard A. Hauser, *Introduction to Rhetorical Theory*, 2nd ed. (Prospect Heights, IL: Waveland Press, 2002), 46. Christian O. Lundberg, "Revisiting the Future of Meaning," *Quarterly Journal of Speech* 101 (2015): 175.

87. See Dilip Parameshwar Gaonkar, "Object and Method in Rhetorical Criticism: From Wichelns to Leff and McGee," *Western Journal of Speech Communication* 54 (1990), 290–316.

88. See Amadae, *Prisoners of Reason* and Philip Mirowski, *Machine Dreams: Economics Becomes a Cyborg Science* (Cambridge: Cambridge University Press, 2002).

89. Kenneth Burke, *The Philosophy of Literary Form: Studies in Symbolic Action*, 3rd ed. (Berkeley: University of California Press, 1973), 5–6.

90. Jacques Lacan, *The Seminar of Jacques Lacan Book X: Anxiety*, ed. Jacques-Alain Miller, trans. A. R. Price (Malden, MA: Polity, 2014), 100–101.

91. Ernesto Laclau, *The Rhetorical Foundations of Society* (New York: Verso, 2014), 119.

92. Becker, "A 19-Year Dialogue on the Power of Incentives," 28.

Chapter 4

1. Todd McGowan, *Enjoying What We Don't Have: The Political Project of Psychoanalysis* (Lincoln: University of Nebraska Press, 2013), 285.

2. "Calculating the Value of Women's Unpaid Work," The FRED Blog, Federal Reserve Bank of St. Louis, https://fredblog.stlouisfed.org/2020/03/calculating-the-value-of-womens-unpaid-work/, March 9, 2020.

3. Patricia Gherovici, *Please Select Your Gender: From the Invention of Hysteria to the Democratizing of Transgenderism* (New York: Routledge, 2010), 140.

4. Moss-Racusin et al. explore the flip side of the signifier "woman" in an experiment on hiring practices. Faculty in an experiment were given CVs of applicants for a laboratory position job; the applications were identical save for a name typically gendered "male" or gendered "female." The names gendered male were reported to be more competent, hirable, and deemed to deserve a higher starting salary than those gendered female. That is, the signifier-ness of "woman" caused the discrepancy in qualifications and pay. See Corinne A. Moss-Racusin, John F. Dovidio, Victoria L. Brescoll, Mark J. Graham, and Jo Handelsman, "Science Faculty's Subtle Gender Biases Favor Male Students," *Psychological and Cognitive Sciences* 109, no. 41 (2012): 16474.

5. "The Wage Gap: The Who, How, Why, and What to Do," National Women's Law Center, https://nwlc.org/resources/the-wage-gap-the-who-how-why-and-what-to-do/, September 27, 2019.

6. Gérard Genette, *Figures of Literary Discourse* (New York: Columbia University Press, 1982), 47.

7. "Lilly Ledbetter Fair Pay Act." *National Women's Law Center*, January 29, 2013, http://www.nwlc.org/resource/lilly-ledbetter-fair-pay-act.

8. There are exceptions and waivers, including an exception for if a worker is unaware of the discrimination, which, it should be noted, is what happened to Ledbetter.

9. "S. 181—Lilly Ledbetter Fair Pay Act," 111th Cong., 2nd sess. January 8, 2009. https://www.congress.gov/bill/111th-congress/senate-bill/181.

10. See Nina Martin, "The Impact and Echoes of the Wal-Mart Discrimination Case," *ProPublica*, September 27, 2013, http://www.propublica.org/article/the-impact-and-echoes-of-the-wal-mart-discrimination-case.

11. The Senate version of the bill, introduced in 2007, was named the "Fair Pay Restoration Act," with no mention of Lilly Ledbetter like in the House bill, but was essentially the same bill.

12. Barack Obama, "Obama Signs Lilly Ledbetter Act," *Washington Post,* http://voices.washingtonpost.com/44/2009/01/29/obama_signs_lilly_ledbetter_ac.html, January 29, 2009.

13. Senator Edward Kennedy, Committee Hearing on Health, Education, Labor and Pensions. "The Fair Pay Restoration Act: Ensuring Reasonable Rules in Pay Discrimination Cases," January 24, 2008, 1.

14. Kennedy, "The Fair Pay Restoration Act," 1.

15. Murray, "The Fair Pay Restoration Act," 4.

16. Mikulski, "The Fair Pay Restoration Act," 6.

17. Mikulski, 6.

18. Ledbetter, "The Fair Pay Restoration Act," 9.

19. Ledbetter, 10.

20. Dorfman, "The Fair Pay Restoration Act," 13.

21. Dorfman, 13.

22. Dorfman, 13.

23. Senator Johnny Isakson, "The Fair Pay Restoration Act: Ensuring Reasonable Rules in Pay Discrimination Cases," January 24, 2008, 3–4.

24. Congressional Record—House, March 27, 2019. The specter of the "trial lawyer" in remunerative legislation deserves fuller attention than a footnote, for opponents consistently invoke this phrase. In the above-cited Congressional record, Republican representatives used the exact phrase twenty-eight times. I interpret the rise of complaints around "greedy" lawyers as an aftereffect of the decline of working-class power and the Democratic Party's abandonment of mass redistributive policies. The shift from collective redistribution to individual lawsuits is both an ideological symptom of neoliberal politics and a convenient ideological alibi against such outcomes since lawyers can be figured as economically parasitic on productive members of society. Although to be self-interested, selfish, and gain-seeking is a positive value in the marketplace, to do so in the legal marketplace qualifies as a moral iniquity. As Fredric Jameson points out, there is a cultural exhaustion for figures of "evil," even serial killers and terrorists are as domesticated as villains motivated simply by greed. See Fredric Jameson, *The Ancients and the Postmoderns: On the Historicity of Forms* (New York: Verso, 2017), 241.

25. Dreiband, "The Fair Pay Restoration Act," 24.

26. Statement of the U.S. Chamber of Commerce before the House Committee on Education and Labor, June 12, 2007.

27. Dreiband, "The Fair Pay Restoration Act," 24.

28. Lacan, *The Seminar of Jacques Lacan, Book XX*, 3.

29. Senator Johnny Isakson, "Congressional Record—Senate," 110th Congress, April 23, 2008, S3279.

30. Republican lawmakers deploy similarly mollifying language to oppose the Paycheck Fairness Act—they unreservedly abhor sexist discrimination but instead locate the cause of it in bills like these rather than by businesses themselves.

31. Barack Obama, quoted in Rachel Weiner, "Lilly Ledbetter Act: Obama Signs His First Bill," *Huffington Post*, February 27, 2009, http://www.huffingtonpost.com/2009/01/27/lilly-ledbetter-act-the-fi_n_161423.html.

32. Becker, *According to Tastes*, 147.

33. William K. Black, "Gary Becker's Treatment of Women Who Work for Pay as 'Deviants,'" *New Economic Perspectives*, June 17, 2014, http://neweconomicperspectives.org/2014/06/gary-becker-treatment-women-work-pay-deviants.html.

34. Febrero and Schwarz, "The Essence of Becker," xxxii.

35. Levitt and Dubner, *SuperFreakonomics*, 45.

36. John List and Uri Gneezy, "A Unified Theory of Why Women Earn Less," *Freakonomics*.com, October 18, 2013, http://freakonomics.com/2013/10/18/a-unifying-theory-of-why-women-earn-less/.

37. Claudia Goldin, "A Grand Gender Convergence: Its Last Chapter," *American Economic Review* 104, no. 4 (2004): 1092.

38. Ramsey Cox, "Senate GOP Blocks Paycheck Fairness Act for the Second Time," *The Hill*, September 15, 2014, http://thehill.com/blogs/floor-action/senate/217775-senate-gop-blocks-equal-pay-bill-again.

39. Other provisions include making discriminatory employers subject to punitive damages, allow women to be gathered in class action lawsuits, and provide negotiation skills training to women and girls.

40. See US Department of Labor, "The Fair Labor Standards Act of 1938, As Amended," May 2011, http://www.dol.gov/whd/regs/statutes/FairLaborStandAct.pdf and "S.2199—Paycheck Fairness Act," https://www.congress.gov/bill/113th-congress/senate-bill/2199.

41. Senators Barbara Mikluski, "Paycheck Fairness," *Congressional Record* 156, no. 150, United States Senate, November 17, 2010, S7295, https://www.congress.gov/congressional-record/2010/11/17/senate-section/article/s7924-1.

42. "S.2199—Paycheck Fairness Act," April 1, 2014, 8. https://www.congress.gov/113/bills/s2199/BILLS-113s2199pcs.pdf.

43. "S.2199—Paycheck Fairness Act," 16.

44. Greenberger, "Paycheck Fairness Act," 16.

45. Greenberger, "Paycheck Fairness Act," 17.

46. Sigmund Freud, "Negation," in *The Freud Reader*, ed. Peter Gay (New York: W. W. Norton & Co., 1995), 667.

47. Freud, "Negation," 667.

48. Bruce Fink, *A Clinical Introduction to Freud: Techniques for Everyday Practice* (New York: Norton, 2017), 43.

49. Sigmund Freud, *Three Case Histories*, ed. Philip Rieff (New York: Touchstone, 1996), 240.

50. McGowan, *Enjoying What We Don't Have*, 27.

51. Freud, *Three Case Histories*, 35.

52. Jean Laplanche and J.-B. Pontalis, *The Language of Psychoanalysis*, trans. Donald Nicholson-Smith (New York: Routledge, 1973), 262.

53. In 1982, female employees of Johnson Controls alleged the company barred women from working in conditions that exposed them to lead because it could potentially harm an "unborn child." The Supreme Court eventually ruled the policy violated Title VII's provision against workplace sex discrimination, but until then, a woman's biological potential worked against her employability: "By assuming the likelihood of accidental pregnancy . . . courts treated all women capable of bearing children as 'potential mothers' although neither court cited

any quantifiable evidence." See Carrie Crenshaw. "The Normality of Man and Female Otherness: (Re)Producing Patriarchal Lines of Argument in the Law." *Argumentation & Advocacy* 32, no. 4 (1996), 170.

54. Olson, "The Paycheck Fairness Act," 28.

55. Olson, 28–29.

56. Sam Levin, "Accused of Underpaying Women, Google Says It's Too Expensive to Get Wage Data," *Guardian*, May 26, 2017, https://www.theguardian.com/technology/2017/may/26/google-gender-discrimination-case-salary-records.

57. The Republican Party advanced an alternative bill to PFA: The GAP Act, or "Gender Advancement in Pay Act," which according to the *University of Cincinnati Law Review*, "creates two new exceptions to a rule which is already full of loopholes." The GAP Act displaces the problem of sex even further by only requiring that any pay disparity be "business related" but not "legitimate" or "genuine," meaning the loopholes that allowed for literal interpretations of "any factor other than sex" to remain, except after passage, they would be ensconced within the discursive shell of "business related." While Stylinski notes that the loopholes would undercut the spirit of the bill, it is equally possible to see that the bill is designed to protect corporations even further by allowing for any factor to become precedent as long as the phrase "business related" is uttered. One forbidden word ("sex") is traded for a trump card ("business related") in this discursive economy. See Brynn Stylinski, "The Gender Advancement in Pay Act: The GAP Act Leaves Some Holes," *University of Cincinnati Law Review*, December 1, 2015, https://uclawreview.org/2015/12/01/the-gender-advancement-in-pay-act-the-gap-act-leaves-some-holes/.

58. Olson, "Paycheck Fairness Act," 22.

59. Sabrina L. Schaeffer, "Paycheck Fairness Act Will Hurt Women," *US News & World Report*, http://www.usnews.com/debate-club/should-the-senate-pass-the-paycheck-fairness-act/paycheck-fairness-act-will-hurt-women, May 4, 2012.

60. Penny Nance, "Act Undercuts Protection, Choices Women Have in J ob Market," *US News & World Report,* http://www.usnews.com/debate-club/should-the-senate-pass-the-paycheck-fairness-act/act-undercuts-protection-choices-women-have-in-job-market, May 4, 2012.

61. Quoted in Stephen J. Dubner, "One Woman's View of the Female Wage Gap," *Freakonomics*.com, http://freakonomics.com/2012/04/17/one-womans-view-of-the-female-wage-gap/.

62. Quoted in Dubner, "One Woman's View of the Female Wage Gap," *Freakonomics*.com.

63. Quoted in Congressional Record—House, H7682, July 31, 2008.

64. Cohen, "Closing the Gap," 43.

65. Samuels, "Closing the Gap," 50.

66. Silvia Federici, *Revolution at Point Zero: Housework, Reproduction, and Feminist Struggle* (Oakland: PM Press, 2012), 16.

67. Slavoj Žižek, "The Real of Sexual Difference," in *Reading Seminar XX: Lacan's Major Work on Love, Knowledge, and Feminine Sexuality*, ed. Suzanne Barnard and Bruce Fink (Albany: State University of New York Press, 2002), 64.

68. See Calum L. Matheson, *Desiring the Bomb: Communication, Psychoanalysis, and the Atomic Age* (Tuscaloosa: University of Alabama Press, 2019).

69. Kevin A. Johnson and Jennifer J. Asenas, "The Lacanian Real as a Supplement to Rhetorical Critique." *Rhetoric Society Quarterly* 32 (2013): 155.

70. Johnson and Asenas, "The Lacanian Real as a Supplement to Rhetorical Critique," 166, 167.

71. Bruce Fink, *The Lacanian Subject: Between Language and Jouissance* (Princeton: Princeton University Press, 1995), 104.

72. Alenka Zupančič, "Sexual Difference and Ontology," *E-Flux* 32, no. 2 (2012).

73. Joshua Gunn, "On Speech and Public Release," *Rhetoric & Public Affairs* 13 (2010): 3.

74. Barbara Biesecker, "Rhetorical Studies and the New Psychoanalysis: What's the Real Problem? Or Framing the Problem of the Real," *Quarterly Journal of Speech* 84 (1998): 222.

75. Gherovici, *Please Select Your Gender*, 126.

76. Lundberg, *Lacan in Public*, 200–201.

77. Lacan, *The Seminar of Jacques Lacan, Book XX*, 103. Lacan's oft-quoted but oft-misunderstood claim of "Woman does not exist" should be read from the perspective of masculine *jouissance*, the logic that poses a "One" to an "other," or the one to the zero. Masculine *jouissance* is incapable of incorporating genuine alterity into its binary logic and instead produces what Lacan called a "semblable," a semblance stemming from speech, or babble. What masculine *jouissance* produces is an image of "femininity" or "womanhood" that does not correspond to actual beings who gendered as women. In effect, Lacan's provocation diagnoses the male fantasy that woman is a play of semblances (Nietzsche), or that she lacks something (Aristotle, Aquinas), as a necessary consequence of the logic of the One and the Other.

78. Lacan, *Seminar XX*, 33.

79. Mary Poovey, *A History of the Modern Fact: Problems of Knowledge in the Sciences of Wealth and Society* (Chicago: University of Chicago Press, 1998).

80. Harkin, "The Fair Pay Restoration Act," 43.

81. Diana Furchtgott-Roth, "Paycheck Fairness Act Is Based on a Misapplied Statistic," *US News & World Report*, http://www.usnews.com/debate-club/should-the-senate-pass-the-paycheck-fairness-act/paycheck-fairness-act-is-based-on-a-misapplied-statistic, May 4, 2012.

82. Senator Michael Enzi, "Closing the Gap: Equal Pay for Women Workers," 6.

83. Nance, "Act Undercuts Protection, Choices Women Have in Job Market."

84. Colette Soler, "Hysteria in Scientific Discourse," in *Reading Seminar XX: Lacan's Major Work on Love, Knowledge, and Feminine Sexuality*, Suzanne Barnard and Bruce Fink, ed. (Albany: State University of New York Press, 2002), 49.

85. Soler, "Hysteria in Scientific Discourse," 49.

86. Zupančič, *What Is Sex?*, 37.

87. Lacan, *Seminar XX*, 7.

88. Suzanne Barnard, "Tongues of Angels: Feminine Structure and Other Jouissance," in *Reading Seminar XX: Lacan's Major Work on Love, Knowledge and Feminine Sexuality*, ed. Suzanne Barnard and Bruce Fink (Albany: State University of New York Press, 2002), 181.

89. Matheson, *Desiring the Bomb*, 32.

90. According to Bruno, while Lacan credits Marx for his discovery of the symptom within the capitalist mode of production (the secret of surplus-value is that it is both "necessary" and "excess," and one cannot manage a system like this without a mystification of this basic fact), Marx does not account for surplus-*jouissance*, or the excessive excess that capitalism tends to generate. See Pierre Bruno, *Lacan and Marx: The Invention of the Symptom* trans. John Holland (London: Routledge, 2020), 15–16.

Chapter 5

1. Barack Obama, "Executive Order: Using Behavioral Science Insights to Better Serve the American People," *The White House*, September 15, 2015, https://www.whitehouse.gov/the-press-office/2015/09/15/executive-order-using-behavioral-science-insights-better-serve-american.

2. Mike Dorning, "Obama Adopts Behavioral Economics," *Bloomberg News*, June 24, 2010, http://www.bloomberg.com/bw/magazine/content/10_27/b4185019573214.htm.

3. William J. Congdon and Maya Shankar, "The White House Social & Behavioral Sciences Team: Lessons Learned from Year One," *Behavioral Science & Policy* 1, no. 2 (2015): 93–104.

4. Tanya Basu, "The White House Is Now Using Behavioral Economics to Improve Policy," *Time*, September 24, 2015, https://time.com/4042689/social-behavioral-sciences-team/.

5. Dorning, "Obama Adopts Behavioral Economics."

6. https://www.whitehouse.gov/ostp/nstc#Documents_Reports. https://sbst.gov.

7. Glenn Thrush and Elaina Plott, "How the Trump Campaign Is Drawing Obama Out of Retirement," *New York Times*, June 28, 2020, https://www.nytimes.com/2020/06/28/us/politics/obama-biden-trump.html, accessed July 20, 2020.

8. "Charter of the Subcommittee on Social and Behavioral Sciences of the Committee on Science, National Science and Technology Council." May 2022.

https://www.whitehouse.gov/wp-content/uploads/2022/06/06-2022-SBS_Recharter.pdf

9. Zeina Afif, " 'Nudge Units'—Where They Came From and What They Can Do," *Let's Talk Development*, October 25, 2017, https://blogs.worldbank.org/developmenttalk/nudge-units-where-they-came-and-what-they-can-do.

10. See Peter Self, *Econocrats and the Policy Process: The Politics and Philosophy of Cost-Benefit Analysis* (London: MacMillan Press, 1975), in particular chapters 1 and 5.

11. Clive Barnett, "Publics and Markets: What's Wrong with Neoliberalism?" in *The Handbook of Social Geography*, ed. Susan Smith, Sallie Marston, Rachel Pain, and John Paul Jones III (London: Sage, 2009), 23.

12. Quoted in Aditya Chakrabortty, "From Obama to Cameron, Why Do So Many Politicians Want a Piece of Richard Thaler?" *Guardian*, July 11, 2008, https://www.theguardian.com/politics/2008/jul/12/economy.conservatives.

13. Matthew Rabin, "A Perspective on Psychology and Economics," Institute of Business and Economic Research Working Paper, Department of Economics, University of California, Berkeley (2002), 659.

14. Thaler and Sunstein, *Nudge*, 5.

15. Cass R. Sunstein, *Why Nudge? The Politics of Libertarian Paternalism* (New Haven: Yale University Press, 2014), 58.

16. See Jeffrey Friedman, "What's Wrong with Libertarianism," *Critical Review* 11 (1993), 426–27.

17. Sunstein, *Why Nudge?*, 28.

18. Sunstein, 26.

19. Sunstein, 27.

20. Riccardo Rebonato, "A Critical Assessment of Libertarian Paternalism," *Journal of Consumer Policy* 37 (2014): 358.

21. Sunstein, *Why Nudge?*, 40.

22. Riccardo Rebonato, *Taking Liberties: A Critical Examination of Libertarian Paternalism* (London: Palgrave Macmillan, 2012), 6.

23. Sunstein, *Why Nudge?*, 31.

24. Thaler and Sunstein, *Nudge*, 3.

25. Thaler and Sunstein, 4.

26. Richard H. Thaler and Cass R. Sunstein, "Behavioral Economics Tips for Home Sellers: How to Price a House," *Nudges.org*, May 14, 2008.

27. Thaler and Sunstein, *Nudge*, 5.

28. Thaler and Sunstein, 4.

29. Thaler and Sunstein, 99.

30. Thaler and Sunstein, 100.

31. Thaler and Sunstein, 6.

32. Thaler and Sunstein, 8.

33. Sunstein, *Why Nudge?*, 57, 59–60.

34. Proponents of nudges use "opt-in"/"opt-out" policies as opportunities for nudges to increase total social welfare with minimal invasiveness. So for retirement plans, organ donations, and so on, the choice architect identifies that an individual's preference for a default setting as the "signified" of their choice, instead of assigning meaning to the choice not to enroll in a company-sponsored retirement plan, for instance. The nudger presumes that the individual is unconscious of the choice they are actually making, and instead are choosing the (signified of the) ease of clicking through on a website more quickly, not that they desire the outcome.

35. Sunstein, *Why Nudge?*, 59. Becker's insistence throughout his work, that price, not changes in preferences, is the primary determining factor in any person's behavior, is followed through here exactly—nudge theorists treat this hypothesis as fact and design policies accordingly.

36. Cass R. Sunstein, *After the Rights Revolution: Reconceiving the Regulatory State* (Cambridge, MA: Harvard University Press, 1990), 106.

37. John P. Swann, "FDA's Origin," http://www.fda.gov/AboutFDA/ WhatWeDo/History/Origin/ucm054819.htm (accessed June 22, 2016).

38. U.S. Environmental Protection Agency Office of Mobile Sources, "Milestones in Auto Emissions Control," August 1994, EPA 400-F-92-014, https:// permanent.fdlp.gov/gpo81172/P10001KM.pdf.

39. "Drinking Water Regulations," United States Environmental Protection Agency, https://www.epa.gov/dwreginfo/drinking-water-regulations (accessed July 12, 2020).

40. Jack Lewis, "The Birth of EPA," *EPA Journal* 12 (1985), 6.

41. At least at the federal circuit court level, the "economic approach" has been enormously influential due to the gargantuan influence of Judge Richard Posner. Indeed, the entire subfield of "law and economics" is one that he largely inaugurated. See Francis J. Ranney, *Aristotle's Ethics and Legal Rhetoric: An Analysis of Language Beliefs and the Law* (Burlington: Ashgate, 2005), particularly chapter 3, "The Things We Say: The Speculations of Legal Science." Richard Coase, another highly influential economist, won a Bank of Sweden prize in economic sciences for work in this vein. According to Landes, Lessig and Solimine, Posner is the single most cited federal appeals judge, followed in third place by his ideological fellow traveler and colleague in at the 7th Circuit, Judge Frank Easterbrook. See William M. Landes, Lawrence Lessig, and Michael E. Solimine, "Judicial Influence: A Citation Analysis of Federal Courts of Appeals Judges," *Chicago Working Paper in Law & Economics* (Second Series) 1998, 23.

42. Sunstein, *After the Rights Revolution*, 78, 81–82.

43. Sunstein, 82.

44. Sunstein, 82.

45. Thaler and Sunstein, *Nudge*, 5.

46. Pierre Dardot and Christian Laval, *The New Way of the World: On Neo-Liberal Society*, trans. Gregory Elliot (New York: Verso, 2014), 93.

47. Cass Sunstein, "Smarter Regulation," The White House, February 7, 2011, https://obamawhitehouse.archives.gov/blog/2011/02/07/smarter-regulation.

48. Dardot and Laval, *The New Way of the World*, 174.

49. Frank Knight, quoted in George Stigler, "Perfect Competition, Historically Contemplated," *Journal of Political Economy* 65 (1957): 12.

50. Schlefler, *The Assumptions Economists Make*, 95.

51. John F. M. McDermott, "Perfect Competition, Methodologically Contemplated," *Journal of Post-Keynesian Economics* 37 (2015): 690.

52. Knight, quoted in Stigler, "Perfect Competition, Historically Contemplated," 12.

53. Black, Hashimzade, and Myles, *Oxford Dictionary of Economics*, 307.

54. George Loewenstein and Peter Ubel, "Economics Behaving Badly," *New York Times*, July 14, 2010, http://www.nytimes.com/2010/07/15/opinion/15loewenstein.html?_r=0.

55. Karl Marx, *Economic and Philosophic Manuscripts of 1844 and the Communist Manifesto*, trans. Martin Milligan (Amherst: Prometheus Books, 1988), 75–78.

56. Lacan, *The Seminar of Jacques Lacan, Book XI*, 205.

57. This is why the French idiom, *la petite mort*, to signify an orgasm, is so auspicious: if one procreates, it does not entail a literal death, but it signifies that one must "pass on." Reproduction is only species-reproduction, for the individual, it is only the production of a new being that is not exactly oneself. Thus it is possible to read the Oedipus complex from the reverse perspective as how one deals with the presence of alterity.

58. See Alenka Zupančič, "Sexual Difference and Ontology," *e-flux* 32 (2012), https://www.e-flux.com/journal/32/68246/sexual-difference-and-ontology/ (accessed August 28, 2020).

59. Lacan, *The Seminar of Jacques Lacan, Book XI*, 204.

60. Slavoj Žižek, "*The Pervert's Guide to Ideology* (transcript/subtitles," *Žižek UK.uk*, December 24, 2016, https://zizek.uk/the-perverts-guide-to-ideology-transcriptsubtitles/.

61. Éric Laurent, "Alienation and Separation (II)," in *Reading Seminar XI*, 30.

62. Bruce Fink, *The Lacanian Subject: Between Language and Jouissance* (Princeton, NJ: Princeton University Press, 1995), 52.

63. This parable serves as a useful example of the death drive in action—the death drive is not about a desire for death but a clinging on to a desire beyond life, or indifferent to life as a neutral concept.

64. Lacan also uses the Hegelian master/slave struggle as an example of the forced choice: when the slave renounces their freedom in the face of death,

they renounce their status as a free being, truly alive. See Lacan, *The Seminar of Jacques Lacan, Book XI*, 212.

65. The "forced choice" of subjectification must be thought of as distinct from both the traditional Althusserian Marxist and the critical/cultural Foucauldian understanding of a subject as the product of discourse. The subject in a Lacanian sense is a gap between signifiers that is then filled in by the activity of the subject's unconscious—hence why subjects react differently to different stimuli. Ideological discourse, like that of the nudge, poses a question, not an answer to a subject, two desirous lacks momentarily coincide; the subject is a logical space that must react to provocations of the symbolic order. They are not simply the passive recipient or product of discourse.

66. Lacan, *The Seminar of Jacques Lacan, Book XI*, 207.

67. Žižek, *For They Know Not What They Do*, 22.

68. The political utility of psychoanalysis is then buttressed by the clinical value thereof: although psychoanalysis refuses methodological individualism, it does take the singular speaking subject's verbal ejaculations seriously (and to the letter). One can find the meaning of the choice not in a statistical regression, but on the couch.

69. Fink, *The Lacanian Subject*, 54.

70. Fink, 54.

71. Lacan, *The Seminar of Jacques Lacan, Book XI*, 188.

72. Lacan, 214.

73. Sigmund Freud, *Jokes and their Relation to the Unconscious*, trans. James Strachey (New York: W. W. Norton & Co., 1960), 137–38.

74. Freud, *Jokes and their Relation to the Unconscious*, 138.

75. See Adam Hill, "Why Nudges Coerce: Experimental Evidence on the Architecture of Regulation," *Science and Engineering Ethics* 24 (2018), 1280. Hill further notes that in an experiment with "hidden" nudges, participants tended to blame laws, rather than regulators, when regulators undertook ineffective nudge strategies to achieve a law's goal. Nudge theory wins coming and going, evading responsibility for their own failures and delivering conceptual body blows to the efficacy of political representation as embodied in legislation.

76. Colette Soler, "The Subject and the Other (II)," in *Reading Seminar XI: Lacan's Four Fundamental Concepts of Psychoanalysis*, ed. Richard Feldstein, Bruce Fink and Maire Jaanus (Albany: State University of New York Press, 1995), 51.

77. Fink, *A Clinical Introduction to Lacanian Psychoanalysis*, 112.

78. Two jokes from the show *Arrested Development* demonstrate the difference between foreclosure and repression. The character Tobias Fünke, a psychiatrist, attempts to explain to Lucille Bluth foreclosure, in which a patient "literally rejects" a thought that is too painful to bear. She replies, "You are a worse psychiatrist than you are a son-in-law, and you will never get work as an

actor because you have no talent." Fünke replies, as if he foreclosed her speech, "Well if she's not going to say anything, I certainly can't help her." By contrast, repression is depicted when Lucille, a wealthy woman, is asked by a server at an American chain restaurant, "Plate or platter?" for her meal size. Lucille replies, "I don't understand the question, and I won't respond to it." The binary signifier is repressed by Lucille as a way to manage her downwardly mobile situation.

79. Antonio Quinet, "The Gaze as an Object," in *Reading Seminar XX: Lacan's Major Work on Love, Knowledge, and Feminine Sexuality*, ed. Suzanne Barnard and Bruce Fink (Albany: State University of New York Press, 2002), 145.

80. Jacques Lacan, "The Neurotic's Individual Myth," *Psychoanalytic Quarterly* 48 (1979), 417.

81. Fink, *The Lacanian Subject*, 58.

82. Žižek, *For They Know Not What They Do*, 135.

83. Fink, *The Lacanian Subject*, 75.

84. Lacan, "The Subversion of the Subject and the Dialectic of Desire," 698.

85. Jacques Lacan, *The Seminar of Jacques Lacan, Book VI: Desire and its Interpretation*, ed. Jacques-Alain Miller, trans. Bruce Fink (Malden, MA: Polity, 2019), 451.

86. Lacan, *Book VI: Desire and Its Interpretation*, 452.

87. Marc De Kesel, *Eros and Ethics: Reading Jacques Lacan's Seminar VII*, trans. Sigi Jöttkandt (Albany: State University of New York Press, 2009), 184.

88. Todd McGowan, *Capitalism and Desire: The Psychic Cost of Free Markets* (New York: Columbia University Press, 2016), 135.

89. The Patient Protection and Affordable Care Act," Public Law 111-148, 111th Congress, March 23, 2010, https://www.congress.gov/111/plaws/publ148/PLAW-111publ148.pdf.

90. "The Patient Protection and Affordable Care Act," 2.

91. As of December 2017, this penalty was repealed, meaning that the federal government no longer can incentivize anyone through a threat or fine to enroll in a health insurance plan.

92. "HealthQuest Rewards Program," Human Resource Management, University of Kansas, https://humanresources.ku.edu/healthquest-rewards-program (accessed July 20, 2020).

93. Quoted in "'I Live Paycheck to Paycheck': A West Virginia Teacher Explains Why She's on Strike," *New York Times*, March 1, 2018, https://www.nytimes.com/2018/03/01/us/west-virginia-teachers-strike.html accessed July 20, 2020.

94. De Kesel, *Eros and Ethics*, 96.

Chapter 6

1. See Paul Samuelson, "The Pure Theory of Public Expenditure," *Review of Economics and Statistics* 36, no. 4 (1954): 387–89.

2. Lacan, *The Seminar of Jacques Lacan, Book XI*, 178.

3. Éric Laurent, "Alienation and Separation (II)," in *Reading* Seminar XI: *Lacan's* Four Fundamental Concepts of Psychoanalysis, ed. Richard Feldstein, Bruce Fink, and Marie Jaanus (Albany: State University of New York Press, 1995), 33.

4. Deirdre McCloskey, *If You're So Smart: The Narrative of Economic Expertise* (Chicago: University of Chicago Press, 1992), 15.

5. US Department of Health and Human Services. *Vaccines National Strategic Plan 2021–2025* (2021) Washington, D.C. https://www.hhs.gov/sites/default/files/HHS-Vaccines-Report.pdf.

6. "US COVID-19 Cases and Deaths by State," USA Facts, June 26, 2022, https://usafacts.org/visualizations/coronavirus-covid-19-spread-map (accessed June 28, 2022).

7. Jodi Dean, "Communicative Capitalism and Revolutionary Form," *Millennium: Journal of International Studies* 47, no. 3 (2019): 331–32.

8. Ella Nilsen and Li Zhou, "What We Know about Congress's Potential $1 Trillion Coronavirus Stimulus Package," *Vox*, March 17, 2020, https://www.vox.com/2020/3/17/21183846/congress-coronavirus-stimulus-package.

9. Katia Dmitrieva and Olivia Rockeman, "Employers Are Baffled as U.S. Benefits End and Jobs Go Begging," *Bloomberg News*, September 20, 2021, https://www.bloomberg.com/news/articles/2021-09-20/employers-are-baffled-as-u-s-benefits-end-and-jobs-go-begging?sref=PJUU2CLn.

10. "Rep. Steube Urges President Trump to Cap Unemployment Benefits and Incentivize Americans to Return to Workforce," *Targeted News Service*, July 11, 2020, https://www2.lib.ku.edu/login?url=https://www.proquest.com/wire-feeds/rep-steube-urges-president-trump-cap-unemployment/docview/2422371422/se-2?accountid=14556.

11. Meijer, colleagues introduce SUPPORT for new workers act to incentivize return to work (2021). Washington: Federal Information & News Dispatch, LLC., June 18, 2021, https://www2.lib.ku.edu/login?url=https://www.proquest.com/other-sources/meijer-colleagues-introduce-support-new-workers/docview/2543441009/se-2?accountid=14556.

12. "Rep. Roy Introduces Legislation to Cut Unnecessary Unemployment Benefits." https://advance-lexis-com.www2.lib.ku.edu/api/document?collection=news&id=urn:contentItem:62Y5-G411-DYG2-R26G-00000-00&context=1516831 (accessed June 19, 2022).

13. Rob Portman, quoted in "On Fox News, Portman Discusses Next COVID-19 Response Package and Highlights Need to Incentivize Returning Safely to Available Jobs," States News Service, July 29, 2020, link.gale.com/apps/doc/A630944030/AONE?u=ksstate_ukans&sid=bookmark-AONE&xid=5ca79ae6.

14. Quoted in "'Bar Rescue' Host Jon Taffer Likens Unemployment Benefits to 'Hungry, Obedient Dogs,'" https://advance-lexis-com.www2.lib.ku.edu/api/document?collection=news&id=urn:contentItem:63C8-CXC1-DY68-12FB-00

000-00&context=1516831 (accessed June 12, 2022). In a statement, Taffer later apologized for the analogy.

15. Jonathan Ponciano, "States Ending $300 Unemployment Benefits Haven't Boosted Labor Market Yet, Morgan Stanley Finds," *Forbes*, July 8, 2021, https://www.forbes.com/sites/jonathanponciano/2021/07/08/states-that-ended-300-unemployment-benefits-havent-boosted-labor-market-yet-morgan-stanley-finds/?sh=e248fa522373.

16. Jed Kolko, "The Impact of Coronavirus on US Job Postings Through June 4: Data from Indeed.com," *Indeed*, June 9, 2021, https://www.hiringlab.org/2021/06/09/job-postings-through-june-4-2021/; Greg Iacurci, "26 States Ended Federal Unemployment Benefits Early. Data Suggests It's Not Getting People Back to Work," *CNBC*, August 4, 2021, https://www.cnbc.com/2021/08/04/early-end-to-federal-unemployment-pay-in-26-states-not-getting-people-to-work.html.

17. "Civilian Labor Force Participation Rate," U.S. Bureau of Labor Statistics," https://www.bls.gov/charts/employment-situation/civilian-labor-force-participation-rate.htm (accessed June 20, 2022).

18. "2021 Small Business Profile," *U.S. Small Business Administration Office of Advocacy*, 2021, https://cdn.advocacy.sba.gov/wp-content/uploads/2021/08/30143723/Small-Business-Economic-Profile-US.pdf.

19. Yu-Ling Chang, "Unequal Social Protection under the Federalist System: Three Unemployment Insurance Approaches in the United States, 2007–2015," *Journal of Social Policy* 49, no. 1 (2019): 193.

20. Ella Koeze, "The $600 Unemployment Booster Shot, State by State," *New York Times*, April 23, 2020, https://www.nytimes.com/interactive/2020/04/23/business/economy/unemployment-benefits-stimulus-coronavirus.html.

21. "Unemployment Benefit Calculator," Missouri Department of Labor and Industrial Relations, https://labor.mo.gov/des/unemployed-workers/benefits-calculator (accessed June 22, 2022).

22. The yearly salary equivalents should be treated only as relational numbers; the benefits were always intended to be temporary, lasting for less than a year each.

23. "Disappearing Incentives; Unemployment Insurance," *Economist*, August 28, 2021, 63.

24. "Generous Unemployment Benefits Are Not Keeping Americans From Work," *Economist*, July 23, 2020, https://www.economist.com/united-states/2020/07/23/generous-unemployment-benefits-are-not-keeping-americans-from-work.

25. "Unemployment Benefits Forever? Treasury Suggests How States Can Continue the Incentives Not to Work," *Wall Street Journal*, August 21, 2021.

26. "Jobs and Unemployment Insurance," University of Chicago Initiative on Global Markets, July 18, 2020, https://www.igmchicago.org/surveys/jobs-and-unemployment-insurance/. To the economists' credit, the question asked of them was double-barreled, suggesting that the benefits should merely be curtailed rather

than eliminated altogether: "Reducing supplemental levels of unemployment benefits so that no workers receive more than a 100% replacement rate would be a more effective way to balance incentives and income support than simply stopping the supplement at the end of this month." The impossibility of parsing the distinction between the multiple options (keep benefits as is, reduce benefits, eliminate entirely) perfectly is nevertheless revealing. Larry Samuelson of Yale suggested that lowering benefits "would help incentives," while Bengt Holmström of MIT suggests that 60 percent is a reasonable compromise.

27. Quoted in Steve Hartsoe, "Pandemic Unemployment Benefits End Sept. 6. It's Not Simple as to What This Will Do to the Labor Market," *Duke Today*, September 1, 2021, https://today.duke.edu/2021/09/pandemic-unemployment-benefits-end-sept-6-its-not-simple-what-will-do-labor-market.

28. See Lacan, "On a Question Prior to Any Possible Treatment of Psychosis," *Écrits*, 458.

29. Lacan, *The Seminar of Jacques Lacan, Book XI*, 203–4.

30. Lacan, *The Seminar of Jacques Lacan, Book XI*, 177.

31. Lacan, *The Seminar of Jacques Lacan, Book XI*, 179.

32. Lacan's "dialectic of the bow" points to the curve that desire must take to achieve its end, as well as the curvature of the earth (and the pull of gravity, itself a relation of rotating bodies in curved space) that one must account for when attempting a shot.

33. Cornelius Castoriadis, *World in Fragments: Writings on Politics, Society, Psychoanalysis and the Imagination* (Stanford, CA: Stanford University Press, 1997), ed. and trans. David Ames Curtis, 151.

34. Lacan, *The Seminar of Jacques Lacan, Book XI*, 154.

35. Matthew Yglesias, "The CARES Superdole Was a Huge Success," *Slow Boring*, December 29, 2020, https://www.slowboring.com/p/the-cares-superdole-was-a-huge-success.

36. Quoted in Juliana Kaplan and Joseph Zeballos-Roig, "Mitch McConnell Says the Labor Shortage Will Be Solved When People Run Out of Stimulus Money Because Americans Are 'Flush for the Moment,'" *Yahoo News*, July 5, 2022, https://news.yahoo.com/mitch-mcconnell-says-labor-shortage-193708143.html.

37. Catherine Chaput, *Market Affect and the Rhetoric of Political Economic Debates* (Columbia: University of South Carolina Press, 2019), 37.

38. This repressed signifier also depends on crowding out the received economic "laws" of supply and demand—workers must be disempowered from earning higher wages in a labor market momentarily tilted in their favor, lest they get the wrong idea about who holds power in the capitalist mode of production.

39. The national focus of Operation Warp Speed, and the refusal to grant patent wavers for vaccine development in countries eager to vaccinate their populations led to what World Health Organization director-general Tedros Adhanom Ghebreyesus called "vaccine apartheid." See Jon Cohen, " 'I'm Still Feeling That

We're Failing': Exasperated WHO Leader Speaks Out about Vaccine Inequity," *Science*, June 18, 2021, https://www.science.org/content/article/i-m-still-feeling-we-re-failing-exasperated-who-leader-speaks-out-about-vaccine.

40. "US Coronavirus Vaccine Tracker," USA Facts, https://usafacts.org/visualizations/covid-vaccine-tracker-states/ (accessed July 10, 2022).

41. "National COVID-19 Preparedness Plan," The White House, https://www.whitehouse.gov/covidplan/ (accessed July 4, 2022).

42. Dardot and Laval, *The New Way of the World*, 11.

43. Dardot and Laval, 243–44.

44. Phillip J. Cooper, *The War against Regulation: From Jimmy Carter to George W. Bush* (Lawrence: University of Kansas Press, 2009), 27–28.

45. Cooper, *The War against Regulation*, 61.

46. Quoted in Cooper, *The War against Regulation*, 78.

47. Al Gore, *From Red Tape to Results: Creating a Government that Works Better and Costs Less*, Report of the National Performance Review (Washington, DC: Government Printing Office, 1993), 7.

48. Hillary Rodham Clinton, *Living History* (New York: Simon & Schuster, 2003), 366.

49. Foucault, *Birth of Biopolitics*, 202.

50. Vee Burke, "The 1996 Welfare Reform Law," *Congressional Research Service*, http://royce.house.gov/uploadedfiles/the%201996%20welfare%20reform%20law.pdf (accessed June 22, 2016).

51. Becker himself was quite enthusiastic about Clinton's welfare reform bill, and specifically noted it in his final column for *BusinessWeek* as an example of how incentive-based programs can be successful.

52. Thaler and Sunstein, *Nudge*, 208.

53. Ted Kolderie, "Beyond Choice to New Public Schools," *Progressive Policy Institute*, 1.

54. Kolderie, "Beyond Choice to New Public Schools," 2.

55. Kolderie, 10.

56. Barack Obama, "The President on 'Race to the Top,'" July 24, 2009, https://obamawhitehouse.archives.gov/blog/2009/07/24/president-race-top.

57. Murray Levine and Adeline Levine, "Education Deformed: No Child Left Behind and the Race to the Top—'This Almost Reads Like Our Business Plans,'" *American Journal of Orthopsychiatry* 82 (2012): 104–113.

58. William G. Howell and Asya Magazinnik, "Presidential Prescriptions for State Policy: Obama's Race to the Top Initiative," *Journal of Policy Analysis and Management* 36 (2017): 505.

59. Joshua Childs and Jennifer Lin Russell, "Improving Low-Achieving Schools: Building State Capacity to Support School Improvement through Race to the Top," *Urban Education* 52 (2017): 236–66.

60. Jonathan Chait, *Audacity: How Barack Obama Defied His Critics and Created a Legacy That Will Prevail* (New York: Custom House, 2017), 151.

61. Chait, *Audacity*, 152.

62. "Maternal CARE Act of 2019," Office of Sen. Kamala Harris, n.d., https://www.harris.senate.gov/imo/media/doc/Maternal%20CARE%20Act%20 of%202019%20background.pdf (accessed July 21, 2020).

63. S.1600—Maternal Care Access and Reducing Emergencies Act, 116th Congress, May 22, 2019, https://www.congress.gov/bill/116th-congress/senate-bill/1600/text (accessed July 22, 2020).

64. Jeff Stein and Chelsea James, "Buttigieg Health Plan Hinges on 'Supercharged' Version of Unpopular Obamacare Mandate," *Washington Post*, December 24, 2019.

65. Stein and James, "Buttigieg Health Plan Hinges on 'Supercharged' Version of Unpopular Obamacare Mandate."

66. Quoted in James Hamblin, "A Mandate, in Other Words," *Atlantic*, March 7, 2017, https://www.theatlantic.com/health/archive/2017/03/no-mandate-youre-the-mandate/518784/.

67. A meaningful difference is that within the ACA and Buttigieg plans, the financial penalty would become government revenue, whereas under the ACHA, the 30 percent premium surcharge as well as the mandated legal penalty would go directly to health insurance companies.

68. Lisa Heinzerling, "Cost-Benefit Jumps the Shark," *Georgetown Law Faculty Blog*, June 13, 2012, https://gulcfac.typepad.com/georgetown_university_law/2012/06/cost-benefit-jumps-the-shark.html.

69. This executive approach to a legislative mandate also points to the critique of representation that nudges and incentives take: even after being given a law to enforce, the economically minded Obama administration evaded this charge and made it an issue of efficiency, and not justice, bypassing a representative regime in favor of an economic one.

70. Žižek uses a joke to illustrate what is at stake in the decline of symbolic efficiency—a man is cured of the delusion that he is a grain of corn but returns to the doctor after seeing a hen, whom he is convinced is going to eat him. After being reassured by the doctor that he knows he is no longer a grain of corn, the man replies, "Yes . . . but *does the hen*?" See Žižek, *The Ticklish Subject*, 393.

71. "Workplace Vaccination Program," Centers for Disease Control and Prevention," November 4, 2021, https://www.cdc.gov/coronavirus/2019-ncov/vaccines/recommendations/essentialworker/workplace-vaccination-program.html#anchor_1615584361592.

72. Jacob Verughese et al., "Increasing Coverage of Appropriate Vaccinations: A Community Guide Systematic Economic Review," *American Journal of Preventative Medicine* 50, no. 6 (2016): 797–808.

73. Pol Campos-Mercade et al., "Monetary Incentives Increase COVID-19 Vaccinations," *Science* 374 (2021): 879–82, November 12, 2021, https://www.science.org/doi/epdf/10.1126/science.abm0475.

74. Lynn Vavreck, "$100 as Incentive to Get a Shot? Experiment Suggests It Can Pay Off," *New York Times*, May 26, 2021, https://www.nytimes.com/2021/05/04/upshot/vaccine-incentive-experiment.html, accessed July 10, 2022.

75. Emily Anthes, "How to Nudge People into Getting Tested for the Coronavirus," *New York Times*, April 5, 2021, https://www.nytimes.com/2021/04/02/health/coronavirus-testing-behavior-hesitancy.html.

76. Ganesh Iyer, Vivek Nandur, and David Soberman, "Vaccine Hesitancy and Monetary Incentives," *Humanities and Social Sciences Communications* 9, no. 81 (2022), http://doi.org/10.1057/s41599-022-01074-y. This survey suggests a causal relationship and "empirical support" for the efficacy of vaccination, however, as with all survey data, it suggests instead the vicissitudes of a promise from both researcher and participant. The researchers offered no monetary reward, and no participants were obliged to follow through on their promises. Additionally, although the researchers argued that $1,000 would suffice for someone to take the vaccine, their entry box had an upper limit of $1,000, which suggests that either individuals would have entered much higher numbers, or in what would confirm the behavioral economic tenet of "anchoring points," that $1,000 would suffice for someone whose desire to avoid vaccination was infinite.

77. Ivan Pereira, "Why COVID-19 Vaccine Incentives Didn't Really Work: Experts," *ABC News*, July 15, 2021, https://abcnews.go.com/Health/vaccine-incentives-best-answer-hesitancy-experts/story?id=78695407.

78. Emily Manley, "Missouri's Vaccine Incentive Program Ends This Week," *FOX 2 Now*, October 5, 2021, https://fox2now.com/news/missouri/missouris-vaccine-incentive-program-ends-this-week/.

79. Allan J. Walkey, Anica Law, and Nicholas A. Bosch, "Lottery-Based Incentive in Ohio and COVID-19 Vaccination Rates," *JAMA* 326, no. 8 (2021): 766–67, http://doi.org/10.1001/jama.2021.11048.

80. Harsha Thirumurthy et al., "Association between Statewide Financial Incentive Programs and COVID-19 Vaccination Rates," *PLoS ONE* 17, no. 3 (2022), https://doi.org/10.1371/journal.pone.0263425.

81. Quoted in Caroline Champlin, "Do COVID-19 Vaccine Incentives Work?" *Marketplace*, October 26, 2021, https://www.marketplace.org/2021/10/26/do-covid-19-vaccine-incentives-work/.

82. Tom Chang et al., "Financial Incentives and Other Nudges Do Not Increase COVID-19 Vaccinations among the Vaccine Hesitant," National Bureau of Economic Research Working Paper no. 29403, October 2021, 8.

83. Quoted in Champlin, "Do COVID-19 Vaccine Incentives Work?"

84. Kate Proctor, "UK Government's Coronavirus Advice—and Why It Gave It," *Guardian*, March 12, 2020, https://www.theguardian.com/world/2020/mar/12/uk-governments-coronavirus-advice-and-why-it-gave-it.

85. Tony Yates, "Why Is the Government Relying on Nudge Theory to Fight Coronavirus?," *Guardian* March 13, 2020, https://www.theguardian.com/commentisfree/2020/mar/13/why-is-the-government-relying-on-nudge-theory-to-tackle-coronavirus.

86. Yates, "Why Is the Government Relying on Nudge Theory to Fight Coronavirus?"

87. There is a further irony in the United Kingdom's initial refusal to implement lockdowns or bans on large gatherings: it is impossible to exert "fatigue" at the cancelation of a football match or concert by attending one.

88. See Robert Baldwin, "From Regulation to Behavior Change: Giving Nudge the Third Degree," *Modern Law Review* 77, no. 6 (2014): 831–57.

89. White, *The Manipulation of Choice*, xiii.

90. White even allows for the individual to be aware that they are making a "bad" choice but demands that they still be free to make it. Only an individual is afforded the ethical dignity of self-reflection; the libertarian position rejects out of hand the ability for a state to determinately self-reflect to produce a better outcome.

91. Diane Davis, "Addressing Alterity: Rhetoric, Hermeneutics, and the Nonappropriative Relation," *Philosophy & Rhetoric* 38 (2005): 193.

92. Davis, "Addressing Alterity," 198.

93. Jacques Lacan, *The Seminar of Jacques Lacan, Book X: Anxiety*, ed. Jacques-Alain Miller, trans. A. R. Price (Malden, MA: Polity, 2014), 315.

94. Sigmund Freud, "Infantile Sexuality," Vol. 7 of *The Standard Edition of the Complete Works of Sigmund Freud*, trans. and ed. James Strachey (London: Hogarth, 1955), 186.

95. Joshua Gunn, "ShitText: Toward a New Coprophilic Style," *Text and Performance Quarterly* 26 (2006): 88.

96. Calum Lister Matheson, Filthy Lucre: Gold, Language and Exchange Anxiety," *Review of Communication* 18 (2018), 257–58.

97. Sigmund Freud, "Character and Anal Erotism," Vol. 9 of *The Standard Edition of the Complete Works of Sigmund Freud*, trans. and ed. James Strachey (London: Hogarth, 1955), 169.

98. Matheson, "Filthy Lucre," 250.

99. From a strict Freudian position, a satisfaction of the oral drive aligns with the paternalist's position that any object is substitutable for another. The major difference between a psychoanalytic approach and that of the paternalist's is that the paternalist's choice of object is not necessarily "genital," or psychologically healthy, but an object that satisfies the political aims of the paternalist herself.

100. White, *The Manipulation of Choice*, 82.

101. Shane Ryan, "Libertarian Paternalism is Hard Paternalism," *Analysis* 78 (2018).

102. Friedrich Hayek, *Studies in Philosophy, Politics and Economics* (Chicago: University of Chicago Press, 1967), 49.

103. Chaput, *Market Affect and the Rhetoric of Political Economic Debates*, 94.

104. Mirowski, *Never Let a Serious Crisis Go to Waste*, 81.

105. Friedrich Hayek, *The Road to Serfdom* (Chicago: University of Chicago Press, 1944), 205.

106. Ryan Calo, "Code, Nudge, or Notice?" *Iowa Law Review* 99 (2014), 795.

107. White, *The Manipulation of Choice*, 106, 110.

108. Sigmund Freud, *Beyond the Pleasure Principle*, trans. C. J. M. Hubback (London: International Psycho-analytical Press, 1922).

109. Žižek, *The Ticklish Subject*, 329.

110. Mark Fisher, *Capitalist Realism: Is There No Alternative?* (Winchester, UK: Zero Books, 2009), 21.

111. "Stories from the Field: Examples of Successful Worker COVID-19 Vaccination Programs," Centers for Disease Control and Prevention, March 28, 2022, https://www.cdc.gov/coronavirus/2019-ncov/community/workplaces-businesses/field-stories.html.

112. Stacy Wood and Kevin Schulman, "Beyond Politics—Promoting Covid-19 Vaccination in the United States," *New England Journal of Medicine*, February 18, 2021, https://www.nejm.org/doi/full/10.1056/NEJMms2033790.

113. This belief has merit, with the capricious ways in which the American legal system disproportionately harms communities of color, working people, people of minoritized sexualities, and every complexly articulated overlap among them. Yet this theory of government must be distinguished from a Marxist perspective that foregrounds class interest as the primary reason why states oppress their populaces. The onerous laws and regulations on people's actions and bodies result from class struggle and ensure social hierarchies; it is never simply dyadic, vertical, or individual.

114. Cass R. Sunstein, *The Ethics of Influence: Government in the Age of Behavioral Science* (Cambridge: Cambridge University Press, 2016), 198.

115. See Juliet Mitchell, *Mad Men and Medusas: Reclaiming Hysteria* (New York: Basic Books, 2000).

116. In 2022, researchers found that, accounting for "publication bias" (the bias toward studies that have positive findings as opposed to no effect or a "null hypothesis") there is no evidence for "nudges" working *at all*. See Maximilian Maier et al., "No Evidence for Nudging after Adjusting for Publication Bias," *PNAS* 119:31 (2022), 1–2, https://doi.org/10.1073/pnas.2200300119.

117. McGowan, *Enjoying What We Don't Have*, 5.

Conclusion

1. Quoted in Tad Friend, "Donald Glover Can't Save You," *New Yorker*, February 26, 2018, https://www.newyorker.com/magazine/2018/03/05/donald-glover-cant-save-you, accessed September 22, 2020.

2. Gilles Deleuze, *Difference and Repetition*, trans. Paul Patton (London: Athlone, 2001), 301.

3. Peter Rusterholz, "On the Crisis of Representation," *Semiotica* 143 (2003): 54.

4. Peter Hallward, *Out of this World: Deleuze and the Philosophy of Creation* (New York: Verso, 2006), 71.

5. Bradford Vivian, *Being Made Strange: Rhetoric Beyond Representation* (Albany: State University of New York Press, 2004), 23.

6. Vivian, *Being Made Strange*, 43.

7. Gayatri Spivak herself has, if not abandoned, at least significantly revised her endorsement of the term "strategic essentialism" that she is credited with coining. See Sarah Danius, Stefan Jonsson, and Gayatri Chakravorty Spivak, "An Interview with Gayatri Chakravorty Spivak," *boundary 2* 20 (1993), 34–35.

8. Jenna N. Hanchey, "Toward a Relational Politics of Representation," *Review of Communication* 18 (2018): 265.

9. Žižek, *Absolute Recoil*, 374.

10. Ernesto Laclau, *The Rhetorical Foundations of Society* (Brooklyn: Verso, 1014), 13–18.

11. Brian J. Hall, "The Pay to Performance Incentives of Executive Stock Options." NBER Working Paper Series. National Bureau of Economic Research (1998), 1.

12. Susan R. Holmberg and Lydia Austin, "Fixing a Hole: How the Tax Code for Executive Pay Distorts Economic Incentives and Burdens Taxpayers." The Roosevelt Institute, July 22, 2013, 2.

13. Polanyi, *The Great Transformation*, 149.

14. One can read the hobbyhorse of decrying "licensing fees" as symptomatic of how few alibis right-wing figures have for explaining income inequality and slow economic growth; the fact that aspiring cosmetologists must acquire fifteen hundred hours of apprenticeship and pay roughly $200 for an examination and license is not a sufficient explanation for persistent and widening income inequality since the 1970s.

15. Lacan, *The Seminar of Jacques Lacan, Book III*, 82.

16. Joshua Gunn, "On Speech and Public Release," *Rhetoric & Public Affairs* 13 (2010), 28.

17. Lacan, *The Seminar of Jacques Lacan, Book III*, 39.

18. Chris Kalaboukis, "How to Incentivize Disruptive Innovation, *Hellofuture*, n.d., https://hellofuture.co/incentivize-disruptive-innovation (accessed October 12, 2020).

19. Arnsperger and Varoufakis note that one's preferences need not be completely independent of context, or "fixed and exogenous," for the discipline. An economist can simply black box the source of one's utility while adhering to the claim that no matter what one desires, one ceaselessly works to achieve it. See Arnsperger and Varoufakis, "What Is Neoclassical Economics?," 9–10.

20. S. M. Amadae, *Prisoners of Reason: Game Theory and Neoliberal Political Economy* (New York: Cambridge University Press, 2016), 32–38.

21. Todd McGowan, *Capitalism and Desire: The Psychic Cost of Free Markets* (New York: Columbia University Press, 2016), 11.

22. Psychoanalysis' warrant for this claim is that our biological drives, our being prior to any conceptualization, come into conflict with our being-with-others. To exist is to be beset on all sides with our own biological needs as well as rules that tell us "no." Civilization is nothing but a negation of a negation, a series of displacements from an inarticulable drive in which we must deny our own innermost needs and deny our aggression about that fundamental dissatisfaction. Signification is one technology that humans deploy to negotiate alterity but is itself allegorical for this original displacement.

23. See Joshua Gunn, "Maranatha," *Quarterly Journal of Speech* 98 (2012): 359–85, and Christian Lundberg, "Enjoying God's Death: *The Passion of the Christ* and the Practices of an Evangelical Public," *Quarterly Journal of Speech* 95 (2009), 387–411.

24. Lacan, *The Seminar of Jacques Lacan, Book XX*, 3.

25. Karl Marx, *Capital*, vol. 1, trans. Ben Fowkes (New York: Penguin, 1990), 333–37.

26. Becker, *The Economic Approach to Human Behavior*, 133.

27. Lacan, *The Seminar of Jacques Lacan, Book XX*, 4.

28. Joseph Schumpeter, "On the Concept of Social Value," *Quarterly Journal of Economics* 2 (1909): 214.

29. Schumpeter, "On the Concept of Social Value, 214, 215. A full discussion of debates around the source of value is beyond the scope of this work, but briefly, from within the framework developed by Léon Walras, Stanley Jevons, Alfred Marshall, and others within the neoclassical tradition, value is determined from a "subjectivist" point of view, meaning that the price of a commodity is determined by one's willingness to pay for it. No commodity has an "innate" value (contra for instance the Physiocrats, who believed land had an innate value), but it is determined by one's desire for it. When a resource is scarce, whoever is willing to pay the highest price for it is the determiner of its value. That is, a purely subjectivist theory of value can logically precede, and absorb, the "law of supply and demand" that often characterizes economics.

30. Schumpeter, "On the Concept of Social Value," 215.

31. Dana L. Cloud, "Hegemony or Concordance? The Rhetoric of Tokenism in 'Oprah' Winfrey's Rags-to-Riches Biography," *Critical Studies in Mass Communication* 13 (1996): 119.

32. Harvey, *A Brief History of Neoliberalism*, 23.

33. Philip Mirowski, *Machine Dreams: Economics Becomes a Cyborg Science* (Cambridge: Cambridge University Press, 2002), 439.

34. Dilip Gaonkar, "Object and Method in Rhetorical Criticism: From Wichelns to Leff and McGee," *Western Journal of Speech Communication* 54 (1990): 290.

35. Many people, rhetoricians included, were horrified at Donald Trump's acceptance speech of the Republican Party's nomination in 2016 for the stark vision of an America beset by violence and decay, along with his plan for addressing it. The empirical truth value of the speech is beside the point: if it is possible to imagine a world in which that speech is possible, there is a sense in which that speech is "true" to a particular group of people. See Donald J. Trump, "Full Text: Donald Trump 2016 RNC Draft Speech Transcript," *Politico*, July 21, 2016, https://www.politico.com/story/2016/07/full-transcript-donald-trump-nomination-acceptance-speech-at-rnc-225974.

36. Marx, *Capital*, 1:163–77.

37. Jodi Dean, *Crowds and Party* (New York: Verso, 2016), 105.

38. Lacan, *The Seminar of Jacques Lacan, Book III*, 161–62.

39. Lacan derives this reading from the fact that Freud's theory of the Oedipus complex was never fully elaborated for women (although Carl Jung attempted to produce an "Electra complex" to make up for this perceived lack in psychoanalytic theory). Rather, the Oedipus complex is a singular process that affects women and men differently. As argued in chapter 5, Lacan theorizes the problem-space of sexual difference from the insight that there is no "human as such," all humans are marked by some original difference from one another.

40. Suzanne Barnard, "Introduction," *Reading Seminar XX: Lacan's Major Work on Love, Knowledge, and Feminine Sexuality*, ed. Suzanne Barnard and Bruce Fink (Albany: State University of New York Press, 2002), 10.

41. Slavoj Žižek, *Absolute Recoil: Towards a New Foundation of Dialectical Materialism* (Brooklyn: Verso, 2014), 242.

42. The Carly Rae Jepsen song "Everything He Needs" demonstrates the overlapping fantasies that organize a "healthy" dyadic relationship. Jepsen's chorus repeats the phrase "He needs me, he needs me, I got everything he needs," in a prayerlike incantation, as if she is convincing herself of the truth of her claim. The bridge reverses the direction of desire by repeating "I can never give him enough, enough of my love," meaning that she acknowledges her own lack. In the chorus, she possesses the thing she imagines he needs; in the bridge, she imagines that he needs something of hers (her lack) and attempts to return it to him. When Lacan tells us that love is giving what we do not have, he means precisely this: We give our "lack" to the other, for we believe them to need it.

43. Chait, *Audacity*, 152.

44. Steve Kelman, "Here We Go Again: 'Diversity Training' and Government Contractors," *Federal Computer Week*, October 2, 2020, https://fcw.com/blogs/lectern/2020/10/comment-kelman-eo-diversity-training.aspx.

45. Kelman, "Here We Go Again."

46. Kelman.

47. Steve Kelman, " 'Reinventing Government,' 25 Years Later," *Federal Computer Week*, December 6, 2017, https://fcw.com/articles/2017/12/06/kelman-25-years-of-acquisition-reform.aspx.

48. "2019 Employer Health Benefits Survey," *Kaiser Family Foundation*, September 25, 2019, https://www.kff.org/report-section/ehbs-2019-section-1-cost-of-health-insurance/.

49. "UnitedHealth Group Revenue 2006–2020," *Macrotrends*, https://www.macrotrends.net/stocks/charts/UNH/unitedhealth-group/revenue (accessed October 10, 2020). Similarly the Kaiser Foundation, a supposedly "nonprofit" health insurance company, posted $2.1 billion in profits in 2009 and in 2019 posted $7.4 billion in profit. See Chris Rauber, "Kaiser Permanente Posts $2.1B in 2009 Profits," *San Francisco Business Times*, February 12, 2010, https://www.bizjournals.com/sanfrancisco/stories/2010/02/08/daily64.html; and Marc Brown, "2019 Financial Results for Kaiser Foundation Health Plan, Hospitals," *Kaiser Permanente*, February 7, 2020, https://about.kaiserpermanente.org/our-story/news/announcements/2019-kaiser-foundation-health-plan-hospitals-financial-results.

50. Levitt and Dubner, *Freakonomics*, 17.

51. Thaler and Sunstein, *Nudge*, 255.

52. Barbara A. Bichelmeyer, "VSIP Participation Follow-Up," University of Kansas Office of the Provost, October 14, 2020.

53. Taylor Pendergrass, "Progress Is Occurring on Prosecutorial Reform, despite Tuesday's Setbacks in California," *American Civil Liberties Union*, June 7, 2018, https://www.aclu.org/blog/smart-justice/prosecutorial-reform/progress-occurring-prosecutorial-reform-despite-tuesdays.

54. Heather Hahn, "Work Requirements in Safety Net Programs: Lessons for Medicaid from TANF and SNAP," *Urban Institute*, April 2018, https://www.urban.org/sites/default/files/publication/98086/work_requirements_in_safety_net_programs.pdf.

55. Will Evans, "How Amazon Hid its Safety Crisis," *Reveal News*, September 29, 2020, https://revealnews.org/article/how-amazon-hid-its-safety-crisis.

56. Evans, "How Amazon Hid Its Safety Crisis."

57. Fink, *The Lacanian Subject*, 9–10.

58. The nature of the unconscious is such that an individual may truly desire their own unhappiness, or the unhappiness of their colleagues for any number of reasons—one may desire the attention of being the proximate cause that prevents the workplace from a reward, or one may engineer an injury to draw attention to poor working conditions. But what is more likely is that most subjects are humdrum neurotics and can never be sure (outside of analysis) what caused them to do what they did: Did I secretly desire to lose the reward? Was I

improperly incentivized? The cause of the action is displaced from the corporation onto the individual's unconscious mind.

59. Castoriadis, *World in Fragments*, 162.

Works Cited

"About SBST." Social and Behavioral Sciences Team. Accessed April 2, 2022. http://www.sbst.gov/.

Adams, Luke. "Players with Incentive Bonuses for 2016/7." *Hoops Rumors* (blog). November 7, 2016. https://www.hoopsrumors.com/2016/11/players-with-incentive-bonuses-for-201617.html.

Afif, Zeina. "'Nudge Units'—Where They Came From and What They Can Do." *Let's Talk Development* (blog). October 25, 2017. https://www.blogs.worldbank.org/developmenttalk/nudge-units-where-they-came-and-what-they-can-do.

AgentShades. "Why I Hate The Phantom Pain's Tranquilizer Gun." *Kotaku.* September 23, 2016. https://www.tay.kinja.com/why-i-hate-the-phantom-pains-tranquilizer-gun-1786994266.

Allais, Maurice. "Nobel Lecture." *Nobel Lectures, Economics* vol. 2 (1981–1990), 233–52. Edited by Karl-Göran Mäler. Singapore: World Scientific Publishing Co., 1990.

Amadae, S. M. *Prisoners of Reason: Game Theory and Neoliberal Political Economy.* Cambridge: Cambridge University Press, 2016.

Anthes, Emily. "How to Nudge People into Getting Tested for the Coronavirus." *New York Times*, April 5, 2021. https://www.nytimes.com/2021/04/02/health/coronavirus-testing-behavior-hesitancy.html.

Aristotle. *Aristotle's Metaphysics.* Translated by Hippocrates G. Apostle. Bloomington: Indiana University Press, 1966.

———. *Aristotle's Physics.* Revised by W. D. Ross. Oxford: Clarendon Press, 1955.

———. *Rhetoric.* Translated by W. Rhys Roberts. www.classics.mit.edu/Aristotle/rhetoric.html.

Arnsperger, Christian, and Yanis Varoufakis. "What Is Neoclassical Economics? The Three Axioms Responsible for its Theoretical Curve, Practical Irrelevance, and, thus, Discursive Power." *Panoeconomicus* 53, no. 1 (2006): 5–18.

Ashraf, Quamrul, and Oded Galor. "The 'Out of Africa' Hypothesis, Human Genetic Diversity, and Comparative Economic Development." *American Economic Review,* vol. 103 (2013): 1–46.

Aune, James Arnt. *Selling the Free Market: The Rhetoric of Economic Correctness.* New York: Guilford Press, 2001.

Baldwin, Robert. "From Regulation to Behavior Change: Giving Nudge the Third Degree." *Modern Law Review* 77, no. 6 (2014): 831–57.

"'Bar Rescue' Host Jon Taffer Likens Unemployment Benefits to 'Hungry, Obedient Dogs.'" *Newsweek.* August 13, 2021. https://advance-lexis-com.www2.lib. ku.edu/api/document?collection=news&id=urn:contentItem:63C8-CXC1-D Y68-12FB-00000-00&context=1516831. Accessed June 12, 2022.

Barnard, Suzanne. "Introduction." In *Reading Seminar XX: Lacan's Major Work on Love, Knowledge and Feminine Sexuality,* edited by Suzanne Barnard and Bruce Fink, 1–20. Albany, State University of New York Press, 2002.

———. "Tongues of Angels: Feminine Structure and Other Jouissance." In *Reading Seminar XX: Lacan's Major Work on Love, Knowledge and Feminine Sexuality,* edited by Suzanne Barnard and Bruce Fink, 171–86. Albany: State University of New York Press, 2002.

Barnett, Clive. "Publics and Markets: What's Wrong with Neoliberalism?" *The Handbook of Social Geography,* edited by Susan Smith, Sallie Marston, Rachel Pain, and John Paul Jones III, 269–97. London: SAGE, 2009.

Basu, Kaushik. *Beyond the Invisible Hand: Groundwork for a New Economics.* Princeton, NJ: Princeton University Press, 2011.

Basu, Tanya. "The White House Is Now Using Behavioral Economics to Improve Policy." *Time,* September 24, 2015. http://www.time.com/4042689/social-behavioral-sciences-team/.

Bates, Jennifer. "Hegel's Inverted World, Cleopatra, and the Logic of the Crocodile." *Phenomenology and Life* 54, no. 3 (2012): 427–43.

Becker, Gary S. *Accounting for Tastes.* Cambridge, MA: Harvard University Press, 1998.

———. "'Bribe' Third World Parents to Keep Their Kids in School." *Business Week,* November 22, 1999, 15.

———. "Changes in Tastes when Preferences Are Stable." In Gary S. Becker Papers, University of Chicago, Special Collections Research Center, Box 2.

———. *The Economic Approach to Human Behavior.* Chicago: University of Chicago Press, 1976.

———. "The Economic Way of Looking at Life." *Prize Lecture* 1992, http://www. nobelprize.org/prizes/economic-sciences/1992/becker/lecture/.

———. "Habits, Addictions, and Traditions." In *The Essence of Becker,* edited by Ramón Febrero and Pedro S. Schwarz, 218–40. Stanford: Hoover Institution Press, 1995.

———. *Human Capital: A Theoretical and Empirical Analysis, with Special Reference to Education.* 3rd ed. Chicago: University of Chicago Press, 1993.

————. "Human Capital, Effort, and the Sexual Division of Labor." *Journal of Labor Economics* 3, no. 1 (1985): S33–S58.

————. "Interview with Gary Becker." n.d. Gary S. Becker Papers, University of Chicago Special Collections Research Center, Box 4.

————. "Is There Any Way to Stop Child Labor Abuses?" *BusinessWeek*, May 12, 1997, 22.

————. "A Note on Restaurant Pricing and Other Examples of Social Influences on Price." *Journal of Political Economy* 99, no. 5 (1991): 1109–16.

————. Phone interview with Roger Arnold, Department of Economics, University of Nevada, Las Vegas, March 16, 1988, 1–10, Gary S. Becker Papers, University of Chicago Special Collections Research Center, Box 22.

————. "The Role of Altruism and Selfishness in Economic Life." George S. Eccles Distinguished Lecture Series, College of Business, Utah State University, 9–14. In Gary S. Becker Papers, University of Chicago, Special Collections Research Center, Box 13.

————. "Understanding Human Behavior." Conference by Becker Center, November 10, 2007, 1–5, Gary S. Becker Papers, University of Chicago, Special Collections Research Center, Box 1.

————. "A 19-Year Dialogue on the Power of Incentives." *BusinessWeek*, July 12, 2004, 28.

Becker, Gary S., and Guity Nashat Becker. *The Economics of Life: From Baseball to Affirmative Action to Immigration, How Real-World Issues Affect our Everyday Life.* New York: McGraw-Hill, 1997.

Becker, Gary S., and Julio Jorge Elias. "Introducing Incentives in the Market for Live and Cadaveric Organ Donations." *Journal of Economic Perspectives* 21, no. 3 (2007): 3–24.

Becker, Gary S., Kevin M. Murphy, and Jörg Spenkuch. "The Manipulation of Children's Preferences, Old Age Support, and Investments in Children's Human Capital," 2013, 1–35. Gary S. Becker Papers, University of Chicago, Special Collections Research Center, Box 1.

Becker, Gary S., and Richard Posner, "Suicide: An Economic Approach," 2006, 1–25. Gary S. Becker Papers, Special Collections Research Center, University of Chicago, Box 14.

Becker, Gary S., and George Stigler. "*De Gustibus Non Est Disputandum.*" In *The Essence of Becker*, edited by Ramón Febrero and Pedro S. Schwarz. 184–208. Stanford: Hoover Institution Press, 1995.

Bentham, Jeremy. *An Introduction to the Principles of Morals and Legislation.* London, Clarendon Press, 1789. http://www.oll.libertyfund.org/titles/278.

Berkshire, Jennifer C. "How Education Reform Ate the Democratic Party." *The Baffler.* November 17, 2017. http://www.thebaffler.com/latest/ed-reform-ate-the-democrats-berkshire.

Bichelmeyer, Barbara A. "VSIP Participation Follow-Up." University of Kansas Office of the Provost, October 14, 2020.

Bidgood, Jess. "'I Live Paycheck to Paycheck': A West Virginia Teacher Explains Why She's on Strike." *New York Times*, March 1, 2018. http://www.nytimes.com/2018/03/01/us/west-virginia-teachers-strike.html.

Biesecker, Barbara. "Rhetorical Studies and the New Psychoanalysis: What's the Real Problem? Or Framing the Problem of the Real." *Quarterly Journal of Speech* 84, no. 2 (1998): 222–240.

Bitzer, Lloyd F. "The Rhetorical Situation." *Philosophy & Rhetoric* 1, no. 1 (1968) 1–14.

Black, John, Nigar Hashimzade, and Gareth Myles. *A Dictionary of Economics.* 4th ed. Oxford: Oxford University Press, 2012.

Black, William K. "Gary Becker's Treatment of Women Who Work for Pay as 'Deviants.'" *New Economic Perspectives* (blog). June 17, 2014. http://www.neweconomicperspectives.org/2014/06/gary-becker-treatment-women-work-pay-deviants.html.

Boswell, Wendy R., Alexander J. S. Colvin, and Todd C. Darnold. "Organizational Systems and Employee Motivation." In *Work Motivation: Past, Present, and Future*, edited by Ruth Kanfer, Gilad Chen, and Robert D. Pritchard, 361–400. New York: Routledge, 2008.

Brown, Marc. "2019 Financial Results for Kaiser Foundation Health Plan, Hospitals." *Kaiser Permanente.* February 7, 2020. http://www.about.kaiserpermanente.org/our-story/news/announcements/2019-kaiser-foundation-health-plan-hospitals-financial-results.

Brown, Wendy. *Undoing the Demos: Neoliberalism's Stealth Revolution.* Cambridge. MA: MIT Press, 2015.

Bruno, Pierre. *Lacan and Marx: The Invention of the Symptom.* Translated by John Holland. London: Routledge, 2020.

Burke, Kenneth. *The Philosophy of Literary Form: Studies in Symbolic Action.* 3rd ed. Berkeley: University of California Press, 1973.

———. *Permanence and Change: An Anatomy of Purpose.* 3rd ed. Berkeley: University of California Press, 1984.

Burke, Vee. "The 1996 Welfare Reform Law." Congressional Research Service. Accessed June 22, 2016. www.royce.house.gov/uploadedfiles/the%201996%20welfare%20reform%20law.pdf.

"Calculating the Value of Women's Unpaid Work." *The FRED Blog*, Federal Reserve Bank of St. Louis. March 9, 2020. http://www.fredblog.stlouisfed.org/2020/03/calculating-the-value-of-womens-unpaid-work/.

Calo, Ryan. "Code, Nudge, or Notice?" *Iowa Law Review* 99, no. 2 (2014): 773–802.

Campos-Mercade, Pol, Armando N. Meier, Florian H. Schneider, Stephan Meier, Devin Pope, Erik Wengström. "Monetary Incentives Increase COVID-19 Vaccinations." *Science,* 374 (2021): 879–82.

Castoriadis, Cornelius. *World in Fragments: Writings on Politics, Society, Psychoanalysis and the Imagination.* Translated and edited by David Ames Curtis. Stanford: Stanford University Press, 1997.

Chait, Jonathan. *Audacity: How Barack Obama Defied His Critics and Created a Legacy That Will Prevail*. New York: Custom House, 2017.

Chakrabortty, Aditya. "From Obama to Cameron, Why Do So Many Politicians Want a Piece of Richard Thaler?" *Guardian*. July 11, 2008. http://www.theguardian.com/politics/2008/jul/12/economy.conservatives.

Champlin, Caroline. "Do COVID-19 Vaccine Incentives Work?" *Marketplace*, October 26, 2021. https://www.marketplace.org/2021/10/26/do-covid-19-vaccine-incentives-work/.

Chang, Tom, Mireille Jacobson, Manisha Shah, Rajiv Pramanik, and Samir B. Shah. "Financial Incentives and Other Nudges Do Not Increase COVID-19 Vaccinations among the Vaccine Hesitant." *National Bureau of Economic Research Working Paper*, no. 29403 (October 2021): 1–15.

Chang, Yu-Ling. "Unequal Social Protection under the Federalist System: Three Unemployment Insurance Approaches in the United States, 2007–2015." *Journal of Social Policy* 49, no. 1 (2019): 189–211.

Chaput, Catherine. "Popular Economics: Neoliberal Propaganda and Its Affectivity." In *Propaganda and Rhetoric in Democracy: History, Theory, Analysis*, edited by Gae Lyn Henderson and M. J. Braun. 157–180. Carbondale: Southern Illinois University Press, 2016.

———. *Market Affect and the Rhetoric of Political Economic Debates*. Columbia: University of South Carolina Press, 2019.

Chaput, Catherine, and Joshua S. Hanan. "Economic Rhetoric as *Taxis*: Neoliberal Governmentality and the Dispositif of *Freakonomics*." *Journal of Cultural Economy* 8, no. 1 (2015): 42–61.

"Charter of the Subcommittee on Social and Behavioral Sciences of the Committee on Science, National Science and Technology Council." *White House*, June 6, 2022. https://www.whitehouse.gov/wp-content/uploads/2022/06/06-2022-SBS_Recharter.pdf.

Chiappori, P. A., S. Levitt, and T. Groseclose. "Testing Mixed-Strategy Equilibria When Players Are Heterogenous: The Case of Penalty Kicks in Soccer." *American Economic Review* 92, no. 4 (2002): 1138–51.

Childs, Joshua, and Jennifer Lin Russell. "Improving Low-Achieving Schools: Building State Capacity to Support School Improvement Through Race to the Top." *Urban Education* 52, no. 2 (2017): 236–66.

Cialdini, Robert B. *Influence: Science and Practice*. 4th ed. Boston: Allyn and Bacon, 2001.

Cicero. *de Oratore*. Translated by H. Rackham. Cambridge, MA: Harvard University Press, 1942.

"Civilian Labor Force Participation Rate." *U.S. Bureau of Labor Statistics*. https://www.bls.gov/charts/employment-situation/civilian-labor-force-participation-rate.htm. Accessed June 20, 2022.

Clinton, Hillary Rodham. *Living History*. New York: Simon & Schuster, 2003.

Cloud, Dana L. "Hegemony or Concordance? The Rhetoric of Tokenism in 'Oprah' Winfrey's Rags-to-Riches Biography." *Critical Studies in Mass Communication* 13, no. 2 (1996): 115–37.

Cohen, Jon. "'I'm Still Feeling That We're Failing': Exasperated WHO Leader Speaks Out about Vaccine Inequity." *Science*. June 18, 2021. https://www.science.org/content/article/i-m-still-feeling-we-re-failing-exasperated-who-leader-speaks-out-about-vaccine.

Congdon, William J., and Maya Shankar. "The White House Social & Behavioral Sciences Team: Lessons Learned from Year One." *Behavioral Science & Policy* 1, no. 2 (2015): 93–104.

Cooper, Melinda. *Family Values: Between Neoliberalism and the New Social Conservatism*. Brooklyn, NY: Zone Books, 2017.

Cooper, Phillip J. *The War Against Regulation: From Jimmy Carter to George W. Bush*. Lawrence: University of Kansas Press, 2009.

Copjec, Joan. *Read My Desire: Lacan Against the Historicists*. New York: Verso, 2015.

Cox, Ramsey. "Senate GOP Blocks Paycheck Fairness Act for the Second Time." *The Hill*. September 15, 2014. www.thehill.com/blogs/floor-action/senate/217775-senate-gop-blocks-equal-pay-bill-again.

Crenshaw, Carrie. "The Normality of Man and Female Otherness: (Re)Producing Patriarchal Lines of Argument in the Law." *Argumentation & Advocacy* 32, no. 4 (1996): 170–84.

Danius, Sarah, Stefan Jonsson, and Gayatri Chakravorty Spivak. "An Interview with Gayatri Chakravorty Spivak." *boundary 2* 20, no. 2 (1993): 24–50.

Dardot, Pierre, and Christian Laval. *The New Way of the World: On Neo-Liberal Society*. Translated by Gregory Elliot. New York: Verso, 2014.

Davis, Diane. "Addressing Alterity: Rhetoric, Hermeneutics, and the Nonappropriative Relation." *Philosophy & Rhetoric* 38, no. 3 (2005): 191–212.

Dean, Jodi. "Communicative Capitalism and Revolutionary Form." *Millennium: Journal of International Studies* 47, no. 3 (2019): 326–40.

———. *Crowds and Party*. New York: Verso, 2016.

De Kesel, Marc. *Eros and Ethics: Reading Jacques Lacan's Seminar VII*. Translated by Sigi Jöttkandt. Albany: State University of New York Press, 2009.

Deleuze, Gilles. *Difference and Repetition*. Translated by Paul Patton. London: Athlone, 2001.

"Disappearing Incentives; Unemployment Insurance." *Economist* 440, no. 9260. August 28, 2021. https://www2.lib.ku.edu/login?url=https://www.proquest.com/magazines/disappearing-incentives/docview/2565467903/se-2?accountid=14556.

Dmitrieva, Katia, and Olivia Rockeman. "Employers Are Baffled as U.S. Benefits End and Jobs Go Begging." *Bloomberg News*. September 20, 2021. https://www.bloomberg.com/news/articles/2021-09-20/employers-are-baffled-as-u-s-benefits-end-and-jobs-go-begging?sref=PJUU2CLn.

Dorning, Mike. "Obama Adopts Behavioral Economics." *Bloomberg News*, June 24, 2010. http://www.bloomberg.com/bw/magazine/content/10_27/b4185019573214.htm.

Drayton, Michael. *Poly-Olbion. or A chorographicall description of tracts, riuers, mountaines, forests, and other parts of this renowned isle of great britaine with intermixture of the most remarquable stories, antiquities, wonders, rarityes, pleasures, and commodities of the same: Digested in a poem by michael drayton, esq. with a table added, for direction to those occurrences of story and antiquitie, whereunto the course of the volume easily leades not.* London, Printed by Humphrey Lownes for Mathew Lownes: I. Browne: I. Helme, and I. Busbie. http://www2.lib.ku.edu/login?url=https://www.proquest.com/books/poly-olbion-chorographicall-description-tracts/docview/2248504116/se-2?accountid=14556.

"Drinking Water Regulations." *United States Environmental Protection Agency*, www.epa.gov/dwreginfo/drinking-water-regulations. Accessed July 12, 2020.

Dubner, Stephen J. "One Woman's View of the Female Wage Gap." *Freakonomics* (blog). April 17, 2012. http://www.freakonomics.com/2012/04/17/one-womans-view-of-the-female-wage-gap.

Earle, Joe, Cahal Moran, and Zach Ward-Perkins. *The Econocracy: The Perils of Leaving Economics to the Experts*. Manchester: Manchester University Press, 2017.

Epstein, Kayla. "'Over Our Dead Bodies': Lindsey Graham Vows Congress Won't Extend Additional $600 Coronavirus-Related Unemployment Benefits, as US Death Toll Crosses the 60,000 Mark." *Business Insider*, April 30, 2020. http://www.businessinsider.com/lindsey-graham-congress-coronavirus-unemployment-benefit-over-our-dead-bodies-2020-4.

Evans, Will. "How Amazon Hid its Safety Crisis." *Reveal News*, September 29, 2020. http://www.revealnews.org/article/how-amazon-hid-its-safety-crisis.

The Fair Pay Restoration Act: Ensuring Reasonable Rules in Pay Discrimination Cases. S. 1843, 110th Cong. 2008.

"The Fair Pay Restoration Act: Ensuring Reasonable Rules in Pay Discrimination Cases." Committee Hearing on Health, Education, Labor and Pensions, United States Senate, January 24, 2008.

Febrero, Ramón, and Pedro S. Schwartz. "The Essence of Becker: An Introduction." In *The Essence of Becker*. Stanford: Hoover Institution Press, 1995.

Federici, Silvia. *Revolution at Point Zero: Housework, Reproduction, and Feminist Struggle*. Oakland: PM Press, 2012.

Fehr, Ernest. *European Economics at a Crossroads*. Edited by J. Barkley Rosser Jr., Richard P. F. Holt, and David Colander. Northampton: Edward Elgar, 2010.

Fine, Ben, and Dimitris Milonakis. *From Economics Imperialism to Freakonomics: The Shifting Boundaries between Economics and Other Social Sciences*. New York: Routledge, 2009.

Fink, Bruce. *The Lacanian Subject: Between Language and Jouissance*. Princeton, NJ: Princeton University Press, 1995.

———. *A Clinical Introduction to Freud: Techniques for Everyday Practice*. New York: Norton, 2017.

Fisher, Mark. *Capitalist Realism: Is There No Alternative?* Winchester, UK: Zero Books, 2009.

Foucault, Michel. *The Birth of Biopolitics: Lectures at the Collège de France*. Edited by Michel Senellart. Translated by Graham Burchell. New York: Palgrave Macmillan, 2008.

Frank, Robert H. *The Economic Naturalist: Why Economics Explains Almost Everything*. London: Virgin, 2008.

Freud, Sigmund. *Beyond the Pleasure Principle*. Translated by C. J. M. Hubback. London: International Psycho-analytical Press, 1922.

———. "Character and Anal Erotism." *The Standard Edition of the Complete Works of Sigmund Freud vol. IX*. Translated and edited by James Strachey. London: Hogarth, 1955.

———. "Infantile Sexuality." *The Standard Edition of the Complete Works of Sigmund Freud*. vol. VII. Translated and edited by James Strachey. London: Hogarth, 1955.

———. *The Interpretation of Dreams*. Translated by James Strachey. New York: Avon Books, 1998.

———. *Jokes and their Relation to the Unconscious*. Translated by James Strachey. New York: W. W. Norton, 1960.

———. "Negation." In *The Freud Reader*. Edited by Peter Gay. New York: W. W. Norton, 1995.

———. *Three Case Histories*. New York: Macmillan, 1996.

Friedman, Jeffrey. "What's Wrong with Libertarianism." *Critical Review* 11, no. 3 (1993): 407–67.

Furchtgott-Roth, Diana. "Paycheck Fairness Act Is Based on a Misapplied Statistic." *US News & World Report*. May 4, 2012. http://www.usnews.com/debate-club/should-the-senate-pass-the-paycheck-fairness-act/paycheck-fairness-act-is-based-on-a-misapplied-statistic.

Gaonkar, Dilip Parameshwar. "Object and Method in Rhetorical Criticism: From Wichelns to Leff and McGee." *Western Journal of Speech Communication* 54, no. 3 (1990): 290–316.

"Generous Unemployment Benefits Are Not Keeping Americans From Work." *Economist*, July 23, 2020. https://www.economist.com/united-states/2020/07/23/generous-unemployment-benefits-are-not-keeping-americans-from-work.

Genette, Gérard. *Figures of Literary Discourse*. New York: Columbia University Press, 1982.

Gherovici, Patricia. *Please Select Your Gender: From the Invention of Hysteria to the Democratizing of Transgenderism*. New York: Routledge, 2010.

Gillespie, Becky Beaupre. "Partnerships and Learning at the Mothership of Law and Economics." *Law School Communications*, July 27, 2017. http://www.law.uchicago.edu/news/partnerships-and-learning-mothership-law-and-economics.

Godelier, Maurice. *Rationality and Irrationality in Economics*. New York: Verso, 2013.

Goldin, Claudia. "A Grand Gender Convergence: Its Last Chapter." *American Economic Review* 104, no. 4 (2004): 1091–19.

Goodnight, Thomas G., and Sandy Green. "Rhetoric, Risk and Markets: The Dot-Com Bubble." *Quarterly Journal of Speech* 96, no. 2 (2010): 115–40.

Gore, Al. *From Red Tape to Results: Creating a Government that Works Better and Costs Less*. Report of the National Performance Review. Washington, DC: Government Printing Office, 1993.

Gorgias. "Encomium of Helen." In *Reading Rhetorical Theory*, edited by Barry Brummett. Fort Worth, TX: Harcourt Brace, 2000.

Greene, Ronald Walter. "Another Materialist Rhetoric." *Critical Studies in Mass Communication* 15, no. 1 (1998): 21–41.

Grossberg, Lawrence. *Cultural Studies in the Future Tense*. Durham, NC: Duke University Press, 2010.

———. "Interview with Lawrence Grossberg, November 14, 2012." Interview conducted by James Hay. Edited by James Hay and Lawrence Grossberg. *Communication and Critical/Cultural Studies* 10, no. 1 (2013): 59–97.

Gunn, Joshua. "For the Love of Rhetoric, with Continual Reference to Kenny and Dolly." *Quarterly Journal of Speech* 94, no. 2 (2008): 131–55.

———. "Maranatha." *Quarterly Journal of Speech* 98, no. 4 (2012): 359–85.

———. *Modern Occult Rhetoric: Mass Media and the Drama of Secrecy in the Twentieth Century*. Tuscaloosa: University of Alabama Press, 2005.

———. "On Speech and Public Release." *Rhetoric & Public Affairs* 13, no. 2 (2010): 1–41.

———. "Refitting Fantasy: Psychoanalysis, Subjectivity, and Talking to the Dead." *Quarterly Journal of Speech* 90, no. 1 (2004) 1–23.

———. "ShitText: Toward a New Coprophilic Style." *Text and Performance Quarterly* 26, no. 1 (2006): 79–97.

Hahn, Heather. "Work Requirements in Safety Net Programs: Lessons for Medicaid from TANF and SNAP." *Urban Institute*. April 2018. http://www.urban.org/sites/default/files/publication/98086/work_requirements_in_safety_net_programs.pdf.

Hall, Brian J. "The Pay to Performance Incentives of Executive Stock Options." *NBER Working Paper Series*. National Bureau of Economic Research, 1998, 1–49.

Hallward, Peter. *Out of this World: Deleuze and the Philosophy of Creation*. New York: Verso, 2006.

Hamblin, James. "A Mandate, in Other Words." *Atlantic*, March 7, 2017, http://www.theatlantic.com/health/archive/2017/03/no-mandate-youre-the-mandate/518784/.

Hanan, Joshua S., Indradeep Ghosh, and Kaleb W. Brooks. "Banking on the Present: The Ontological Rhetoric of Neoclassical Economics and its Relationship to the 2008 Financial Crisis." *Quarterly Journal of Speech* 100, no. 2 (2014): 139–62.

Hanchey, Jenna N. "Toward a Relational Politics of Representation." *Review of Communication* 18, no. 4 (2018): 265–83.

Harpham, Edward J., and Richard K. Scotch. "Economic Discourse, Policy Analysis, and the Problem of the Political." *Handbook of Political Theory and Policy Science*. Edited by Edward Bryan Portis and Michael B. Levy. New York: Greenwood, 1988.

Hartsoe, Steve. "Pandemic Unemployment Benefits End Sept. 6. It's Not Simple as to What This Will Do to the Labor Market." *Duke Today* (blog). September 1, 2021. https://today.duke.edu/2021/09/pandemic-unemployment-benefits-end-sept-6-its-not-simple-what-will-do-labor-market.

Harvey, David. *A Brief History of Neoliberalism*. Oxford: Oxford University Press, 2007.

Hauser, Gerard A. *Introduction to Rhetorical Theory*. 2nd ed. Long Grove: Waveland, 2002.

Hayek, Friedrich. *The Road to Serfdom*. Chicago: University of Chicago Press, 1944.

———. *Studies in Philosophy, Politics and Economics*. Chicago: University of Chicago Press, 1967.

Hazlitt, Henry. *Economics in One Lesson*. New York: Pocket Books, 1952.

"HealthQuest Rewards Program." Human Resource Management, University of Kansas. http://www.humanresources.ku.edu/healthquest-rewards-program. Accessed July 20, 2020.

Higden, Ranulf. *Polychronicon Ranulphi Higden Monachi Cestrensis*. London: Longman & Co., 1865.

Heilbroner, Robert. *The Worldly Philosophers: The Lives, Times, and Ideas of the Great Economic Thinkers*. 7th ed. New York: Touchstone, 1999.

Heinzerling, Lisa. "Cost-Benefit Jumps the Shark." *Georgetown Law Faculty Blog*. June 13, 2012. http://www.gulcfac.typepad.com/georgetown_university_law/2012/06/cost-benefit-jumps-the-shark.html.

Hill, Adam. "Why Nudges Coerce: Experimental Evidence on the Architecture of Regulation." *Science and Engineering Ethics* 24, no. 4 (2018): 1279–95.

Hirshleifer, Jack. "The Expanding Domain of Economics." *American Economic Review* 75, no. 6 (1985): 53–68.

Holmberg Susan R., and Lydia Austin. "Fixing a Hole: How the Tax Code for Executive Pay Distorts Economic Incentives and Burdens Taxpayers." *The Roosevelt Institute*, July 22, 2013, 1–11.

Hook, Derek. "Toward an Erotics of Truth: Commentary on Session I." In *Reading Lacan's Seminar VIII: Transference*, 1–14. Edited by Gautam Basu Thakur and Jonathan Dickstein. Cham, Switzerland: Palgrave Macmillan, 2020.

Hoover, Kevin D. "Causality in Economics and Econometrics." In *The New Palgrave Dictionary of Economics,* 2nd ed., edited by Steven N. Durlauf and Lawrence E. Blume, 719–28. London: Palgrave Macmillan, 2008.

Howell, William G., and Asya Magazinnik. "Presidential Prescriptions for State Policy: Obama's Race to the Top Initiative." *Journal of Policy Analysis and Management* 36, no. 3 (2017): 502–31.

Humphrey, Paul. "Metaphysics of Mind: Hylomorphism and Eternality in Aristotle and Hegel." PhD diss., State University of New York at Stony Brook, 2007.

Hunter, Andy. "Ivory Coast Given Incentive to Transform Elephants' Forgettable Record." *Guardian*, June 23, 2014. http://www.theguardian.com/football/2014/jun/23/elephants-ivory-coast-world-cup-greece.

Iacurci, Greg. "26 States Ended Federal Unemployment Benefits Early. Data Suggests It's Not Getting People Back to Work." *CNBC*. August 4, 2021. https://www.cnbc.com/2021/08/04/early-end-to-federal-unemployment-pay-in-26-states-not-getting-people-to-work.html.

"Incentive." *Oxford English Dictionary.* https://www-oed-com.www2.lib.ku.edu/view/Entry/93397?redirectedFrom=incentive#eid. Accessed September 18, 2021.

Isakson, Johnny. "Congressional Record—Senate." 110th Congress, April 23, 2008, S3279.

Iyer, Ganesh, Vivek Nandur, and David Soberman. "Vaccine Hesitancy and Monetary Incentives." *Humanities and Social Sciences Communications* 9, no. 81 (2022): 1–10.

Jameson, Fredric. *An American Utopia: Dual Power and the Universal Army.* Edited by Slavoj Žižek. New York: Verso, 2016.

———. *The Ancients and the Postmoderns: On the Historicity of Forms.* New York: Verso, 2017.

"Jobs and Unemployment Insurance." University of Chicago Initiative on Global Markets. July 18, 2020. https://www.igmchicago.org/surveys/jobs-and-unemployment-insurance/.

Johnson, Kevin A., and Jennifer J. Asenas. "The Lacanian Real as a Supplement to Rhetorical Critique." *Rhetoric Society Quarterly* 32, no. 2 (2013): 155–76.

Kalaboukis, Chris. "How to Incentivize Disruptive Innovation." *Hellofuture* (blog). http://www.hellofuture.co/incentivize-disruptive-innovation. Accessed October 12, 2020.

Kelman, Steve. "'Reinventing Government,' 25 Years Later." *Federal Computer Week*. December 6, 2017. http://www.fcw.com/articles/2017/12/06/kelman-25-years-of-acquisition-reform.aspx.

———. "Here We Go Again: 'Diversity Training' and Government Contractors." *Federal Computer Week*. October 2, 2020. http://www.fcw.com/blogs/lectern/2020/10/comment-kelman-eo-diversity-training.aspx.

Keri, Jonah. "The Duncan Way: How Cardinals Pitchers Continue to Dominate by Exploiting Hitter Tendencies." *Grantland*, May 21, 2014. http://www.grantland.com/the-triangle/st-louis-cardinals-pitchers-dave-duncan-adam-wainwright-michael-wacha/.

Khan, Victoria Ann. *Rhetoric, Prudence, and Skepticism in the Renaissance*. Ithaca, NY: Cornell University Press, 1985.

Kim, Hyun-Ah. *The Renaissance Ethics of Music: Singing, Contemplation and Musica Humana*. New York: Routledge, 2015.

Klamer, Arjo. *Speaking of Economics: How to Get into the Conversation*. New York: Routledge, 2007.

Klein, Ezra. "I want to be clear: I don't think getting rid of the filibuster will usher in some new era of bipartisanship." January 26, 2021. http:www.twitter.com/ezraklein/status/1354134416377827328.

Klein, Naomi. *The Shock Doctrine: The Rise of Disaster Capitalism*. New York: Picador, 2007.

Koeze, Ella. "The $600 Unemployment Booster Shot, State by State." *New York Times*, April 23, 2020. https://www.nytimes.com/interactive/2020/04/23/business/economy/unemployment-benefits-stimulus-coronavirus.html.

Kolderie, Ted. "Beyond Choice to New Public Schools." *Progressive Policy Institute*. Accessed August 2, 2017. http://www.files.eric.ed.gov/fulltext/ED327914.pdf.

Kotsko, Adam. *Neoliberalism's Demons: On the Political Theology of Late Capital*. Stanford: Stanford University Press, 2018.

Lacan, Jacques. "The Function and Field of Speech and Language in Psychoanalysis." In *Écrits*, 197–268. Translated by Bruce Fink. New York: W. W. Norton, 2006.

———. "The Instance of the Letter in the Unconscious, or Reason since Freud." In *Écrits*, 412–41. Translated by Bruce Fink. New York, W. W. Norton, 2006.

———. "The Neurotic's Individual Myth." *Psychoanalytic Quarterly* 48, no. 3 (1979): 405–25.

———. "On a Question Prior to Any Possible Treatment of Psychosis." In *Écrits*, 445–88. Translated by Bruce Fink. New York, W. W. Norton, 2006.

———. "Presentation on Psychical Causality." In *Écrits*, 123–58. Translated by Bruce Fink. New York: W. W. Norton, 2006.

———. "Science and Truth." In *Écrits*, 726–45. Translated by Bruce Fink. New York: W. W. Norton, 2006.

———. *The Seminar of Jacques Lacan, Book III: The Psychoses, 1955–1956*. Edited by Jacques-Alain Miller. Translated by Russell Grigg. London: Routledge, 2013.

———. *The Seminar of Jacques Lacan, Book V: Formations of the Unconscious*. Edited by Jacques-Alain Miller. Translated by Russell Grigg. Malden, MA: Polity, 2017.

———. *The Seminar of Jacques Lacan, Book VI: Desire and its Interpretation*. Edited by Jacques-Alain Miller. Translated by Bruce Fink. Malden, MA: Polity, 2019.

———. *The Seminar of Jacques Lacan, Book VII: The Ethics of Psychoanalysis, 1959–1960*. Edited by Jacques-Alain Miller. Translated by Dennis Porter. New York: W. W. Norton, 1988.

———. *The Seminar of Jacques Lacan, Book VIII: Transference*. Edited by Jacques-Alain Miller. Translated by Bruce Fink. Cambridge: Polity, 2015.

———. *The Seminar of Jacques Lacan, Book X: Anxiety*. Edited by Jacques-Alain Miller. Translated by A. R. Price, Malden, MA: Polity, 2014.

———. *The Seminar of Jacques Lacan, Book XI: The Four Fundamental Concepts of Psychoanalysis*. Edited by Jacques-Alain Miller. Translated by Alan Sheridan. New York: W.W. Norton, 1998.

———. *The Seminar of Jacques Lacan, Book XX: On Feminine Sexuality: The Limits of Love and Knowledge (Encore, 1972–1973)*. Edited by Jacques-Alain Miller. Translated by Bruce Fink. New York: W. W. Norton, 1999.

———. "The Subversion of the Subject and the Dialectic of Desire in the Freudian Unconscious." In *Écrits*, 671–702. Translated by Bruce Fink. New York: W. W. Norton, 2006.

———. *Talking to Brick Walls: A Series of Presentations in the Chapel at Sainte-Anne Hospital*. Translated by A. R. Price. Medford, MA: Polity, 2017.

Laclau, Ernesto. *The Rhetorical Foundations of Society*. New York: Verso, 2014.

Landes, William M., Lawrence Lessig, and Michael Solimine. "Judicial Influence: A Citation Analysis of Federal Courts of Appeals Judges." *Chicago Working Paper in Law & Economics* (2nd series), 1998.

Laplanche, Jean, and J. B. Pontalis. *The Language of Psychoanalysis*. Translated by Donald Nicholson-Smith. New York: Routledge, 1973.

Laurent, Éric. "Alienation and Separation (II)." *Reading Seminar XI: Lacan's Four Fundamental Concepts of Psychoanalysis*, 29–38. Edited by Richard Feldstein, Bruce Fink, and Marie Jaanus. Albany: State University of New York Press, 1995.

Levin, Sam. "Accused of Underpaying Women, Google Says It's Too Expensive to Get Wage Data." *Guardian*, May 26, 2017. http://www.theguardian.com/technology/2017/may/26/google-gender-discrimination-case-salary-records.

Levine, Murray, and Adeline Levine. "Education Deformed: No Child Left Behind and the Race to the Top—'This Almost Reads Like Our Business Plans.'" *American Journal of Orthopsychiatry* 82, no. 1 (2012): 104–13.

Levitt, Steven D., and Stephen J. Dubner. *Freakonomics: A Rogue Economist Explores the Hidden Side of Everything*. New York: William Morrow, 2005.

———. *SuperFreakonomics: Global Cooling, Patriotic Prostitutes, and Why Suicide Bombers Should Buy Life Insurance*. New York: William Morrow, 2009.

———. *Think Like a Freak: The Authors of Freakonomics Offer to Retrain your Brain*. New York: William Morrow, 2014.

Lewis, Jack. "The Birth of EPA." *EPA Journal* 12, no. 9 (1985): 6–11.

Lilly Ledbetter Fair Pay Act of 2009, 111th Cong. s. 181, 2009.

"Lilly Ledbetter Fair Pay Act." National Women's Law Center. January 29, 2013. http://www.nwlc.org/resource/lilly-ledbetter-fair-pay-act. Accessed September 19, 2014.

"Linking Staff Incentives with Frequent Reporting and Target Hitting." *Be the Business* (blog). http://www.bethebusiness.com/productivity-insights/linking-staff-incentives-with-frequent-reporting-and-target-hitting. Accessed September 9, 2020.

List, John, and Uri Gneezy. "A Unified Theory of Why Women Earn Less." *Freakonomics* (blog). October 18, 2013. http://www.freakonomics.com/2013/10/18/a-unifying-theory-of-why-women-earn-less/.

Longaker, Mark Garrett. "Adam Smith on Rhetoric and Phronesis, Law and Economics." *Philosophy & Rhetoric* 47, no. 1 (2014): 25–47.

Lundberg, Christian O. "Enjoying God's Death: *The Passion of the Christ* and the Practices of an Evangelical Public." *Quarterly Journal of Speech,* 95, no. 4 (2009): 387–411.

———. *Lacan in Public: Psychoanalysis and the Science of Rhetoric.* Tuscaloosa: University of Alabama Press, 2012.

———. "Revisiting the Future of Meaning." *Quarterly Journal of Speech* 101, no. 1 (2015): 173–85.

MacLean, Nancy. *Democracy in Chains: The Deep History of the Radical Right's Stealth Plan for America.* New York: Viking, 2017.

Maier, Maximilian, Frantisek Bartos, T. D. Stanley, and Eric-Jan Wagenmakers. "No Evidence for Nudging after Adjusting for Publication Bias." *PNAS* 119, no. 31 (2022): 1–2.

Mak, Aaron. "Here Are the Outrageous Incentives That Losing Cities Offered Amazon for HQ2." *Slate,* November 14, 2018. http://www. slate.com/technology/2018/11/amazon-hq2-incredible-incentives-losing-cities-offered.html.

Mankiw, N. Gregory. *Principles of Macroeconomics.* 5th ed. Mason: South-Western Cengage Learning, 2008.

Manley, Emily. "Missouri's Vaccine Incentive Program Ends This Week." *FOX 2 Now,* October 5, 2021. https://fox2now.com/news/missouri/missouris-vaccine-incentive-program-ends-this-week/.

Martin, Nina. "The Impact and Echoes of the Wal-Mart Discrimination Case" *ProPublica.* September 27, 2013. http://www.propublica.org/article/the-impact-and-echoes-of-the-wal-mart-discrimination-case.

Marshall, Alfred. *Principles of Economics.* Vol. 1. New York: Macmillan, 1895.

Marx, Karl. *Economic and Philosophic Manuscripts of 1844 and the Communist Manifesto.* Translated by Martin Milligan. Amherst: Prometheus, 1988.

———. *Capital.* Vol. 1. Translated by Ben Fowkes. New York: Penguin, 1990.

"Maternal CARE Act of 2019." Office of Sen. Kamala Harris. http://www.harris.senate.gov/imo/media/doc/Maternal%20CARE%20Act%20of%202019%20background.pdf. Accessed July 21, 2020.

Matheson, Calum. *Desiring the Bomb: Communication, Psychoanalysis, and the Atomic Age*. Tuscaloosa: University of Alabama Press, 2019.

———. "Filthy Lucre: Gold, Language and Exchange Anxiety." *Review of Communication* 18, no. 4 (2018): 249–64.

———. "'What Does Obama Want of Me?' Anxiety and Jade Helm 15." *Quarterly Journal of Speech* 102, no. 1 (2016): 133–49.

McCloskey, Deirdre. *If You're So Smart: The Narrative of Economic Expertise*. Chicago, University of Chicago Press, 1992.

———. *Knowledge and Persuasion in Economics*. Cambridge: Cambridge University Press, 1994.

———. *The Rhetoric of Economics*. Madison: University of Wisconsin Press, 1998.

McDermott, John F. M. "Perfect Competition, Methodologically Contemplated." *Journal of Post-Keynesian Economics* 37, no. 4 (2015): 687–703.

McDonald, Robert. "*Freakonomics* as a Discourse of Perversion." *International Journal of Žižek Studies* 11, no. 2 (2017): 1–20.

McGowan, Todd. *Capitalism and Desire: The Psychic Cost of Free Markets*. New York: Columbia University Press, 2016.

———. *Enjoying What We Don't Have: The Political Project of Psychoanalysis*. Lincoln: University of Nebraska Press, 2013.

McKenna, Stephen J. *Adam Smith: The Rhetoric of Propriety*. Albany: State University of New York Press, 2006.

McKenzie, Richard B., and Dwight R. Lee. *Managing Through Incentives: How to Develop a More Collaborative, Productive, and Profitable Organization*. Oxford: Oxford University Press, 1998.

Mehmood, Sajit. "The $159 AirPod price tag is really for your own sake." September 7, 2016. http://www.twitter.com/smehmood/status/773596786434961408.

"Meijer, Colleagues Introduce SUPPORT for New Workers Act to Incentivize Return to Work." Washington, DC: *Federal Information & News Dispatch, LLC*. June 18, 2021. https://www2.lib.ku.edu/login?url=https://www.proquest.com/other-sources/meijer-colleagues-introduce-support-new-workers/docview/2543441009/se-2?accountid=14556.

Mikluski, Senator Barbara. "Paycheck Fairness." *Congressional Record* 156, no. 150, United States Senate, S7295. November 17, 2010. http://www.congress.gov/congressional-record/2010/11/17/senate-section/article/s7924-1.

Mills, Dan. "'Set and Characters' and 'The Metaphor of Love: Phaedrus'—Commentary on Sessions II and III." In *Reading Lacan's Seminar VIII: Transference*, edited by Gautam Basu Thakur and Jonathan Dickstein, 15–42. Cham, Switzerland: Palgrave Macmillan, 2020.

Milton, John, Elijah Fenton, and Samuel Johnson. *Paradise Lost*. Cambridge, MA: Harvard University Press, 1821.

Mirowski, Philip. *Machine Dreams: Economics Becomes a Cyborg Science*. Cambridge: Cambridge University Press, 2002.

————. *More Heat than Light: Economics as Social Physics, Physics as Nature's Economics (Historical Perspectives on Modern Economics)*. Cambridge: Cambridge University Press, 1991.

————. *Never Let a Serious Crisis Go to Waste: How Neoliberalism Survived the Financial Meltdown*. New York: Verso, 2014.

Mirowski, Philip, and Dieter Plehwe, eds. *The Road from Mont Pèlerin: The Making of the Neoliberal Thought Collective*. Cambridge, MA: Harvard University Press, 2009.

Mitchell, Juliet. *Mad Men and Medusas: Reclaiming Hysteria*. New York: Basic Books, 2000.

Moss-Racusin, Corinne A., John F. Dovidio, Victoria L. Brescoll, Mark J. Graham, and Jo Handelsman. "Science Faculty's Subtle Gender Biases Favor Male Students." *Psychological and Cognitive Sciences* 109, no. 41 (2012): 16474–479.

Nance, Penny. "Act Undercuts Protection, Choices Women Have in Job Market." *US News & World Report*, May 4, 2012. http://www.usnews.com/debate-club/should-the-senate-pass-the-paycheck-fairness-act/act-undercuts-protection-choices-women-have-in-job-market.

"National COVID-19 Preparedness Plan." *The White House*. https://www.whitehouse.gov/covidplan/. Accessed July 4, 2022.

Nilsen, Ella, and Li Zhou. "What We Know about Congress's Potential $1 Trillion Coronavirus Stimulus Package." *Vox*. March 17, 2020. https://www.vox.com/2020/3/17/21183846/congress-coronavirus-stimulus-package.

Obama, Barack. "Executive Order: Using Behavioral Science Insights to Better Serve the American People." *The White House*, September 15, 2015. http://www.whitehouse.gov/the-press-office/2015/09/15/executive-order-using-behavioral-science-insights-better-serve-american.

————. "Obama Signs Lilly Ledbetter Act." *Washington Post*, January 29, 2009. http://www.voices.washingtonpost.com/44/2009/01/29/obama_signs_lilly_ledbetter_ac.html.

————. "The President on 'Race to the Top.'" July 24, 2009. http://www.obamawhitehouse.archives.gov/blog/2009/07/24/president-race-top.

Office of Science and Technology Policy. "National Science and Technology Council." http://www.whitehouse.gov/ostp/nstc/#Documents_Reports. Accessed August 4, 2022.

Ogbonnaya, Chidiebere, Kevin Daniels, and Karina Nielsen. "Research: How Incentive Pay Affects Employee Engagement, Satisfaction, and Trust." *Harvard Business Review*. March 15, 2017. http://www.hbr.org/2017/03/research-how-incentive-pay-affects-employee-engagement-satisfaction-and-trust.

Ogden, C. K., and I. A. Richards. *The Meaning of Meaning*. San Diego: Harcourt, 1927.

O'Gorman, Ned. *The Iconoclastic Imagination: Image, Catastrophe and Economy in America from the Kennedy Assassination to September 11*. Chicago: University of Chicago Press, 2015.

"On Fox News, Portman Discusses Next COVID-19 Response Package and Highlights Need to Incentivize Returning Safely to Available Jobs." *States News Service*, July 29, 2020. link.gale.com/apps/doc/A630944030/AONE?u=ksstate_ukans& sid=bookmark-AONE&xid=5ca79ae6.

Parsons, Talcott. "The Position of Sociological Theory." In *Classical Sociological Theory*, edited by Craig Calhoun, Joseph Gertels, James Moody, Steven Pfaff, and Indermohan Virk. 405-411. 2nd ed. Malden, MA: Blackwell, 2007.

The Patient Protection and Affordable Care Act, Public Law 111-148, 111th Congress. March 23, 2010. http://www.congress.gov/111/plaws/publ148/PLAW-111 publ148.pdf.

"Paul A. Samuelson—Facts." *Nobelprize.org*. http://www.nobelprize.org/nobel_ prizes/economic-sciences/laureates/1970/samuelson-facts.html. Accessed September 22, 2015.

Peacham, Henry. *The Garden of Eloquence*. 1577. http://www.gateway.proquest. com.www2.lib.ku.edu/openurl?ctx_ver=Z39.88-2003&xri:pqil:res_ver=0.2& res_id=xri:lion&rft_id=xri:lion:ft:pr:Z200728358. Accessed February 1, 2016.

Pendergrass, Taylor. "Progress Is Occurring on Prosecutorial Reform, despite Tuesday's Setbacks in California." *American Civil Liberties Union*. June 7, 2018. http://www.aclu.org/blog/smart-justice/prosecutorial-reform/progress- occurring-prosecutorial-reform-despite-tuesdays.

Pereira, Ivan. "Why COVID-19 Vaccine Incentives Didn't Really Work: Experts." *ABC News*, July 15, 2021. https://abcnews.go.com/Health/vaccine-incentives- best-answer-hesitancy-experts/story?id=78695407.

Peters, John Durham. *Speaking into the Air: A History of the Idea of Communi- cation*. Chicago: University of Chicago Press, 1999.

Plato. *Gorgias*. http://www.classics.mit.edu/Plato/gorgias.html.

———. *Phaedrus*. http://www.classics.mit.edu/Plato/phaedrus.html.

———. *Symposium of Plato*. Translated by Tom Griffith, engraved by Peter Forster. Berkeley: University of California Press, 1989.

Plutarch. *Moralia*. Translated by W. M. Helmbold. Vol. 4. Cambridge, MA: Har- vard University Press, 1939.

———. *The Philosophie, Commonlie Called, the Morals Written by the Learned Philosopher Plutarch of Charonea*. Translated by Philemon Holland. London: Arnold Hatfield, 1603.

———. *Plutarch's Morals*. Translated by Several Hands, corrected and revised by William W. Goodwin. Vol. 2. Little, Brown, 1878.

Polanyi, Karl. *The Great Transformation*. Boston: Beacon, 1944.

Ponciano, Jonathan. "States Ending $300 Unemployment Benefits Haven't Boosted Labor Market Yet, Morgan Stanley Finds." *Forbes*, July 8, 2021. https:// www.forbes.com/sites/jonathanponciano/2021/07/08/states-that-ended-300- unemployment-benefits-havent-boosted-labor-market-yet-morgan-stanley- finds/?sh=e248fa522373.

Poovey, Mary. *A History of the Modern Fact: Problems of Knowledge in the Sciences of Wealth and Society.* Chicago, University of Chicago Press, 1998.

Powell, Benjamin. "Private Property Rights, Economic Freedom, and Well Being." Mercatus Center, George Mason University, Working Paper 19. www.mercatus.org/system/files/Private-Property-Rights-Economic-Freedom-and-Well-Being.pdf. Accessed September 10, 2020.

"The Prize in Economics 1992—Press Release." *Nobelprize.org.* Nobel Media. October 13, 1992. http://www.nobelprize.org/nobel_prizes/economic-sciences/laureates/1992/press.html.

Proctor, Kate. "UK Government's Coronavirus Advice—and Why It Gave It." *Guardian*, March 12, 2020. http://www.theguardian.com/world/2020/mar/12/uk-governments-coronavirus-advice-and-why-it-gave-it.

Puttenham, George. *The Art of English Poesy, A Critical Edition*, edited by Frank Whigham and Wayne A. Rebhorn. Ithaca, NY: Cornell University Press, 2007.

Quinet, Antonio. "The Gaze as an Object." In *Reading* Seminar XI: *Lacan's Four Fundamental Concepts of Psychoanalysis*, edited by Richard Feldstein, Bruce Fink, and Maire Jaanus. 139–48. Albany: State University of New York Press, 1995.

————. *Lacan's Clinical Technique: Lack(a)nian Analysis.* London: Karnac, 2018.

Quintilian. *Quintilian's Institutes of Oratory: or, Education of an Orator.* Vol. 2. Translated and revised by John Shelby Watson. London: George Bell & Sons, Ltd., 1891.

Rabin, Matthew. "A Perspective on Psychology and Economics." *Institute of Business and Economic Research Working Paper.* Department of Economics, University of California, Berkeley, 2002.

Ranney, Francis J. *Aristotle's Ethics and Legal Rhetoric: An Analysis of Language Beliefs and the Law.* Burlington, VT: Ashgate, 2005.

Rauber, Chris. "Kaiser Permanente Posts $2.1B in 2009 Profits." *San Francisco Business Times*, February 12, 2010. http://www.bizjournals.com/sanfrancisco/stories/2010/02/08/daily64.html.

Rebonato, Riccardo. "A Critical Assessment of Libertarian Paternalism." *Journal of Consumer Policy* 37 (2014): 357–96.

————. *Taking Liberties: A Critical Examination of Libertarian Paternalism.* London: Palgrave Macmillan, 2012.

Remer, Gary A. *Ethics and the Orator: The Ciceronian Tradition of Political Morality.* Chicago: University of Chicago Press, 2017.

"Rep. Roy Introduces Legislation to Cut Unnecessary Unemployment Benefits." *Targeted News Service, LLC.* June 18, 2021. https://advance-lexis-com.www2.lib.ku.edu/api/document?collection=news&id=urn:contentItem:62Y5-G411-DYG2-R26G-00000-00&context=1516831.

"Rep. Steube Urges President Trump to Cap Unemployment Benefits and Incentivize Americans to Return to Workforce." *Targeted News Service.* July 11, 2020.

https://www2.lib.ku.edu/login?url=https://www.proquest.com/wire-feeds/
rep-steube-urges-president-trump-cap-unemployment/docview/2422371422/
se-2?accountid=14556.

Rickert, Thomas. *Acts of Enjoyment: Rhetoric, Žižek, and the Return of the Subject.*
Pittsburgh: University of Pittsburgh Press, 2007.

Rusterholz, Peter. "On the Crisis of Representation." *Semiotica* 143 (2003): 53–60.

Ryan, Shane. "Libertarian Paternalism is Hard Paternalism." *Analysis* 78, no. 1
(2018): 65–73.

"S. 100–Closing the Gap: Equal Pay for Women Workers." 100th Cong., 1st sess.
April 12, 2007.

"S. 181—Lilly Ledbetter Fair Pay Act." 111th Cong., 2nd sess. January 8, 2009.
http://www.congress.gov/bill/111th-congress/senate-bill/181. Accessed June
10, 2014.

"S.2199—Paycheck Fairness Act." http://www.congress.gov/bill/113th-congress/
senate-bill/2199.

"S.1600—Maternal Care Access and Reducing Emergencies Act." 116th Congress,
May 22, 2019. http://www.congress.gov/bill/116th-congress/senate-bill/1600/
text. Accessed July 22, 2020.

Samuelson, Paul. *Economics: An Introductory Analysis,* 4th ed., New York: McGraw-
Hill, 1955.

———. *Foundations of Economic Analysis Enlarged Edition.* Cambridge, MA:
Harvard University Press, 1983.

———. "The Pure Theory of Public Expenditure." *Review of Economics and
Statistics* 36, no. 4 (1954): 387–89.

Samuelson, Paul, and William D. Nordhaus. *Economics,* 19th ed. New York: Tata
McGraw-Hill, 2010.

Schaeffer, Sabrina L. "Paycheck Fairness Act Will Hurt Women." *US News & World
Report,* May 4, 2012. http://www.usnews.com/debate-club/should-the-senate-
pass-the-paycheck-fairness-act/paycheck-fairness-act-will-hurt-women.

Schlefer, Jonathan. *The Assumptions Economists Make.* Cambridge: Belknap, 2012.

Schroeder, Jeanne Lorraine. *The Triumph of Venus: The Erotics of the Market.*
Berkeley: University of California Press, 2004.

Schumpeter, Joseph. "On the Concept of Social Value." *Quarterly Journal of Economics* 2 (1909): 213–32.

Self, Peter. *Econocrats and the Policy Process: The Politics and Philosophy of
Cost-Benefit Analysis.* London: Macmillan, 1975.

Sen, Amartya K. "Rational Fools: A Critique of the Behavioral Foundations of
Economic Theory." *Philosophy and Public Affairs* 6, no. 4 (1977): 317–44.

The Simpsons. "'Tis the Fifteenth Season." December 14, 2003. http://www.simpsons.
fandom.com/wiki/%27Tis_the_Fifteenth_Season.

Smith, Noah. "101ism." *Noahpinion* (blog), January 21, 2016. http://www.noah-
pinionblog.blogspot.com/2016/01/101ism.html.

Soler, Colette. "Hysteria in Scientific Discourse." In *Reading Seminar XX: Lacan's Major Work on Love, Knowledge and Feminine Sexuality*, edited by Suzanne Barnard and Bruce Fink, 47–56. Albany: State University of New York Press, 2002.

———. "The Subject and the Other (II)." In *Reading* Seminar XI: *Lacan's Four Fundamental Concepts of Psychoanalysis*, edited by Richard Feldstein, Bruce Fink, and Maire Jaanus, 45–54. Albany: State University of New York Press, 1995.

"Sorry Ma'am—We Just Didn't See it Coming." *Associated Press*, July 26, 2009. http://www.nbcnews.com/id/32156155/ns/business-world_business/t/sorry-maam-we-just-didnt-see-it-coming/#.X1Z5vnlKg2w.

Spence, Patricia. "Sympathy and Propriety in Adam Smith's Rhetoric." *Quarterly Journal of Speech* 60, no. 1 (1974): 92–99.

Stein, Jeff, and Chelsea James. "Buttigieg Health Plan Hinges on 'Supercharged' Version of Unpopular Obamacare Mandate." *Washington Post*, December 24, 2019. https://www.washingtonpost.com/business/economy/buttigieg-health-plan-hinges-on-supercharged-version-of-unpopular-obamacare-mandate/2019/12/24/415ae876-21bb-11ea-9146-6c3a3ab1be6c_story.html.

Stigler, George. "Perfect Competition, Historically Contemplated." *Journal of Political Economy* 65, no. 1 (1957): 1–17.

"Stories from the Field: Examples of Successful Worker COVID-19 Vaccination Programs." *Centers for Disease Control and Prevention*. March 28, 2022. https://www.cdc.gov/coronavirus/2019-ncov/community/workplaces-businesses/field-stories.html.

Streuver, Nancy S. *Theory as Practice: Ethical Inquiry in the Renaissance*. Chicago: University of Chicago Press, 1992.

Stylinski, Brynn. "The Gender Advancement in Pay Act: The GAP Act Leaves Some Holes." *University of Cincinnati Law Review*. December 1, 2015. http://www.uclawreview.org/2015/12/01/the-gender-advancement-in-pay-act-the-gap-act-leaves-some-holes/.

Sunstein, Cass R. *After the Rights Revolution: Reconceiving the Regulatory State*. Cambridge, MA: Harvard University Press, 1990.

———. *The Ethics of Influence: Government in the Age of Behavioral Science*. Cambridge: Cambridge University Press, 2016.

———."Smarter Regulation." The White House. February 7, 2011. https://obamawhitehouse.archives.gov/blog/2011/02/07/smarter-regulation.

———. *Why Nudge? The Politics of Libertarian Paternalism*. New Haven, CT: Yale University Press, 2014.

Swann, John P. "FDA's Origin." http://www.fda.gov/AboutFDA/WhatWeDo/History/Origin/ucm054819.htm. Accessed June 22, 2016.

Thaler, Richard H., and Cass R. Sunstein. *Nudge: Improving Decisions about Health, Wealth and Happiness*. New York, Penguin, 2009.

————. "Behavioral Economics Tips for Home Sellers: How to Price a House." *Nudge* (blog). May 14, 2008. https://nudges.wordpress.com/tips-for-home-sellers-how-to-price-a-house/.

Thirumurthy, Harsha, Katherine L. Milkman, Kevin G. Volpp, Alison M. Buttenheim, and Devin G. Pope. "Association between Statewide Financial Incentive Programs and COVID-19 Vaccination Rates." *PLoS ONE* 17, no. 3 (2022): 1–7.

Thompson, Derek. "The Economics of Penalty Kicks in Soccer." *The Atlantic.* June 10, 2010. http://www.theatlantic.com/business/archive/2010/06/the-economics-of-penalty-kicks-in-soccer/58001.

Thrush, Glenn, and Elaina Plott. "How the Trump Campaign Is Drawing Obama Out of Retirement." *New York Times,* June 28, 2020. http://www.nytimes.com/2020/06/28/us/politics/obama-biden-trump.html.

Trump, Donald J. "Full Text: Donald Trump 2016 RNC Draft Speech Transcript." *Politico.* July 21, 2016. http://www.politico.com/story/2016/07/full-transcript-donald-trump-nomination-acceptance-speech-at-rnc-225974.

"Unemployment Benefit Calculator." *Missouri Department of Labor and Industrial Relations.* https://labor.mo.gov/des/unemployed-workers/benefits-calculator. Accessed June 22, 2022.

"Unemployment Benefits Forever? Treasury Suggests How States Can Continue the Incentives Not to Work." *Wall Street Journal,* August 21, 2021. https://www.wsj.com/articles/unemployment-benefits-forever-janet-yellen-marty-walsh-11629494576?mod=mhp.

"UnitedHealth Group Revenue 2006–2020." *Macrotrends.* http://www.macrotrends.net/stocks/charts/UNH/unitedhealth-group/revenue. Accessed October 10, 2020.

"Updated: More Misleading Information from Bloomberg's Everytown for Gun Safety on Guns." Crime Prevention Research Center (blog). September 1, 2014. http://www.crimeresearch.org/2014/09/more-misleading-information-from-bloombergs-everytown-for-gun-safety-on-guns-analysis-of-recent-mass-shootings/.

"US Coronavirus Vaccine Tracker." *USA Facts.* https://usafacts.org/visualizations/covid-vaccine-tracker-states/. Accessed July 10, 2022.

"US COVID-19 Cases and Deaths by State." *USA Facts.* https://usafacts.org/visualizations/coronavirus-covid-19-spread-map. Accessed June 26, 2022.

US Department of Labor. "The Fair Labor Standards Act of 1938, As Amended." May 2011. http://www.dol.gov/whd/regs/statutes/FairLaborStandAct.pdf.

US Environmental Protection Agency Office of Mobile Sources. "Milestones in Auto Emissions Control." EPA 400-F-92-014. August 1994. http://www.permanent.fdlp.gov/gpo81172/P10001KM.pdf.

"Vaccines National Strategic Plan 2021–2025." US Department of Health and Human Services. https://www.hhs.gov/sites/default/files/HHS-Vaccines-Report.pdf. Accessed August 4, 2022.

van Haute, Philippe. *Against Adaptation: Lacan's "Subversion" of the Subject*. Translated by Paul Crowe and Miranda Vankerk. New York: Other Press, 2002.

Varro, Cato. *On Agriculture*. Translated by W. D. Hooper. New York: Loeb Classical Library, 1934.

Vavreck, Lynn. "$100 as Incentive to Get a Shot? Experiment Suggests It Can Pay Off." *New York Times*, May 26, 2021. https://www.nytimes.com/2021/05/04/upshot/vaccine-incentive-experiment.html.

Verughese, Jacob, Sajal K. Chattopadhyay, David P. Hopkins, Jennifer Murphy Morgan, Adesola A. Pitan, John M. Clymer, Community Preventative Services Task Force. "Increasing Coverage of Appropriate Vaccinations: A Community Guide Systematic Economic Review." *American Journal of Preventative Medicine* 50, no. 6 (2016): 797–808.

Vivian, Bradford. *Being Made Strange: Rhetoric Beyond Representation*. Albany, State University of New York Press, 2004.

"The Wage Gap: The Who, How, Why, and What to Do." National Women's Law Center. September 27, 2019. http://www.nwlc.org/resources/the-wage-gap-the-who-how-why-and-what-to-do/.

Walkey, Allan J., Anica Law, and Nicholes A. Bosch. "Lottery-Based Incentive in Ohio and COVID-19 Vaccination Rates." *JAMA* 326, no. 8 (2021): 766–67.

Wallich, Henry C. *The Cost of Freedom: A New Look at Capitalism*. New York: Harper, 1960.

Weiner, Rachel. "Lilly Ledbetter Act: Obama Signs His First Bill." *Huffington Post*, February 27, 2009. http://www.huffingtonpost.com/2009/01/27/lily-ledbetter-act-the-fi_n_161423.html.

White, Mark D. *The Manipulation of Choice: Ethics and Libertarian Paternalism*. New York: Palgrave Macmillan, 2013.

Wolfgang von Goethe, Johann. "Der Rattenfänger." *Stade Hameln*. www.hameln.de/en/thepiedpiper/thepiedpiper/pied-piper-by-goethe. Accessed October 1, 2020.

Wood, Stacy, and Kevin Schulman. "Beyond Politics—Promoting Covid-19 Vaccination in the United States." *New England Journal of Medicine*. February 18, 2021. https://www.nejm.org/doi/full/10.1056/NEJMms2033790.

"Workplace Vaccination Program." *Centers for Disease Control and Prevention*. November 4, 2021. https://www.cdc.gov/coronavirus/2019-ncov/vaccines/recommendations/essentialworker/workplace-vaccination-program.html#anchor_1615584361592.

Yates, Tony. "Why Is the Government Relying on Nudge Theory to Fight Coronavirus?" *Guardian*. March 13, 2020. http://www.theguardian.com/commentisfree/2020/mar/13/why-is-the-government-relying-on-nudge-theory-to-tackle-coronavirus.

Yglesias, Matthew. "The CARES Superdole Was a Huge Success." *Slow Boring* (blog). December 29, 2020. https://www.slowboring.com/p/the-cares-superdole-was-a-huge-success.

Žižek, Slavoj. *Absolute Recoil: Towards a New Foundation of Dialectical Materialism.* New York, Verso, 2014.

———. *For They Know Not What They Do: Enjoyment as a Political Factor.* New York: Verso, 1991.

———. "The Pervert's Guide to Ideology (transcript/subtitles, *ŽižekUK.uk*, December 24, 2016, zizek.uk/the-perverts-guide-to-ideology-transcript subtitles/. Accessed October 24, 2020.

———. "The Real of Sexual Difference." In *Reading Seminar XX: Lacan's Major Work on Love, Knowledge and Feminine Sexuality.* Edited by Suzanne Barnard and Bruce Fink, 57–76. Albany: State University of New York Press, 2002.

———. *The Sublime Object of Ideology.* New York, Verso, 1989.

———. *The Ticklish Subject: The Absent Centre of Political Ontology.* New York: Verso, 1999.

Zupančič, Alenka. "Sexual Difference and Ontology." *E-Flux* 32, no. 2 (2012). http://www.e-flux.com/journal/32/68246/sexual-difference-and-ontology/.

———. *What Is Sex?.* Cambridge, MA: MIT Press, 2017.

"2019 Employer Health Benefits Survey." Kaiser Family Foundation. September 25, 2019. http://www.kff.org/report-section/ehbs-2019-section-1-cost-of-health-insurance/.

"2021 Small Business Profile." U.S. Small Business Administration Office of Advocacy. https://cdn.advocacy.sba.gov/wp-content/uploads/2021/08/30143723/Small-Business-Economic-Profile-US.pdf. Accessed June 1, 2022.

Index

Milton Keynes UK
Ingram Content Group UK Ltd.
UKHW040319080224
437360UK00004B/239